SAVING KARL BARTH

SAVING KARL BARTH

HANS URS VON BALTHASAR'S PREOCCUPATION

D. STEPHEN LONG

Fortress Press
Minneapolis

SAVING KARL BARTH

Hans Urs von Balthasar's Preoccupation

Cover images: Hans Urs von Balthasar © Archiv Hans Urs von Balthasar, Basel. Karl Barth © STR/Keystone/Corbis

Cover design: Laurie Ingram

Library of Congress Cataloging-in-Publication Data

Print ISBN: 978-1-4514-7014-7

eBook ISBN: 978-1-4514-7972-0

The paper used in this publication meets the minimum requirements of American National Standard for Information Sciences — Permanence of Paper for Printed Library Materials, ANSI Z329.48-1984.

Manufactured in the U.S.A.

This book was produced using PressBooks.com, and PDF rendering was done by PrinceXML.

For Rebecca who inherits and lives with an inspiring faithfulness the tensions noted in this work.

CONTENTS

Introduction

Hans Urs von Balthasar's presentation and interpretation of Karl Barth's theology has fallen on hard times. Once heralded as a landmark analysis of Barth's theology (even by Barth himself), and a breakthrough in ecumenical relations, Balthasar's interpretation finds fewer and fewer takers. Significant Protestant theologians charge him with an inaccurate periodization and understanding of Barth's conversion(s) from liberalism, as well as an inadequate recognition of Barth's central theological insight. Balthasar failed to see the radical implications Barth contributed to theology when he placed the doctrine of election within the doctrine of God. Significant Catholic theologians claim that Barth misled Balthasar. His preoccupation with Barth resulted in the loss of a robust doctrine of nature and a rejection of metaphysics, especially the *analogia entis*, as the condition for theology. The following work defends Balthasar's interpretation of, and preoccupation with, Karl Barth against these significant theological voices. The charges miss the heart of Balthasar's interpretation of Barth and divert attention away from the significant ecumenical and theological achievement their friendship and work produced. What follows is more than a defense of the specific argument Balthasar presented in his 1951 published work, *Karl Barth: Darstellung und Deutung Seiner Theologie* (*Karl Barth: Presentation and Interpretation of His Theology*); it defends the theological and ecumenical fruit of their friendship and conversation. Balthasar's preoccupation with Barth, beginning in the 1930s and extending until the end of his life, led to a remarkable theological achievement.[1]

My argument does not defend Balthasar or Barth's theology per se; it defends Balthasar's preoccupation with understanding, presenting, and discussing the "enigmatic cleft" between Catholic and Protestant Christianity Barth identified. Balthasar acknowledged Catholicism lost something significant with this cleft, and he refused a self-satisfied Catholic theology that dismissed the Reformed Barth out of hand. His refusal brought attacks upon him from both Catholic and Protestant sides. A lesser person might have given up trying to present Barth to Catholics, and Catholicism to Barth, and thereby to Protestants in general. Some theologians think Balthasar did give up after Barth's death and turned away from the Catholic-Protestant rapprochement

1. Hans Urs von Balthasar, *Karl Barth: Darstellung und Deutung Seiner Theologie* (Köln: Jakob Hegner, 1951).

1

present in his early work. But that too, I think, misstates Balthasar's post—Vatican II concerns. It was because of his engagement with Barth that he worried about Vatican II developments. Rather than dismissing him as a conservative reactionary who abandoned his earlier preoccupation, his preoccupation with Barth helps make sense of his later concerns. The following argument, then, is not an example of Barthian or Balthasarian scholasticism. Neither of them is innocent of theological and moral errors. It is, instead, a defense of the conversation between them and of a way of doing theology that involves friendship rather than conquest. Significant theological fruit came from their conversation. I fear that conversation is not being taken up and built upon by contemporary theologians. Instead, we find a retrenchment to positions prior to their conversation that now threatens their ecumenical fruit, a fruit that often occurred despite them.

In order to defend Balthasar's preoccupation with Barth and its ecumenical fruit, six steps are necessary. The first step is to tell the story of that friendship; it is not well known, largely because Balthasar never publicly acknowledged the difficulties he had in presenting and interpreting Barth's work.[2] Chapter 1, "An Unlikely Friendship: Balthasar's 'Conversations' with Barth," tells that story up to the publication of Balthasar's book on Barth in 1951 and a brief reaction to it in 1953. The history ends at that point because a second step in the story is necessary before properly situating their ongoing conversations in the 1950s and 1960s. The complexity of Balthasar's interpretation must be recognized in all its fullness, and this is what some of the charges brought against Balthasar neglect. Chapter 2, "Presenting and Interpreting Karl Barth," offers a careful analysis of Balthasar's published book on Barth, placing that book within its long and complicated history prior to its 1951 publication. Situating the book within that history results, I hope, in a different and more nuanced reading than interpretations that focus either on Balthasar's supposed twofold periodization of Barth's conversions (where Balthasar merely restates Barth's own words) or one that wrongly suggests Balthasar loses a Catholic understanding of nature. Only after these two steps are accomplished can the third be taken. Chapter 3, "Collapse of Balthasar's Interpretation," examines the reasons contemporary Protestants and Catholics critique and/or dismiss Balthasar's presentation and interpretation of Barth; it also questions, in light of chapters 1 and 2, if they

---

2. One significant exception is Manfred Lochbrunner's "Die Schwere Geburt Des Barth-Buches von Hans Urs Von Balthasar: Ein Betrag Zur Werkgenese," in Manfred Lochbrunner, *Hans Urs von Balthasar und seine Theologen-Kollegen: Sechs Beziehungsgeschichten* (Würzburg: Echter, 2009), 406–49. Although I was able to do some archival research in Basel that adds to his story, I remain deeply indebted to Lochbrunner's archival research published in this excellent book.

have taken into account the nuances of Balthasar's interpretation. The purpose of this chapter is primarily negative. It addresses the question if the new, modern interpretation of Barth's theology leads us toward the retrenchment and widening of the cleft between Catholic and Protestant positions that repeats where Barth and Balthasar began, but never arrives where they concluded.

The next three steps in the argument are more constructive. They address the question of what positive theological gains arose from Balthasar and Barth's theological friendship. Balthasar identified the essential issue between himself and Barth as the "realm" within which theologians pursue knowledge of God and ethics. He was both for and against Barth in identifying the proper realm for theology and ethics. He learned from Barth's christological renaissance even when he critiqued him for a christological "constriction." Because of the latter, Balthasar argued, Barth failed to take into account ecclesial agency. The advances occurring from their friendship, then, are found in the doctrine of God, theological ethics and—to a lesser extent—ecclesiology, each of which is discussed in the final three chapters.

Balthasar's preoccupation with Barth did not end with his 1951 publication. In some sense, it only began. They continued to discuss theology, vacation together, and address the perplexing division between Protestants and Catholics. Their ongoing friendship in the 1950s and 1960s will be taken up in the final three chapters. However, Balthasar's preoccupation with Barth did not end with Barth's death in 1968. Toward the end of his life, Balthasar was still presenting Barth's work and arguing that his doctrine of God set forth God's glory better than most theologians ancient or modern. Chapter 4, "The Realm of God," explains what Balthasar saw in Barth: the overcoming of a nominalist doctrine of God that could not adequately express God's glory. Balthasar found Barth's doctrine of the divine perfections in *Church Dogmatics* 2.1 beautiful; that he did so is unsurprising. Anselm's aesthetic approach to theology appealed to Barth, and he cited its beauty as essential for understanding his dogmatic turn. Balthasar took Barth at his word. Chapter 5, "The Realm of Ethics," shows how Barth offered something of a theological revolution, or perhaps retrieval, in Christian ethics. What Balthasar does to moral theology is similar. Because theology is no rigid system with carefully ordered propositions based on an adequate method, but an endeavor to set forth the proper form and tone of God's address to creation in Christ, any sharp distinction between theology and ethics is rendered problematic. No neutral realm of nature exists where ethics can be done as if God had not spoken in Christ. Barth's putative opposition to natural theology presumes a rejection of a doctrine of pure nature. He did not oppose natural theology; he thought it didn't exist. One may as well oppose flying pumpkins. If everything is created in, through, and for Christ, then there is no independent nature that can assess his claims on creation, as it were, from the outside. Where would such an outside be?

Protestant and Catholic approaches that recover a christological ethic owe a great debt to Barth and Balthasar's friendship. Their friendship began with some initial meetings that culminated in Barth inviting Balthasar to attend his 1941 seminar on the Council of Trent. It ended with Barth's last lecture in 1968 on the unity of the church, which was delivered in tandem with Balthasar. The "Protocols" from the 1941 seminar set the stage for an intriguing discussion on the ecclesial differences between them, a discussion to which they returned again and again during their twenty-seven-year friendship. It bore, and still promises to bear, ecumenical fruit. Central to what follows is a presentation of that fruit. Although it will be implicit throughout, the final chapter, "The Realm of the Church: Renewal and Unity" addresses it explicitly. The final chapter does not resolve the key differences between Barth and Balthasar on the relationship between Christ and his church for the simple reason that such differences have not been resolved. It does assist, I hope, in highlighting those differences and exploring what is at stake in them. For Balthasar, Christ and the church constitute a single, albeit differentiated, reality. For Barth, Christ always stands over and against his church, even though he too will call the church Christ's flesh. This difference remains irresolvable, but highlighting the reasons for it and posing critical questions about it might prove salutary.

Balthasar remains, I am convinced, an excellent guide through Barth's theology, both in how he interprets and presents Barth's work as well as how he developed and supplemented it with his own. Contemporary criticisms of Balthasar's reading of Barth are insufficiently patient with it. Sometimes they come from a deeply committed Protestant theology that is incapable of hearing well theological voices outside our tradition, which is understandable. It was Barth's initial approach to Catholics and ecumenical dialogue. Ecumenical dialogues are to be engaged, he said in 1931, with "dogmatic intolerance."[3] Barthians like to adopt Barth's *enfant terrible* disposition (the ascription comes from Balthasar). Dogmatic intolerance is where he began his ecumenical engagements, and oddly enough his approach bore fruit, but it is not where he concluded. We should neither begin nor conclude with dogmatic intolerance. It would not be Barthian in the best sense, for it would deny the considerable ecumenical gains he accomplished, surprising as that was to him.

---

3. Eberhard Busch, *Karl Barth: His Life from Letters and Autobiographical Texts*, trans. John Bowden (Philadelphia: Fortress Press, 1976), 215.

If an entrenched Protestantism critiques and dismisses Balthasar's reading of Barth, a reactive Catholicism accuses Balthasar's preoccupation with Barth's theology of significant errors. A similar reactive Catholic theology prohibited Balthasar's Barth book from being published for over a decade. I suspect, and worry, that current trends in Protestant and Catholic theology may be repeating the entrenched Protestant and Catholic positions that made Barth and Balthasar's friendship so unlikely and yet theologically necessary. They were always puzzled by the "enigmatic crack" that separated Catholics and Protestants for five hundred years. Although both eschewed any liberal sentimentality for healing this rift—"what's five hundred years of anathemas among friends"—they nonetheless were drawn to each other's work because that rift was theologically unintelligible and unsustainable. Telling the story of their friendship might offer a witness that prevents Catholics and Protestants from once again merely repeating, and thereby widening, that "enigmatic crack."

This book has been a long time in preparation. It began during my graduate studies in the late 1980s when several Protestant colleagues formed a Barth reading group: Willie Jennings, Charles Campbell, and David Matzko McCarthy (who since became Catholic); and several Catholic colleagues formed a Catholic reading group: Frederick Bauerschmidt, Michael Baxter and William Cavanaugh. These were never competing reading groups. We were and remain friends listening to and appreciating the distinct tones found among the different theologies. For us theology was always a practice of friendship. These friendships initiated me into the massive works of Barth and Balthasar, which I read over several decades—first at the Jesuit St. Joseph's University in Philadelphia and then at Garrett-Evangelical Theological Seminary. When the latter hired me I was asked to teach the "dead white theologians." I was told at the time that the seminary students knew the criticisms of that generation of theologians, but did not know those theologians, so I was encouraged to teach a course comparing and contrasting Barth, Tillich, Rahner, and Balthasar, and tracing their lineage through James Cone, Elizabeth Johnson, Rosemary Ruether, Gustavo Gutiérrez and others. I also taught a graduate seminar on Barth and Balthasar. For all the students who worked through that material with me, I remain indebted.

Through friendship, courses taught and the insurmountable task of reading the volumes Barth and Balthasar published I became increasingly fascinated with their friendship. My appointment at Marquette University gave me the opportunity to pursue this interest at a deeper level. I am grateful to my friend Sven Grosse, who was a visiting scholar at Marquette, and encouraged me to apply for a grant from the *Schweizerischer Nationalfonds zur Förderung der Wissenschaftlichen Forschung* (SNF), which I received. Sven introduced me to Georg Pfleiderer, professor of theology and ethics at the University of Basel, who graciously agreed to host my research. Although neither of them is responsible for what follows, this work would not have been possible without their hospitality. I remain in their debt. Hans Anton Drewes assisted me at the Barth archives in Basel and offered invaluable suggestions. I am grateful to him for conversation and for providing a copy of Barth's 1941 Council of Trent protocols. Reading the students' handwritten German from those protocols was laborious. My colleagues Ulrich Lehner and Lyle Dabney assisted me in that task, for which I remain grateful. Ms. Claudia Capol welcomed me to the Balthasar archives and arranged a meeting with Bishop Peter Henrici. I could not have discovered much that is in this work without them. Their kindness and warmth remain much appreciated. I have never met Manfred Lochbrunner, but his own archival work and publications made my efforts much more manageable. Many others read the manuscript and provided wise counsel. I'm grateful to Rick Barry, David Luy, Joseph Mangina, Chad Pecknold, John Wright, and Kenneth Oakes. I am especially grateful to Anne Carpenter who read the manuscript with a discerning Catholic eye and saved me from several misstatements.

Barth and Balthasar have been constant companions to me as a theologian. Their work appears in nearly everything I've done. I am somewhat embarrassed to confess it, for it is cliché, but a copy of Grünewald's crucifixion, picked up in Colmar, hangs above my desk. How else could one be inspired to write on Barth and Balthasar's friendship and its theological significance? Balthasar was called the most cultured man in Europe. Barth's knowledge was encyclopedic. I am neither cultured nor possess that breadth of knowledge. For that reason I always felt, and still feel, inadequate to this project. I'm sure much more needs to be done, but I remain grateful for the little I have seen they tried to declare and show to us and hope some of that is present in what follows.

1

An Unlikely Friendship: Balthasar's "Conversations" with Barth

Barth and Balthasar's friendship was unlikely, but theologically significant. The friendship was unlikely for several reasons. When they first met Karl Barth was already fifty-four years of age, a well-known theologian and a professor with an international reputation. Having been removed from his teaching post at the University of Bonn in 1935, he had resided in his birthplace, Basel, Switzerland, for five years, taking up a position at the University of Basel. From Basel he was politically active in the church struggles, writing, lecturing, and forming associations to challenge the church's accommodation to National Socialism. Balthasar was thirty-four, a Jesuit, and taking his first appointment as campus minister at the same university. He was much less visible than Barth, and much less engaged in the political struggles of the times. As a Jesuit it was difficult, even illegal, to do so in Switzerland. He was not disengaged. He even worked to find places for Jewish refugees. Both Barth and Balthasar recognized that resistance to National Socialism was a Christian obligation.

Barth was staunchly Reformed, Balthasar a devout Roman Catholic. Balthasar was known for encouraging, sometimes goading, Catholic laity to profess the evangelical counsels (poverty, celibacy, obedience) and for making converts from Protestantism to Roman Catholicism. Converting Barth had to be at least in the back of his mind when he arrived in Basel. Balthasar came to Basel from working with the Jesuit Erich Przywara in Munich. When Barth was teaching at the University of Münster, he had invited Przywara to his 1929 seminar. Three years later Przywara would publish the first volume of his *Analogia Entis*, setting forth the metaphysics of Christianity. During that same year Barth published his well-known introduction to the first volume of the *Church Dogmatics*, where he claimed that the *analogia entis* was the reason he could never become Roman Catholic.[1] Balthasar arrived in Basel prepared to show Barth how he misunderstood this essential Catholic teaching.

If this were the sole reason for not being Catholic then to show Barth his error would take away that singular reason. The discussion that ensued never found agreement on whether Barth understood the *analogia entis* or whether it contained the grave theological errors Barth attributed to it in the 1930s. After Vatican II, Balthasar expressed concern about its misuse, but he never relented on its importance for Catholic theology. Their debate has generated ongoing discussion for nearly a century now. Resolution is not forthcoming, which is unsurprising.[2] As we shall see, Catholics disagree among themselves whether Przywara was correct in his claim about the *analogia entis*. Devout Thomists still disagree on exactly what the *analogia entis* is. If Thomists themselves don't agree, surely Barth could be forgiven for misunderstanding a debate about which there is still great misunderstanding and controversy? The debate may have been misplaced altogether. Balthasar thought Barth misidentified the error Barth rightly sensed in modern Catholicism. It was not the *analogia entis*; Balthasar thought Barth tacitly affirmed it throughout his *Church Dogmatics* even if he failed to admit it as such. Instead, the error was a doctrine of pure nature.[3]

Balthasar would learn the hard way that the *analogia entis* was not the only reason Barth rejected Catholicism. At the 1948 World Council of Churches, Barth argued, in good Swiss Protestant fashion, that no freedom-loving person

1. We have no evidence Barth read Przywara's *Analogia Entis.* According to Hans Anton-Drewes, Barth most likely gave it to a student to read and inform him about it, who was living with him at the time, Frederick Herzog. Keith Johnson has demonstrated, however, that Barth and his students read carefully through the first two sections of Przywara's *Religionsphilosophie* and discussed it, along with his teaching of the *analogia entis*, prior to Przywara's visit to his seminar. See Keith Johnson, *Karl Barth and the* Analogia Entis (London: T & T Clark, 2010), 87–88.

2. Keith Johnson argues Barth did understand it and rejected it for essentially Reformed theological reasons. The *analogia entis* failed to acknowledge the sinfulness of human beings and argued to God from an analysis of human consciousness. It also failed to maintain that God always remains in control of God's revelation and never gives it over to human agency, including that of the church. See Johnson, *Karl Barth and the* Analogia Entis, 87–99, 119. Johnson assumes Przywara's interpretation of the *analogia entis* is accurate. As will be demonstrated below, many Thomists challenge this assumption and disagree over the kind of analogy the *analogia entis* is. John Betz argues Barth never understood Przywara's teaching. He writes that one of Barth's "first and oft-repeated criticism of the *analogia entis* has remarkably little to do with Przywara's actual doctrine—either in its early or its mature form." See "After Barth: A New Introduction to Erich Przywara's *Analogia Entis*" in *The Analogy of Being: Invention of the Antichrist or the Wisdom of God?*, ed. Thomas Joseph White, OP (Grand Rapids, MI: Eerdmans, 2011) 72.

3. Although Johnson would disagree with Balthasar, he nonetheless seems to restate rather than refute Balthasar's central claim. In explaining Barth's later position on the *analogia entis*, he writes, "For Barth, the key question is not whether an *analogia entis* exists; the question is whether an *analogia entis* is understood in light of the particularity of God's grace in Jesus Christ." Johnson, *Karl Barth and the* Analogia Entis, 190.

could become Catholic. In 1954, much to the chagrin of Balthasar, he told a Protestant audience that no "decent person" could convert to Catholicism. All this occurred while Balthasar attempted to get Catholics to read Barth sympathetically. Barth did not make it easy. Nor was he ever consistent in his comments about Catholicism. He stated in 1924 that if Schleiermacher were right about Protestantism, the only option would be to become Catholic. Toward the end of his life, he told Balthasar that he could not convert but if he were born Catholic he would have remained such. Finding the thread that holds Barth's statements for and against Catholicism together is impossible, which makes his preoccupation with Catholicism and his friendship with Balthasar all the more interesting. It proves Ralph Waldo Emerson correct: "A foolish consistency is the hobgoblin of small minds, adored by little statesmen and philosophers and divines." No such foolishness is to be found in the divines Barth and Balthasar.

There were other types of foolishness to be sure. Both had, to say the least, unconventional relationships with women. Balthasar lived in the Kaegi household after the conversion of Adrienne von Speyr in 1940 (Mrs. Kaegi) from Protestantism to Catholicism. Barth's relationship with Charlotte von Kirschbaum and the stress it caused his own family is now well known and will not be repeated, nor excused, here. Such arrangements undoubtedly caused family tensions. The friendship between Barth and Balthasar often included Speyr and Kirschbaum. The four of them listened to Mozart, discussed theology, and vacationed together. Both Barth and Balthasar took advantage of patriarchal benefits. Yet, in admittedly strange ways, both also gave voice to women as theologians.[4]

Despite their differences that made for an unlikely friendship, they also had commonalties that made it theologically significant. Both loved Mozart, and even more importantly, Jesus Christ. That may seem too pious a way of putting it, but it best describes the common love that forged their friendship. Both had a painting of Grünewald's crucifixion hanging over their desk; Balthasar's was a gift from Barth. Both pursued theology from the heart of the Christian mystery, the incarnation. Both were attentive to the "form" theology should take, although they differed in expressing that form. Balthasar saw in Barth's theology a beautiful "system," albeit metaphysically deficient. Barth, however, found "systematic theology" to be "problematical." It is a "pattern of thought constructed on the basis of a number of concepts chosen in accordance with the

---

4. For important discussions on Balthasar and feminism see Karen Kilby, *Balthasar: A (Very) Critical Introduction* (Grand Rapids, MI:, Eerdmans, 2012), 123–47, and Tina Beattie, *The New Catholic Feminism: Theology and Theory* (London: Routledge, 2006), 81–100.

criteria of a particular philosophy and developed in accordance with a method appropriate to it."[5] He was neither preoccupied with such consistency nor with method. Instead, theology is "responsible to the living command of the Word of God——and to no other authority in heaven or on earth." Because theology was responsible to the Word, it was not a "free science," but one "bound to the sphere of the church."[6] Here is another important agreement. Both agreed on theology's ecclesial location, although they differed most profoundly on what that meant because they differed on how to express Christ's relationship to his church.

This first chapter tells why Barth and Balthasar's friendship was unlikely and how, despite opposition, it came to be.

Conversation(s) with Karl Barth

Hans Urs von Balthasar first met Karl Barth on April 29, 1940, soon after Barth published *Church Dogmatics* 2.1, which Balthasar read, as he put it, "with great interest." Its teaching on God's perfections would remain central to Balthasar's own work throughout his life. Balthasar had moved to Basel in December 1939. Once he arrived he wrote Barth seeking a face-to-face conversation, acknowledging he already had many "conversations" with him in his imagination. Some of those conversations were in print. Balthasar published a chapter on Barth in his 1937–39 three-volume work, *Apokalypse der deutschen Seele*; a 1938 review, "The Crisis of Protestant Theology";[7] and a 1939 essay that bore the same title as his 1948 lectures, "Karl Barth and Catholicism."[8] Before meeting him, Balthasar was already preoccupied with Barth.

Balthasar's interest in Barth came through his teachers, first and foremost through the influence of Erich Przywara. They became acquainted during Balthasar's two years studying philosophy in Pullach near Munich in the early 1930s. They were reacquainted the two years he worked with him for *Stimmen der Zeit* in Munich, 1937–1939. Balthasar went straight from his mentorship to Przywara in Munich to be the campus minister at the University of Basel. Balthasar had also studied with the French Jesuits from 1933 to 1937 in Lyons

---

5. Cited in Eberhard Busch, *Karl Barth: His Life from Letters and Autobiographical Texts*, trans. John Bowden (Philadelphia: Fortress Press, 1976), 211.

6. Busch, *Karl Barth*, 211–12.

7. Hans Urs von Balthasar, "Die Krisis der protestantischen Theologie," *Stimmen der Zeit* 132 (1938): 200–1.

8. Hans Urs von Balthasar, "Karl Barth und der Katholizismus," *Theologie der Zeit* 3, no. 2 (1939): 126–32.

at Fourviére, the Jesuit seminary, which became known as a hotbed of *nouvelle théologie*, but Balthasar found nothing of it during his time there.[9] These six years studying with the Jesuits and working for *Stimmen der Zeit* accounted for six of the ten years Balthasar lived outside Switzerland. He returned to his native country in December 1939 to become campus minister at Basel. He had been given the opportunity to be professor for ecumenical theology at the Gregoriana in Rome or campus minister in Basel.[10] He chose the latter and would spend the rest of his life in Switzerland, most of it in Basel, except for a six year period, 1950–1956, when he left the Jesuits and was required to leave Basel.

Having settled in Basel, Balthasar took the publication of Barth's *Church Dogmatics* 2.1 as an opportunity to send a letter requesting a meeting with Barth. Balthasar opened his letter with these words: "With great interest I have read your earlier work and also the new volume of your *Dogmatics*." He immediately challenged Barth's interpretation of Catholicism; Barth's argument with the *analogia entis* is "not satisfying in every respect" because it really hasn't confronted the "ultimate Catholic position."[11] So begins a conversation, a disagreement and a friendship that lasts until Barth's death.

Shortly after their first meeting, Balthasar sent Barth a lengthy ten-page letter. He wrote, "I have for many years envisioned a conversation with you, because the 'conversations' [*Gespräche*] which I have already held with you are numerous."[12] Balthasar placed *Gespräche* in quotations for a reason. Now that he resided in Basel, the virtual conversations he already had with Barth could become the personal conversations he desired. The first book he wrote on Barth, which was never published in its original form, was entitled, *Analogie: Ein Gespräch mit Karl Barth* (*Analogy: A Conversation with Karl Barth*). Writing a book on Barth must have been on his mind prior to this personal encounter since he was able to complete it so quickly. Balthasar's "conversations" with Karl Barth would shape his work and undoubtedly influence Barth's as well.

Barth's work may very well have saved Balthasar's theological vocation. Perhaps that puts it too strongly, but Balthasar's dissatisfaction with the "sawdust

---

9. See Peter Henrici, SJ, "Hans Urs von Balthasar: A Sketch of His Life," in *Hans Urs von Balthasar: His Life and Work*, ed. David Schindler (San Francisco: Ignatius, 1991), 12.

10. See Urban Fink, "'Ihr stets im Herrn ergebener Hans Balthasar:' Hans Urs von Balthasar und der Basler Bischof Franziskus Streng," in *Hans Urs von Balthasar—ein grosser Churer Diözesan*, ed. Peter Henrici (Fribourg: Academic, 2006), 96.

11. Manfred Lochbrunner, *Hans Urs von Balthasar und seine Theologenkollegen: Sechs Beziehungsgeschichten* (Würzburg: Echter, 2009), 267.

12. Ibid., 269.

Thomism" fed him during his Jesuit formation is too well known to retrace here.[13] Barth provided him with a more dramatic, biblical, and patristic theological "form" than the "School" theology he received during his Jesuit formation. Barth invited Balthasar to attend his seminar on the Council of Trent in 1941 and the *Protokolle* demonstrate that he was a regular contributor to the discussion.[14] Manfred Lochbrunner suggests this seminar "placed in the shadows the poor Scholastic theology of his neoscholastic formation."[15] Balthasar searched for something that captured the glory of Christian revelation better than that form, and one important place he found it was Barth's theology. The other was of course his Jesuit friend and mentor, Erich Przywara.[16] The fact that Barth and Przywara opposed each other constituted the aporia Balthasar's life and work sought to resolve.

Beginning in 1946, Balthasar also became increasingly convinced he could not pursue his theological vocation within the Jesuit order as well as he could through the secular, lay institute he established in Basel. That community still exists. This also puts it much too strongly, but Balthasar bequeathed to us a religious community within the Catholic Church that received his work whereas Barth bequeathed an argument, especially as to how best to interpret him, that primarily has its home in the university. By that I mean Balthasar's work continues to exist, in part, in the hands of people who gather together and pray, the *Johannesgemeinschaft* (the Johannine community). He was more interested in forming lay institutes than in contributing to academic life. Barth clearly inspired people to form Christian community as well. His work with the Confessing Church offered something similar to Balthasar's community, but it fell apart. Barth's Reformed theology lacked a home within an institutional structure that could receive and preserve his work in the same way the *Johannesgemeinschaft* preserves Balthasar's. Nonetheless, Barth's work had an undeniable influence on Protestant and Catholic institutional structures, not least of all because of Balthasar's preoccupation. He constantly pushed Barth on such questions, encouraged him to go with him to Rome and personally presented his book on Barth to Pius XII. Barth's last lecture, delivered in tandem with Balthasar in 1968, discussed the "structures" that make possible "church renewal." If Barth's theology is to be something more than scholastic wrangling

13. See Edward T. Oakes, SJ, *Pattern of Redemption: The Theology of Hans Urs von Balthasar* (London: Continuum, 1997).

14. *Protokolle* are the students' notes that record the conversation. Each week a different student is assigned to record the seminar. Their discussion will be examined in chapter 6.

15. Lochbrunner, *Hans Urs von Balthasar und seine Theologenkollegen*, 284.

16. See Henrici, "A Sketch of His Life," 13.

about how best to interpret him, it may be because of the questions Balthasar put to him. In this sense, Balthasar saved Karl Barth; he gave his work a much-needed ecclesial form outside of the academic setting to which it was and always will be alien, but upon which it often depends for its viability.[17]

If Barth 'saved" Balthasar's theological vocation, Balthasar sought to return the favor, not only interpreting his theology to Catholics and finding a place for it within a Catholic ecclesial home, but also seeking to find a place there for Karl Barth himself. There can be little doubt that converting Karl Barth to Catholicism was part of Balthasar's mission in Basel. He sought to do this theoretically, showing Barth the errors in his interpretation of Catholicism, and how it accomplished what he himself desired. He also attempted it personally. The relationship between them was not one-sided, as if Balthasar thought Catholic theology had the answers and Barth only needed correction. Barth had something to say to Catholics and Balthasar did not shy away from suggesting as much even when he suffered for it. Engaging Barth as he did during the forties was risky for a Catholic theologian. During this time the Roman Catholic Church was fearful of modernism, and despite how Barth might have been interpreted in Protestant circles, in Catholic ones, he was viewed as modernist. Balthasar strove to convince them otherwise.

SUFFERING CATHOLICISM

In his preoccupation with Karl Barth, Balthasar initiated an ecumenical conversation he thought needed to occur without in any way diminishing Catholic truth. Barth had something to contribute to the recognition of the latter that too many Catholics overlooked. Balthasar thought Catholics misunderstood Barth, and Barth misunderstood the heart of Catholicism. One part of his vocation was to remedy the misunderstanding on both sides.

In 1942, Balthasar followed up a conversation with Barth by an innocent, yet theologically loaded, suggestion that Barth read the theology of Oskar Bauhofer in order to understand Catholicism better. Barth, however, was already more familiar with Bauhofer's work than Balthasar could have known.

17. Both Barth and Balthasar were unusual academics. Balthasar had no desire to be a university theologian and turned down such posts when they were offered. He wanted to reunite what had been lost—holiness and a theological vocation—and did so within the secular community he and others formed. Barth began as a Reformed pastor and was literally called out of the pastorate to take a university post, for which by his own account he was ill prepared. Nonetheless I find Georg Pfleiderer's argument persuasive that Barth's work assumed an "elite vanguard," and especially an academic one, for its viability. See Pfleiderer, *Karl Barths praktische Theologie* (Tübingen: Mohr Siebeck, 2000), 135–40, 260, 389, 393–99. 449.

He had a very public disagreement in 1932 with his former colleague Georg Wobbermin over the conversions to Catholicism of Oskar Bauhofer and Erik Peterson. In published editorials against Wobbermin Barth outlined why he took Catholicism seriously, how he sought to offer a Protestant alternative, and why this required rejecting Wobbermin's appeal to Schleiermacher. The exchange with Wobbermin provides an illuminating structure for Barth's engagement with Catholicism.

Balthasar entered into a conversation with Barth about Catholicism that Barth had not only already engaged but about which he had already adopted firm commitments. Early in his theological work, Barth chose, in his words, to "suffer" Catholicism. It was a worthy adversary. But if Barth suffered Catholicism, Balthasar returned the favor. Balthasar persisted, in his words, in a "preoccupation with Barth," for which he too suffered. Balthasar was convinced, perhaps to the end, that if Barth understood Catholicism properly he would see it presupposed and completed what Barth sought to accomplish with his turn to dogmatics. Barth's misunderstanding, Balthasar acknowledged, was not always his fault; much of modern Catholic theology was exactly what Barth critiqued it for being. Balthasar constantly presented Catholic theology to Barth that he thought would assuage his qualms. If he truly understood Pryzwara, or would read Bauhofer, Barth would find the "heart" of Catholicism, and with it the "presupposition for the single most interesting confrontation between" Protestants and Catholics: the *soli Deo Gloria* (the glory of God alone) of Calvin versus the *omnia ad majorem Dei gloriam* (all things to the greater glory of God) of Ignatius Loyola. These two theologians, who had actually been classmates for a brief time, represented for Balthasar the decisive difference.

Balthasar acknowledged that Calvin's *soli Deo Gloria* was itself "Catholic." Glory was to be given to God *alone*, and "glory," of course, formed the heart of Balthasar's theology. Calvin, like Protestantism, pointed in the right direction, but it was incomplete and even theologically detrimental if it was not supplemented by Loyola's *omnia ad*—"everything to." For this reason Balthasar wrote, "The *soli* is catholic, but the exclusion and suspicion of the *omina ad* is not."[18] Balthasar's own dogmatics began where Barth and Calvin did—glory belonged to God alone revealed in the Person of Christ. Everything radiated out from this center, but in so radiating everything was directed to it—*omnia ad*— and this he thought Barth neglected because he had an inadequate account of nature.

18. Letter from Balthasar to Karl Barth, Aug. 12, 1942, in Lochbrunner, *Hans Urs von Balthasar und seine Theologenkollegen*, 289.

That Balthasar encouraged Barth to read Oskar Bauhofer has more than a bit of irony. Neither Balthasar nor Barth mentioned in their 1942 exchange that Barth already had an unfortunate encounter over Bauhofer. A decade earlier, Georg Wobbermin, Barth's former colleague from his Göttingen days (1921–1925), accused him, and dialectical theology, of being responsible for Oskar Bauhofer and Erik Peterson's conversions to Catholicism. On May 31, 1932 Wobbermin published an editorial, "A New Case: Peterson" ("Ein neuer Fall: Peterson"), that compared the significance of Bauhofer and Peterson's conversions to that of John Henry Newman. Wobbermin argued against those who claimed that Peterson and Bauhofer's conversions "illuminated the situation of the time" like Newman's did his. Their conversions did illumine something about the present state of theology, he suggested, but what they illumined was the baleful influence of Karl Barth. He offered three reasons for such a judgment. First, Bauhofer and Peterson acted on the "assumption" of Barth's "dialectical theology." Second, both lacked a proper understanding of the Reformed doctrine of faith, which was "a heartfelt confidence in the grace and goodness of God, revealed and experienced through the Word" that then takes precedence over and arranges "dogmatic formulations." Third, this gave rise to an "unevangelical version and evaluation [of faith] in the Catholic-Scholastic sense" with its "claim of an infallible papist church."[19] Wobbermin reminded his readers he had warned Barth and others about this a year earlier in 1931.[20] He acknowledged he had evaluated somewhat positively Bauhofer's earlier 1930 work, *Das Metareligiöse, eine kritische Religionsphilosphie*. Much in it was positive, but it already pointed in a dogmatic Catholic direction, and explicitly drew on dialectical theology. Karl Barth laid the seeds for Bauhofer's un-Reformed appreciation of dogma and therefore his conversion. Now with the conversions of Bauhofer and Peterson, Wobbermin found his warning justified.

Barth, who was now teaching at Bonn, replied on May 31, 1932 with an editorial refuting Wobbermin. Wobbermin's accusation and "construction" were so thoroughly untrue Barth wrote, "Its origin I do not know how to explain under the presupposition of good will on your side."[21] Barth reminded

---

19. Karl Barth, *Offene Briefe 1909–1935*, ed. Diether Koch, vol. 5 of *Gesamtausgabe* (Zürich: Theologischer Zurich, 2001), 214.

20. Wobbermin, "Das Wort Gottes und der evangelische Glaube," in *Vom Worte Gottes: Bericht über den dritten Theologentag in Breslau vom 5. bis 8. Oktober 1930*, ed. Ernst Lohmeyer (Göttingen: Vandenhoeck & Ruprecht 1931), 46–65. This conference seems to have been in response to Peterson's "Was ist theologie?" See Barth *Offene Briefe 1909–1935*, 214.

21. Karl Barth *Offene Briefe 1909–1935*, 216.

Wobbermin what Peterson wrote against him in his 1925 essay, "Was ist Theologie?" Far from acting on the assumption of dialectical theology, Peterson rejected it. His rejection led him to Rome, not his affirmation. Likewise Barth now publicly told Wobbermin something he could not have known. Barth was asked to recommend Bauhofer's 1930 book, but he wrote, "I very wisely declined."[22] Barth gave no credence to Wobbermin's accusations. He bore no responsibility for their conversions.

Wobbermin did not back down. He recalled a "long conversation" they had while colleagues at Göttingen after Peterson published his famous essay. They agreed it "was to be taken seriously and not something to be hushed up," but for diametrically opposed reasons. Barth supposedly "praised it" for the way it established the problem of dogma and called for a "theological objectivism." Wobbermin agreed it must be taken seriously, but for a very different reason. He lamented it. It wrongly set up the problem and the solution. He also lamented Barth's own "hardening" of Christian doctrines and facile rejection of Schleiermacher. Wobbermin accused Barth of sharing this rejection with Peterson and Bauhofer, and found in the rejection of Schleiermacher the true loss of Protestantism. Schleiermacher developed it as was needed; Barth was leading Protestants away from Schleiermacher and therefore back to Rome. Those were the options. Barth argued that same year, in his introduction to the first volume of the *Church Dogmatics*, that they were not options at all, but two sides of the same coin. Barth's quip about the *analogia entis* as the antichrist, and its similarity to Schleiermacher's theology, cannot be understood separate from his public encounter with Wobbermin.

Barth questioned Wobbermin's recollection of a conversation they had seven years earlier and repeated the phrase, "there is no proof," in the face of Wobbermin's accusation. Barth then wrote something, which reveals important theological themes and preoccupations in his work that unfold from 1932 on. This quote shows how he "suffered" Catholicism, the firm commitments he developed in his response to it, and what the structure would be by which he engaged it. Barth wrote:

> I want to say to you, and concerning this I become acerbic, I don't take matters of Catholicism as a joke. I take it as an incredibly strong and deep conversation partner; to be the only real conversation partner Protestant theology can take seriously. I hold idealism, anthroposophy, folk religion and the death of God movement [*Gottlosenbewegung*] for children in comparison to this opponent. I

22. Ibid.

am seriously affected [*leide*] about this, [especially] that Protestant theology is here blind; that it does not recognize to what intellectual and spiritual insignificance it has descended on the line, which you Herr Colleague, hold as salvific, [and] how little it has grown internally today to Catholicism. My entire work asks the desperate question (yes: to our long and completely desperate methods used in these two hundred years) about a Protestant theology, which would oppose Catholicism, which I hold as great heresy——as *theology* and as a worthy *Protestant* theology.[23]

This exchange reveals key elements in Barth's theology and its relationship to Catholicism. The first is the role "dialectic" plays. On the one hand, Wobbermin unjustifiably associated Peterson and Bauhofer with Barth's dialectic. Peterson railed against it, arguing despite Barth's own affirmations, it "cannot give God the glory" because it provides no "concrete knowledge" nor "concrete authority" nor "concrete obedience."[24] But Wobbermin should be excused for misunderstanding the situation. As Barbara Nichtweiß demonstrates, early on Peterson was considered a "dialectical theologian," and while he rejected Barth's version of dialectic, he never abandoned a different version, which is necessarily the case for every theologian who employs analogy under the influence of Thomas Aquinas as Peterson did. Analogy and dialectic are not opposed; rather, dialectic is a moment in analogy that must be affirmed and then surpassed. It forms the very structure of the "objections" and "on the contrary" that then seek resolution in the "I answer that" of the Thomistic method. It is especially central to the affirmation of attributes to God that are then negated (*remotio*), only to be reaffirmed by the way of eminence.

Dialectic was not alien to Peterson's own work, but he found various reasons to critique Barth's dialectic. Not only did it avoid concrete obedience, but it was a species of "Greek mythology" and indebted to "Father Kant."[25] Nonetheless, Peterson also recognized dialectic's inevitability. He acknowledged Thomas Aquinas was a "dialectical thinker," and that such an approach was necessary because of his "enhypostatic understanding of Christology."[26] Likewise, it must be remembered that Balthasar never rejected

23. Ibid.

24. Peterson, "Was ist Theologie?," in *Theologische Traktate* (Munich: Kosel, 1950), 18.

25. See Barbara Nichtweiß, *Erik Peterson: Neue Sicht auf Leben und Werk* (Herder: Freiburg im Breisgau, 1992), 586, 591.

26. The doctrine of the enhypostaton teaches that in the incarnation the Person of Christ does not have a human "hypostasis," but exists as a Person in the divine hypostasis, uniting humanity and divinity

dialectic completely. In an essay published in 1944 that came from the first edition of the Barth book, Balthasar acknowledged a place for dialectic in theology (as he also did in his 1951 Barth book), but he rejected it when it was understood as a "contradiction"; then it was nothing but a failed "demonic attempt" at analogy.[27] If he occasionally stated that Barth abandoned dialectic, he overstated his case. What he wrote elsewhere is more nuanced. Barth abandoned dialectic as the sole method, and as the kind of method that dominated his *Romans* phase. But Balthasar, like Peterson, never rejected dialectic. It has a place in theology within analogy, never as its replacement. Chapters 2 and 3 discuss Balthasar's interpretation and the place it has for dialectic.[28]

A second important theme in Barth's response to Wobbermin is the question of the ecclesial location of "theology." Wobbermin admonished him for failing to be a follower of Schleiermacher. Here Barth was guilty as charged. In his 1928 essay, "Roman Catholicism: A Question to the Protestant Church,"

---

into one without either ceasing to be distinctly human or divine; humanity is not divinity nor vice versa, but Christ's two natures exist in one Person who is the acting subject. See Barbara Nichtweiß, *Erik Peterson*, 657. The "outline" for Peterson's lectures on Thomas Aquinas in 1923–1924, which Barth attended, was based on the claim, as Peterson put it, "Thomas weiß genau, daß alle theologischen Begriffe in einem dialektischen Zusammenhang miteinander stehen. . . . Der Glaube lebt nicht aus dem logisch Ausgeschlossenen, sondern in der dialektischen Spannung der Begriffe." The importance of this should not be missed. Barth attended Peterson's lectures and became acquainted through them with a more patristic Christology. Amy Marga recognizes this in her *Karl Barth's Dialogue with Catholicism in Göttingen and Munster: Its Significance for His Doctrine of God*, Beitrage zur Historischen Theologie (Tübingen: Mohr Siebeck, 2010). She acknowledges that this qualifies Bruce McCormack's thesis that Barth learned the anhypostatic-enhypostatic distinction primarily from Heppe. Instead, she writes, "He clearly had some previous exposure to this Christological pattern through Peterson's lectures," which were on Aquinas (32).

27. Hans Urs von Balthasar, "Analogie und Dialektik: Zur Klärung der theologischen Prinzipienlehre Karl Barths," *Divus Thomas* 22 (1944): 173.

28. Any nuanced discussion of the place of dialectic in twentieth-century theology should take into account that proponents of the so-called *nouvelle théologie* saw dialectic contributing to the scholasticism they found arid and lifeless. See Henri de Lubac, *Medieval Exegesis*, vol. 1: *The Four Senses of Scripture*, trans. Mark Sebanc (Grand Rapids, MI: Eerdmans, 1998), 61–63. De Lubac traces a shift, albeit not an opposition, in the interpretation of Scripture to the "dialectic" that emerged with the "new questions" that were being asked by the dialecticians in the eleventh century which worked against the more allegorical model of Augustinianism. What is this dialectical model? According to those of a more Augustinian persuasion, the dialecticians "presumed to submit the mysteries of God himself or his action in the world to the laws which rule the nature of things." Ironically, de Lubac finds the Scholastic method of dialectic accomplishing precisely what Barth saw in the *analogia entis*.

Barth explained in a footnote why he felt more "at home" in Catholicism than in the Reformed tradition. He wrote,

> If I today became convinced that the interpretation of the Reformation on the line taken by Schleiermacher-Ritschl-Troeltsch (or even by Seeberg or Holl) was correct; that Luther and Calvin really intended such an outcome of their labours; I could not indeed become a Catholic tomorrow, but I should have to withdraw from the evangelical Church. And if I were forced to make a choice between the two evils, I should, in fact, prefer the Catholic.[29]

That of course is not high praise for Catholicism, but it is even less so for modern Protestantism. It helps us understand his opposition to Wobbermin.

Barth found Wobbermin's Protestantism incapable of challenging Catholicism in *theological* terms. He envisioned a robust Protestant theology that would be as grounded upon the solid truth of dogma as Catholicism, but he meant something different by "dogma" than did Peterson and the Roman Catholics. Wobbermin failed to take that into account. If Balthasar's presentation of Barth's work has any validity, it is in his insight that Barth's later work fulfilled something always present from his earlier *Romans* phase but inadequately expressed: Christian theology takes its form from its christological dogmas. Balthasar interprets Barth's turn in his latter work as, in the words of Lochbrunner, a "slight turn," which Balthasar described as "from the vision of humanity to the vision of Christ, from dialectic to sacrament, from a unity of opposition to a veiling of revelation." He referred to it as a "consistent path" because the latter was only the "becoming explicit of the presuppositions ignored in the initial form."[30] For Balthasar, Barth presented Christian theology in its true "ratio," in the true "form and tone of revelation." Balthasar rightly understood the important dogmatic implications entailed in Barth's doctrine of God, which we will take up in chapter 4. But the "ratio" Barth recognized also had implications for Christian ethics, which was what mattered most in the

---

29. "Roman Catholicism: A Question to the Protestant Church," in *Theology and Church: Shorter Writings: 1920–28*, trans. Louise Pettibone Smith (New York: Harper and Row, 1962), 314n1. This was also a lecture delivered in Bremen Mar. 9, in Osnabrück Mar. 15, and the Lower Rhine Pastor's Conference in Düsseldorf, Apr. 10, 1928. Barth made a similar claim in his lectures on Schleiermacher in 1923–1924. Karl Barth, *The Theology of Schleiermacher*, trans. Geoffrey Bromiley (Grand Rapids, MI: Eerdmans, 1982), 259.

30. Lochbrunner, *Hans Urs von Balthasar und seine Theologenkollegen*, 264

convoluted nature-grace debates. For Barth "dogma is ethics." It may be Barth's most significant insight. It will be taken up in chapter 5.

A third theme in Barth's response to Wobbermin is how he suffers Catholicism. Catholicism haunted Barth both practically and theoretically. He sought a Protestant theology able to address the formidable developments of Catholicism, both since Schleiermacher as well as those that occurred toward the end of his life at Vatican II. Catholics were capable of cleaning house in a way Protestants were not. They had become self-satisfied, content to repeat shibboleths from Father Schleiermacher, which is why Barth must become "acerbic" with Wobbermin. Barth wanted a Protestant theology as robust as what he saw taking place in Catholicism.

Censoring Balthasar's Barth Book: Catholic Opposition

Balthasar provides no evidence that he knew of Barth's exchange with Wobbermin or his accusation that Barth was responsible for the Catholic conversions of Bauhofer and Peterson. Barth's engagement with Catholicism already caused him to be suspect by Protestants like Wobbermin. Balthasar's preoccupation with Barth also provoked suspicion. When he sat in on Barth's 1941 spring semester course on the Council of Trent, Barth told his students, "The enemy is listening in." Referring to Balthasar, he also stated, "He hears many critiques but still offers no actual, impressive resistance. Perhaps he read too much in my *Dogmatics*. (He tows especially 2/1 in his briefcase around like a cat her youth)."[31] The expression, "the enemy is listening in," was a well-known Swiss public advertisement reminding Swiss citizens in the midst of World War II that spies could be anywhere and they had to be careful with what they said.[32] But it was not only Protestants who were suspicious of Balthasar; Catholic theologians also found his preoccupation with Barth problematic.

Soon after Barth's 1941 seminar on Trent, Balthasar completed his monograph on Barth's work and presented it to him. It was never published in the form first presented. Few people have read it, perhaps no one still living.[33] No one yet has compared it to the 1951 book and identified similarities and differences. We know he showed it to Karl Rahner and Dominikus Thallhammer.[34] It was also sent to his Jesuit provincial, Gutzwiller, and then

31. Ibid., 279.

32. I am indebted to Hans-Anton Drewes for this information in a conversation at the Karl Barth Archiv, Apr. 21, 2011.

33. Only one copy of it remains and it can be found in the Balthasar archives in Basel. Once it is open to the public, it will be important for someone to go through this manuscript and compare it to the 1951 book.

on to at least four censors, including Mario von Galli, Franz Lakner, Johannes Umberg and Dominikus Thallhammer.[35] They were neoscholastics, and for that reason suspicious of Karl Barth and Balthasar's preoccupation with him. None of them consented to its publication without significant revisions. Lochbrunner notes that the objections fell into two classes.[36] First were the theological objections; the primary and consistent one was that Balthasar did not uphold Vatican I's teaching of the twofold order of knowledge, where both faith and natural reason provided knowledge of God. Galli expressed concern that the book would be seen as an "enemy of scholastic theology." Lakner found his interpretation of nature and grace to be "incompatible" with Catholic teaching, and deficient in its understanding of natural morality. It lacked the clarity of Catholic theology because it used Barth's terminology. It was also guilty of "traditionalism," a position that claimed knowledge of God was only available to faith. Traditionalism had already been rejected in Catholic theology. For Lakner, Balthasar's work was "too influenced" by Barth, especially the latter's "voluntarism" and "personalism." Umberg cites the antimodernist oath that stated God's existence can be demonstrated "by the light of natural reason," and accuses the book of failing to uphold natural reason. He wrote, "The author must present clearly and unambiguously the consistent teaching of the ecclesial teaching office concerning the power of knowledge from human reason." The book was guilty of modernism. Dominikus Thallhammer also expressed concerns about Balthasar's understanding of natural knowledge of God and natural morality.[37] There is some irony in the censoring of Balthasar's book on Barth for this first concern. In his 1932 preface to the first volume of the *Church Dogmatics*, Barth had allied the teaching of Vatican I with Schleiermacher's theology. For Barth, both the *Vaticanum* (Vatican I) and a Protestant theology running "from Schleiermacher by way of Ritschl to Herrmann" contributed to a "secular misery" from which he sought liberation. Balthasar's Barth book challenged this claim. Barth was right about Schleiermacher, but wrong about Catholicism.[38] He defended Vatican I against Barth's accusations. Roman censors were unconvinced. Balthasar had

---

34. Lochbrunner, *Hans Urs von Balthasar und seine Theologenkollegen*, 410

35. Ibid., 413.

36. Ibid., 413.

37. Ibid., 444–47.

38. As will be shown in chapter 6, Balthasar feared Barth might be correct about developments in Catholicism after Vatican II. His fear was that Catholics had unwittingly embraced Schleiermacher's theology.

not adequately defended Catholic teaching. They remained suspicious of Barth and of any rapprochement between him and Catholicism.

The second concern was the precarious position of Catholicism, and especially the Jesuits, in Switzerland. Was this the appropriate time for an engagement and argument with a Protestant theologian who was himself controversial among Protestants? Balthasar's provincial, Gutzwiller, supported his work, but feared after publication it would be placed on the Index. For this reason he counseled him to publish a few chapters as essays in order to get his work before the public. At first Balthasar refused because the work was a "unity," but eventually he agreed, publishing two of three planned essays in the Dominican journal in Fribourg, *Divus Thomas*, in the 1940s.[39]

As Lochbrunner notes, given the difficulties it caused Balthasar, a lesser person would have given up working on Barth altogether. It is also remarkable that Balthasar expresses little of this when he finally publishes the Barth book in 1951. The only evidence of the difficulties is a veiled reference on page ten that the English version mistranslates. Balthasar wrote, "The author has meditated upon his theme for almost twenty years."[40] In other words, the book is not new but bears the mark of two decades of reflection and debate with Catholics and Protestants. Balthasar alludes to this history, but does not state it explicitly.[41] It is a sign of Balthasar's obedience. He was clearly frustrated at the censor's reviews and thought they misunderstood what he and Barth were doing, but he did not publicly challenge them. He revised the work over the next decade until an appropriate time was present for it to be published. Rather than diminishing his interest in Barth's theology, the time taken to publish it only increased his desire to engage Barth and Protestantism. During the year 1950, when he left the Jesuits, it became increasingly important to him not only to engage Barth, but also Protestantism.

---

39. Lochbrunner, *Hans Urs von Balthasar und seine Theologenkollegen*, 422.

40. Fr. Oakes's excellent English translation misleads us here such that the difficulty of the Barth book is even more hidden from English readers. He translates, "Der Verfasser hat sein Thema seit bald 20 Jahren meditiert" as "The author of this book has mediated on this theme since the early 1920s." Hans Urs von Balthasar, *The Theology of Karl Barth,* trans. Edward T. Oakes, SJ (San Francisco: Ignatius, 1992), xviii.

41. I would not have recognized the significance of this statement if Lochbrunner had not pointed it out. See Lochbrunner, *Hans Urs von Balthasar und seine Theologenkollegen*, 408 where he states that given how Balthasar put this one reference to the difficulty he had in publishing the book, it is not surprising that readers don't ask "why" the "great manuscript" had not been published earlier.

CENSORING BALTHASAR'S SERMON: PROTESTANT OPPOSITION

While Balthasar's Catholic colleagues expressed strong concerns about his preoccupation with Barth, Barth's colleagues were also worried about Balthasar's interest in their friend. Such worries arose from existing Protestant suspicions of Jesuits in Switzerland, suspicions supported by law. The "Jesuit paragraph" in the Swiss constitution, first set forth in the 1848 constitution and then maintained in the 1874, forbade Jesuits from teaching and preaching in "church and school." It was not rescinded until 1974. It was not always enforced, which upset Protestants such as Arthur Frey, who was Barth's close friend and publicist. [42] Ironically, in Barth's study beneath a picture of Mozart given to him by Balthasar hangs a picture of Barth and Frey standing side by side. Frey thought the Jesuits represented a serious threat to Swiss liberty, and he lobbied for the enforcement of article 51, the Jesuit paragraph. Frey was known in the Catholic press as a "Protestant agitator" against Catholicism. On September 7, 1953, while Balthasar was living in exile in Zürich, Frey addressed the Zürich Canton Council on the "Jesuit question." He acknowledged that Catholics felt "insulted" by article 51, and he distanced his critique of the Jesuits from Catholicism in general. However, he argued, the Jesuits were "absolutist" Catholics and if given freedom they would lead Switzerland into an absolutist state. He cited Ignatius Loyola's rule 13 of the *Spiritual Exercises* as evidence for their dangerous absolutism, where Loyola admonished Jesuits to confess, "I believe that the white that I see is black if the hierarchical church so defines it."[43] For Frey rule 13 was evidence of Jesuit absolutism. He argued every absolutist state was a Catholic state. It is "no accident," he wrote, that the "first dictator originated in Catholic Italy. It is also no accident, that none of the great dictators has been a child of Protestantism."[44] Likewise he argued that it is only Catholic states that fall prey to communism, whereas Protestant states such as "Finland, Reformed Switzerland, Holland and the Anglo-Saxon World" resist it.[45] Switzerland enjoyed its freedom because it rejected the Jesuit order and any Catholic nuncio, but lately the government had become lax in its enforcement of paragraph 51. Some Swiss officials were heeding the call to overturn it because it offends Catholic sensibilities. Moreover Jesuits now

42. Barth published his works, beginning with *Church Dogmatics* 1.2, with Frey's press Zollikon after the Nazis forbade his works being published in Germany with his previous publisher Christian Kaiser Verlag. See Busch, *Karl Barth*, 285.

43. Arthur Frey and Max Fischer, *Zeitgenössische Betrachtungen zur Jesuitenfrage* (Zurich: Evangelischer Ag., 1953), 70.

44. Ibid., 71.

45. Ibid., 72.

violate the prohibition everywhere with impunity. They are teaching in church and school, and even preaching on the radio. He wrote, "There are Jesuits preaching for many years, issuing instructions for converts, and doing in fact everything that the constitution forbade until finally the government becomes aware of this activity and conducts an investigation."[46] Such investigations are necessary, Frey argues, and despite the concern for Catholic feelings of offense, Swiss freedom requires the continuation of the prohibition against the Jesuits. Frey concluded his address with two statements. First, he reaffirmed the rich diversity of languages and religions that constitute Switzerland. This diversity will be threatened if Catholic nuncios are set up and the Jesuit order permitted. Second, he recognized that he himself "has been situated in the Catholic press for a decade as a Protestant agitator."[47] He claimed this misunderstood his position; nonetheless, Swiss freedom demands agitation.

Seven years earlier, on Christmas Eve 1946, Balthasar was one of those Jesuits violating paragraph 51 with impunity. He was scheduled to deliver a sermon on Swiss radio from Basel. At the last minute the Swiss Federal Council banned it. Balthasar's family waited around the radio in his hometown of Lucerne only to wonder what had happened. What had happened was the enforcement of article 51. As Lochbrunner notes, this "stirred up much dust in public." We have no evidence Frey was behind the ban, but someone had lobbied the Federal Council. Balthasar thought the Reformed pastor and president of the Basel Church Council, Alphons Koechlin, whom Barth knew from his college days, was responsible.[48] He sent a letter to Koechlin and copied Barth. Barth responded in good humor, but questioned Balthasar about the facts; he did not believe Koechlin was responsible.[49] Barth questioned the "tone" of Balthasar's letter, and jokingly suggested Balthasar's tone fell under one of the seven deadly sins so that he should acknowledge it next time he goes to confession. Balthasar responded that if he is wrong, he will make a pilgrimage on his knees to *Martinskirchplatz* in Basel, but if he is right, then his tone in this letter is "elegant." Moreover he tells Barth he has done no more in this incident than write one letter, and will do no more. He will not "raise any state action."[50]

Karl Barth disagreed with paragraph 51, which is evident by his support of ten public lectures Balthasar gave in Basel in 1948 on Barth's theology. Eberhard Busch describes those lectures this way: "In the winter of 1948–49

46. Ibid., 75.

47. Ibid., 83.

48. Eberhard Busch, *Karl Barth*, 36

49. Lochbrunner, *Hans Urs von Balthasar und seine Theologenkollegen*, 307.

50. Ibid., 308

Hans Urs von Balthasar gave ten much-discussed lectures on 'Karl Barth and Catholicism', resulting later in his book *Karl Barth*, published in 1951, which attracted even more attention."[51] The chronology is incorrect. Those lectures did not result in Balthasar's book, but the book gave rise to the lectures. The book had not yet appeared only because Balthasar's Catholic colleagues censored it. Much like the book, Balthasar's lectures were controversial. The Basel bishop, Franziskus von Streng, and the Protestant layman Frey opposed their public presentation. [52] Nonetheless Balthasar proceeded to deliver his lectures on Barth in Basel. Barth attended and sat on the front row.

Several months prior to Balthasar's lectures, Barth had offended many Catholics by his comments at the first meeting of the World Council of Churches in 1948. Barth's comments show that he was not immune from promulgating some of Frey's anti-Jesuit ideas, which of course made Balthasar's presentation and interpretation of Barth to Catholics all the more difficult.

J. L. Witte, SJ, the editor of the Amsterdam Catholic weekly for the Jesuit periodical *America*, interviewed Barth on September 25, 1948 during the Amsterdam Conference, little more than one month before Balthasar, still a Jesuit, was scheduled to present his first public lecture on Barth back in Basel. Witte found Barth refreshingly honest and blunt. He also agreed with him that much occurring at the World Council was "utter nonsense." Then he raised the issue of the offense Barth caused.

> Yet something in your opening discourse has hurt me, and many non-Catholics with me. It was the passage in which you mentioned "alleged Christianity" and "precisely Rome and Moscow" who refuse any contact with the World Council. You must have suspected that we would immediately link Moscow with communism and not think only of the Orthodox Church.

Witte then reported the following statement by Barth:

> "Indeed, I did," Barth said very frankly. "For I see a link there. I always felt Catholicism to be in agreement with communism. Both are totalitarian, both claim the whole man. Both reason from a closed circle. Communism uses about the same methods of organization;

---

51. Busch, *Karl Barth*, 362.

52. Lochbrunner, *Hans Urs von Balthasar und seine Theologenkollegen*, 422. Those lectures were not written down but delivered from shorthand notes according to Balthasar's secretary, Ms. Capol, recounted to me on Apr. 20, 2011, at the Balthasar archives in Basel.

it learned them from the Jesuits. Both alike stress the visible. But for Protestantism the more dangerous of the two is Catholicism. Communism will pass; Catholicism will remain."

Fr. Witte then offered a criticism of Barth's "spiritualistic conception of the Church," and posed this question to Barth: "If that is your idea about the Catholic Church, do you mean that the World Council of Churches should develop into an anti-Catholic bloc?" Barth responded, "I regret that it isn't." Fr. Witte then asked why he couldn't find more of a place for Catholicism as the Anglicans and Greek Orthodox do? Barth responds, "I know the Catholic Church better than those sentimental Americans and that mystical Florovsky. I know that the Catholic Church is not content with a place next to the others. If I were Pope, I should demand the same recognition which the Catholic Church now demands." Witte concluded his essay lamenting Barth's influence at the Council; it is a source of "tragedy." If the WCC is to be "really ecumenical" it could not include Barth's "closed circle of Reformed theology." If it continues in Barth's direction, its purpose will be limited. "If the Council continues in Barth's direction, the question will come whether cooperation with several other groups can be permanent. Already at Amsterdam the Greek Orthodox as well as the Anglicans, and even the Lutherans, have felt him as a menace."[53] In response to receiving Balthasar's essay "Preoccupation with Karl Barth," Barth sent Fr. Witte's interview from *America* to Balthasar, with the ironic claim that it showed he and Pius XII now "stick together." Barth referred to his claim that if he were pope, he too would refuse to think of Catholicism as one church among many. Barth and the pope shared this in common: neither compromise on the truth of their position.

Two decades later, after Vatican II, Karl Barth has a significant conversion away from his 1948 statements at Amsterdam. He explicitly denounces the Jesuit paragraph, and distances himself from the kinds of claims he made in 1948. Commenting on the Second Vatican Council Barth wrote,

> In looking at it we can only wish that we had something comparable, if it could avoid at least the worst mistakes we have made since the sixteenth century. I would be happy to see the words "Protestant" and "Protestantism" disappear from our vocabulary——and along with them the backwards article of exception in our Swiss constitution. The Pope is not the Antichrist![54]

---

53. J. L. Witte, SJ, "A Talk With A Giant," in *America*, Sept. 25, 1948.

Surely Balthasar's patient preoccupation, friendship and influence moved Barth toward a more appreciative understanding of Catholicism.

Frey certainly would have taken comfort in Barth's earlier condemnation of Jesuitism and Catholicism and scratched his head over these later comments. Perhaps this explains his surprise when three months after the 1948 Council Barth comes to Balthasar's defense and tells him not to respond to Balthasar.

Barth's comments at the World Council made Balthasar's engagement with his work all the more perplexing to leading Swiss Catholic intellectuals. In November 1948 Victor von Ernst, the Roman Catholic Canon Professor of Theology and editor of the *Kirchen-Zeitung* in Lucerne, published an editorial entitled "Karl Barth und kein Ende."[55] It began by recalling the scandalous statements of a liberal Protestant pastor who questioned the doctrine of the Trinity at the 1948 Amsterdam World Conference of Churches.[56] Ernst then said, "And the liberal direction holds undoubtedly in a still greater majority [of Swiss Protestantism] despite Barth and the so-called dialectical theology, which seems to find popularity among the youth." The subtext of Ernst's editorial is that Barth's dialectical theology and recovery of "strict Calvinism" does not provide any substantive alternative to this unfortunate liberal direction. In fact, it ends up denying the heart of Christian truth, not only through his denunciation of infant baptism, but also because Christ becomes disconnected from the world.

> Barth comes with his over-tensioned dialectical theology, with his disjunction of the world and men from God as from a "complete

---

54. Karl Barth, *Ad Limina Apostolorum: An Appraisal of Vatican II*, trans. Keith R. Crim (Richmond, VA: John Knox Press, 1968), 17.

55. *Kirchen-Zeitung Luzern*, Nov. 25, 1948, 116.

56. Ernst had commented on this in an earlier edition of *Kirchen-Zeitung* in a one-page piece entitled, "Der 'Welkonferenz' von Amsterdam" (October 14, 1948, 49). He began by saying that the *Kirchen-Zeitung* took no position on the "World Church Conference of Amsterdam" but were waiting on the Protestant side. Then he wrote, "As far as we saw, it has slightly broken down." The conference attempted to unify the 147 churches represented under the title: "Christus, unser Gott und Erlöser." Ernst rightly noted, "But this minimum of the Christian substance of faith could not serve as a basis of a theological-dogmatic agreement." Ernst would welcome a "religious deepening of Protestantism," but he doesn't see this occurring. He cited two French Protestants, one who wrote "blasphemously" of the Trinity. Ernst quoted him as saying, "I do not personally feel the need to fragment divinity in three parts in the manner of a puzzle . . . but if I were catholic, I would certainly attempt to add to the Father, Son and Holy Spirit a fourth piece, which would be reserved for the holy Virgin, regrettably forgotten." Ernst is also puzzled by Barth's objections to the conference: "Barth designated the entire conference as superfluous: one must leave everything to God. What is the purpose then for theologians, pastors and Barth himself?"

other" [*ganz andern*] finally to a denial of any divine revelation. Scripture and Church are not for him concrete structures of divine authority, but rather products of human darkness, even Christ himself had according to him no relationship to the world and church.

What Ernst found most disconcerting was the positive reception Barth's work had among Catholics. "It is astonishing that despite this absolute radicalization of theology by Barth there are still catholic theologians who offer their compliments and celebrate and still celebrate him as a great theologian."[57]

Shortly after the publication of Ernst's editorial, on November 12, 1948, Balthasar gave the first of his ten lectures at the Bernoullianum in Basel. After several of the lectures were given, Arthur Frey reprinted Ernst's essay in the *Evangelischen Pressedienst* on December 1, 1948, obviously attempting to show the distance between Karl Barth and Roman Catholicism. He introduced the reprint with the following comments: "The article shows how little unity there is in Catholicism about Karl Barth. Prof. Viktor von Ernst virtually vents his anger in the article that Karl Barth is recognized also by Catholics. He especially takes Dr. Urs von Balthasar to task, who in Basel holds no less than ten lectures about Barth and his theology."[58] Ernst had not mentioned Balthasar by name in his editorial; he only made an explicit reference to Jean Daniélou. Arthur Frey made sure to make any implicit connection explicit. Balthasar now felt obligated to defend himself and did so in an editorial entitled, "Preoccupation with Karl Barth" (*Beschäftigung mit Karl Barth*).[59] He sent a copy to Barth, stating it came from the "two fronts of the war movement." He found himself caught between the Protestant Frey and the Catholic Ernst. The danger for Balthasar was that his "preoccupation with Barth" would be interpreted as an opposition to other Catholics, confirming the fears many Catholics had about his work. After Frey republished Ernst's editorial with his own introductory comments, Balthasar responded by explicitly denying Frey could drive a "wedge" between Catholic theologians, and publicly affirmed that on "foundational dogmatic questions" he and Ernst would be in "complete agreement." The first part of his article set forth his unquestionable loyalty to Ernst and Catholicism, but the second took a different tone.

Balthasar challenged Ernst's interpretation of Barth, and in so doing interpreted Barth to Catholics: "But who does not gradually know, that Barth

---

57. *Kirchen-Zeitung Luzern*, Nov. 25, 1948, 116.

58. Lochbrunner, *Hans Urs von Balthasar und seine Theologenkollegen*, 311.

59. Ibid., 311. Balthasar published this on Dec. 11, 1948, in the Lucerne Magazine, *Vaterland*.

enjoys playing *das enfant terrible* in order to set the unsuspecting bourgeois not only in amazement but in fear? But can we not distinguish the *Person und Sache* and then suppose that a theology of the dimension of Barth's has nothing to say to Catholics?"[60] In fact, Barth had something "essential" to say. He questioned why Ernst still referred to Barth's "dialectical theology," which, "since the beginning of the *Dogmatics* disappeared from Barth's thought." He also questioned why he placed Barth within a revival of strict Calvinism, since Barth devoted his *Dogmatics* "only to the refutation of the basic positions of Calvin." He referred to Barth's work as "the first thoroughly consistent formed Protestant dogmatic, which at numerous passages outgrows the limitations of the earlier confessions." Balthasar admits Barth's doctrine of baptism is "Anabaptist" and he does not "share" it, but then he asks why the author writes that Barth "denies revelation, Scripture and Church as products of human darkness and claims Christ to have no connection to the world and church?" Clearly he thought Ernst misunderstood Barth. He encouraged him to begin again and read Barth anew. There is so much misunderstanding between Protestants and Catholics that Balthasar openly questioned whether the time was ripe in Switzerland for a confessional conversation, but he also asked if such a conversation was in fact "already in progress" over Barthian theology. Rather than speaking of *Karl Barth und kein Ende*, Barth's work was the beginning of such a conversation, its first fruits. Balthasar does not want this fruit at any price. He confessed that four hundred years of division were a short time given what is at stake, but a "heavy responsibility lies on us, that one must always presuppose in love, there is something to do."[61]

Balthasar sent a copy of his editorial to Barth, who thanked him for his "preoccupation with me" (*Beschäftigung mit mir*). Barth then intervened and supported Balthasar in his precarious position. He admonished his friend Arthur Frey to avoid any response to Balthasar's editorial. Barth was in a difficult position to admonish Frey because he had earlier opposed Frey over the question of censorship. Barth's own preaching had been censored in Bonn, and Barth consistently opposed Swiss censorship during the war, which kept him in difficulties with the Swiss authorities.[62] This opposition to censorship was one of two major differences he had with his good friend Arthur Frey, who thought some censorship in wartime was necessary.[63] Given these facts, Barth's earlier

---

60. Lochbrunner, *Hans Urs von Balthasar und seine Theologenkollegen*, 312.

61. Ibid., 313.

62. See Frank Jehle's *Ever Against the Stream: The Politics of Karl Barth 1906–1968*, trans. Richard and Martha Burnett (Grand Rapids, MI: Eerdmans, 2002).

response to the censoring of Balthasar's radio sermon in 1946 seemed mild. He supported Balthasar, and did not appear to support the Jesuit paragraph, but he certainly did not lead any movement to get it removed from the Swiss constitution at that point. He explicitly condemned it after Vatican II. In fact, Barth's reaction did not seem to possess the kind of outrage one would expect given the events that transpired. His opposition to the censorship of Balthasar's public sermon did not have the conviction he showed two years later when he came to Balthasar's defense and in turn silenced his friend Arthur Frey. He began his letter to Frey saying, "You know that your literary independence is sacred to me." He then proceeded, as Frank Jehle notes, to silence Frey.[64] He tells him that he will "exegete these remarkable texts" (Balthasar's lectures) and explain Balthasar's position, but it is not up to them to "participate in nor endorse" this intra-Catholic debate. They are "not in the peculiar position that [Balthasar] is" in that he endorses *Church Dogmatics* 1.1–2.2, and affirms Catholicism at the same time. He admonished Frey with 2 Sam. 18:5—"Deal gently for my sake with the young man Absalom."[65]

Frey did not respond to Balthasar in print, but he did share his "deep displeasure" with Barth.[66] He found Balthasar's editorial, especially in its first part, "classically Jesuit," which meant it was dishonest, equivocating on what he really believed in order to make himself acceptable to his Catholic confreres. He wrote, "The man was knocked out of the bush and now you take the gun out of my hand." He was particularly upset with the telephone call they had where Barth suggested Balthasar had to walk a thin line in his response. Frey responds,

> Dear Karl, what shall become of our poor world, when it looks thus in the church? You told me on the telephone that there is of course in Balthasar's article a deceit, but it would be in this case Catholics who are deceived. That may be, it does not make the thing more beautiful! Probably you and von Ernst are the ones deceived. But that this entire situation is for you still discussable, for that I have for the time being no explanation. But I must recall how narrow once was the way for you in the German *Kirchenkampf* about which you

63. Frank Jehle, "Karl Barth und der Publizist Arthur Frey. Zur Geschichte einer Freundschaft" in *Karl Barth im europäischen Zeitgeschehen (1935–1950): Widerstand-Bewährung-Orientierung*, ed. Michael Beintker, Christian Link and Michael Trowitzsch (Zurich: Theologischer, 2010), 219–23.

64. Ibid., 227.

65. Lochbrunner, *Hans Urs von Balthasar und seine Theologenkollegen*, 314.

66. This is how Jehle puts it. Frank Jehle, "Karl Barth und der Publizist Arthur Frey. Zur Geschichte einer Freundschaft," 227.

allowed no discussion. I thought you were then right. And now the worst hypocrisy is discussable. The air becomes so heavy one can no longer properly breathe.[67]

Why did Barth silence his friend? Perhaps because Barth thought Balthasar used his work as a "trojan horse" within Catholicism to reform it.[68] To that extent, he misunderstood Balthasar's purpose. Balthasar affirmed truth wherever it was found, even in Protestantism, but he always thought Catholicism, rightly understood, recognized and incorporated such truths. Such "integration" was what made it Catholic.

LEAVING THE JESUITS: ENGAGING PROTESTANTS

Balthasar's attempt to present Barth's work found few friends anywhere. Catholics like Ernst opposed it. Protestants such as Frey worried about it, and Barth himself only made matters worse. Indeed, Balthasar spent much of the 1940s trying to find an audience for his interpretation of Barth. It took incredible tenacity for him finally to succeed. When he left the Jesuits, Balthasar's task was made all the more difficult. The years between Balthasar's censored sermon (1946) and his public lectures on Barth (1948) were also years in which he experienced a crisis of vocation that culminated in his leaving the Jesuits (1949).

Two years before his public lectures on Barth that the bishop of Basel Streng opposed, Streng expressed his concern about Balthasar's work in Basel. In 1946, at the same time Balthasar started to wonder if he could fulfill his vocation through the Jesuits, the bishop began investigating Balthasar's secular institute, "the Johannine community."[69] The secular institute had no official standing. Balthasar petitioned for it to come under the province of the Jesuits, but the petition did not succeed. For that reason, the institute came under the authority of the Basel bishop. He kept his eye on it for some time, and expressed concerns about Balthasar's reliance upon the mystical visions of Adrienne von Speyr. His concerns were exacerbated when an event happened that caused Bishop Streng "to deal concretely" with the community. Urban Fink explains the incident:

67. Ibid.

68. Busch, *Karl Barth*, 362.

69. Urban Fink states that "already in August 1946" Balthasar and Adrienne von Speyr were a point of reference for Streng. Fink, "'Ihr stets im Herrn ergebener Hans Balthasar,'" 109. I am grateful to Bishop Henrici for the gift of this book.

> Triggering that was the circumstance, that the daughter of a respectable Solothurner family, who maintained close contact with Bishop von Streng, joined the *Johannesgemeinschaft*. This daughter answered her parents' question about the aim, purpose, and tasks of the *Johannesgemeinschaft* that she was not able to give, or did not know, the overall information.[70]

The parents appealed to Streng for information on July 15, 1947. Streng then questioned the Jesuit provincial about the status of Balthasar's community and discovered it had no official status. Nonetheless, he told the provincial he would do nothing as long as Balthasar remained with the Jesuits. Balthasar told him he would appeal to General Janssens of the Jesuits for official status for the institute. The general's response was that Balthasar's Jesuit vows were "unconditional."[71] The Provincial Thüer then instructed Balthasar to remove himself completely from the community on *Wettsteinplatz* so Streng could investigate it "unhindered." Balthasar did so, but when Streng investigated he was unhappy with Balthasar's ongoing influence on the community, even from a distance.

On March 20, 1948, Thüer met with Balthasar and encouraged him to take his Jesuit vows "without conditions." Fink notes that he conveyed to Balthasar, "Should [he] not consent to this step, he must ask for dismissal from the society." Balthasar did not want to accept the conditions, and responded that this could only mean his "exit from the order."[72] Thüer seemed puzzled by his response and "promised Balthasar all means and ways to keep him in the society." He knew Streng would not accept him in the diocese for "reasons of conscience" if he left the Jesuits, and so he asked him, "How will you continue your pastoral work without a canonical mission?"[73] In fact, Thüer prophetically described Balthasar's life from 1950 to 1956 when he worked without a canonical mission because he could not find a bishop who would incardinate him. To avoid this potential outcome, Thüer recommended Balthasar go to Lyon and undergo a retreat with P. Donatien Mollatt, SJ. Balthasar did so and returned convinced "obedience to God" was to be preferred to remaining in the order. On July 31, 1949, on the feast day of St. Ignatius, he sent a request to be released from the order.[74] Balthasar explained why he left: "I carry within me the incontrovertible certainty to be called to a task for which the required freedom is not able

70. Ibid., 110.
71. Ibid., 111.
72. Ibid., 116.
73. Ibid., 117.

to be given in the order. What kind of task this is, you know, if you read the little essay about 'Laity and Religious Life.'"[75] In that essay Balthasar was convinced that the "present hour" required a lay apostolate in the "form of the life of the counsels." Through the establishment of "secular institutes," which were affirmed in 1947 by Pius XII's encyclical *Provida mater*, laypersons would engage in Christian mission by professing vows of poverty, chastity, and obedience.[76] For Balthasar, secular institutes provided the best means for the Christian mission to the modern world. Convinced this was his mission, Balthasar chose the institute over the Jesuits.

Despite *Provida mater*, Balthasar's Johannine community had no official standing. Once Balthasar left the Jesuits neither did he. The Basel Bishop Streng banned him not only from his official work but also from living in the city, and the Jesuit Provincial Karl Thüer prohibited his lecturing there.[77] He was an exile. He moved to Zürich and spent six years in an irregular relationship with the Catholic Church. (Recall that Arthur Frey addressed the Zürich Canton Council in 1953 about the Jesuit question. Balthasar was living in Zürich at that time.) No bishop would take him in until 1956, when Bishop Christian Caminada of the Chur diocese did, granting him incardination.

Prior to his incardination, Balthasar was granted two temporary three-year terms in the diocese of Chur. The bishop allowed him to say Mass and hear confession. During his time in Zürich he corresponded with Streng explaining his position. Balthasar did not seem bitter or angered by Streng's decisions. For Balthasar, Streng did what he thought "best for the Church" even if it caused Balthasar pain to find a "closed door" in his home diocese.[78] When Balthasar sought incardination with the bishop of Fribourg, he told him to inquire with Streng as to the reason he left Basel. He did so and Streng responded. His response is measured. He thinks Balthasar's residence in Basel would have negative effects, but he also hopes he will find incardination in a foreign diocese and notes that he is "morally blameless."[79] Balthasar suffered these decisions obediently. He was finally granted incardination at the insistence of some influential laity on February 2, 1956.[80] Having left the Jesuits in 1949,

74. Manfred Lochbrunner, "Hans Urs von Balthasar und seine Verbindung mit dem Bistum Chur," in *Hans Urs von Balthasar—ein grosser Churer Diözesan,* ed. Henrici, 58.

75. Ibid., 63.

76. Hans Urs von Balthasar, *The Laity and the Life of the Counsels: The Church's Mission in the World,* trans. Brian McNeil, CRV, with D. C. Schindler (San Francisco: Ignatius, 1993), 58.

77. Manfred Lochbrunner, "Hans Urs von Balthasar und seine Verbindung mit dem Bistum Chur," 59.

78. Fink, "'Ihr stets im Herrn ergebener Hans Balthasar,'" 121.

79. Ibid., 124.

and given temporary rights to say the Mass and hear confession, he was finally received as a diocesan priest in 1956. He could now return to Basel, and take up his work again along with his personal conversations with Karl Barth. He moved into the Kaegi household.

Balthasar and Barth continued to correspond during Balthasar's exile. In fact they had agreed to travel to Rome together on November 1, 1950, for the Feast of the Bodily Assumption of Mary, and already had reservations at St. Peter's Basilica.[81] Balthasar's precarious ecclesial situation forced him to cancel. However, the following year, while still in an irregular canonical situation, his book on Barth finally found publication. He sent it to Barth on the feast day of Dionysius, and presented it to Pope Pius XII during a private audience in May 1952. He had finally presented and interpreted Barth to the Catholic world.

When Balthasar left Basel in 1950, he went on a lecture tour throughout Germany, largely to raise an income, for in leaving the Jesuits he also left all financial support behind. In seeking to get his Barth book past the censors, he wrote to the chancellor of the Roman Catholic diocese of Chur and explained why it was so important. "My travel throughout Germany has shown me that today, at the present moment, nothing is more urgent that a good, serious argument [Auseinandersetzung] with Protestantism."[82] This was not out of any irenic desire, but because of the scandal of disunity and the truth of the gospel. For this reason he refused a position offered to him by the Chur Chancellor Johannes Vanderock to assist in the Kurort St. Moritz in Engadin. He needed the time in the summer of 1950 to finish the Barth book so he could engage Protestantism, which is of the "highest importance."[83] He cites the Instruction from the Holy Office on December 20, 1949, on the importance of engaging Protestantism as the motivation for his work. When his book finally passes the censors in 1951, Robert Grosche will cite this Instruction as evidence for its catholicity.[84]

With the publication of Humani generis on August 12, 1950, publishing on Barth was made even more difficult. A November 1950 essay by a Lucerne Dominican, "Zur Enzyklika Humani Generis: Geschichte und Verurteilung der 'Neuen Theologie'" ("On the Encyclical Humani Generis: The History and Condemnation of the 'New Theology'") prompted Balthasar, even though the

80. Lochbrunner, "Hans Urs von Balthasar und seine Verbindung mit dem Bistum Chur," 62

81. Lochbrunner, Hans Urs von Balthasar und seine Theologenkollegen, 322.

82. Lochbrunner, "Hans Urs von Balthasar und seine Verbindung mit dem Bistum Chur," 70.

83. Lochbrunner, Hans Urs von Balthasar und seine Theologenkollegen, 427.

84. Ibid., 431.

book was already in the process of going to print, to call it back and once again revise it to make sure it did not conflict with *Humani generis*.[85]

Balthasar's Barth book had now passed the censors and found publication. Its publication, however, did not put an end to the controversies that accompanied his preoccupation with Barth since the 1930s. In many ways, they were only exacerbated. In 1953, an Innsbruck Jesuit, Gutwenger, raised the same issues that the censors had raised more than ten years earlier. For him, a key controversial passage was the following sentence in Balthasar's book:

> Questions about marriage, community, the State, our relation to a God who might not have revealed himself in his personal, interior life, the necessity for prayer in a natural state (which many people deny, for good reasons), the eschatological fate of the soul, resurrection of the body, Last Judgment, eternal bliss: all such questions addressed to pure nature are simply unanswerable.[86]

Gutwenger questioned Balthasar's "agnosticism" on these questions and challenged the "convolution" between nature and supernature in Balthasar and de Lubac.[87] Gutwenger concluded, "So we believe that Balthasar in his zeal to understand our Protestant brothers let himself be led away."[88]

Balthasar responded in an essay entitled, "The Concept of Nature in Theology." He began by noting, "The controversy about the concept of nature among today's theologians is not in the least an academic dispute. Behind apparently subtle, life-distancing distinctions stand decisions that touch many life nerves of Catholic theology and are important for ethics and apologetics."[89] He then accused Gutwenger of "philosophizing with a hammer" and restated his position on the relationship between nature and supernature, making subtle distinctions Gutwenger avoided. He argued that Gutwenger divided, as did modern theology, philosophy and theology too decisively, overlooking the "really existing" supernatural nature, and the one alone that "can be the object of philosophy, such that the theologian (and he alone) has the competence to abstract nature from this supernatural modality, in order to extract the pure antonym to supernature."[90] Following Barth, Balthasar built theology on the

---

85. Lochbrunner, "Hans Urs von Balthasar und seine Verbindung mit dem Bistum Chur," 72.

86. Balthasar, *The Theology of Karl Barth*, 283.

87. Engelbert Gutwenger, "Natur und übernature," *Zeitschrift für katholische Theologie*, 75 (1953): 82–97.

88. Gutwenger, "Natur und übernature," 97.

89. Balthasar, "Der Begriff der Natur in der Theologie," *Zeitschrift für katholische Theologie* 75 (1953): 452.

"really existing" creature God redeemed in Christ and not a hypothetical one philosophically built by abstraction. Against Barth, Balthasar acknowledged the role theology must play in identifying the creature to whom God comes in Christ in his or her *nature*, a being who is analogous, not univocal, to God's own being, a being who is made in God's image.

Balthasar did not discount Barth's criticism of Catholicism, but he did find Barth misidentified the error. The crucial issue dividing them was not the *analogia entis*, but the doctrine of pure nature. To Protestants, Balthasar insisted on the necessity of the *analogia entis* rightly understood, which meant that it never replaced Christology but worked within and from it. To Catholics, Balthasar insisted that Barth's christological renaissance captured the glory of God that best fit their tradition. Barth and Balthasar's friendship continued over the next fifteen years until Barth's death. What the history of their friendship demonstrates to this point is how much the controversy over Balthasar's engagement with Barth repeats itself. Gutwenger's objections have returned more than fifty years later. The contemporary Catholic theologian, Steven A. Long, refers to the same quotation Gutwenger identified in Balthasar's Barth book as problematic and also uses it to argue against Balthasar's catholicity, and to denounce Barth's baleful influence on Balthasar and Catholicism. Like Gutwenger, he argues Balthasar's preoccupation with Barth led him astray. Likewise some contemporary Protestant theologians abandon Balthasar's interpretation of Barth's work. For them, Balthasar presented Barth too much as a traditional theologian sympathetic to Catholic concerns, and lost, or failed to recognize, Barth's modernity. Returning Barth to Schleiermacher will supposedly bear more fruit than following lines set forth in Balthasar's interpretation of his work. Catholic theologians return to neoscholasticism, Protestants to Schleiermacher. The story of the contemporary difficulties of Balthasar's preoccupation with Barth, and its difficult reception in the present, awaits the reader in chapter three. But before engaging in those controversial discussions, the complexity and substance of Balthasar's interpretation must be carefully presented. Only then can the adequacy of those criticisms be assessed.

90. Ibid., 453. The next chapter provides a fuller discussion of Balthasar's position and its relationship to his interpretation and presentation of Barth.

2

Presenting and Interpreting Karl Barth

Throughout the 1930s and 1940s, Balthasar presented Barth's work to a Catholic audience, offering a nuanced interpretation along with affirmative and negative evaluations. His conversations with Barth, his struggles with the censors, and the constant critiques from Catholic and Protestant theologians resulted in his 1951 publication: *Karl Barth: A Presentation and Interpretation of His Theology.*[1] It is a complicated work. It had to be if it were to achieve its goal of presenting a convincing presentation of Barth's theology, an ecumenical "rapprochement," and at the same time demonstrate fidelity to Vatican I. In fact, Balthasar's preoccupation, interpretation, and presentation of Barth's work is much too broad, dynamic, and changing to be encapsulated in any single formula such as "from dialectic to analogy."

This chapter chronologically traces the development of Balthasar's interpretation of Barth's theology. It is a detailed discussion of the shifts and turns by which Balthasar traced the "ways" Barth broke through to a substantive dogmatic theology, which Balthasar claimed came closest to the Catholic approach because it adhered so closely to Christ. Although the details in this chapter might try the patience of the reader, they are necessary in order to make the arguments in the succeeding chapters. The next chapter assesses the abandonment of Balthasar's interpretation by Catholics and Protestants. If any theologian is to follow this abandonment, he or she should at least be clear on what is being abandoned. The stakes are high in abandoning Balthasar's interpretation for our understanding of Barth, of Balthasar, and of the ecumenical fruit their friendship bore. For this reason, Balthasar's interpretation must be set forth in all its complexity. Once that has been done,

---

1. I have translated Balthasar's book on Barth more literally than the English translation because the literal translation better expresses Balthasar's intent to present and interpret Barth's work to a Catholic audience and to Barth himself.

the appropriateness or inappropriateness of this call for abandonment can be calmly assessed.

The structure of this chapter is straightforward. It begins by examining four essays Balthasar published dealing with Barth in the 1930s, including his lengthy chapter on Barth in his dissertation, *Apokalypse der deutschen Seele* (*Apocalypse of the German Soul*). Barth is the only theologian to appear in that book, and it is there where Balthasar first states that Barth identifies the wrong Catholic error. It is not the *analogia entis* that should concern him, but a doctrine of pure nature. Each of these essays was written before Balthasar met Barth. After their personal conversations, some of the themes in these essays will remain, such as Balthasar's claim Barth misidentified the Catholic error, and some of the themes will disappear, such as Balthasar's use of *Gesetz* to express the form of the basic Christian principle, the incarnation. The second step in this chapter examines Balthasar's two published essays in the 1940s, "Analogy and Dialectic" and "Analogy and Nature." These two essays were chapters from the original 1941 manuscript that were published at the suggestion of Balthasar's Jesuit provincial. In a third step, each of the essays will be compared to relevant sections of the 1951 publication, *Karl Barth: Darstellung und Deutung Seiner Theologie*, which also provides the occasion to set forth Balthasar's complicated presentation and interpretation of Barth's theology. The final step draws some conclusions, tracing the similarities and differences in Balthasar's reading of Barth during his two-decades-long preoccupation.

Interpreting Barth in the 30s

Balthasar's earliest interpretations of Barth are the 1939 publications "Karl Barth," in the third volume of *Apokalypse der deutschen Seele*, which is subtitled *The Apotheosis of Death* (*Die Vergöttlichung des Todes*);[2] and a short essay that same year that bore the same title as the 1948 public lectures in Basel, "Karl Barth and Catholicism" ("Karl Barth und der Katholizismus").[3] A third 1939 publication, "Patristics, Scholastics, and Us" is not explicitly about Barth's theology, but it addressed Barth and set Balthasar's interpretation of him in the context of theological concerns about the Fathers, Scholastics, and moderns. It is a programmatic essay for both Balthasar's own work and his presentation of Barth. He also had a brief review in 1938 of Helmut Thielicke's *Die Krisis der Theologie* that was more about Barth than Thielicke.

---

2. *Apokalypse der deutschen Seele: Studien zu einer Lehre letzten HaltungenBand III: Die Vergöttlichung des Todes* (Leipzig: Erst Ausgabe Anton Pustet, 1939, and Einsiedeln: Johannes , 1998).

3. "Karl Barth und der Katholizismus," *Theologie der Zeit* 3, no. 2 (1939): 126–32.

In the Thielicke review, Balthasar took up Thielicke's accusation that Barth's theology contained a secret philosophical ideology, an *Identitätsspekulation.* Barth's theology sought to secure God's sovereignty but resulted in, as Thielicke put it, "a monologue of God with himself." Balthasar agreed with Thielicke's accusation, but only as it referred to the early Barth. The accusation did not fit Barth's *Credo, Theological Existence Today,* or the *Church Dogmatics.* He wrote, "In Barth's new phase, the economy of salvation is still an unconditioned monologue of God: no longer as the *dia* of the dialectic of God and world, but rather as the *dia* of the dialogue of the Father and Son, in which dialogue the world is enclosed in silence."[4] He saw in Barth's work since *Credo* (1935) an "analogy" between "God's love for us and our offered love for God."[5] Balthasar mentioned Barth's "conversation with Catholicism" and directed the reader to his forthcoming *Apocalypse of the German Soul* for a fuller interpretation of Barth. The review is only two pages long. However, it shows Balthasar's consistent interpretation that Barth turned from the *Romans* phase, where he could do little but deconstruct, to a dogmatic one, where Christian dogma makes a positive contribution.

Balthasar began the more substantive essay, "Karl Barth and Catholicism," acknowledging how difficult it is to interpret Barth, especially with respect to his attitude toward Catholicism, "because he constantly, often noticeably, often not, keeps changing." He described Barth's theology as "a strange, dazzling position between Old Protestantism and Catholicism, which is difficult to bring into an unambiguous formula."[6] Although setting forth Barth's theology is difficult, setting it forth was his major concern in this essay. It could not be done through a few propositions, but was more like finding the right way to present Mozart. "Karl Barth and Catholicism" cannot be well understood without setting it in the context of Balthasar's programmatic essay, "Patristics, Scholastics, and Us," and his interpretation of Barth in his *Apokalypse.*

FINDING FORM

Finding the proper form to Barth's theology preoccupied Balthasar in his *Apokalypse,* where he referred to Barth's work as a *Gesetz der Umkehrung* (a law of conversion or reversal). The term *Gesetz* is key to understanding Balthasar's complicated interpretation and evaluation of Barth, as can also be seen in the

---

4. Hans Urs von Balthasar, "Die Krisis der protestantischen Theologie," *Stimmen der Zeit* 132 (1938): 200–1.

5. Balthasar, "Die Krisis der protestantischen Theologie," 501.

6. "Karl Barth und der Katholizismus," 126.

essay "Patristics, Scholastics, and Us." It uses this term to render intelligible three epochs, the patristic, scholastic, and modern.[7] Balthasar identified each epoch's structuring law (*Gesetz*) and compared it to the fundamental law of the gospel. Such a procedure arose from his long interest in music. He could hear and see form in creation and sought to explicate it.[8]

The "Patristik" essay first posed a problem, and then laid out a method to address it. The problem is "we live in a time of the toppling of divine images and idols."[9] Notice the ambiguity of the problem. Idols are falling down, but along with them the image of God falls as well. Balthasar stated, "The spiritual and cultural traditions of the Western religion have become questionable, indeed even more, they are being liquidated rapidly and relatively painlessly."[10] This occurs like "a tree that loses its leaves [*Blätter*] in the fall in order to be renewed." He plays on the term *Blatt*, which can be a leaf, or a page in a book. The tree of culture is losing its leaves, its "spiritual and cultural" pages. Here Balthasar, like Barth in his *Romans* commentaries, sounds a note of crisis. Like Barth his response to this crisis is not reactionary. He eschews those who would blame the Scholastics for the crisis of modernity, abandon them entirely, and turn only to the Fathers. Nor did he affirm those who see the modern as only a decadent turn from the Scholastic era's purity and thus call for a return to the Scholastics. He directly challenged both responses, which could be understood first as that of the *nouvelle théologie*, and second that of neoscholasticism. Instead of romanticizing one epoch against the others, he looked for that which was worth preserving and critiquing in all three.

The method used to evaluate them is to "break through" to their "innermost structural law" (*innersten Strukturgesetz*) and compare it to the "structural law of the Christian (*Strukturgesetz des Christlichen*) as it encounters us in the gospel."[11] Balthasar's work here, which has resonances in both his *Apokalypse* and *Trilogy*, is to identify first the form or law of the gospel and then see how it radiates out into every epoch. Sometimes an epoch receives

---

7. "Patristik, Scholastik und wir," *Theologie der Zeit* 3, no. 2 (1939): 65–10. From here on this essay will be referred to as "Patristik."

8. Aidan Nichols traces the importance of "form" in Balthasar's earliest essay, "Die Entwicklung der musickalishen Idee," in Nichols, *Scattering the Seed* (London: T & T Clark International, 2006) 3–7. Balthasar had perfect pitch and had the ability to look at a musical score and hear the music. According to Ms. Capol, he would travel by taking the score with him. By looking at the score, he could hear the music.

9. "Patristik," 65.

10. Ibid., 65.

11. Ibid., 68.

the structural law of Christianity improperly. The epoch becomes a simulacrum that might need to be pruned because it distorts the center; other times the form of the gospel illumines an epoch showing us something we have not yet seen. Balthasar takes the reader through two forms of the law of the Gospel: "the fundamental law of the Christian: in Christ" (*Das Grundgesetz des Christlichen: in Christus*) and "the fundamental law of the Christian: in the church (*Das Grundgesetz des Christlichen: in der Kirche*).

The "fundamental law" of the Christian is based on the incarnation. Jesus is both God and human, without confusing the natures. God enters into that which is not God without ceasing to be God. Thus we do not have identity alone. Humanity is not God (theopanism) and God is not humanity (pantheism), but in Christ both natures are united without conflating one with the other. These themes from Przywara help Balthasar identify the basic *Gesetz* of the gospel. Reminiscent of Przywara, he states, "The more we recognize God, which says that we are in God for we only recognize God through God, the more we know we are not God."[12] For every similarity, there is revealed a greater dissimilarity. This statement expresses, for Balthasar, the *analogia entis*. But this fundamental law also shows Barth's influence: we only know God inasmuch as we participate in God. Like Barth, Balthasar thinks "enhypostatically."

The two temptations of theopanism and pantheism identified in the "Patristik" essay also represent the two forms by which the "apocalypse of the German soul" distorted the gospel that Balthasar traced in his *Apokalypse*. Here is another version of the "crisis" before modern theologians. The desire to empty God into humanity and thereby do away with God is similar to the "Promethean" temptation Balthasar identified in *Apokalypse*. Likewise to raise humanity into God, and thereby do away with human nature, is akin to the temptation he called "Dionysian." While he recognized Barth avoids the Promethean, his early dialectical work fell prey to the Dionysian. Both the Promethean and Dionysian lapse into an identity that prohibits genuine love, for only if there is otherness can there be a summons to love. As he puts it, "Only where there is non-identity is love possible."[13]

---

12. Ibid., 71.

13. Ibid., 71. He also writes, "Similarity in a radical difference is as such the formal foundation (*Grundriß*), the nature of every possible creature, and every gracing (*Begnadung*) on the side of God does not destroy this relation and does not cancel it (*aufheben*), but rather completes it through the elevation (*Erhöhung*), which it brings to it. Gratia non destruit sed perficit et extollit naturam." Ibid., 72.

In the "Patristik" essay Balthasar also identified a "law of nature" (*Gesetz der Natur*). It is a longing for God where the human creature seeks not to be similar to God, but to be God.[14] The longing itself is either good or evil depending on how it finds fulfillment. Nature is not pure because it has this longing. It can never complete itself. Only the incarnation properly fulfills it. Nature then, requires the incarnation for its fulfillment, but without collapsing nature into supernature, which would succumb to the *Dionysian* temptation; a temptation to which the early Balthasar found Barth succumbing. He did so because he identified the wrong error in Catholic theology.

In the *Apokalypse* Balthasar explicitly argued Barth misidentifies the source of error in Catholicism. It was neither in the *analogia entis* nor the *potentia oboedientialis*, both of which are "essential" to Catholicism, and were teachings Barth mistakenly rejected. Barth failed to realize that the true source of the error present in Catholicism is the doctrine of *natura pura*, which is nonessential and only results from the overreach of the Counter-Reformation. Balthasar writes, "We have then made no 'concessions' to Barth, but rather only demonstrated the *analogia entis* problematic as not identical and not indissolubly connected to a *natura pura* problematic, which first obtained broad theological validity since the Counter-Reformation."[15] Barth's real enemy should be this doctrine of pure nature, but Barth mistook it for the *analogia entis* and *potentia oboedientialis*. If Barth understood the latter properly, he would realize his own work already expressed them. Barth never seems to have heard, and Balthasar never tired of presenting, this criticism. If Barth had heard Balthasar the conversation he bequeathed us would have looked very different. It would focus less on the *analogia entis* and the correlative methodological and epistemological questions it gives rise to, which were of course always secondary for Barth, and more on the shape dogma gives to the practical living out of the Christian life, the main concern Barth and Balthasar shared.

After Balthasar explained, in his *Apokalypse*, the "slight turn" Barth made from dialectic to dogmatics, he then queried how Barth's dogmatic turn did not "presuppose and express the *analogia entis*?" For Balthasar it did, and Barth always had a version of it, even in the *Romans* phase, because his theology was first and foremost a "theology of Christ." Here is where Balthasar thought Barth should have recognized his consanguinity with Catholicism properly understood. Both Barth and some Catholics miss the fact that the "formal principle" of Catholicism is not an abstraction, but the incarnation. Barth

14. Ibid., 69.
15. *Apokalypse* 380.

too sought to do theology within this formal principle, but his early work kept slipping into the idealist tradition of "identity" in its Dionysian version by eliding human nature into the divine, especially because of the influence of the Reformed doctrine of predestination. Yet for Balthasar, the Dionysian identity was always on the surface of Barth's work, a tangent he was bound to correct because of his profound Christology and its role in his revision of predestination.

In his *Apokalypse*, Balthasar traces a turn in Barth's theology occurring in the late 1920s, especially 1928 and 1929 (before the Anselm book), when the term "dialectic" begins to disappear.[16] Balthasar recognized a dialectic remains after this turn. Barth, unlike Hegel, never sought a synthesis to his dialectic; it always remained open. Because it remained open, Barth's dialectic is more akin to Nietzsche, who played a crucial role in volume 2 of *Apokalypse*. As Aidan Nichols explains it, volume 2 takes place "under the sign of Nietzsche," moving from the Prometheanism of idealism to the Dionysianism of a philosophy of life. Nichols writes, "In Hegel's wake——and above all with Nietzsche——we hear a 'No' to Idealism and a corresponding 'Yes' to the heroic situation of life lived in conscious contradiction."[17] This conscious contradiction refuses any resolution to the thesis-antithesis differentiation. It was a heroic look at the crisis in modernity that refused to turn away from its contradictions by ameliorating them through an attempted synthesis.

Balthasar recognized, and explicitly cited, the ethical reasons why Barth affirmed this version of dialectic. It maintained the appropriate difference between God and creatures, something liberal Protestantism failed to do with its comedic performance of Christianity, reducing theology to ethics or consciousness in order to have a synthesis. If we synthesize God and creatures, then Christian theology gets reduced to ethics. Anthropology becomes its primary occupation, and ethics becomes building the kingdom of God on earth. We lose Christianity's apocalyptic dimension. The loss of a Christian apocalyptic concerned Balthasar in 1939; it concerned him as well after Vatican II. Although Balthasar affirmed Barth's reasons to avoid Hegel's synthesis and leave the dialectic open, he argued Barth's dialectic nonetheless fell into a Dionysian *contradiction* that denied God's presence in the created order. It still smacked of a deformed Platonism, with a faulty understanding of participation, where grace only comes when creation is destroyed. This destruction is the apocalypse present in much of German literature, which did not seek creation's

16. Ibid., 366. Balthasar makes the same claim in "Karl Barth und der Katholizismus," 126.

17. Aidan Nichols, *Scattering the Seed*, 133.

redemption, but its annihilation. It is the "deification of death," and does not fit the fundamental law of the Christian. Balthasar wrote, "This complete awarding of the great negative experience as the only thing that grace brings before the eyes, makes Barth's eschatology still Dionysian. It is not the redemption *of* this world, but rather nearly a transfiguration of a most painful ecstasy."[18]

Balthasar asked "whether this dialectic really corresponds" to the basic structure of Christianity, and therefore whether it truly "gives God the glory" and maintains God's "freedom?"[19] But he does not linger long in answering this question because "Barth himself has given the answer." That answer is found in the third part of Balthasar's interpretation of Barth in the *Apokalypse*, which he titled, "Theology of Christ" ("Theologie Christi").[20] The two previous sections were named, respectively, "The Conversion" ("Die Umkehrung") and "Dionysian Theology" ("Dionysische Theologie"). In 1939 Balthasar claimed Barth had already moved from the Dionysian identity of humanity with God present in the German apocalypse to a much more profound articulation of what mattered most to both of them: Christology with an analogy between God and creatures that prevented identity.

BRINGING BARTH IN CONVERSATION WITH THE FATHERS, SCHOLASTICS, AND MODERNS

Balthasar's "Patristik" essay, his *Apokalypse*, and the essays he would publish from his 1941 Barth book after it was censored bear a striking resemblance in terms of their overall structure. He correlates Barth's work to the three epochs assessed in the "Patristik" essay. In Balthasar's 1944 essay, "Analogy and Dialectic," which he reluctantly published at the request of his Jesuit provincial, he traced a similar threefold development in Barth's thought by seeing in it the "fruit of a certain retracing of Western theology," a retracing that followed closely the three epochs in the "Patristik" essay. Barth's first stage is similar to the "Greek patristic period in its native Platonizing and Neoplatonizing." It suffers

---

18. *Apokalypse*, 364. Balthasar's own position in his *Theodrama* comes close to such a transfiguration, which we will discuss in chapter 5.

19. "Man wird sich also angesichts dieses Ergebnisses fragen müssen, ob diese Dialektik wirklich dem Gesetz der Umkehrung entspricht, welches Gott die Ehre und Gott die Freiheit geben wollte, welches alle innerweltliche Notwendigkeit an der einzigen 'Nezessität' Seines Verfügens und Ermessens aufhängen wollte, — oder ob hier nicht vielmehr die Kreatur und ihre Problematk und Zerrissenheit selber prometheisch in den Himmel versetzt werde, ob die christliche 'Zuversicht,' mit der immer wieder 'Identität' gesprochen wird, wirklich noch *christlich* Zuversicht ist. Aber wir brauchen nicht lange zu fragen: Barth selbst hat die Antwort erteilt." *Apokalypse*, 365.

20. Ibid., 365.

from the error of "identity," which Barth reproduced in his *Romans* 1. At this stage, Barth was insufficiently dialectical. The second stage is an "Augustinian correction" in *Romans* 2, which can also be seen in Calvin and Baius.[21] It was dialectical, but an overcorrection. The third stage was Thomistic analogy, which he found Barth accomplishing by thinking with and through the true form of the Gospel. In fact with the third stage Barth approached

> probably for the first time, a Protestant radicalization of Thomas (not in the sense of a Scholastic systematic, which the Protestant scholastics already attempted—but rather a thorough formation or development [*Durchformung*] of the entire material knowledge of theology from a final simplicity and height of its principle.[22]

The correspondence between Balthasar's "Analogy and Dialectic" and the "Patristik" essay is not exact, but the strong similarities cannot be overlooked. In both essays, Thomistic analogy is the antidote to the overreach of identity and dialectic. Balthasar interprets Barth as a Thomist, but not in the Scholastic sense. He is a radical Thomist because, like Thomas, he consistently thinks the form of Christianity: the incarnation.

Just as Balthasar is for and against each of the three epochs in the "Patristik" essay, so he is for and against Barth in each of his stages. Balthasar's interpretation is not "Hegelian."[23] He does not read the three epochs through a thesis and antithesis resolved in a synthesis. Each epoch endures, and cannot be synthesized with the others. Balthasar found the patristic epoch present in Barth's dialectical phase, but like the fathers, Barth's dialectic suffers from a too-Platonic understanding of participation.[24] The Fathers, like Barth, took on too much of the Platonic *exitus-reditus* schema.[25] Balthasar does not want to be misunderstood here. He distanced himself from Harnack's Hellenization thesis, where ancient metaphysical categories corrupted Christian dogma.[26] Harnack and "other Protestant researchers" miss the important "relation of symbols" used by the Fathers and fail to see how they used these terms as "pedagogical

---

21. Balthasar, "Analogie und Dialektik: Zur Klärung der theologischen Prinzipienlehre Karl Barths" *Divus Thomas* 22 (1944): 173–74.

22. Ibid., 174.

23. Here I would differ with Benjamin Dahlke's interpretation of Balthasar in his *Die katholische Rezeption Karl Barths* (Tübingen: Mohr Siebeck, 2010), 197–200.

24. "Patristik," 90.

25. Ibid., 86.

26. Ibid., 82.

background" (*Erziehung*) for Christianity. The Fathers used symbols this way because like Catholics and unlike Protestants, they did not reject categorically the "eros" that moved the supernatural world of antiquity. Although such an eros was not "totally perverted," it was, nonetheless, "colored" by original sin to which the Fathers did not always attend.[27] Such a "coloring" can lead to a worldliness or "secularization" (*Verweltlichung*) already present in the Fathers that works itself out in time leading to the current crisis, both in its promise and peril.[28]

The promise was in the Fathers' realization, at Nicea and afterward, that the basic movement of Christian theology is "descent" and not "ascent." The eros present in creation was incomplete in itself; it needs Christ's descent. The peril was that this Christology did not find its way sufficiently into Christian spirituality, which still works too much through "mystical ascent" that bears the marks of the Dionysian eros. Mystic ascent is not directed to the Trinitarian God but to "an absolute simple essence of God that stands at the height of the Platonic period."[29] Balthasar should not be misunderstood here. Unlike many contemporary theologians neither he nor Barth denied God's simplicity. Both recognized such a denial would turn God into a mythical creature. The problem is not with simplicity, but simplicity distinguishable from Trinity. What thoroughly excited Balthasar about Barth's *Church Dogmatics* 2.1 is his skill at maintaining both, as we shall see in chapter 4. But what troubles him about Barth is his doctrine of creation; he finds it too Platonic, too patristic.

In the "Patristik" essay Balthasar identified similar errors in Buddhism, Platonism, Gnosticism, and "consistent Protestantism," by which he meant Barth. They all redeem by "destroying" nature.[30] Such destruction is the structural law of all great heresies. He wrote,

> This is the meaning of all great Christian heresies from Docetism and Origenism of antiquity to Joachinism of the Middle Ages up to the Protestant spiritualism of modernity. The *Gesetz* of the incarnation as the decisive highlighting of nature in its finality and for all times in the required sense is cancelled. The true incarnation in the flesh would be denied overall because it would be unworthy of God as pure spirit (Docetists), because it would be impossible for the holy God (consistent Protestantism, perhaps with Karl Barth) that in

27. Ibid.
28. Ibid., 83.
29. Ibid., 87.
30. Balthasar returns to this theme in his *Epilog* (Johannes Verlag: Einsiedeln, 1987).

Christ's act of redemption this nature is thought to be for all time overcome or raised up. Thus Christ is situated not in the *Gesetz* of Christ himself, but rather in the *Gesetz* of a spiritual-pneumatic existence, not in the tension of the old and new Aeons, but rather in a "spiritual kingdom."[31]

This spiritual-pneumatic *Gesetz* "bears the form of original sin."[32]

It is interesting to note Balthasar wrote, "*perhaps* with Karl Barth." In 1939 Balthasar was ambivalent in his interpretation. *Perhaps* his doctrine of creation bore the gnostic marks of a too-thoroughly Platonic anthropology and spirituality present in the Fathers that contributed to secularization. Balthasar's ensuing friendship with Barth two years later did much to alleviate his ambiguity. The 1939 essay reflects one of the virtual "conversations" he had with Barth before they met in person.

Given Balthasar's well-known dissatisfaction with neoscholasticism, and his penchant for de Lubac's theology, what comes next in the "Patristik" essay is surprising. He considered how the Scholastics offered "a necessary clarification of the foundational structure (*Grundstrukturen*), which in the realm of the patristics, could not arrive at full insight because of a certain lack of conceptual material."[33] The Scholastics turned from Plato to Aristotle, and therefore from participation to "causality," which "emphasized the self-movement of the creature."[34] Aristotle's philosophy better captured the fundamental law of the Christian, particularly as Aquinas developed it. Balthasar wrote, "Thomas recognized the paradox in its complete acuteness, as he expressed the principle, the closer a creature stands to God, the more it would be able, to move itself."[35] The self-movement of the creature is something Balthasar constantly affirmed, especially in his *Theo-Drama*, and it is something that always concerned him about Barth, but even more so about the Reformed doctrine of predestination, which Balthasar accused of Gnosticism and claimed Barth remedied. The Scholastics, unlike the Fathers, secured the proper place for "nature." But now a different temptation set in: "rationalism."

As Balthasar did with the epochs of the Fathers and moderns, he likewise does to the Scholastics; he poses a critical question: "Does not Scholasticism soon degenerate into an overestimation of natural reason and its capacity?" He

31. "Patristik," 75.
32. Ibid., 75.
33. Ibid., 92.
34. Ibid.
35. Ibid.

answered, "We do not deny this immanent danger nor the partial degeneration of late Scholasticism in a rationalistic subtilizing of the form of revelation."[36] Nonetheless, he argued, it misinterprets the Scholastics to see them developing a "pure philosophy." Only the late medieval and modern Scholastics developed a "pure philosophical 'system' of logical stringency."[37] Once again, the problem is not Scholasticism per se, but the doctrine of pure nature it generated and the form theology took once that doctrine predominated.

Balthasar affirmed the modern for its "progressive elimination of the Platonic-Hellenistic residues of the Scholastics," but he faulted it for a number of its changes, largely motivated by nominalism. Epistemology replaced ontology. The concept of universality "loses its ontological dignity" and became nothing but a "bare auxiliary for knowledge." The "individual" became the "only real existent." This "drive" then "degenerates further as empiricism, rationalism, deism, materialism, and historicism." Protestant "actualism" and its "theology of crisis" participated in this degeneration.[38] Although Barth is not mentioned by name, Balthasar sharply critiques him. Similar to a criticism he levied against him in the *Apokalypse*, the early Barth is both too ancient and too modern. However, in each of these criticisms Balthasar professed Barth already answered his critics in his turn to dogmatics; it is Barth's "breakthrough."

CATHOLICIZING BARTH

Balthasar consistently asserted throughout all these conversations with Barth that he "broke through" his earlier dialectic phase, and in so doing, Barth made a decisive break with Calvin, as his editorial response to Ernst showed in the first chapter. That is an overstatement. Barth adhered to much of Calvin's work. (He also adored him, having three pictures of him in his house and study.) But Balthasar is correct at one point. Barth broke with Calvin on the question of predestination. For Balthasar this was the decisive break with Calvin, one that overcame old confessional boundaries.[39] For this reason, in his "Karl Barth and Catholicism," Balthasar affirmed Barth as "the most significant Protestant thinker of modernity, perhaps since Luther and Calvin generally."[40] Nonetheless, Barth confused two important questions. The first concerned "the

---

36. Ibid., 93.

37. Ibid., 94.

38. Ibid., 96–97.

39. Matthias Gockel points out how this breakthrough bears affinities with Schleiermacher. See his *Barth & Schleiermacher on the Doctrine of Election: A Systematic-Theological Comparison* (Oxford: Oxford University Press, 2006).

40. "Karl Barth und der Katholizismus," 127.

relation of the sinful world to the gracious God," the second the "relations of the natural world to the God of revelation."[41] Balthasar contrasted Barth's confusing position on these two questions with "a short development of the Catholic solution," which allowed him to explain how Barth is both for and against Catholicism, and by implication how Catholics should be for and against Barth. It was one of the first times he "catholicized" Barth. He does so by taking up Paul and Augustine.

On first glance, Balthasar admits, both Paul and Augustine seem to support Barth's criticisms of Catholic teaching on nature. Paul claimed the wisdom of the world is foolishness; Augustine argued "pagan virtues are splendid (glittering) vices." But, Balthasar objects, we can interpret Augustine's position in two ways. First, these virtues are not virtues at all. This would be more akin to Barth's Protestant solution. Second, they are virtues but only as they are "hidden in Christ." We do not *naturally* recognize them as such without recognizing them in Christ. This second accords with a "Catholic interpretation" because they would not be virtues if God did not take them up into God's mercy and make them something they are not in themselves. Then Balthasar made an interesting and important turn. The world we actually inhabit is a place where this has always already been accomplished. "Neither Paul nor Augustine say, however, in these statements, what actually is, but rather what would be if God did not take mercy on us. They press on from an inner proper relation between God and the sinner to no actual relation. Because in truth, God has taken mercy."[42]

Thus these natural or pagan virtues provide no "point of contact" between God and creatures that one can seize and use to move from nature to God. Eros does not work with this direction of ascent. Here Balthasar sided with Barth against neoscholasticism, which was the reason Balthasar's work brought suspicion on him from certain Catholic quarters before and after his Barth book. But nor are these virtues, like nature itself, simply to be contradicted and destroyed so that all that remains is a "supernature" that demolishes "nature." Here he sided with Thomas against the early Barth and Reformed doctrines of predestination, which Balthasar identified as a species of Gnosticism. Insofar as Barth reminds us of the need for the "repudiation of the sinful world and behind it conceives the abundant precedence of grace before nature," he too expresses a Catholic disposition. But insofar as Barth teaches that "it lies in the essence of nature to be remote from God," he cannot be made consistent with a Catholic position. He confused the "sinful world" with "nature" and

41. Ibid.
42. Ibid., 128–29.

"grace" with "supernature."[43] The result is an inadequate doctrine of both. Nature becomes nothing but a crater, an empty hole (an expression from Barth's *Romans* commentary—*Hohlraum*—that always troubled Balthasar). Grace then would simply be a supernatural intervention that makes no contact with nature. Balthasar categorically rejects this understanding of nature and grace. If it were true, grace would not be "objective." It would have no nature to which it came because nature would be nothing but a crater.[44]

Nature as an empty hole was Barth's stated position in his *Romans* phase, but Balthasar denied Barth ever consistently held it—even then. If he had, "it would necessarily lead to a complete negation of the world" and the "loss of the incarnation."[45] Barth never intended to negate the world or lose the incarnation and so the *Romans* interpretations of nature always sat uneasily with Barth's best insights. In his dogmatic turn he accentuated the place for the incarnation, which brought a more positive account of creation (and nature) that made it something other than sin, producing a rapprochement with Catholicism.

> In his *Church Dogmatics* Barth has on several occasions expressed Catholic positions. In place of the old Lutheran subjectivism is now a stronger move toward objectivity. Revelation appears in an objective church, through a visible donor in objectively efficacious sacraments. Indeed, to this visible entrance of revelation in the realm of the world corresponds now a positive taking up of nature itself: a self-efficacy of human reason and freedom internal to faith, a recognition of "created grace." Here and in many individual issues, Barth has broken through the foundation of his dialectic.[46]

That Barth had "objectively efficacious sacraments" in an "objective church," is certainly questionable, but defensible, as chapter 5 and 6 below will argue. Balthasar sees this objectivity as a necessary consequence of Barth's dogmatic turn. Theology lives from its object.[47]

43. Ibid., 130.

44. Balthasar categorically rejected understanding "nature" as a *Hohlraum*, which suggests Steven A. Long's critical interpretation of Balthasar as turning nature into a "vacuole" for grace is in error. See Steven A. Long, *Nature Pura: On the Recovery of Nature in the Doctrine of Grace* (New York: Fordham University Press, 2010), 52–110.

45. "Karl Barth und der Katholizismus," 131.

46. Ibid., 131.

47. Hans Urs von Balthasar, *Karl Barth: Darstellung und Deutung Seiner Theologie* (Cologne: Jakob Hegner, 1951), 13. Balthasar, *The Theology of Karl Barth,* trans. Edward T. Oakes, SJ (San Francisco: Ignatius, 1992), 25.

Throughout Balthasar's 1930 essays, he affirmed Barth's "priority of grace to nature."[48] He questioned, however, if for Barth this grace *comes* to a nature, which is the Catholic solution, or if it exists only in supernature, which then made it inappropriate for creatures. The latter was a Protestant solution that returned nature to the "nothingness" (*Nichtigkeit*) of the Protestant dialectic.[49] Grace would then be only supernatural and all it could do is come to a bare nothingness. As previously noted, Balthasar recognized why Barth adopted this dialectical method against liberal Protestantism: "The grounds on which Barth so stubbornly wards off any positivity of nature are ethical grounds."[50] For Barth, our "natural" ethics failed and precipitated a crisis that then required his dogmatic turn. Like Balthasar, Barth recognized the dire consequences of reducing theology to ethics. Such a reduction prohibited the priority of grace to nature or culture. Ethics was then read off the world as it is. For Barth, this fell apart in the political scene in the early twentieth century. Now we had to ask the question again, "What Shall We Do?" This question produced the *crisis* that his theology addresses; it is the ethical reason he emphasized dialectic. Balthasar affirmed Barth's concerns about the reduction of theology to ethics, but he found Barth capitulating too much to the "nothingness" that precipitated this crisis. In his 1951 book Balthasar will write, "The second *Römerbrief* is—in a dangerous proximity to Nietzsche—'dynamite' (R 238)."[51] We should not forget that Balthasar already examined and questioned the "apocalyptic soul" of German literature, wondering if it ultimately could do anything other than affirm death.

INTERPRETING BARTH IN THE 40S

Hans Urs von Balthasar's life and vocation entered into its own crisis in the mid to late 1940s, but this did not deter his preoccupation with Barth. After the censors rejected his manuscript, he turned it into essays and published "Analogy and Dialectic: On the Clarification of the Theological Principles of Karl Barth" in March 1944, and "Analogy and Nature: On the Clarification of the Theological Principles of Karl Barth" in March 1945. These essays offer a glimpse into the unpublished 1941 manuscript. Unlike the 1930 essays, they also bear the fruit of Balthasar's personal conversations with Barth. The 1944 essay states that any "fruitful engagement" with Barth's theology must attend to its

48. "Karl Barth und der Katholizismus," 131.

49. Ibid., 132.

50. Ibid.

51. Hans Urs von Balthasar, *Karl Barth: Darstellung und Deutung Seiner Theologie*, 75

"formal principles." Much as we saw in the "Patristik" essay, Balthasar remained concerned with "form." But Barth had explicitly denied that the incarnation could be called a *Gesetz*, and that term, although still used in these essays, largely disappears from the 1951 Barth book, in which Balthasar most often refers to the "*Denkform*" (thought form) of Barth's work rather than its *Gesetz*. Nonetheless, here is where Barth and Balthasar may never have had a "fruitful engagement." Barth simply didn't see why the conversation should begin here; it was too speculative, too philosophical. It is a starting point to which he never consented and Balthasar never relented. In 1962 Balthasar published a second edition of his Barth book. The same approach began the book, comparing the "thought forms" of Barth and Catholicism. A year earlier, on Christmas Eve 1961, he added a long foreword acknowledging Barth had not changed his basic polemical position or Balthasar his main criticism. Balthasar sent the revisions to Barth and confessed he did so cautiously because "it will probably not make for any pure joy," and then concluded his letter saying, "May it not displease you too much!"[52] After vacationing and having broken his right arm, Barth responded by referring to a novel he had read that explained their relationship. They are "ships that meet at night." Like those ships they meet and pass in opposed directions "without forgetting and without grief." Then he stated:

> You were not able to find yourself in my persistent traveling on the theological one-way street. Who knows whether you might not have already been close to those monks of the nitrischen desert? I in turn am able neither to join nor be inclined to your high altitude flight in a beyond of philosophy and theology. I understand you as a Catholic Tillich (and as such much more interesting and full). It goes without saying that I will henceforth accompany you and your work—in a bewildering participation or rather in a participating bewilderment—and look forward to every contact with you.[53]

Balthasar responded expressing concern for Barth's broken arm and his hope that it was not the only thing broken.[54] He renewed his affirmation of "the christological and theological brackets" Barth places around philosophy but also his opposition to Barth's take on philosophy in general.[55] However Barth could

---

52. Lochbrunner, *Hans Urs von Balthasar und seine Theologenkollegen: Sechs Beziehungsgeschichten* (Würzburg: Echter, 2009), 348.

53. Ibid., 349.

54. Ibid., 350.

not avoid philosophy and the question of form. He had identified the Catholic form, *analogia entis*, as the antichrist.

Form mattered for Balthasar because it divided Barth and Przywara, Protestantism and Catholicism. After emphasizing the "formal principle" in the 1944 essay, Balthasar then mentioned the "paradox" Barth and Przywara represented to each other. Barth accused Catholicism of laying hands on God by the form its theology takes: the *analogia entis*. Przywara reproached Barth for the same thing by the form his theology takes: dialectic. "Dialectic is for him [Przywara] the titanic attempt to jump over the creaturely distance to God in a kind of theological pantheism."[56] Balthasar then concluded that this paradox, where both "hurl the same reproach against each other . . . stimulates a renewed consideration of these formal principles."[57] For Balthasar, Barth could not refer to the *analogia entis* as the antichrist and then neglect a significant engagement with the "form" of theology.

Balthasar largely defended Barth's theological form in the 1944 essay. Barth's work, he suggested, developed along three stages: first a "theology of identity," then "contradiction," and finally "analogy" (*Identitätstheologie, Widerspruchstheologie, Analogie*). These stages roughly correspond to the publication of *Romans 1*, *Romans 2*, and the *Christian* and *Church Dogmatics*. But this three-stage development did not represent any decisive breaks. To the "finely tuned ear," Balthasar states, each of the latter stages can be heard in the former. They represent the "*Gesetz* of a progressive discovery of theology."[58] This musical analogy will be further expanded in the 1951 book.

Balthasar heard "dialectic" and "analogy" in each stage. He did not dismiss dialectic but distinguished dialectic as method from dialectic as ontological contradiction. The latter was particularly found in *Romans 2*, which was a "demonic attempt to think contradiction through all the way to the end."[59] Once Barth thought it through, without "short-circuiting" or "evasion," then it inevitably led to the "horizon of analogy" because dialectic as ontological contradiction is a dead end—literally. All it can do is deny and destroy creation; it is one more instance of German apocalypse. For this reason, dialectic alone cannot express well the basic form of Christianity, the incarnation.[60] What Balthasar and Barth shared in common, a commitment to the incarnation as

---

55. Ibid.
56. "Analogie und Dialektik," 171.
57. Ibid., 172.
58. Ibid., 173.
59. Ibid.
60. Ibid., 174.

the form of theology, is also what caused their deepest disagreements. For Balthasar, Barth was never merely a dialectical thinker because he was always a Christocentric theologian. Even in the early period, analogy was tacitly necessary. The issue between Catholicism and Barth, and thus between Catholicism and Protestantism, did not really take the form of analogy versus dialectic. That was misleading. Both agreed, given the incarnation, "analogy" is the necessary form Christian theology must take. The real difference was whether the analogy is of being (*entis*) or of faith (*fidei*). This difference mattered. Balthasar named it "the last essential difference" between Catholicism and Protestantism. It had a "deadly seriousness" and was something much more than "idle theological bickering."[61]

Balthasar may have always heard analogy in Barth's dialectic, but he also heard "identity" even in the "contradiction" of *Romans* 2, albeit "horribly distorted." In other words, these stages were not progressive advances. They were failed attempts to express adequately the Christian form. As he had argued in the 1939 essay "Karl Barth and Catholicism," so he argues here: Barth's early work collapsed creaturely being into guilty and sinful being. Thus he lacked an adequate concept of nature. His anthropology did not take the form of the *fall* of a nature, but the *nature* of fallenness. This left nothing for creatures to do but be negated. This was how dialectic as contradiction collapsed back into identity. If creation can only be negated, then it contributed nothing in the soteriological drama. God will be the lone actor. Balthasar acknowledged this is not what Barth sought to affirm, but it was the logical consequence of dialectic as contradiction if it were consistently carried through.

THE BURNING MATTER OF DISPUTE: LOSING NATURE TO GRACE

Balthasar took up this concern again in his 1945 essay, "Analogy and Nature." If the "last essential difference" between Catholicism and Protestantism was found in the distinction between analogy of being or faith, Balthasar now established why it mattered. The "burning matter of dispute a priori decides the realm (*Gebiet*) of the natural knowledge of God and ethics."[62] The difference mattered because of the "realm" within which natural knowledge of God and ethics would be pursued. The importance of this dispute cannot be overstated.

Balthasar began the 1945 essay summarizing the findings from the 1944 one. The earlier essay made "agreement" with Barth possible because the "right

61. Ibid.

62. Balthasar, "Analogie und Natur: Zur Klärung der theologischen Prinzipienlehre Karl Barths," *Divus Thomas* 23 (1945): 3.

understanding of the concept of dialectic in Barth is able to subordinate it to analogy." Notice he did not reject dialectic, or argue Barth moved decisively away from dialect to analogy. Instead the conclusion from the first essay brought over into the second was that Barth subordinated dialectic to analogy and that made for a possible agreement between Protestantism and Catholicism. This agreement is limited, however, because "the possibility of subordination (through which the door to a true agreement is opened) depends on the recognition of the concept of creaturely nature."[63] A proper understanding of analogy required a robust concept of "creaturely nature." Balthasar must now examine this decisive difference, which is the reason for the title to his second published essay, "Analogy and Nature." Balthasar sets forth his basic position right away. Without the concept of "the independence of nature," which required the *analogia entis* as a *"philosophical principle* as a *presupposition* of the relationship of revelation between God and creation," the *analogia fidei* cannot be adequately represented.[64] The analogy of faith without the presupposition of the analogy of being was impossible. Balthasar then developed his position in two sections, which have four and three subsections respectively. First he explained "Analogy in the Concept of Nature," and then "The Analogy between Nature and Grace."[65]

In the first subsection, "On the Question," in the section, "Analogy in the Concept of Nature," Balthasar presented the Catholic concept of nature, beginning with a traditional understanding where it is, following Augustine and "all the Fathers," a "physical ontological unity" of "creaturely essence and grace." But such a unity was never "necessary." "It belongs to the essence of the creature that it is of course creature, but never that it must be an elevated, graced creature."[66] So the synthesis between grace and nature is "factual," but not "necessary." Grace is not owed to nature; it is always a gift. Balthasar argues that Baius, Jansenism, and Protestantism takes what is a fact and makes it necessary because the fall not only disrupted the synthesis, but also destroyed the nature. Once the nature is destroyed, the only agency possible for its redemption is God's. Grace becomes nature with the latter making no contribution. From Trent to Vatican I, the Catholic *duplex ordo cognitionis,* which Balthasar unequivocally defends, sought to safeguard "grace" from its "naturalizing." It is

63. Ibid.

64. Ibid. Emphasis original.

65. Much of this material found its way into the 1951 Barth book in the third part, the "Thought-Form in Catholicism," under the sections, "The Concept of Nature in Catholic Theology" and "Christocentrism."

66. "Analogie und Natur," 5.

"naturalized" when grace is made the necessary feature of human nature. This is akin to Eutychianism where the divine and human are reduced to a single nature.

In effect Balthasar defended a hypothetical pure nature. We know from abstraction that grace is not nature, even though factually we do not know of a human nature that has not been graced. Initially his essay posed a sharp question to Barth and Protestantism, "Where is your doctrine of nature?" But he then made an interesting turn, posing a question to Catholicism: "But now Barth asks us a question: What about the entirely unevangelical possibility of a *natura pura*? Even of a natural theology?"[67] Of course, Barth never actually raised this question. His question was primarily about the *analogia entis*. But as we have seen, Balthasar was convinced that Barth misunderstood it even when he pointed in the right direction of the critical question that should be addressed to Catholicism. Balthasar put in Barth's mouth the question he thought Barth should have asked. The real problem is the nonessential teaching of *natura pura*, not as a hypothetical abstraction from factual reality but as an actual reality that then defines the realm within which the natural knowledge of God and ethics gets determined, especially when (or if) Catholicism assumes such knowledge can be known with precision, prescinding from the revelation in Jesus Christ.

Balthasar never opposed a *duplex ordo* where grace and nature, like theology and philosophy, overlap without being changed into each other. He never veered from Chalcedon whenever he presents the relationship of nature and grace. Scripture and tradition, rather than Aristotle's *Posterior Analytics,* always have the first and last word. He did not think theology within, or upon the ground floor of, philosophy, but philosophy within theology. This approach created a two-pronged disagreement. Against Barth and Protestantism, he challenged an anthropological monophysitism that could not distinguish nature from grace, philosophy from theology, and collapsed them into an identity. Against neoscholasticism, he challenged an anthropological Nestorianism that distinguished them as discrete realms.

THE BURNING MATTER OF DISPUTE: LOSING NATURE TO NATURE

To explain the distinction between grace and nature well, Balthasar argued for a more theologically transformed understanding of nature in the second subsection, "The Concept of Nature in Philosophy and Theology." He began with a textbook definition of nature, determined philosophically from Aristotle and found in the Latin manuals and Scheeben (someone whom Barth admired),

---

67. Ibid., 6.

as "*constitutive, consecutive* and *exigitive*."[68] A nature is what it is constitutively, consecutively, and appetively. In other words, a nature follows from a nature (*consecutive*), makes that nature what it is and not something else (*constitutive*), and in desiring its proper end (*exigitive*) always has the means intrinsic to it to attain that end. As was the case with Aristotle, the Stoics and Scholastics, this means a nature is born or generated from an original source (*nascitur*). It is static and dynamic at the same time because it can be recognized for what it is, but it can primarily be so as it continues the movement of that which it is, which is also the goal toward which it naturally aims. Balthasar found this definition of nature hampering Christian theology. Like *hypostasis* and *physis*, it could only be used once it was theologically transformed. When he speaks of a theological conception of nature over and against a philosophical one, he refers to this necessary transformation.

Balthasar finds both Protestantism and Catholicism hampered by this late Scholastic definition of nature. Baius, and by implication Protestantism, took this philosophical definition of nature and applied it to the factual synthesis of the graced creature, which made Adam's appointment to the end of blessedness intrinsic to his nature. When he lost that end, which he did in the fall, he lost his nature. In so doing Baianism reduced theology to philosophy without recognizing it had done so. A philosophical definition of nature defined it even in its graced state. Against this, Balthasar emphasized

> that the grace of the children of God cannot lie in the concept of creation, that it indeed must stand to it in a certain opposition. Creaturely being as such is called servant-being. Grace is called freedom, progeny, and friendship. The revelation of God that lies in the fact that he brings forth creation is in no way conceptually identical with that revelation of God in which he raises creatures to a participation in his personal, inner, divine life.[69]

---

68. Ibid., 8, 10. Barth referred to Scheeben as "the greatest figure which the Roman Catholic Church has recently produced in the German sphere." See Eberhard Busch, *Karl Barth: His Life from Letters and Autobiographical Texts*, trans. John Bowden (Philadelphia: Fortress Press, 1976), 13. Balthasar is much more critical. Scheeben also defines nature philosophically and doesn't see that the term "nature" must undergo a metamorphosis when it arises theologically rather than philosophically. For a very similar discussion to the section here in the 1945 essay, see *The Theology of Karl Barth*, 270–82.

69. "Analogie und Natur," 14. Notice that Balthasar makes this argument prior to *Humani generis*, which calls into question John Milbank's interpretation where Balthasar, like de Lubac, concedes too much to the encyclical. See *The Suspended Middle* (Grand Rapids, MI: Eerdmans, 2005).

If nature is philosophically defined as "constitutive aut consecutive aut exigitive," then it could not possibly be equated with a theological concept of nature. For then, supernature would be defined simply as the negation of this philosophical concept of nature as

"quidquid non pertinent ad naturam aut constitutive aut consecutive aut exigitive" (whatever does not pertain to nature constitutively or consecutively or appetitively).[70] For Balthasar, this definition will not do. The trouble with the Catholic manuals, including Scheeben, is that they start with this philosophical definition of nature from Aristotle and then define supernature and grace in opposition to it. Balthasar affirms a concept of nature independent of grace, but the method to attain it should be theological. The concept of nature is derived from the "vocation to the vision of God" (*Berufung zur Anschauung Gottes*), and not the other way around.[71] Balthasar fears this is what the manualist tradition has done, even Scheeben, and it distorts the realm within which the natural knowledge of God and ethics is then pursued.

Although nature is derived from grace and not vice versa, we do nonetheless know something about nature, both in its formal and material concepts (subsections three and four in the first section in the 1945 essay). We know it however, not by simply observing nature, but by abstracting nature from the graced economy. This is also the purpose of the *analogia entis*, and it shows the antinominalist thrust of Balthasar's argument. What does the formal concept of nature show us? "God can reveal himself as a Person, not stones, plants, or animals."[72] If we did not have the formal theological concept of natures, we would not be able to make such claims. If, as Aristotle taught, nature is the desire for an end consistent with the means to achieve it, then the incarnation is no more fitting to human creatures than it would be to a donkey. Each creature has all it needs to achieve its proper end immanent to the creature. But the human creature has a supernatural end that then provides intelligibility to its nature that makes incarnation fitting. Stones, plants, and animals are not capable of incarnation because they do not have the natural requisites for being a person aware of its longing for God. God could not have become incarnate in a donkey (which is not to say he cannot speak through an ass). Balthasar then cited numerous places in Barth's work where he too assumed such a formal, theological concept of nature. God's incarnation in Christ is fitting because human creatures desire an end that exceeds their nature without

70. "Analogie und Natur," 11.

71. Ibid.

72. Ibid., 18.

that end demanding grace as an essential part of that nature, as occurred with Baianism.

Balthasar made explicit his two-pronged challenge to Protestantism and neoscholasticism in his concluding observations on the "material concept of nature." He first affirmed the scholastic argument that grace cannot be a nature, but is its mode.[73] As a mode of nature, it so pervades nature that it renders impossible any pure nature because there is actually no place in this word that is a "piece of *natura pura.*"[74] Balthasar asserted this was the common teaching of the church until the later Middle Ages. He cited Pryzwara as his source:

> Erich Przywara thinks here in the sense of all the Fathers and the Scholastics when he says, "Accordingly there is in real existence no pure natural religion, no pure natural morals, no pure natural culture, no pure natural science, no pure natural politics, but rather all without exception . . . bear explicitly or implicitly, consciously or unconsciously, in the highest or lowest measure, on the one supernatural God in Christ in the church as a final form."[75]

Real existence has no neutral, natural space, no religion, ethics, culture, science or politics that is somehow free from the either-or of this one order.

Here is Balthasar at his most Barthian, and at the same time Przywarian. Both provide a dramatic character of real existence where the *single order* of the divine economy permeates every aspect of life. The single order mattered to him because in "the newer theology a certain tendency exists to secure the realm of nature through which one isolates it also factually from the order of grace."[76] What is this "newer theology"? Balthasar may be playing on the critique against the *nouvelle théologie* at this point. The innovation in theology is not attributable to them, but to those who take what was hypothetical and render it factual, dividing God's single economy into two orders, one ruled by "nature" and another by "grace," that comes to it through some kind of divine fiat. For this reason the Reformation and Counter-Reformation were mirror images of a common error. The Reformation provided "a false concept of grace that factually more or less became an essential part of the human person" and thus destroyed nature. The Counter-Reformation recognized the mistake and rightly "believed in the integrity of nature even in the sinner,"

73. Ibid., 23.
74. Ibid., 24.
75. Ibid.
76. Ibid., 25.

but it overreacted and affirmed this "not only through a factual delimitation of nature over and against sin and grace, but also through a far-reaching, factual separating out of this natural sphere." The result is the modern era, in which, with Descartes, we attain a "finally independent natural ethic and knowledge of God."[77] That Descartes is identified as constituting this shift agrees with Barth's own assessment, as he made clear in the conclusion to his book on Anselm.

Balthasar began his essay letting the reader know what mattered most was "deciding" the "realm" within which the knowledge of God and ethics resides. By the time we get to the end of his first section, we discovered he decided for and against Barth. But if his decision is correct, then both Protestantism and Counter-Reformation Catholicism need reform. And what the one needs the other can provide in part by correction (which is not how Balthasar would have put it). Protestantism lost any natural ethical and theological agency by annulling it and lifting nature up solely into grace. This occurred primarily in double predestination where the human being's fate is decided by an absolute decree prior to the Trinitarian economy. Grace does, or does not do, everything. Election becomes the singular doctrine within which everything gets conceived. Nature is no longer intelligible, but in practice it still exists, so whatever it might still be, it is left to its own immanent devices. Paradoxically, a pure nature returns. Counter-Reformation Catholicism protected grace from its dissolution into nature, and nature into grace, but it posited two real orders where grace and nature possess independent spheres of operation. The result was the very "secular misery" Barth rightly divined afflicted modern theology.

GRACE SUPPOSES, ELEVATES, AND PERFECTS NATURE

In the second section in his argument, "The Analogy between Nature and Grace," Balthasar clarified why this single order requires the use of analogy. Thomas Aquinas provided the key elucidations, but for Balthasar the key is that they are *elucidations*; no single formula will do. Thomas taught that *gratia supponit, extollit, non destruit, perficit naturam* (grace supposes or posits, elevates, does not destroy and perfects nature.) The multiplicity of verbs shows "the impossibility of an unambiguous formulation of this analogy."[78]

The verbs suggest three analogies that together form a "factual unity" even if the logical moments in them can be abstracted. All of these analogies bear on the question of the "realm" within which natural knowledge of God and

77. Ibid.
78. Ibid., 34.

ethics unfold and in which they should be pursued. The first analogy is found in creation. It bears "an untraceable tension . . . between a complete passivity (in the act of being *created*) and relative activity (in the act of *being* created)." Our freedom to move ourselves and to act emerges from the complete passivity that constitutes our being. In other words, receptivity is at the same time an activity. The second analogy is found in the relation between God and creation. God remains both transcendent over the creature while at the same time immanent to it. This provides a twofold ontology where the creature is on the one hand a being-in-itself (*In-sich-sein*), but on the other a being-beyond-itself *(Über-sich-hinaus-sein)* directed to God. Most important is the third analogy; since the fall, only from the perspective of the third analogy can we glimpse the first two.

> The analogy of nature and grace exists concretely—since the fall—only as an analogy of sinful nature and redeeming grace in Christ and his church, and [only] insofar as Christ as God becoming man represents the final appropriate unity of God and creation, only as an analogy between divine and human nature in the full soteriological concreteness in Christ himself.[79]

These three analogies elucidate Thomas's statement that grace perfects nature when we acknowledge they only work backward. The first does not necessitate the second or the third, but the third necessitates the second and first. Only because we know the third do the other two emerge. Balthasar then exegeted each of the verbs in Thomas's statement, explaining how they should be read in terms of the direction of the three analogies. He concluded from this the necessity of the *potentia oboedientialis*.[80] It is a *natural* possibility. This, he acknowledges, "irritates" Barth, but it should do so only when the direction of analogy gets reversed and philosophy conditions theology.

> That here (as Barth tirelessly with right emphasizes) reality [*Wirklichkeit*] goes before possibility [*Möglichkeit*] as its basis so that this reality is so very much from God, that it presupposes as

79. Ibid., 35.

80. Balthasar explained how this potency does not in any sense give the creature a "natural" ability to claim God. Like Barth, he agrees the creature is helpless and cannot initiate his own redemption. But this "helplessness . . . is not able to change in the least that the creature is as such always available (in potency) to the creator. The *potentia oboedientialis* must be accounted already for the ground structure of the first (philosophical) analogy between God and creation. It is thus here so little the expression of a natural ability of the creature, that it is much more just the adequate expression of his final inability (*Nichtkönnens*) (*d.h. sich-nicht-entziehen-Könnens*)." Balthasar, "Analogie und Natur," 40–41.

corresponding no naturalistic potency, ability, structure, desire, preparation, resignation, or existential brokenness and despair in the creature; instead with the reality is brought along the possibility.[81]

Balthasar concludes his essay with a further articulation of his insistence on the Ignatian *omnia ad*. The last section is titled, "Omnia in ipso constant" (in him all things consist). In it he explains the twofold consequence of his argument. First: "Every natural human and worldly thing is able to be understood and interpreted finally only from Christ: *in ipso omnia constant*. Every ontology, epistemology, ethic, and aesthetics has its decisive measure in him, . . . and not as a crowning to an already fixed nature." Second: "Insofar as Christ is this measure not in the unity of a single divine–human nature (*gottmenschlichen Natur*), but rather in the distinction between God and men through the unity of his person, there is in the nature also its measure as nature, established in the proper distance to grace. He became 'flesh.'"[82] Balthasar always thinks existence, as did Barth, within the context of the incarnation, and that requires thinking human contemplation and action within that same context. Never does Balthasar argue that philosophy or metaphysics conditions revelation. That would assume a doctrine of pure nature that actually does work. Never does he suggest that theology renders philosophy null and void, nor that it should venture into a postmetaphysical epoch. That would reject the possibility for the actual divine economy and render it gnostic by grace negating rather than positing and perfecting nature.

KARL BARTH: PRESENTATION AND INTERPRETATION OF HIS THEOLOGY: THE 1951 BARTH BOOK

Balthasar reproduced substantial portions of the 1944 and 1945 essays, with some variation, in the long awaited 1951 publication. Comparing the 1951 publication to those earlier essays does not result in much new content, but does show how Balthasar reordered his argument to answer his critics. The comparison demonstrates that most of the key arguments were already present in the 1940s. Balthasar did not alter his main commitments because of *Humani generis*. He did not think he needed to do so because he never imagined he was in violation of it. He consistently argued from the 1930s through the 1950s that a *philosophical* doctrine of pure nature was an innovation in Catholic theology. A *theological* definition of nature was, contra Barth, necessary in order

81. Ibid., 44.
82. Ibid., 52.

to safeguard the gratuity of grace. What did change was the structure of his argument. He fine-tuned his presentation of Barth and set it within a context where Barth's *Dogmatics* rendered intelligible the *Romans* commentary and not vice versa. This different context led Balthasar to make a similar criticism of Barth that he made of the Scholastics. Just as they had not sufficiently transformed Aristotle's teaching on nature through theological realities, Barth's early work had not accomplished a sufficient christological transformation of dialectic.

The following chart shows where the sections from the 1944 essay were incorporated into the 1951 book, illuminating the shifts and similarities in Balthasar's argument. After some discussion of the significance of this reordering and the content of these sections in the 1944 essay, the 1945 essay will then be compared to the 1951 book and discussed as well.

1944 "ANALOGY AND DIALECTIC" COMPARED TO 1951 KARL BARTH: PRESENTATION AND INTERPRETATION OF HIS THEOLOGY

1944 essay "Analogy and Dialectic" 1. "On the Question" (171–77)	1951 Barth book, Part II: Presentation 1. "On the Interpretation" (67–71)
2. "Dialectic as Method" (177–86) A. "Pretheological Dialectic" B. "Dialectic as Warning" C. "Dialectic as Indication"	2. "The Dialectical Period" (71–93) A. "Romans 1" B. "Romans 2" C. "The Task of Dialectic"
3. "Dialectic as Ontological Contradiction?" (186–201) A. "Romans I" B. "Romans II" C. "The Turn to Analogy"	3. "The Turn to Analogy" (93–124) A. "The *Christian Dogmatics in Outline*" B. "Paths to the Breakthrough" C. *"Analogia Fidei"*
4. "Sin and Analogy" (201–16) A. "Sin" B. "The Form of Analogy"	3. "The Full Form of Analogy" (124–81) A. "Christological Foundations" B. "Creation and Covenant"

C. "Grasping after God"	C. "The Partner of God"
	D. "Faith and Knowledge"
	E. "Sin"
	F. "*Analogia entis*"

Much of the material in the 1944 essay in "On the Question" (1944 essay, #1 above) remained the same in the 1951 book. Its context, however, changed. Balthasar's reading of Barth no longer begins with a question, but an interpretation. He now argues that the first step in properly interpreting Barth hinges on whether we read the *Dogmatics* through *Romans* or *Romans* through *Dogmatics*. Balthasar asked:

> How should Barth be interpreted? Should the *Church Dogmatics* be understood in terms of his *Romans* commentary or vice versa? Like the Big Bang that initiated the universe, is the immense work of his later years but the expansion of the first intense, explosive insight of his early years, the long-reverberating echo of thunder after the initial flash of lightning? Or—to change the metaphor—is his early work a chaotic, cacophonous prelude, much like the odd sounds orchestra members emit when they tune their instruments before beginning to play the masterly music of the symphonies?[83]

Balthasar answers Catholics critics, such as Ernst, who were mystified why a Catholic theologian would be preoccupied with a Reformed theologian like Barth, whose dialectical maneuverings seemed to prohibit an adequate expression of Catholic truth. If Barth were read according to the "Big Bang" metaphor, the Catholic critics might be correct. Barth will be read primarily through the *Romans* commentaries, and dialectic remains the structural form within which the later dogmatics makes sense. But Balthasar does not read Barth in terms of this historical, efficient causation, in which the *Romans* phase is the initial cause and all that comes after stems from it as effects from the cause. He interprets Barth aesthetically, through the metaphor of music. The final performance gives form to the earlier notes.

For Balthasar *everything* hinges on whether an interpreter adopts the "Big Bang" approach, and then *Romans* renders intelligible the *Church Dogmatics*, or the aesthetic approach; then *Church Dogmatics* renders intelligible *Romans*. Given the preoccupation of Barth scholarship with Barth's historical

83. *The Theology of Karl Barth*, 59.

development in the 1920s, most contemporary Protestant interpreters adopt the "Big Bang" approach. The "bomb" of the *Romans* commentary exploded in the playground of the theologians, generating effects that are then sketched out historically. What matters most is getting the historical stages right. Balthasar's interpretation is less dependent upon this historical staging because he finds the 1920s was primarily a time of tuning instruments and practicing scales for Barth. We hear the later beauty in the former cacophony, but the later beauty of his dogmatic turn cannot be made dependent upon the cacophony of the dialectical early stages like an effect from a cause. If we do not have the latter beauty, we are left with cacophony.

The two possible interpretations reordered Balthasar's previous argument. In the 1944 essay a broad discussion of "dialectic" led into his critique of *Romans* 1 and 2. That broad discussion, which was previously placed in the section "Dialectic as Method" (1944 essay, #2 above) shifts in the 1951 book so that it now follows after the critique of *Romans* 1 and 2, and is renamed "The Task of Dialectic" (1951 book, 2C above). Because Balthasar read Barth backward from the *Church Dogmatics* to *Romans*, the former redeems the latter and places *Romans* in its proper context. It does so by showing us the appropriate "task" of dialectics. This too must be emphasized. Balthasar's interpretation of Barth never rejected dialectics, but properly situated it.

Before explaining the proper task of dialectic within theology, Balthasar posed a question about Barth's use of it and the philosophy undergirding it, which is similar to the question he posed to the use of philosophy by the Scholastics and Fathers. "Is this Platonism, this actualism, this mysticism of identity only a pointer and a method, or is it the whole point of his theology, which has to be taken literally?"[84] Dialectic as "pointer and method" is its proper task. After all, that is what the *dia* does; it points to a between that requires something more for its intelligibility. If dialectic becomes the form of theology rather than a "pointer and method," then the content of revelation gets subordinated to a dialectical form. Theologians, despite what they say, would only be doing philosophy. Balthasar asked if Barth "subordinates revelation to a philosophical system?"[85] Much like Balthasar called on Thomists to transform Aristotle's philosophical definition of nature by the theological reality of the incarnation, he challenges Barth to think dialectic only within the context of that same reality.

84. *The Theology of Karl Barth*, 72.
85. Ibid., 72.

Balthasar's criticisms of *Romans* 1 and 2 are nearly identical in the 1944 essay and 1951 book. Unlike most "Big Bang" interpreters, Balthasar never found much value in Barth's *Romans* phase in itself because it was entirely too philosophical. Recent interpretations emphasizing Barth's neo-Kantianism during his *Romans* phase restate rather than refute Balthasar's criticism, although he finds Hegelianism more influential on the early Barth than Kantianism. His primary criticism of *Romans* is that it subordinated dogmatic content to philosophical form. For Balthasar *Romans* 1 set forth a "dynamic eschatology" that was a version of "right-wing" (or religious) "Hegelianism," in which history progresses inevitably through a dialectical movement to a synthesis where everything concludes by God's providence with little drama, little risk. The actual is the rational. Balthasar sees similarities between Barth's dynamic eschatology and Origen's Platonic apocatastasis.[86] Balthasar became clearer as to the inadequacy of Barth's *Romans* phase. The entire section, "The Dialectical Period," in the 1951 book situated Barth's *Romans* commentaries within the context of a new question: Is the philosophy in service to revelation or revelation in service to the philosophy?[87] The answer is the latter. Barth reduced theology to a philosophical form that did not do justice to Christianity's dogmatic content, and in so doing failed to fulfill dialectic's proper task within theology.

Przywara set forth dialectic's appropriate task, which is twofold—human and divine. Dialectic is a method of human reasoning that brings two things together, mediating them via a *dia* that can be both a rendering of something into pieces (*dia als zer*) and pointing to something beyond (*dia als hindurch*). As a human task, dialectic is an ancient discipline for approaching an "intraworldly domain" (*innerweltlichen Bereich*), and has "three stages of motivation." That is to say, it preserves three important steps in human understanding. First, it reminds us that the knower as subject must be distinguished from the known as object, one proper use of the *dia*. True knowledge is to know the object as it really is, but this only takes place within a subject who always differs from that object. Dialectic preserves the necessary historical movement that acknowledges the ongoing task of achieving knowledge of the real. Dialectic here is "conventional" (*üblich*). The second human use of dialectic reminds the knower of her or his "inadequacy" before the object, and the third of the

---

86. Ibid., 67. See "Analogie und Dialektik," 187, and *Karl Barth: Darstellung und Deutung Seiner Theologie*, 73.

87. *Karl Barth: Darstellung und Deutung Seiner Theologie*, 80.

"impossibility" of comprehending it completely.[88] This human use of dialectic is, for Balthasar, unexceptional.

Balthasar then unequivocally states that moving from human knowledge to revelation only intensifies the need for dialectic. It becomes "methodologically necessary."[89] Here too he provides three reasons. First, revelation is an "event" (*Geschehen*) that "only God can speak." Dialectic preserves the reality that human creatures cannot subordinate the event of revelation to their own finite limits. Second, dialectic is a means of indicating (*Hinweis*). Citing an essay from Barth's *Theological Existence Today*, Balthasar draws on the image of John the Baptist pointing to Christ. Given that Grünewald's painting of the crucifixion hung in both their studies, readers cannot help but see an allusion to that painting. Balthasar explained why this matters in the third task of divine dialectics, which has to do with the "form" of theology. Theology, he laments, too often "siphons off the content of revelation and shucks the form. But by doing this, it also eviscerates the content, which cannot be separated from the form. Revelation ceases to be revelation when it is summoned to the bar of reason or of the various human sciences as a kind of universally available truth."[90] A proper task for dialectics is to act like John the Baptist's finger pointing to the shocking image of Christ. These are all dialectical tasks Balthasar affirmed, drawing upon Pryzwara, Barth, and others.

Balthasar once again explains Barth's good reasons for dialectic in his early theology. The first reason is the "absolute actuality of God's revelation." The second is the human creature's utter sinfulness.[91] In order to set forth the truth of these two reasons, which Balthasar does not reject, Barth adopted a "style" that brought the form and content together. Its purpose was to present the "dramatic" character of God's revelation, which Barth did through a "static" and "dynamic" dialectic.[92] The "static" is Kierkegaard's "infinite qualitative difference." The dynamic is a Hegelian "total reversal" of "being and history" in the cross and resurrection. Balthasar lodges no objection. He objects when dialectic is not a task but the exclusive form within which the content of revelation gets presented. Then it fails.

> At just the point where dialectics sees itself as the absolute, we once more encounter absolute identifications (whether static or dynamic).

---

88. Ibid., 73.
89. Ibid., 82.
90. *The Theology of Karl Barth*, 80.
91. Ibid., 81.
92. Ibid., 82.

First, God is identified (in all his aseity!) with his revelation. Then the creature is defined as the pure opposite of God and thus is identified with nothingness. And finally when the creature is retrieved by God through revelation and brought back to God through a dynamic movement (which is an absolute, because divine, movement), creation is then equated with God himself, at least in its origin and goal.[93]

As the "absolute" form expressing revelation, dialectic cannot adequately distinguish between the immanent and economic Trinity; God gets identified with his revelation (the Hegelian dynamic). God is the only actor in redemption, which reduces the creature to nothingness. Redemption no longer distinguishes between God's actions and that of creatures. Oddly enough, dialectic as theology's absolute form inevitably leads to identification between God and creation, to univocity.

If dialectic were only a method or indication pointing to something still more, it would fulfill its task. But in Barth's *Romans* phase, it was the absolute form and ironically accomplished the opposite Barth intended. He wanted to "do pure theology," but theology became *aufgehoben* (superseded) by an "unbiblical theopanism." Much as we saw in the *Apokalypse*, Balthasar critiques Barth's early work as woefully inadequate because it did not avoid the philosophical tendencies of the "German soul." Philosophy superseded theology. But now, after the *Church Dogmatics*, the *Romans* commentaries can be redeemed. In other words, if we interpret Barth via the "Big Bang" approach, then his dialectical philosophy gets the better of the content of revelation, distorting Christian dogmatics. Barth never intended to distort theology through philosophy. When he traced the dialectic out to its logical consequence, he realized it could not sustain the proper form of Christianity, the incarnation. Gradual transitions occurred where Barth switched from philosophy giving form to revelation, to revelation giving form to philosophy. There is no single moment when this occurred according to Balthasar. It took place through many different "paths"; notice the plural in section 3B of the 1951 book: "Paths to the Breakthrough" (*Wege im Umbruch*).[94]

---

93. Ibid., 84.

94. This gets translated by Fr. Oakes as "The Breakthrough," which is certainly accurate. There is a breakthrough. But it loses the sense of the various paths that led to it. There was not one single path, but many, which were more "slight turns," as Balthasar said in *Apokalypse* 3.

Balthasar made a surprising claim in the 1951 book at the end of the section, "The Task of Dialectic," before moving to the next section, "The Turn to Analogy." He wrote,

> The later path (*Weg*) of Barth is a paradoxical rehabilitation of the *Romans* commentary insofar as it now becomes clear, what this odd book *actually wanted to say*: [it was] not a theologically disguised philosophy, but rather a philosophically disguised, and by that, detachable theology. Only when this safeguard, which may bear the name analogy, is fixed in theological thinking, does the problem of the rights and limits of dialectic arise anew once more on an entirely different plane.[95]

Dialectics has its "rights," which are also its "limits." The dialectic of *Romans* 2 had its purpose. It sought to maintain the distinction between God and creation and to challenge liberal Protestantism's subjectivization of the knowledge of God, but it did not adhere to dialectic's rights and limits. If left to its own devices, dialectic as theology's form would destroy creation in an apocalyptic blaze that becomes uncontrollable. However, if we interpret the earlier Barth from the perspective of the *Church Dogmatics*, the *Romans* commentary can be salvaged.

At this point in his argument, Balthasar traces Barth's turn to analogy as a "slow and interlaced [*vielverzweigte*] history of the changes" between 1922 and 1932, where what Balthasar named as the "most important document" came right in the middle of this ten-year period, the 1927 *Christian Dogmatics*.[96] The essays in the mid 1940s did not give such prominence to Barth's *Christian Dogmatics* as does the 1951 book. Nonetheless, Balthasar never identified a single, or even a double, cause to Barth's "breakthrough." There were many "ways" to it, and they were "interlaced." Along with the many ways to Barth's breakthrough, Balthasar did speak of Barth's "two conversions," the first from liberalism to "Christian radicalism," and the second from the "dross of philosophy" to an "independent theology." Bruce McCormack challenges this periodization of Barth interpretation. But in speaking of two conversions,

---

95. *Karl Barth: Darstellung und Deutung Seiner Theologie*, 93.

96. "Will man die langsame und vielverzweigte Geschichte der Wandlungen Barths vom 'Römerbrief' zur 'Kirchlichen Dogmatik' also die Epoche 1922 bis 1932 übersehen, so wird man nach dem wichtigsten Dokument in ihrer Mitte greifen, dem ersten Entwurf der Dogmatik, dessen erster und einziger Band 'Die Lehre vom Worte Gottes, Prolegomena zur christlichen Dogmatik,' 1927 erschien." *Karl Barth: Darstellung und Deutung Seiner Theologie*, 93.

Balthasar only honored Barth's own words about his development. He quoted Barth's 1948 statement that "the actual document of this departure from the remains of a philosophical, that is to say, anthropological justification and explanation of theology is not the much-read little book '*Nein*' against Brunner from 1934 but rather the book appearing in 1931 on the proofs of God's existence by Anselm of Canterbury."[97] Note that Barth spoke of the "remains" of a philosophical-anthropological approach to doctrine that lingered from the *Romans* phase, and affirms the "proofs of God's existence" in Anselm. The latter is what Barth thought Schleiermacher replaced in a previous scholastic theology with his turn to consciousness. *Barth* periodized the decisive change with the Anselm book, and in so doing assumed the prior Scholastic approach against Schleiermacher. Balthasar neither invented nor rejected this; he took Barth at his word and merely restated Barth's autobiographical account. But Balthasar also supplemented it. "The most important document," he asserted, was less the Anselm book and more the 1927 *Christian Dogmatics.* He did not dismiss Barth's own words about the importance of the Anselm book. It too is "interlaced" in his gradual, slow manifold changes. Balthasar took Barth's own words about his twofold conversion and complicated them by tracing his manifold ways to his "breakthrough."

A striking difference between the 1944 and 1951 interpretation is the substantive role *The Christian Dogmatics* played in the latter. Balthasar did not mention it in his *Apokalypse*; nor is it listed in the sources for his 1944 essay.[98] In the 1951 book it has its own section (3A above), which Balthasar devoted to no other of Barth's work except the *Romans* commentaries. Why is it so important? Because in it Barth addressed the question Balthasar raised about the *Romans* commentaries, the question that framed his interpretation and reordered it. Balthasar wrote, "Above all, one sees Barth preoccupied to find and emphasize undiluted that 'principle' that delimits and builds up a Christian theology on the one side from philosophy, metaphysics, and religion in general, and on the other side within the Church from the word of proclamation and Scripture and the word of God."[99] In 1927 more clearly than before, Barth took up what always interested him: "the content of dogmatics," which is "the concrete Word of God as it became man in Jesus Christ."[100]

---

97. Ibid., 102.

98. He did not cite nor mention it in his list of works referenced in the 1944 essay. See 171n1, which contained a near identical list of Barth sources as he used in the *Apokalypse* except for the addition of "*Gotteserkenntnis und Gottesdienst*, 1938," and "*Zeitschrift zwischen den Zeiten*, 1924ff."

99. *Karl Barth: Darstellung und Deutung Seiner Theologie*, 94.

Barth now had the right "point of resolution or termination" (*Lösungspunkt*), but the 1927 breakthrough is still only partial because the "staring point" (*Ausgangspunkt*) of the philosophical system of idealistic monism from *Romans* still "fascinates" him.[101] Balthasar characterized this system "as a dynamic-actualistic theopanism or a monism as the beginning and end (protology and eschatology), of which an encompassed dualistic-dialectic world-reality and world-time, in the mathematical point of the miracle of a reversal, is overcome."[102] Nowhere does Balthasar state so succinctly, albeit opaquely, his main critique and concern of Barth's *Romans* phase. God shows up at the beginning of creation and at the end. In the end, primarily through a will-to-miracle, God effects an unexpected reversal. What occurs in the time between these times, however, lacks dramatic import. What is the problem with Barth's *Romans* phase? His God is a nominalistic power who only works miraculously at the end of time with no attention to the goodness, truth, or beauty of creaturely being. Balthasar explicitly refers to "nominalism" several pages later when he charts Barth's decisive overcoming of the monistic dynamic-actualism with the publication of *Church Dogmatics* 2.1, a book that had a profound effect on Balthasar. In charting this overcoming, he cites Barth's own words, "The concept of analogy is in fact unavoidable (3, 254)." Now Barth refuses both "identity" and "total dissimilarity."[103] God is neither identified with creation, nor so completely other that no resemblance between God and creation exists. The various ways Barth travelled to the *Church Dogmatics* led him beyond this to address what really mattered all along.

If Barth has made his breakthrough, so Balthasar argued, he must recognize a place for worldly truth, a truth of God expressed in our language. Balthasar sets up an important quote from Barth by first stating,

> Analogy is an ultimate relational term: it cannot be explained by any more fundamental identity or nonidentity. But the words that we use of God are not independent of the relationship *that God establishes*. Therefore, it is not something one already finds present in nature as

100. Ibid. Balthasar noted that the incarnation is no general law, no *Gesetz*. It is interesting to note how Balthasar's own language has shifted. He no longer speaks, as he did in "Patristik," about a *Gesetz*.

101. *Karl Barth: Darstellung und Deutung Seiner Theologie*, 102

102. "Diese ist zu kennzeichnen als ein dynamisch-aktualistischer Theopanismus oder Monismus als Anfang und Ende [Protologie und Eschatologie], welcher eine dualistisch-dialektisch verstandende Weltwirklichkeit und Weltzeit umgreift und—im mathematischen Punkt des Wunders der Wende—überwindet." *Karl Barth: Darstellung und Deutung Seiner Theologie*, 102.

103. *The Theology of Karl Barth*, 109.

> part of its innate laws but is a relation founded on revelation. The truth contained in our concepts is—corresponding to their objects—a created, relative finite truth. To pertain to God, *God* must produce from within himself the relation between temporal truths and his divinity. He chooses our truth to express his truth. But this action by God—and this is important—is no arbitrary act as the Nominalists would have it. Rather his act of appropriating our truths is founded in the fact that our truth already belongs to God, just as our being belongs more to him than to us, since we are entirely his creations, the product of his decision to create.[104]

Only because our being and truth already belong to God can we avoid the nominalist temptation, where God arbitrarily and unexpectedly appears as a sheer act of will reversing creaturely being and commandeering our language miraculously from the outside such that nothing identifiably human remains of it. If Barth fell prey to this temptation in *Romans*, he now resists it. He has a more substantive place for "worldly truth" that overcomes the "nominalism" present in his previous "dynamic-actualistic theopanism." Having provided this context for interpreting Barth, Balthasar then cites a long statement from *Church Dogmatics* 2.1, in which Barth explained how God makes our truth God's truth without it ceasing to be our truth.

Although the 1927 *Christian Dogmatics* was central for Barth's turn to analogy, Balthasar did not find it the only turning point. Balthasar flanked his discussion of it with a number of other important Barth essays prior and posterior to the 1927 publication that were relevant for saving creation from a fiery, dialectic apocalypse via the "Big Bang" approach. Barth comes to see how "unchristian" that approach was, and sought to save the "world-reality" of "culture and philosophy," "ethics," and "church." Barth's efforts to salvage world reality through each of these constituted a distinct, albeit interlaced, way (*Weg*) contributing to his breakthrough.

THE PATH THAT LED THROUGH CULTURE AND PHILOSOPHY

Barth's essays, "Church and Culture" (1926) and "Fate and Idea in Theology" (1929), sought to save culture and philosophy. The 1926 essay already contained much of what Barth later developed in the *Church Dogmatics*, but without the christological foundations. In it, Balthasar wrote, "we encounter Barth talking about a natural theology justified—indeed, necessary—inside revealed

---

104. Ibid., 109. Emphasis original.

theology."[105] Had he maintained this more rigorously he would have spared himself the unfortunate "rift" with Brunner and his "polemic against Catholicism" would at least have been "more nuanced."[106] In this essay Barth spoke of the "undestroyed image of God" which for Balthasar was similar to the Catholic "*potentia oboedientialis.*" But all of these important themes were "strangled in the cradle by Barth's monistic framework."[107] Nature and culture did not find an adequate theological rendering. Barth wanted to save them, but did not yet have the tools. In essence they became untheological. In so doing, Barth repeated a version of the doctrine of pure nature.

The 1929 essay, "Fate and Idea in Theology," was nearly identical to Przywara's argument that realism and idealism cannot get along without each other. For both of them, the use of such philosophical concepts in theology is inevitable, but Barth radicalizes Przywara's argument, finding in these philosophies an attempt to usurp theology. For this reason Barth questioned whether the Word or some "philosophical first principle" does the heavy lifting in such theologies. So far Balthasar agreed. Neither idealism nor realism alone provides the necessary form to express Christian content. Yet Barth, unlike Pryzwara, found philosophy to be "nothing but a theology alienated from itself and grown weary of remaining obedient to its true source." Philosophy was collapsed into theology, and theology into God's actualism such that "the presence of faith cannot really be detected."[108] Faith is only God's free choice and we are left with nothing but a doctrine of predestination, one Balthasar acknowledged Barth could not finally affirm and would revise. We are on the way to the breakthrough, but we are not there yet.

THE PATH THAT LED THROUGH ETHICS

That Balthasar traced multiple *paths* from the dialectic of *Romans* to the analogy in the *Dogmatics* is clear when discussing Barth's ethics. Balthasar wrote, "A second path (*Weg*) leads from the path of ethics to the *Church Dogmatics.*" Here three important essays flank Barth's *Die christliche Dogmatik*: "The Problem of Ethics Today" (1922), "Keeping the Commandments" (1927), and "The First Commandment as a Theological Axiom" (1933). Much as with philosophy, Barth did not originally find sufficient space for ethics. It only precipitated crisis, but these three essays move from existentialist crisis rendering ethics

---

105. Ibid., 96.
106. Ibid.
107. Ibid. 97.
108. Ibid., 99.

impossible, through Barth's emphasis on God's concrete command, which made God's ethical agency possible but rendered human agency impossible, to the christological foundations of Christ's two natures that finally gave "history and temporal being their due."[109]

THE PATH TO THE CHURCH

Along with his efforts to save culture, philosophy, and ethics, Barth also endeavored to save the "church." Three essays Barth wrote during his Münster days provided a third way from *Romans* to the *Church Dogmatics*. The first, "Church and Theology" (1926), responded to Erik Peterson's "What Is Theology?" Two others were "The Concept of the Church" (1927) and "Roman Catholicism as a Question in Protestant Theology" (1928). During this time, Barth attempted an ecclesiology that was set over and against Catholicism. He was unsuccessful, according to Balthasar, because all these essays were still permeated by "dynamic actualism." Barth did nonetheless find a way (*Weg*) beyond the "catastrophic ecclesiology" of *Romans* where the church was nothing but "the great negation of revelation."[110] Balthasar attributed this movement to the "influence of Barth's dialogue with Catholics." Barth "accepts all the essential attributes of the Catholic Church and radicalizes and reworks them through dynamic actualism."[111] For Barth this means that the only authority for the church is God, and no human participates in this authority. The church was merely a conduit through which God works. The problem remained the same. The philosophical structure of actualism prevented him from making the dogma of the incarnation the real center of his theology. Balthasar restated the central problem with Barth's actualism:

> Actualism, with its constant, relentless reduction of all activity to God the *actus purus*, leaves no room for any other center of activity outside of God. In relation to God, there can only be passivity. So the church is "holy insofar as she obeys, not insofar as she commands." She is "infallible as she seeks for what has been told her, but what she says cannot lay claim to divine authority." (299). Once more everything collapses into that unholy dualism of *Romans*: viewed from above, the Church completely coincides with God's Word; but,

---

109. Ibid., 103.

110. Ibid., 104, *Karl Barth: Darstellung und Deutung Seiner Theologie*,113.

111. *Karl Barth: Darstellung und Deutung Seiner Theologie*, 113.

viewed from below, all her attempts to give expression to this Word are radically fallible.[112]

Barth's philosophical limitation failed to account for actors other than God in the realm of grace. Balthasar sought a place for human actors in the theodrama, but he also recognized it was a problem not easily resolved. For if God is who the church has traditionally confessed him to be: simple, perfect, immutable, impassible, omniscient, omnipotent, and so on, what role could there be for any other actors once God appeared on the historical stage? One way to answer this question is simply to limit God in order to make space for others. Despite theologians who either affirm or criticize Barth and Balthasar for supposedly offering this answer, it was not a way either took. Another answer is to distinguish nature and grace so sharply that we have two different spaces for the drama: one takes place in a realm of pure nature and the other in that of grace. Balthasar feared the Barth of *Romans* and neoscholasticism (not Scholasticism per se) adopted this solution through different paths. However the result was the same. The realm within which the divine economy works—the hypostatic union—was neglected as that which renders creation intelligible. Recognizing that graced-nature ordered to the beatific vision is the *one* realm within which the drama unfolds, and yet this *one* realm must not collapse grace into nature, nature into grace, or hold them as decisively separated, is Balthasar's overriding concern in his *Trilogy*. He takes this up in the *Theo-Drama* when he asks the question, how can there be other actors when God shows up on the scene? His answer to this question brings into a tightly woven unity the traditional perfections of God's oneness and the doctrine of the Trinity. These questions and their solution in the Trinity owe their genesis to Karl Barth, especially *Church Dogmatics* 2.1. Barth did not give him the answer in full, but he pointed toward it, because of his answer to the question of the proper "realm" for the natural knowledge of God and ethics. Here in 1951 Balthasar's preoccupation with Barth set the context for the question Balthasar's *Trilogy* will answer.

Balthasar reordered the material from the 1944 essay in the 1951 book and set that earlier essay within a new context, established by his illuminating question whether we should read Barth in terms of a causality that traces his later work as an effect from the cause of *Romans*, or a musical aesthetic that works teleologically, making sense of what really mattered all along in *Romans*, and thereby saving it, through the later perspective of the *Church Dogmatics*. He consistently critiqued Barth's work on *Romans* as too idealistic, losing the

---

112. *The Theology of Karl Barth*, 105.

dramatic character of the divine economy. If Barth were to be interpreted with an immanent causality from the *Romans* phase onward then, for Balthasar, he cannot escape the charge that he is the one who subordinates theology to philosophy and produces a form that lays hands on God. What is at stake in this conversation is the "realm" within which the natural knowledge of God and ethics are to be known and enacted. It is this latter concern that he developed in his 1945 essay that also gets reordered and supplemented in the 1951 book.

1945 "ANALOGY AND NATURE" COMPARED TO 1951 KARL BARTH: PRESENTATION AND INTERPRETATION OF HIS THEOLOGY

As noted above, Balthasar challenged textbook definitions of nature, including Scheeben's, which assumed Aristotle's definition where nature is "*constitutive aut consecutive aut exigitive.*" Such a philosophical definition posited that a nature must have an end proportionate to its natural means to attain it. After the incarnation, this definition could no longer condition theology. Now we know that human nature can be united to a nature that exceeds it, the divine nature, which becomes its true end without evacuating human nature. How is this mystery to be explained philosophically? It will require a close cooperation between theology and philosophy where standard philosophical terms will need to be transformed, as the church fathers did at Chalcedon. Balthasar fears the more rigorous Thomism of the innovative neoscholastics failed to achieve this, and in so doing misinterpreted the *Vaticanum*, unnecessarily widening the crack between Catholics and Protestants. Such a misinterpretation fell into the hands of Barth, who of course, accused it of leading theology into a "secular misery." The chart below shows the similarities and differences between sections in the 1945 essay and similar material in the 1951 book.

1945 essay "Analogy and Nature"	1951 Barth book
A. "Analogy in the Concept of Nature"1. "On the Question" (3–8)	A. "The Concept of Nature in Catholic Theology"1. "Historical Transitions" (278–82)
2. "The Concept of Nature in Philosophy and Theology" (8–17)	2. "Objective Ambiguity" (282–94)
3. "The Formal Concept of Nature" (17–23)	3. "Formal and Material Concept of Nature "(294–314)

4. "The Material Concept of Nature" (23–33)	4. "Nature in the *Vaticanum*" (314–35).
B. "The Analogy between Nature and Grace"1. "The Form of Analogy of Nature and Grace" (33–38)	B. "Christocentrism"1. "Christ: the Ground of Creation" (336–44)
2. "*Potentia oboedientialis*" (38–49)	2. "Nature and History" (344–53)
3. "*Omnia in ipso constant*" (49–56)	3. "Nature and Grace" (353–67)
	4. "Justice and Redemption" (367–72)

As Balthasar incorporated the material from the 1945 essay into the 1951 book, he maintained a twofold structure that began with "nature," but the second element of that structure has been renamed from 1945, "The Analogy between Nature and Grace," to 1951, "Christocentrism." Balthasar brings out more fully the Christocentric foundation for the analogy. He also prefaces the material in the 1951 book with a new section, "The Problem of a Catholic Thought-Form" (264–278) that continues his criticisms of a Catholic doctrine of pure nature. Two crucial additions are made between the 1945 essay and its incorporation into the 1951 book. First, Balthasar makes more explicit the reason he opposes any doctrine of pure nature with an important paragraph added to "The Formal Concept of Nature" (A3). The fact that he added this section after *Humani generis* shows that he was not trying to assuage his critics who thought that his preoccupation with Barth, and rejection of pure nature, violated Vatican I. Second, he had an extended section on the *Vaticanum* explaining how his position, which remained the same as the one he adopted before *Humani generis*, was not guilty of violating either. Both sections contributed to his overarching concern—to show how Barth pointed in the direction of theology's proper form, but did not quite attain it. These additions show more clearly the consequences of Balthasar's criticism of the doctrine of pure nature, why he insists on emphasizing the importance of form for theology, and how his work fits within a proper interpretation of Vatican I.

The first crucial addition makes clearer the consequences of his criticism of the doctrine of pure nature than did the 1945 essay. This passage is not found in the 1944 or 1945 essay. It is the one Gutwenger and Long object to. Gutwenger was convinced it violated Trent, Vatican I and *Humani generis*. The previous chapter cited it in part; here is the full quote published in 1951:

> Now common sense claims to know what nature is. But the more exactly it tries to grasp it, the more difficult—nay impossible—it becomes to isolate it neatly from the other dimension: supernatural grace. But it is equally difficult to espy the negative effects on the realm of nature of the loss of grace. The questions, for example, of how far "ignorance and hardship belong to natural existence," how much concupiscence, disease, death (and the form that death takes) are the result of sin or are part of the definition of being human and animal; but also questions about marriage, community, the State, our relation to a God who might not have revealed himself in his personal, interior life, the necessity for prayer in a natural state (which many people deny, for good reason), the eschatological fate of the soul, resurrection of the body, Last Judgment, eternal bliss: all such questions addressed to pure nature are simply unanswerable.[113]

With this argument Balthasar blurs any sharp boundary divisions between the disciplines of theology, philosophy, and ethics. Faith and reason, theology and philosophy, grace and nature, dogma and ethics cannot be divided into neat, segregated compartments. The real economy within which they all work is one where such neat distinctions do not exist. If theology takes the form of such distinctions, as it did in the manualist tradition, it loses the glory of the divine economy.[114]

The importance of what Balthasar has done here, and its relation to Barth and the neoscholastics, should not be lost on the reader. Barth is right in practice, but wrong in theory. Ethics, politics, and even our knowledge of God can never arise from a "pure nature." Natural theology and an ethics based upon natural law alone have been seriously curtailed if they are understood as emerging from an Aristotelian philosophy of nature that has not been theologically transformed. Just as the Fathers had to revise what was mean

---

113. *The Theology of Karl Barth*, 283; *Karl Barth: Darstellung und Deutung Seiner Theologie*, 294.

114. Most contemporary theological textbooks, including those of the "Ressourcement Thomists," reveal that Barth and Balthasar carried the day on the question of the form theology should take. A simple comparison of the theological form of those who would defend the manualists, such as Steven A. Long, Reinhard Hütter, Romanus Cessario, or Thomas Joseph White, with that of Joseph Gredt's *Elementa Philosophiae Aristotelico-Thomisticae* will show how vastly different theological "form" is today from the time of the manualists. Their form resembles much more that of Barth and Balthasar than the propositional structure of the manuals.

by *physis* (nature) and *hypostasis* (person) at Chalcedon to render intelligible the mystery of the incarnation, so Aristotle's philosophical definition of nature must be revised based on the creature's vocation to the vision of God. The doctrine of God, including the so-called natural love of God, and ethics will not be pursued within the manualist tradition's Aristotelianism, where each nature has an end proportionate to that nature. Theology will have a more determinative role in explaining nature. This revision does not do away with nature; it can even affirm Aristotle in part, but Aristotle cannot define the realm within which "nature" is understood completely, for he did not know the call to the beatific vision. Positing a twofold end to the human creature, one purely natural and identical to Aristotle's definition of nature, and the other supernatural, will not do, for such a twofold end neglects the *theologically* derived concept of nature that revelation demands. Balthasar does not reject the manualist tradition, however, for he finds in it a second definition of nature that does derive from grace. Balthasar affirms it, but it sits in tension with the Aristotelian-derived definition.

Balthasar's theological definition of nature will work itself out in his *Trilogy*, and will have significant implications for the doctrine of God and for ethics. Balthasar will, like Barth, place ethics within the dogmatic, dramatic communication of the Triune God (see chapter 5). But a nature is still required for intellectual and ethical practice, even if it is a nature intelligible only within the vocation to the beatific vision. This concept of nature also means we cannot move from nature to grace. As he stated in the 1945 essay and repeated identically with emphasis in the 1951 book: "*The positive definition of grace can only through grace itself be given.*"[115] Theology and philosophy cannot move from Aristotle's teaching on God and ethics to Aquinas, but only the other way around. Otherwise, a nature that does not exist, a nature not called to the beatific vision, establishes the acting arena within which the divine economy works.

Balthasar's analysis of nature and grace does not dispense with philosophy, but it poses a limit on what philosophy accomplishes. Philosophers cannot move "from the world to God," at least not based on the assumption of pure nature.[116] Grace determines nature and not nature grace, which is why "analogy" matters so much. Aristotle's philosophical definition of nature can be affirmed, but only analogically. Nature functions somewhat like he suggests, but how it functions must be corrected and completed by the creature's true end. Because

---

115. *The Theology of Karl Barth*, 279.

116. "Analogie und Natur," 14.

it functions analogically, grace and nature cannot be decisively distinguished. If grace and nature were easily distinguished in practice, analogy would not be necessary. Either identity or equivocation would suffice. Because they cannot be divided up precisely into distinct fields, we must use analogy. As an example Balthasar referred to the resurrection of the body and death. Would Aristotle have thought the human body has a nature capable of resurrection? Of course not, yet theologically we know this pertains to it—"I believe in the resurrection of the body." The body noted here is not some "supernatural" body; it is the resurrected natural body. To which does bodily resurrection belong? Grace? Nature? Balthasar wrote, "At one time it is considered with the eyes of reason, at another with the eyes of faith, and therefore seen under a different perspective. Because the material object which reason has before it is already not a bare nature, but rather is already elevated."[117] There is no "pure reason" (contra Kant) anymore than there is pure nature. Thus there is also no neutral reason; every account of reason always already stands within a "teleology of faith or unfaith."[118]

The new and revised sections show more clearly Balthasar's concerns as to why Barth should be more attentive to the importance of form and style as theological categories. Balthasar defended the form of Barth's theology as beautiful even when Barth showed little interest in the question of form. Barth was unable to take form into account because he feared attention to form posited an "essence" to Christianity, which would threaten God's inexhaustibility. Balthasar readily conceded that there is no "essence" to Christianity or Catholicism, and in so doing tried to assuage Barth's concern about "form." To find a form is not to locate an essence. Form is no static essence, but like nature it has a history (consecutive) that flows into other forms such that no single one expresses the truth once and for all. There is no singular essence, but there is "form," and it is symphonic.[119] Balthasar wrote,

> The kinetic variety of forms and styles used to express the truth also arises because of the unimaginable fullness of individual traits in peoples, epochs and personalities in their unique talents and missions. Just as there is not only a "history of style" for beauty, there is also one for the true. And what is astonishing in both is that the most felicitous expressions, the most personal, the ones most touched by

---

117. This is the beginning of the argument in the 1945 essay that then gets expanded in the quotation from the 1951 book noted above.

118. "Analogie und Natur," 15.

119. *The Theology of Karl Barth* 251; *Karl Barth: Darstellung und Deutung Seiner Theologie,* 263.

genius, are precisely the ones that are the most universally valid. And consequently they are the forms that are most easily brought into relation with other unique forms, which in their juxtaposition let new and yet more fruitful aspects of the beautiful and the true come to light.[120]

Here again we see how programmatic the "Patristik" essay was for Balthasar. Each epoch had something to offer, as did Barth, to a properly attuned ear. Balthasar offered the best interpretation of the Catholic "both-and" that concerned Barth.

Catholicism's "both-and" answered Barth's concern about God's inexhaustibility. Catholicism never "holds fast to a closed-off and finished system." It held a place for dialectic, but never as the final and definitive form; something more than dialectic alone must be said.[121] Recognizing this was Aquinas's genius. He offered a "form" open to both past and future.[122] This was also what made him a transitional figure from the patristics to the Scholastic and modern. He held together the *unicus ordo concretus spiritualis* [the one and only concrete spiritual order] of the patristic epoch with the future *duplex ordo naturalis et supernaturalis* of the modern. Like the "Patristik" essay, Balthasar does not side with one of these orders against the other; the symphonic form of Catholicism should affirm both. But others did not hold them together; they turned them into an either-or. The two forms Aquinas united became divided. Despite all the difficulties raised by the neoscholastic censors concerning Balthasar's book, he still raised a critical question that could only confirm those censors' worries: "Yet we can still ask whether the sense in Catholic theology for its *propria principia*, its *propria methodus*, has always been sufficiently vigorous and fruitful after the stress that was put on nature in the Middle Ages, in the Counter-Reformation and in the nineteenth century."[123]

Balthasar was willing to be critical of the tradition. On the one side, Counter-Reformation Roman Catholicism clung so tightly to nature and reason it truncated the form, dividing nature and grace, philosophy and theology. Two decades later, as will be shown below, he still critiques Aristotle's influence on Catholicism. Because Aristotle had no conception of sin, in following him, the manualist tradition confused nature with fallen nature, which was also one of his criticisms of Barth.

120. *The Theology of Karl Barth*, 251.
121. Ibid., 253.
122. Ibid., 252.
123. Ibid., 266.

Protestants like Barth sought a *"scientia de singularibus . . . where, in other words, the essence of event as well as doctrine is embedded in the person and activity of Jesus Christ."*[124] This science of singularity may have been the "theological point" nominalism, and with it Protestantism, sought to emphasize. Balthasar affirms its "Christocentrism." In fact, he now included a section entitled "Christocentrism" in his argument, arguing Catholics are every bit as Christocentric as Protestants. If Christocentrism is what Barth, nominalism, and Protestantism sought to achieve, it was worth pursuing, but for Balthasar Protestantism "failed" in its attempt to accomplish this. Its Christological constriction failed to read creation in and through Christ. As we shall see, Balthasar also acquits Barth of the charge of nominalism, but here he counters Protestant nominalism with the Catholic charge to "maintain the foundation and full conceptual panoply [of philosophy] for explicating the theological *datum*."[125]

Along with showing the consequences of his criticism of the doctrine of pure nature, and emphasizing the importance of form for theology, Balthasar added a lengthy discussion on "Nature in the *Vaticanum*" in the 1951 book. This new material explicitly addressed Balthasar's censors and potential critics. He began with a concession that a straightforward reading of the decree on the natural knowledge of God would seem to "call into question" all he had written so far: "Holy Mother Church holds and teaches that God, the origin and end of all things, can be known with certainty by the *natural* light of human reason from the things that he has made."[126] How then can he argue, "Such questions addressed to pure nature are simply unanswerable"?[127] His answer is found in a question. Is "natural" in the decree to be understood as philosophical or theological?

> Does the statement here pertain to "philosophical" nature as a counterpoint to the revelation of the *Word* but not to the whole supernatural order outright, or is it referring to the whole supernatural order that is left over as an (unperceivable) "residual concept" [*Restbegriff*] after the process of subtraction has been completed?[128]

124. Ibid. 266. Emphasis original.
125. Ibid. 266.
126. Ibid., 302. Emphasis original.
127. Ibid., 283. *Karl Barth: Darstellung und Deutung Seiner Theologie*, 294.
128. *The Theology of Karl Barth*, 303. *Karl Barth: Darstellung und Deutung Seiner Theologie*, 314. Emphasis original.

If it were the first, then nature would be pure and not ordered to the supernatural. It would only be a "counterpoint" to revelation; Aristotle's definition would stand without transformation as the condition for theology. If the latter, and he obviously is indebted to Rahner on the point he makes, then nature is a "residual concept" that is only known from grace. What then follows is a careful and lengthy exegesis of Vatican I that bore the fruit of Balthasar's decade-long conversation with Barth and his Catholic critics.

The *Vaticanum*'s natural knowledge of God was only concerned with God as origin and end. In this respect, it acknowledged what is undeniable. Some people demonstrated God existed as origin and end without any explicit appeal to the Christian mystery. It did not say this knowledge is redemptive or even necessary, it just said it is possible and in fact has occurred. What is not at stake in Vatican I, Balthasar wrote, was this: "It should be explicitly noted that the Council exercised the caution of not speaking of *pure* nature, and thus it did not in the least broach the question of its possible realization."[129] If they had, he could not have argued it was "unessential" Catholic teaching. Far from making knowledge of God predicated upon the certainty of what pure nature could achieve, it set the "certainty" of such knowledge in a "dialectical" relationship to the "moral *necessity* of revelation." The certainty of natural reason was set forth only *de jure* and as potential. In a "fallen state" revelation was *de facto* and "actual knowledge."[130] The council decided the *de jure*. Natural knowledge is possible, but it "left open" the *de facto*, which meant the extent to which revelation was necessary even for the *de jure* was not a matter of dogma. In other words, it did not teach knowledge of God via a pure nature was *de facto* knowledge. Balthasar concluded,

> Nothing prevents the theologian from maintaining,—not only for his own reasons but also according to Vatican I—that all natural knowledge of God occurs *de facto* within the positive and negative conditions of the supernatural order. Thomas Aquinas was of the opinion that in corresponding to the fact that man possesses only one single supernatural goal, every human being who has reached the age of reason must make a choice for or against the God of grace. . . . The Council only decided this issue: that *within* this concrete supernatural context, exaltation and transformation, human nature is not destroyed or turned into its opposite. On the contrary,

---

129. *The Theology of Karl Barth*, 306. Emphasis original.
130. Ibid. Emphasis original.

the natural capacity of a human being to know God continues to function.[131]

Here we find another important instance of the Catholic "both-and": Balthasar affirms both the analogy of being and of faith, which also affirms both Aquinas and Barth. He made this clear in his conclusion:

> Thus it becomes clear once more that Vatican I has in no way anticipated in its decisions the whole complex of questions we have described as the structure of Karl Barth's thought: thinking from the most concrete reality of being and history in order *from this perspective* to go on to describe the conditions for their possibility. It is really not possible to construct any genuine contradiction between Barth's statements in his anthropology about the capacity of human nature to know God within the concrete order of revelation (in *all* its conditions) and the statements of Vatican I.[132]

That statement may have come as a surprise both to Barth and neoscholastic interpreters of the Vatican I decree. Barth had asked who would free us from the "secular misery" Schleiermacher and Vatican I foisted upon the church. Balthasar answered by showing how Vatican I did not contradict Barth and Barth did not contradict it. Perhaps, however, Balthasar's argument surprises more Barth's interpreters than Barth himself; for as we shall see in the next chapter, he confessed under certain conditions he could sign the modernist oath that grew out of these Catholic convictions.

If Balthasar is correct, a decisive reason (at least for Barth) for Protestants to remain Protestant and Catholics Catholic has been removed. Balthasar argued Catholics could learn something from this as well as Protestants. He wrote, "We will see in the next chapter that the radical Christocentric vision that serves as the foundation for Barth's *Church Dogmatics* is a completely open possibility for Catholics too."[133] The "form" of Barth's theology, even if he did not affirm it as such, and the Catholic form are mutually enriching. But Balthasar never capitulated to Barth's criticism of the *analogia entis*. If we lose the *analogia entis*, we will also lose the *analogia fidei*. In the 1945 essay he told us this was the "burning" issue between Protestants and Catholics, and it was an issue that affected the realm within which knowledge of God and ethics

---

131. *The Theology of Karl Barth*, 306–7. Emphasis original. He cites ST 1/2 q. 89 a 6 c.

132. *Theology of Karl Barth*, 308. Emphasis original.

133. *Theology of Karl Barth*, 309.

are pursued. In a telling passage, Balthasar writes in 1951, "But every time we use faith in its specific (supernatural, Christian) meaning, human reason is addressed and challenged to its very roots. But nothing unnatural is required of it. On the contrary, grace calls on reason to fulfill the most natural aspects of its identity."[134] The first part of that statement acknowledged the radical character of Barth's analogy of faith. Faith challenges human reason "to its very roots." In that sense, we could say it "disrupts nature" in its distorted shape, which is a primary shape in which we know it. Faith then does not lay on top of a nature already sufficient in itself. Everything is changed. But what is changed remains *natural*. Otherwise we fall back into a Promethean identity where grace replaces nature.

In 1951 Balthasar addressed yet again the "burning dispute" between Protestants and Catholics. He bluntly set forth the crucial issues that animated Barth, dividing him from liberal Protestantism; for Barth ethics and theology were pursued in a common, dogmatic realm, not divided into two different spheres. But this is also what divided him from certain interpretations of Roman Catholicism, which looked to Barth as if they simply mirrored the errors present in liberal Protestantism. It is the question of the *Gebiet*, the realm in which human creatures pursue natural knowledge of God and ethics. Balthasar recognized that for Barth dogma is ethics. Knowledge of God and ethical agency are brought together. No neutral, purely natural sphere remains where one can act as if he or she were not directed to the supernatural end of friendship with God. It reorders everything. Balthasar made this explicit:

> We have here an exact parallel [with the fact that implicit knowledge of God needs its supernatural goal] to the fact that, in the ethical sphere, acts of natural morality are possible to the sinner but that he is not only incapable of *keeping* the natural order as such but is also unable to *direct* the individual moral act in the direction of the concrete supernatural *goal*. He therefore remains, in the Augustinian sense, "off target" (*peccatum*). And this is because a moral act in the *full* sense of that word, even the natural one, includes a *total* and free *decision* of man toward his *final* goal and salvation.[135]

Balthasar addressed the difference between Protestants and Catholics by being for and against Barth. He is for him in that ethics must be done within the

---

134. *Theology of Karl Barth*, 311.
135. *Theology of Karl Barth*, 323. Emphasis original.

context of dogmatics. He is against him in that what must be done within the context of dogmatics is *ethics*, and that includes a robust understanding of human freedom and ethical agency in all its *natural* reality.

We should not overlook how central human ethical agency is in Balthasar's dramatic theology. Although his theology begins in contemplation and vision, with "seeing the form," theology must then issue in dramatic, ethical agency. Much like Aquinas, Balthasar's ethics depends upon the dogmatic vision of God first set forth. Barth may have blazed a trail in the twentieth century to embed ethics in dogma, but for Balthasar he lacked the riches of the philosophical tradition that could truly make such an embedding a dramatic event in which something was *actually* at stake and a free human agency truly mattered. As long as he was bound to a dynamic actualism, he could not avoid a Reformed version of nominalism.[136] Nominalism can only know the singular event. It lacked an adequate narrative construal of history and its significance. History dissolved into the moment, as if it all could have been created five minutes ago complete with an intuition of a past that may or may not have existed. Its dramatic import, then, cannot be realistic. Balthasar wrote, "Theology, as a true science of singulars that are nonetheless general and normative, needs a philosophy in which the essential and realistic aspects are effectively protected as Thomas had done: the Incarnate Logos is the norm and fulfillment of all authentic *logoi* in nature and history."[137] Unlike neoscholasticism and more like Barth, Balthasar does not fear "history" as a decisive category within which the divine economy unfolds. Unlike Barth, Balthasar does not fear metaphysics as a realm about which we know something so that genuine human freedom can be exercised in all truth, beauty, and goodness. Catholicism can affirm "historicity" as thoroughly as Barth without degenerating into Hegelianism.[138] Like Barth, Balthasar also spoke of God's being as his deed but without losing God's nature and collapsing it into history.[139]

CONCLUSION

None of Balthasar's 1930s essays contain the sophistication of his 1940s essays or the 1951 publication. That stands to reason. Balthasar had not yet held personal

---

136. Balthasar wrote, "It was a misfortune that the Reformers wanted to build their theology on a philosophical nominalism." *The Theology of Karl Barth,* 336.

137. Ibid.

138. Ibid. For a compelling account of how Balthasar is discontinuous with, and an antidote to, Hegel, see Cyril O'Regan's *The Anatomy of Misremembering,* vol. 1: *Balthasar and the Specter of Hegel* (New York: Herder & Herder, 2011).

139. *The Theology of Karl Barth,* 342.

conversations with Barth, nor refined his arguments in light of the Catholic and Protestant objections to them. Those 1930s essays do show common themes that reappear in the later work. First, Balthasar finds both continuity and discontinuity in Barth's early and late theology. There is no decisive break. The continuity is found in Barth's preoccupation with Catholicism and in his Christocentrism. Balthasar understood Barth suffered Catholicism and took that suffering as an opening for conversation. He also spoke early and late of Barth's "Catholic side," which he presented to Catholics and Protestants, to mixed reviews. Continuity is also found in Barth's major concern, Christology, and his doctrine of revelation. For Balthasar, the glory of Christ was always present in Barth's theology even in his *Romans* phase, but it shines through with increasing intensity as Barth turns to dogmatics. Balthasar understands the ethical reasons behind Barth's *Romans* phase. Barth wrote during a time of "crisis." Although Balthasar affirmed and understood the ethical reason for Barth's *Romans*, he lamented its theology. Identifying a crisis resolved nothing. Something more positive needed to be said and done. Balthasar interpreted Barth as recognizing this and making a more theological turn. It produces the discontinuity. As Barth turns from a dialectical method that dominated *Romans* to a dogmatic one in his *Die christliche Dogmatik*, the Anselm book, *Credo*, and then the *Church Dogmatics*, he intensifies the dogmatic shape he gives to theology: first from God as a bare essence (still present in the *Romans* phase) to God as Triune, and second from a theology of the Word to one of Jesus Christ.

As Barth deepened his dogmatic theology, so Balthasar argues, he approached Catholicism. He retrieved elements Catholics themselves neglected, such as a Triune rendering of God's perfections that did not play God's unity against Trinity or vice versa. Balthasar saw in Barth the proper "form" theology should take. His fundamental agreement with Barth is that creation must be understood through the dynamic structure of the hypostatic union, in which divinity and humanity are a single acting subject without this absolute unity ceasing to be the ever greater distance between divinity and humanity. For Balthasar the dynamic of the hypostatic union formed the *analogia entis*, but called into question any doctrine of pure nature. He took up this form and developed his own *Trilogy* based on it, supplementing that form where he thought Barth too narrowly constricted it. On this crucial point Barth failed to recognize the true difficulty in modern Catholic theology. It was never the *analogia entis*. Instead it was the innovative doctrine of pure nature in the late medieval and early modern eras that had deleterious consequences for the doctrine of God and ethics.

In 1951 Balthasar fulfilled his desire to make his preoccupation with Barth public. His preoccupation, however, was not with Barth alone but also with a divided Christianity: "A House Divided." It was indeed one of the most important "overtures" to "ecumenical dialogue" in the twentieth century. What makes it unique, however, is that it never compromised on the Catholic form in which dogmatic content must be expressed. Balthasar never denied Trent or Vatican I, or any essential Catholic teaching. Still he thought variations on the main theme were possible without losing that form. Barth provided one such possible variation. This made possible a "rapprochement" between Catholicism and Protestantism. By hearing Barth backward from his *Dogmatics* to *Romans*, Balthasar heard a form that harmonized with Catholicism and Catholicism with it. In so doing, his interpretation and presentation served the purpose of convincing Protestants that their own best insights move them in a Catholic direction. Likewise it served the purpose of admonishing Catholics that what they failed to develop as fully as should have been developed at the end of the Middle Ages and beginning of modernity can be seen by a careful, albeit critical, engagement with Karl Barth—Catholicism's proper form. Aristotle's definition of nature, when it conditioned theology, neglected this proper form. Hans Urs von Balthasar interpreted Karl Barth's theology to Catholics, to Protestants, to Swiss Christians, and perhaps most importantly to Barth himself. Balthasar was a Catholic Barthian who offers to Protestant Christianity a "form" that could provide a counter to its "formlessness," which as he warned, could only "prove disastrous for Christianity."[140]

140. Balthasar wrote, "The demand for such formlessness and sightlessness in contemporary Protestantism—which among other things has made Barth's own genius and accomplishment increasingly misunderstood—is disastrous for Christianity in the world, and I am fully convinced that I was, in my own way, a 'Barthian' when I wrote *Prayer* (1955). And I am just as Barthian in the work of theological aesthetics I have recently begun." "Afterword," in *The Theology of Karl Barth*, 400.

3

Collapse of Balthasar's Interpretation

In a moving passage defending why both he and Catholics should engage in "conversation" (*Gespräch*) with Karl Barth, Balthasar wrote:

> There is another reason why we want to begin a dialogue with Karl Barth: his theology is beautiful [*schön*]. I do not mean merely that stylistically Barth writes well, though he does. But the beauty of his prose emerges more because he unites two things: passion and impartiality. He is passionately enthusiastic about the subject matter of theology, but he is impartial in the way he approaches so volatile a subject. Impartiality means being plunged into the object, the very definition of objectivity. And Barth's object is God, as he has revealed himself in Jesus Christ, to which revelation Scripture bears witness.[1]

Because Barth expressed theology from its object, he captured the beautiful form of the transcendentals. His theology was aesthetic, founded upon a metaphysical realism where the object and its representation were brought together and presented in the form of glory. Barth returned theology to a necessary objectivity, but without the inessential doctrine of pure nature upon which a previous scholastic theology was built. Balthasar saw this metaphysical realism and theological aesthetics in Barth. Yet an important question remains: Has Balthasar provided us with an interpretation and presentation of Barth that fits better Balthasar's vision than Barth's proclamation? Many Barth interpreters now qualify, abandon, or reject Balthasar's interpretation in favor of a much

---

1. I maintained Fr. Oakes's interpretation here except that I substituted "beautiful" for "lovely" as a translation of *schön*. Balthasar, *The Theology of Karl Barth*, trans. Edward T. Oakes, SJ (San Francisco: Ignatius, 1992), 25. *Karl Barth: Darstellung und Deutung Seiner Theologie,* (Cologne: Jakob Hegner, 1951), 13.

more modern, postmetaphysical Barth. Catholic theologians who reject Barth take comfort in this thoroughly modern Barth. It makes their rejection easier.

This chapter examines the collapse of the Balthasar interpretation. The argument first examines contemporary Catholic calls to distance Catholic theology from Barthian influence in favor of a stricter observance of Aristotelian Thomism, now often called "Thomist Ressourcement." Those calls will sound quite familiar; they resonate with Gutwenger and the censors who dismissed Balthasar's appropriation of Barth for failing to adhere to Vatican I's twofold order of knowledge. Thomas Aquinas, interpreted as a strict Aristotelian, they shall argue, is a much better source for Catholic theology than Barth.

The second step in the argument traces the modern, Protestant objection to Balthasar's Barth interpretation. Although these Barthian theologians remain appreciative of Balthasar's work, it contains two errors: First, a historical error. Balthasar periodized Barth's breakthrough erroneously. Second is a related theological error. Because he did not fully understand what Barth was doing, he missed the true heart of the dogmatic material content—Barth's theological ontology of election. The primary theologian interpreting and presenting Barth in terms of this alternate breakthrough is Bruce McCormack. His Barth appears very different from Balthasar's, if not incommensurable with it. His Barth is also thoroughly modern and Kantian, which leads to the final stage in the argument that addresses the question, How Kantian was Barth? Is he a modern theologian revising Christian tradition to answer modern epistemological concerns, or is he a metaphysically realist theologian who retrieves the glory of God? If he is the former, then Balthasar greatly misunderstood him. If he is the latter, the Protestant affirmation of a modern Barth, and Catholic rejection of the same, becomes more difficult. It throws into question both the rejection of him by the resurgent Catholic neoscholasticism and the affirmation of his modernism by recent Reformed theologians, who are undergoing their own Schleiermachian *ressourcement* through Barth. The Catholic rejection, and Protestant affirmation, of the modern Barth feed off each other. It makes the retrenchment on both sides much easier.

Neoscholastic Reaction against a Kantian Barth

Thomas Joseph White and Steven A. Long are two important contemporary Catholic theologians who find Barth a baleful influence in Catholic theology. White begins his masterful book, *Wisdom in the Face of Modernity*, criticizing Kierkegaard and Barth. Their work fails to affirm wisdom, and capitulates to modernity, because they teach three things. First, "natural knowledge of God is not an authentic foundation for understanding human life with God." Second, "philosophical interest in such a natural inspiration is in fact morally problematic." Third, "such knowledge is not possible."[2] Barth's insistence on revelation as the only locus for the knowledge of God is, for White, not antimodern, but another version of Kant's stricture against natural theology, against the possibility of moving from creation to an authentic knowledge of God. Barth remains Kantian in his epistemology, and for this reason he cannot develop an adequate ethic founded upon nature.[3] This undercuts any proper response to grace. "The graced actualization of the human person in an authentic response to divine revelation is possible only if the human person is naturally capable of knowledge of God."[4] The realm within which that natural knowledge occurs is confusing in White's work. Does it occur within grace, or is natural knowledge a presupposition that conditions grace?

White calls for theologians to retrieve much of what twentieth century Catholic theology left behind: Reginald Garrigou-Lagrange's neoscholastic theology, which was the kind of theology responsible for the modernist oath.[5] Garrigou-Lagrange saw the oath as a logical consequence of the twofold order of knowledge affirmed by Vatican I; God can be known by both reason and faith. What is known by reason is not that God is Triune or incarnate, but that God is "origin and end of all things." That God is origin and end is not a matter of faith, but of reason. Vatican I, and the modernist oath, affirmed a metaphysical knowledge with respect to God's existence, directed against errors known as "fideism" and "traditionalism." They were Catholic positions that claimed God can only be known by faith.[6] Garrigou-Lagrange also understood the oath as a condemnation of Kant. He wrote,

---

2. Thomas Joseph White, OP, *Wisdom in the Face of Modernity: A Study in Thomistic Natural Theology* (Ave Maria, FL: Sapientia Press, 2009), xvii–xviii.

3. Ibid., xxi.

4. Ibid., xx.

5. The modernist oath, first issued by St. Pius X on Sept. 1, 1910, was an oath required of all Catholic clergy, religious, and seminary professors. It began, "I profess that God, the origin and end of all things, can be known with certainty by the natural light of reason from the created world." It was rescinded in 1967.

6. If Barth's position is that God is only known from revelation, then there is nothing new about it. It had already been taught in a Catholic school known as "traditionalism."

There is no doubt that the Council in this definition[7] and its corresponding canon condemned Fideism. But the question may be asked: "Is the Kantian doctrine also involved in this definition?" Kant maintained that the speculative proofs for the existence of God are not convincing, that metaphysics is an impossibility, and there are no other proofs for the existence of God except those of the practical or moral order, productive of *moral faith*, which is sufficiently certain, subjectively considered, but objectively considered, is insufficient. . . . For the present we may say that the Vatican Council, in condemning Fideism and Traditionalism, also had in view the Kantian theology.[8]

Garrigou-Lagrange makes it unmistakably clear that the modernist oath rejected Kant's postmetaphysical denial of any natural knowledge of God's existence.

White agrees with Garrigou-Lagrange's criticism of Kant, and finds Barth's work too much taken by Kant's postmetaphysical denials of natural theology, but White doesn't simply repristinate Garrigou-Lagrange. He acknowledges Garrigou-Lagrange did not develop his argument for God's existence adequately. His "insufficiencies" made him susceptible to the critique of "being" found in Kant and Heidegger, which has come to be known as "ontotheology." As White puts it, "His portrayal of analogy risks treating God as a subject within the study of being."[9] Such an understanding of analogy was behind Barth's rejection of the *analogia entis*.[10] It assumes we know "that God is" primarily from the being God and creatures supposedly share in common. Early on Barth interpreted the "analogy of being" along these lines, but this has little to do with "analogy." It is actually a form of "univocity." Barthians have a tendency to confuse the two. White argues for a much more analogical

7. The definition to which he refers is this: "Human reasoning has the power to prove the existence of God with certainty." This passage from Vatican I was included in the modernist oath.

8. Reginald Garrigou-Lagrange, OP, *God: His Existence and His Nature; A Thomistic Solution of Certain Agnostic Antinomies*, trans. Don Bede Rose (St. Louis: B. Herder, 1946), 10.

9. White, *Wisdom in the Face of Modernity*, 20.

10. The most careful analysis of Barth's rejection is John Betz's "After Barth: A New Introduction to Erich Przywara's *Analogia Entis*," in *The Analogy of Being: Invention of the Antichrist or the Wisdom of God?*, ed. Thomas Joseph White (Grand Rapids, MI: Eerdmans, 2011). Betz suggests five reasons Barth rejected it. It established continuity between God and creation (72). It allows a human epistemology access to knowledge of God (78). It is based upon a Mariology that fails to take sin seriously (80). It is "an illegitimate philosophical anticipation of the incarnation" (80). It predetermines Christ's place through an ontological order such that he cannot be the Lord of his Church (83).

understanding of being than what Barth critiques or Garrigou-Lagrange presented.

White's criticism of Barth fits well any interpretation that makes Barth a "modernist." In fact, he is well aware of the Schleiermacher renaissance among contemporary Reformed theologians and the similarities they see between Schleiermacher and Barth, and therefore between Barth and modernity. For White, however, these similarities justify rejecting Barth. The similarities have to do with the characteristically modern assertion that we are now postmetaphysical and therefore must abandon any metaphysics taught prior to Kant. But if this is Barth, then White rightly asks, how can Barth sustain Chalcedon? For if there is no metaphysics, how can we speak of two "natures"? White thinks Barth, like Schleiermacher, cannot sustain the metaphysics necessary for Chalcedon. The Reformed theologian Bruce McCormack agrees, but with a very different conclusion. Barth had no interest in sustaining the *metaphysics* of Chalcedon. McCormack understands Balthasar's interpretation of Barth as erroneous because he supplemented Barth's Christology with his own metaphysical presuppositions and not Barth's revised "theological ontology in the light of election." Balthasar incurs no blame for this; his 1951 book did not yet have access to the later *Church Dogmatics* where Barth's radical revision occurred. Balthasar rightly saw the dogmatic shift to the hypostatic union, but Barth did not have an ontology for it until later, so Balthasar erred by providing Barth with his own ontology, a more traditional, Chalcedonian one.[11]

If Barth's breakthrough is, as McCormack and Balthasar agree, retrieving the christological doctrine of the anhypostaton and enhypostaton, then White asks, how can it at the same time adhere to Kant's postmetaphysical conditions for knowledge, how could it make sense of the ancient metaphysics necessary for a "hypostasis"? White does not think it can. Like Schleiermacher, Barth then can at most have an "accidental" union between Christ's two natures and not a substantial one.[12] McCormack also does not think Barth can make sense of a pre-Kantian metaphysics, and is untroubled by it. Chalcedonian metaphysics needs to be revised.

White, however, finds this giving up too much (as do I). He points in the direction of an analogy that maintains Barth's Christocentric concerns without abandoning metaphysics, through "rethinking *from within Christology* about our

---

11. McCormack, "Karl Barth's Version of an 'Analogy of Being': A Dialectical No and Yes to Roman Catholicism," in White, *The Analogy of Being*, 114–15.

12. White, "Classical Christology after Schleiermacher and Barth: A Thomistic Perspective," *Pro Ecclesia* 20 (Summer, 2011): 229–63.

natural capacities for knowledge of God." In suggesting such a direction, he recognizes his indebtedness to Balthasar's interpretation. He writes,

> In making this argument, I am indebted in part to the thinking of Hans Urs von Balthasar in his seminal work *The Theology of Karl Barth*, trans. Edward Oakes, S.J. (San Francisco: Ignatius Press, 1992), esp. pp. 267–325. Balthasar makes the case that a natural ontology and metaphysical theology are possible, and even necessary within the framework of a Christological doctrine of God-world analogy and a Catholic consideration of the relations of nature and grace. I am suggesting here something potentially complementary but distinct, and more classically Thomistic: because an analogical ontology of creation and God are possible and necessary within Christology, therefore a natural theology is necessary that is distinguishable from Christology. And without a distinct metaphysical reflection on God that is philosophical in kind, true Christological reflection becomes intrinsically impaired.

White suggests this "complements" Balthasar, but it may do more than that, especially if he adopts a nonchristological "natural" theology that then conditions Christology. The troubling move is from a "possible and necessary" analogy "within Christology" to the unwarranted conclusion, "therefore a natural theology is necessary that is distinguishable from Christology."[13] The steps from the former to the latter are missing in White's work. In what sense could "nature" be distinguished from Christ if *omnia in ipso constant* (in him all things consist). In other words, has White assumed a realm of pure nature, untouched from Christology that is more than hypothetical? Does nature-distinguished-from-Christ do actual work in theology? If so, it would have to be more than hypothetical, and a theologian or philosopher who uses it would have to inhabit this realm in order to make it work. Balthasar's question is: Where is this space? In which realm must one stand to do theology from the perspective of a pure nature?

Unlike White, Steven A. Long leaves no doubt he disagrees with Barth and Balthasar. Balthasar must be abandoned as a resource for Catholic theology because Barth's influence led him, and Catholic theologians who follow him, into profound error. Whereas Balthasar dismissed the doctrine of "pure nature" as an inessential Catholic teaching about which one could hold diverse opinions, and argued it was Barth's real Catholic enemy, Long makes it essential

---

13. White, "Classical Christology after Schleiermacher and Barth," 256n64

to Catholic thought. Balthasar's critique of *natura pura* is a disease inflicting serious harm in contemporary Catholic theology. Long critiques Balthasar and then states that if his "analysis is true, then critical aspects of the systematic contemplation, and of the prudence, of a generation and more of theologians is rendered suspect and in need of corrective mediation in order to serve the tradition."[14] In particular, Henri de Lubac and Balthasar are "rendered suspect" and "corrected." They are corrected by turning from the "enormous complication and confusion following the Second Vatican Council" back to the classical doctrine of pure nature in Thomas Aquinas set forth in Vatican I and *Aeterna patris*.[15]

For Long, de Lubac and Balthasar are largely responsible for the modern errors afflicting Catholic theology, the primary one being the inability to recognize the ontological density in nature. De Lubac comes off better than Balthasar in Long's analysis, but the judgment against him is equally severe: "It is not the first time that a physician unintentionally has communicated the plague he nobly sought to resist."[16] De Lubac's work plagues modern Catholic theology not because of his opposition to extrinsicism; here Long would side with him, but because he did not understand properly the Catholic teaching on *potentia oboedentialis*. He only read it with the Franciscans as "susceptibility to miracle," and thus envisioned it as a potency that is at best nonrepugnant to a grace that comes to it as miracle and elevates it without fundamentally engaging nature.[17] This neglects "specific obediential potency" which is "a diverse range of actuation" that "corresponds to the purely passive potency of each nature in relation to a distinct active agency, including the agency of God."[18] In other words, there is an "aptness" of nature to its proportionate end imprinted upon a creature, which occurs always within the context of God's providential action, but is nonetheless purely natural. This aptness is a natural end that need not refer to any supernatural one for its intelligibility. Long advocates a pure Aristotelian nature that Balthasar thought did serious damage to Catholic theology and ethics.

If de Lubac unwittingly "communicated the plague," Balthasar was the means by which it was propagated. Of course, as we saw in the previous chapter, Balthasar affirmed the *potentia oboedentialis* against Barth. He and Long

14. Steven A. Long. *Natura Pura: On the Recovery of Nature in the Doctrine of Grace* (New York: Fordham University Press, 2010), 199.

15. Ibid., 211.

16. Ibid., 44.

17. Ibid., 28.

18. Ibid., 32.

would agree on this point, but for Long Balthasar went horribly wrong on nature and grace in his book on Barth. Because he denied the "hypothetical state of pure nature," he also rejected the claim that nature could be known in "precision from the order of grace."[19] For Long, Balthasar's putative rejection of a hypothetical pure state of nature reduces nature to a "vacuole" for grace. As evidence for the reduction of nature to a "vacuole," Long cites the same quote Gutwenger raised against Balthasar's Barth book in 1953. Balthasar, like Barth, denies that nature alone renders intelligible "questions about marriage, community, the State."[20] Balthasar concedes the point to Barth that nature alone cannot provide an adequate ethics or politics. It is one of the most important passages in Balthasar's book, which chapter 5 will explain through Barth's claim that "dogmatics is ethics." Long agrees it is significant, but negatively so.

Long's interpretation of Balthasar is unconvincing. His first objection to Balthasar is obviously misinformed. As noted in the previous chapter, Balthasar never denied a "hypothetical state of pure nature." He explicitly affirmed it. His second objection, however, is correct. Balthasar did deny that we could know "nature" with "precision" by abstracting if "from the order of grace." For Balthasar, pure nature was "hypothetical." Of course a hypothetical pure nature cannot be known with precision; it does not exist. Long obviously makes pure nature much more than hypothetical, for he claims to know it with "precision." What Balthasar denied, but Long affirms, is that "hypothetical states" actually do theological and ethical work. They do quite a bit of work in Long's moral theology, and the question is to what end? Why do Ressourcement Thomists cling so tenaciously to a hypothetical doctrine of pure nature making it nothing short of a *status confessioni*? The obvious answer has to do with a theology that has the power to rule. Pure nature allows them to acknowledge a natural love for God that is not rooted in faith, but in the natural virtue of justice and should be enshrined in law. The Roman Catholic magisterium then has the responsibility of educating the citizenry on that natural love and the justice it entails. In other words, it gives them a basis to engage in culture war.

Such a harsh criticism is warranted by how Long uses pure nature. For Long the denial of pure nature and its ability to be known with precision distorts our understanding of God, moral theology, and the church's evangelical mission. Balthasar contributed to all three distortions. First, in wrongly employing the *analogia entis* he loses the importance of the divine perfections, distorting the doctrine of God. The problem resides in his "denial of the

19. Ibid., 61.

20. Ibid., 68. Long does not demonstrate sufficient knowledge of Balthasar's corpus. Balthasar is clear that the "nature" he critiques is a philosophical nature independent of theology.

abstractive intelligibility of proportionate nature in relation to the analogy of being."[21] For Long, Aquinas's treatise on God's unity *de deo uno*, which is known via a natural reason that can arrive at those perfections without revelation, is a necessary condition for the treatise on the Trinity, *de deo trino*. Because natural theology conditions revealed theology, and Balthasar did not adequately maintain this relation, he lost the perfections *de deo uno* as the basis for the Trinity. Following Barth, he read the divine perfections too much through revelation. Long is correct about Balthasar's understanding of the relationship between the *de deo uno* and *trino*, but misses the theological reason he refuses to concede the *de deo uno* is a philosophical treatise that conditions Trinitarian theology. The next chapter explains the reason Balthasar followed Barth in this rejection.

Barth and Balthasar's neglect of natural theology contributes to the second distortion Long finds in Balthasar. Balthasar neglected "the role of natural virtue and natural law within the life of grace."[22] He chides Balthasar for denying that in a statue of pure nature creatures would not know the need for prayer. He then states, "As Aquinas shows, with masterful orthodoxy, public worship and prayer is owed to the Creator from whom every public and private benefit is derived, and the virtue of religion falls under the natural good of justice."[23] Long so insists on these natural ends that they condition the possibility of theology. His thesis is provocative because without this particular understanding of nature, we supposedly cannot make sense of the incarnation. He writes, "To hold that human nature is not intelligible in its species in distinction from grace is to make the Nicene doctrine the doctrine that, in Christ, God assumes a 'who knows what?'"[24] He means Chalcedon rather than Nicea, and overlooks the fact that, as Balthasar pointed out, the language of *hypostasis* and *physis* had to be theologically transformed before it could be used.[25] The Fathers did not adopt a metaphysics sufficient unto itself and let it condition theology. Metaphysical terms were transformed by theology before being serviceable for expressing Christian mysteries. Long is forcing upon us an ahistorical unpalatable either-or. Either we know nature in distinction from

21. Ibid., 93.
22. Ibid., 96–97.
23. Ibid., 69.
24. Ibid., 74.
25. Long makes the utterly outlandish claim that "the doctrine of *natura pura* is an essential requisite of the Nicene formula" (Ibid., 210). How is that possible when none of the church fathers present knew of such a doctrine? Long's metaphysics works without any sense of history precisely because it remains so thoroughly abstract.

grace or we cannot understand the Chalcedonian Definition. Certainly we cannot make sense of the incarnation if we cannot distinguish between the nature of a human being and that of a donkey. As we saw in the previous chapter, Balthasar affirmed a theologically derived definition of nature precisely for this kind of distinction, but he never thought we had access to this nature apart from grace, for that kind of nature defined no actually existing being. It was *hypothetical*. Apart from grace we would not know that the human creature, rather than a donkey, is the means by which God redeems the world.

Given that Long argues for an ontologically dense nature, known by reason without faith, the crucial consequence of his argument comes as a surprise, and here is where it is a means of rule. Balthasar's third distortion relates to the church's mission. Because he denied the "abstractive intelligibility of proportionate nature" he unwittingly contributed to a "certain antinomian rejection of the Church's intelligibly authoritative direction in moral teaching: the magisterium in *faith* and *morals*."[26] That would certainly come as a shock to Balthasar who was, throughout his life, nothing but obedient to the magisterium. It was never his intention to reject the church's magisterium. Despite his intention, for Long, if we lose *natura pura*, we lose the necessary role of the magisterium. The correlation between a rejection of *natura pura* and the magisterium seems counterintuitive. If this nature is imprinted on creatures as a specific obediential potency known through reason alone, why must the magisterium explain or superintend it? How can Long move so quickly from the realm of nature to the necessary office of the magisterium? Long recognizes the question and asks, "How is this rejection an implication of the denial of *nature*?" But his answer is unsatisfying. Moral matters require "the essential mediation of subordinated teleologies."[27] The argument seems to go like this. We must first assume it is possible to know moral matters by nature alone. They are impressed upon everyone through God's providence in creation, and that is what gives them their universality. Everyone should know them simply by the use of natural reason. Such knowledge is what allows for laws about such matters that can be universally binding. But then, because of sin, which seems to manifest itself especially in historicism, fideism, and "hypertrophic Hegelian relationality," which he finds as the cause of nearly every contemporary theological error, we no longer recognize nature for what it is. Because we do not recognize it, we must acknowledge the necessary role of the magisterium as the tutor of the moral law. Its teaching on morals is

---

26. Ibid., 98. Emphasis original.
27. Ibid.

not an exercise in grace but nature. So sin is insufficient to damage the use of our natural reason. For that reason, all rational persons should acknowledge Catholic moral teaching. But sin is sufficiently damaging that nonetheless the magisterium is necessary for it to be *naturally* known. A not-so-subtle subtext in Long's work is that the Catholic teaching on the natural love of God and on ethics should be acknowledged in law. Long's discussion of state-sponsored prayer and the possibility of confessional states suggests as much.[28]

Long's work calls for a return to the manualist tradition of Thomism before theologians like de Lubac and Balthasar, who contributed so much to Vatican II, distorted it. They went awry in part because they engaged Protestant theologians. Long writes, "Perhaps it all resolves to this: St. Thomas Aquinas remains, at the end, a richer and more profound dialogical partner and teacher than Karl Barth."[29] That may be so, but certainly Balthasar and de Lubac thought Barth had something to contribute. For Long, that is part of the problem with contemporary Catholic theology. It has a "lack of critical philosophic distance from, essentially Protestant modes of theology."[30] Long's analysis, of course, makes any ecumenical conversation impossible. The only Protestant response is complete surrender or a return to counterpolemics.

Long presents a much more rigorist critique of Barth than White; however, both Long and White agree at a decisive point. They see Barth as a modern fideist incapable of affirming the doctrine of the incarnation because of his rejection of the *analogia entis*. Their arguments are reminiscent of the charges Ernst and Gutwenger brought against him sixty years earlier, and by which they also challenged Balthasar's preoccupation with Barth. White nonetheless finds Balthasar's Barth book pointing in a positive direction; Long does not. Where they would agree is that Barth capitulates to modern modes of thought, especially to those that are putatively postmetaphysical, and in so doing can no longer make sense of terms such as *hypostasis* or *nature* or *essence*. In this sense they offer a very different interpretation of Barth than Balthasar, who read Barth as retrieving a traditional dogmatics within a realist metaphysics. Long and White's interpretation is one that fits with some modern Protestant Barth research. They agree on one aspect of Barth interpretation; he is thoroughly modern. They differ, however, on the evaluation.

28. Ibid., 146–50, 178
29. Ibid., 108.
30. Ibid., 142.

PROTESTANT OPPOSITION TO THE BALTHASAR INTERPRETATION

If significant Roman Catholic theologians call into question Balthasar's interpretation and presentation of Barth because it distorts Catholic theology, Protestants call it into question because it distorts Barth's modern, Reformed theology. Bruce McCormack interprets Barth as an orthodox and modern theologian, and for this reason he makes the strongest argument among Protestants for abandoning Balthasar's interpretation.[31] There is much about Balthasar's work he appreciates and affirms. "It is a simply brilliant book," he states, "one that rests on a real depth of understanding."[32] Its errors are not Balthasar's fault; he did not have access to the materials now available that render his interpretation unconvincing. McCormack's concern is less with Balthasar, and more with those who still read him as their source for knowledge of Barth. Balthasar's interpretation remains too influential among English-speaking theologians because they are unaware of contemporary German Protestant interpretations, especially the work of Jüngel, Spieckermann, and Beintker, that calls for the abandonment of Balthasar's interpretation. The contemporary German interpretation reveals that Balthasar erred historically and theologically.[33] First, he erred historically through his periodization of

---

31. McCormack, *Karl Barth's Critically Realistic Dialectical Theology: Its Genesis and Development 1909–1936* (Oxford: Oxford University Press, 1997), 16, 21.

32. McCormack, "Karl Barth's Version of an 'Analogy of Being,'" 108.

33. McCormack overstates the case for these interpreters. The influential studies he cites find more to appreciate in Balthasar's interpretation than McCormack himself does. In his influential essay "*Dialektik zur Analogie*" Jüngel cites Balthasar favorably as an interpreter of Barth and writes, "Barth's own dialectical way breaks off where he recognizes that there is theology because God has spoken and so human creatures can speak of God. This fundamental, theological insight of Barth's has rightly been named 'from dialectic to analogy.'" (Jüngel, "Von Dialektik zur Analogie: Die Schule Kierkegaards und der Einspruch Petersons," in *Barth-Studien* (Zurich: Benzinger, 1982), 129. Jüngel cites Balthasar's *Karl Barth: Darstellung und Deutung Seiner Theologie*, 93ff). Jüngel offered amendments to Balthasar's interpretation, including a nuanced account of dialectic, but he did not abandon it. Beintker did not abandon the Balthasar interpretation, or call for such, either. He writes, "This thesis of Balthasar's has much to recommend it and provides a plausible key for characterizing the distinction between the time of the *Romans* commentary and the position of the *Church Dogmatics* and of the time lying in between in the process of change. For that reason it has, irrespective of the necessary corrections and modifications, found broad agreement." (Beintker, *Der Dialektik in der "dialetischen Theologie" Karl Barths: Studien zur Entwicklung der Barthschen Theologie und zur Vorgeschichte der "Kirchlichen Dogmatik,"* [Munich: Chr. Kaiser, 1987], 245.) Balthasar's interpretation is less abandoned than corrected and modified. Beintker argues, "The thesis of a turn of Barth's from the *Denkform* of dialectic to the *Denkform* of analogy consequently lacks not only the sharpness in view of Barth's *Church Dogmatics*, where a determined coexistence of logic, dialectic, and analogy is demonstrable. It also lacks the sharpness in view of Barth's dialectical phase, in which after all the awareness of the problem for analogy is recognizable." (Ibid., 280).

Barth's "breakthrough." He failed to see "analogy" in *Romans* and "dialectic" in the *Dogmatics*, and thus misinterpreted Barth's shifts. Second, he never presented Barth's most revolutionary thesis: his theological ontology determined by the doctrine of election.

BALTHASAR'S HISTORICAL ERROR

For McCormack, Ingrid Spieckerman identified the historical error in her 1985 *Gotteserkenntnis*, when she discovered an "analogy of the cross" in *Romans* that provided a consistent lens through which Barth's dominant concern—epistemology—was addressed. Spieckermann situates Barth's work within the question of epistemology raised by Kantian philosophy. She acknowledges that Barth's answers to the Kantian question are not Kant's; instead he turns to a "theological objectivity."[34] This seems congruent with Balthasar's interpretation. After all, Barth's theology is beautiful for Balthasar because it lives from its object. However, for Spieckermann and McCormack, this objectivity is not based on a realist metaphysics as it was for Balthasar; Balthasar wrongly supplied a traditional metaphysics to Barth's work. Barth, however, followed Kant, whose epistemology demolished any traditional metaphysics. Here is one important place where the criticisms of the Ressourcement Thomists and the modern Barthians meet. Both agree Barth affirmed Kant's critique of metaphysics. Both agree Barth was postmetaphysical. The Ressourcement Thomists find that sufficient reason to reject Barth because their theology is a premodern retrieval of Thomas Aquinas, while the modern Barthians think Kant frames the questions that must be answered anew, and they cannot be answered by retrieving a defunct metaphysics. Barth's answers are not Kant's answers, but his questions are Kant's questions. For Barth, like Kant, the knowing subject is trapped within the phenomenal world of his or her own making, and the only way beyond it is a dialectical interplay that on the one hand acknowledges the epistemological circle within which we are caught, while on the other hand recognizes that we cannot get out of it. This dialectical interplay calls into question all our phenomenal expressions, so that something else might appear and interrupt the circle, which of course we cannot escape by

---

Like Beintker, Ingrid Spieckermann still finds value in Balthasar's interpretation, although she is critical of it. (See Spieckermann, *Gotteserkenntnis: Ein Beitrag zur Grundfrage der neuen Theologie Karl Barths* [München: Chr. Kaiser, 1985], 12 and 141–42.) Although McCormack can speak well of Balthasar's work, he calls for a more radical break with Balthasar than these others because of the "genetic method" he uses resulting in an alternative historical narration of Barth's development.

34. Spieckermann, *Gotteserkenntnis*, 73.

ourselves. Barth's dialectic responds to Kant's epistemology with a doctrine of justification by faith alone, now understood as an epistemology.

Balthasar acknowledged this dialectic interplay was present in the early Barth. He accused such a dialectic of "torture." It required a willingness to contradict everything human, to place everything creaturely and divine "on the rack," in order to penetrate beyond the phenomenon and peer behind it to the real, which will nonetheless elude us because we have no human means to make sense of it. Behind the torturer's mask Balthasar saw Hegel more so than Kant. He wrote, "The end result of this relentlessness is to stretch out all the mysteries of God on the rack of this method, to tear them apart in the harsh glare of dialectics that gives to them an immediacy that paradoxically destroys them as mysteries. Clearly, Hegel is at work."[35] Balthasar pointed out how Barth's theology could not endure this "harsh glare of dialectics," because it rendered the incarnation unthinkable. This peculiar dialectic exceeded its task and worked against Barth's primary concern: to think theology from its object. Spieckermann disagrees. Contra Balthasar, she writes,

> Its meaning is not an aweless penetration into "'the secrets of God" which it "forces by the method on the rack" but rather an interruption in the dialectic, "consequently remaining as a dialectic" in the *Gotteserkenntnis*. Thus it becomes *Erkenntnis Gottes*, a letting itself be disturbed in the undisturbed crisis of dogmatics and ethics, and thus it would be a common indication to the inscrutable secret, that in Christ the *soli Deo gloria* is erected among men.[36]

Knowledge of God emerges from God's knowledge, dialectically disturbing human knowing and making possible something completely other. Human knowing is trapped in a phenomenal bind, identified by Kant, where all human concepts are just that—human concepts. The "analogy of the cross" interrupts the human creature's phenomenal bind by dialectically challenging those concepts, destabilizing them. For Spieckermann, Barth's use of analogy always serves his dialectical interest. Balthasar's interpretation neglected Barth's lectures in Göttingen, where this "analogy of the cross" showed up already in his dialectical phase. There was development in Barth's analogy, but it was from the knowledge of God as an "impossible possibility" to a "possible reality." It was not from dialectic to analogy; analogy was present long before the Anselm book and dialectic remained long after. Barth's work is therefore inadequately

---

35. *The Theology of Karl Barth*, 72; *Karl Barth: Darstellung und Deutung Seiner Theologie*, 79.

36. Spieckermann *Gotteserkenntnis*, 139

described as "from dialectic to analogy" (*der Dialektik zur Analogie*) and better described as "the dialectic of analogy" (*der Dialektik aus Analogie*).[37]

McCormack remains indebted to Spieckermann's interpretation for his historical periodization of Barth's development. He summarizes its importance this way: "In sum: the 'analogy of the cross' is a highly actualistic form of analogy that results in a conformity of human knowledge of God to God's knowledge of himself."[38] The analogy of the cross provides a "formal" continuity throughout Barth's work, although the "material" dogmatics informing it intensifies. The intensifying material dogmatics points to Balthasar's theological error. He misses Barth's theological ontology of election, which gradually informs Barth's *Church Dogmatics*. Before making sense of their very different dogmatic interpretations of Barth, McCormack's more thorough criticism of Balthasar's historical reading of Barth needs to be explained.

McCormack considers Balthasar's historical periodization of Barth's *Umbruch* or "radical change" confusing. He is undoubtedly correct, as the previous chapter affirmed. Balthasar's tracing of the diverse and circuitous ways leading to Barth's conversion(s) are confusing, but intentionally so. Balthasar confessed this when he began to trace those "ways." He explicitly claimed Barth's thought unfolded in a "slow and interlaced" way. In other words, if Balthasar's account of Barth's conversions is confusing it may be because those conversions were in fact confusing, and not easily identified historically. The early Barth was "cacophonous." A straight line of historical development cannot be traced from cacophony to harmony. There are elements that point in one direction, and others that point in different directions. Only by reading (or hearing) retrospectively can we determine harmony. Here is an essential, if not incommensurable, difference in McCormack and Balthasar's interpretation. Balthasar approached Barth aesthetically, making sense of the earlier "cacophonous" notes by what he heard later. He read Barth much like he read the theological tradition in his programmatic "Patristik" essay. No singular course of historical development unfolds, but a slow, meandering development with all kinds of loose ends. McCormack reads Barth diachronically, tracing with precision when he made his most significant steps historically, which then lead to a singular theological revolution—a revised doctrine of election that supplants metaphysics. From the revised doctrine of election, everything else unfolds. Because of McCormack's emphasis on the singular doctrine of election

---

37. Ibid., 141–42. Exactly how the cross functions as an "analogy" remains confusing to me. That knowledge of God arises, or does not arise as the case may be, through the cross, would not per se make it an analogy.

38. McCormack, "Karl Barth's Version of an 'Analogy of Being,'" 93.

as key to interpreting Barth, he does not find the breaks in Barth's thought Balthasar did. From *Romans* on, Barth is on a trajectory toward a theological ontology of election. McCormack's interpretation points in a future-oriented, and therefore modern, direction that must now be completed.

McCormack traces Balthasar's historical error to the story of Barth's "conversions." He begins with Balthasar's first sentence after announcing Barth's *Wege im Umbruch* (translated as "Breakthrough") in the 1951 book. Balthasar wrote, "Wie Augustin zwei Konversion durchgemacht hat . . ." (As Augustine underwent two conversions . . .) and then set forth Barth's two conversions.[39] The first was from liberalism to radical Christianity during the time of the *Romans*. The second was from a philosophically grounded theology to a Christocentric theology liberated from the "remnants" of any such philosophy. Balthasar did not impose this interpretation on Barth; he restated Barth's own words. Balthasar draws here upon statements Barth made in his 1939 *Christian Century* essay, "How My Mind Has Changed," but McCormack sees the source of the historical error here. Barth did not use the term "conversion" but of a "farewell to" the "remnants."[40] This distinction seems to split hairs. To say "farewell" to something requires turning away from it. Yet McCormack's point is that Balthasar neglected the context within which Barth explained his "farewell," and thus misinterpreted Barth. He failed to see that Barth spoke of a "deepening" and "application" of the knowledge he learned 1928–1938 rather than a conversion. Balthasar did not, however, argue for a break that was not also a deepening of Barth's main concern. As the previous chapter demonstrated, Balthasar acknowledged that Barth's work during this time pointed in many "ways" (*Wege im Umbruch*) to Barth's dogmatic turn, which was always a deepening of Barth's primary concern, Christology. For Balthasar Barth's "breakthrough" and "conversions" were always intensifications of what mattered most to him. The melody was always there. Balthasar never claimed a complete rupture in Barth's conversions. He simply started his interpretation by quoting Barth's own words.

Balthasar's interpretation has the advantage of making sense both of Barth's affirmation of his Anselm book, and why he affirmed it. Schleiermacher lost the Scholastic proofs for the existence of God and replaced them with an analysis of consciousness. Barth found in Anselm a way to affirm those proofs and make them the basis for theology that Kant's criticism did not touch.[41]

---

39. *Karl Barth: Darstellung und Deutung Seiner Theologie*, 101.

40. See Barth, "How My Mind Has Changed," in *Christian Century*, Sept. 20, 1939, 37–38. Balthasar, *Karl Barth: Darstellung und Deutung Seiner Theologie,* 101, and McCormack, *Critically Realistic*, 3.

McCormack's alternative reading of Barth has the difficult task of explaining one key historical point. Barth never questioned Balthasar's interpretation on the two issues McCormack argues matter the most: his historical analysis and his theological ontology. If the latter were the heart of his work, should we not expect Barth to have told us? Barth and Balthasar were in conversation up until Barth's death. Barth had no fear of criticizing Balthasar when he thought it was necessary, and as we shall see in the final chapter, he often did so on the question of ecclesiology. Why did he never write privately or publicly and say, "Balthasar has understood much of what I am doing, but he failed to see how decisive my turn was in *Church Dogmatics* 2.2 when I made theological ontology dependent upon the doctrine of election." We have no such statement, not even a vague approximation. So we have two historical narrations, one that has Barth's *imprimatur* (Balthasar's) and another that cannot produce *historical* evidence for it from Barth's own comments (McCormack's).[42] This absence of a

41. This point will be discussed below, but it should note be forgotten that in the 1951 book on Barth, Balthasar affirmed his work for returning to the Scholastics. He argues that while Catholics during the twenties were fleeing scholasticism and embracing the "jejeune trendiness" of modern philosophical developments such as "existentialism," Barth "was moving toward Anselm and Thomas Aquinas." (*The Theology of Karl Barth*, 40.)

42. Barth's "imprimatur" is present in 1958 in the second edition to his book on Anselm, where he wrote, "Only a comparatively few commentators, for example Hans Urs von Balthasar, have noticed that my interest in Anselm was never a side issue for me. . . . Most of them have completely failed to see that in this book on Anselm, one encounters if not *the* key, then certainly *a* very important key to understanding the movement of thought which has urged itself upon me more and more in the *Church Dogmatics* as the only one appropriate to theology" (*Anselm: Fides quaerens intellectum*, trans. Ian W. Robertson (London: SCM Press, 1960), 11. Emphasis original. This does not entail Barth agreed with everything in Balthasar's interpretation, but if he thought Balthasar had glaringly missed something in his dogmatic turn, should we not have expected some kind of statement to that effect? One of the more puzzling aspects of McCormack's interpretation is his rejection of Barth's own words on the importance of the Anselm book. For McCormack it is Barth's adoption of the doctrine of the anhypostatic and enhypostatic union in Christ, which he learns from Henrich Heppe in 1924 as he planned a cycle of lectures on dogmatics in Göttingen, that is decisive against Balthasar's interpretation (*Critically Realistic*, 19.) McCormack claims this is the "ultimately conclusive argument" against Balthasar. But why it is so is confusing. He writes, "The major influence was not Anselm of Canterbury but Heinrich Heppe's *Reformed Dogmatics*" on the "decisive turn" from Romans 2 in 1924 (*Critically Realistic*, 23.) We now know Barth attended Peterson's lectures on Aquinas a few years later when they were colleagues in Münster, and that Aquinas via Peterson was also the source of Barth's understanding of the anhypostasis/ enhypostasis doctrine. (See Barbara Nichtweiß, *Erik Peterson: Neue Sicht auf Leben und Werk* [Herder: Freiburg im Breisgau, 1992], 703; and Amy Marga, *Karl Barth's Dialogue with Catholicism in Göttingen and Münster: Its Significance for His Doctrine of God*, Beitrage zur Historischen Theologie [Tübingen: Mohr Siebeck], 2010, 34). Far from challenging Balthasar's interpretation, this lends support to it. What was decisive for Barth's move from dialectics to dogmatics was a better informed Christology. Balthasar

clear statement by Barth supporting McCormack's interpretation does not make it wrong, but clearly it bears the burden of proof.

McCormack finds Balthasar presenting two different historical periodizations of Barth's conversion. In the first he locates Barth's turn from dialectic to analogy primarily with the publication of the Anselm book. Thus the decisive point is 1931. The second locates the "turn to analogy" at two different stages. The first is during the years 1927–1938, followed by "analogy in its fully developed form" after 1938, which of course coincides with *Church Dogmatics* 2.1, which was so influential on Balthasar.[43] The second break, McCormack argues, misses Barth's development completely. He writes, "If there is one point on which all recent Barth scholarship agrees, it is that Balthasar's belief in a second 'break' in Barth's development cannot be sustained."[44] But that overstates Balthasar's messy historical narration. Balthasar wrote,

> Barth did not suddenly replace dialectics with analogy. We cannot isolate any one particular text as *the* sign of this shift, for it happened gradually. Not even mentioned in the first volume of the *Church Dogmatics*, the second volume (1938) merely notes it without having the opportunity to test it. But with the third volume (*The Doctrine of the Word of God*, 1940) and his contemporaneous essays (especially "Credo", 1935; and "Confessing God, Serving God", 1938) it starts to take on definitive form, so that the doctrine of analogy unfolds more and more clearly with each succeeding volume. Indeed so victorious does it become that by the time of the later volumes on creation, Incarnation and providence (1945, 1948 and 1950), it has become the central theme of his theology.[45]

Attentive readers must *hear* what Balthasar writes here. Barth's early work was a cacophony of various themes, some coming to the surface, others remaining hidden, but gradually, like any good symphony, a proper form emerges that renders the various themes harmonious.

---

claimed Barth's familiarity with Catholic teaching had a salutary effect on his retrieval of a christological rather than a philosophical grounding of material dogma (*The Theology of Karl Barth*, 40.) He consistently argued Barth only told Catholics what they already knew about their faith, even if they neglected it.

43. McCormack, *Critically Realistic*, 4.

44. Ibid., 14.

45. *The Theology of Karl Barth*, 107. Emphasis original.

Balthasar's interpretation of Barth's *Umbruch* is much messier than even McCormack narrates. It simply did not matter to Balthasar to identify precisely when in the 1920s Barth made his turn. What mattered was that Barth liberated theology from a modern philosophical foundation on which even Catholic theologians were desperate to build during the twenties. McCormack seeks a more precise account of how Barth's theology developed historically and finds Balthasar's work, along with its influence on theologians such as Hans Frei and T. F. Torrance, misleading. He writes, "The riddle of how Barth's theology developed will not be solved along this line. Fortunately, there is a better way."[46] This way is Spieckermann's, who discovered in Barth "a continuous unfolding of a single material intention through different models of explication."[47] This shows the stark difference between the two interpretations. Balthasar worked explicitly against reading Barth from *Romans* to the *Dogmatics*. McCormack insists it is the "better way" to make sense of Barth. The result is a preoccupation with Barth's historical development in the 1920s. Barth's work is the "unfolding of a single material insight," that was "dogmatic," and produces a "new paradigm" for understanding Barth's historical development. Once we understand that "new paradigm," Barth's radical revision of theological ontology comes to light. The differences between Balthasar and McCormack are not antiquarian squabbling; the different histories serve different dogmatics, one an orthodox modern neo-Protestantism, the other Catholic. As the next chapter will show, these two interpretations will have profound differences in understanding Barth's doctrine of God.

BALTHASAR'S DOGMATIC ERROR

The different dogmatics served by Balthasar and McCormack's interpretations of Barth bring us to McCormack's account of Balthasar's theological error. As previously mentioned, McCormack claims Balthasar missed Barth's theological ontology, and substituted his own more traditional metaphysics in its place. Balthasar can be excused for this because Barth himself did not fully recognize it. The radical turn in his theological ontology begins in *Church Dogmatics* 2.2, where the doctrine of election reorders everything, and is only completed in the later volumes in Barth's doctrine of reconciliation. Now God is not only the subject of election in Jesus Christ, but also the "object."[48] This will require rethinking the doctrine of God in a postmetaphysical direction that Barth began

---

46. McCormack, *Critically Realistic*, 14.

47. Ibid.

48. McCormack, "Karl Barth's Version of an 'Analogy of Being,'" 122.

but did not complete, and Balthasar only vaguely recognized in his theology of Holy Saturday.

Jüngel first identified the "pivotal role of divine election" in Barth's theological ontology.[49] A single material dogmatic insight from *Church Dogmatics* 2.2, Jesus Christ is the electing God, now requires radical revisions in theological developments from the Fathers, including Nicea and Chalcedon, through the Middle Ages. None of these epochs or councils recognized how radically ontology must be changed if we are to make sense of the mystery of the incarnation. If Long and White argue the incarnation makes no sense without the metaphysical language of nature, substance, and hypostasis, McCormack argues it makes no sense with them. They must be jettisoned for a theological ontology found in election. This is the singular material insight present in Barth from *Romans* through his *Dogmatics* that gets intensified.

That Barth's work develops this single dogmatic insight means, as McCormack puts it, "that Barth was from first to last a theologian (and not a philosopher turned theologian as Balthasar and those who followed in his wake seem to imply)." To be fair to Balthasar, we must remember *it was Barth* who confessed he had to rid himself of the—in his own words—"remnants of a philosophical or anthropological grounding and exposition of Christian doctrine." Balthasar may have leveled that charge, but in so doing he quoted Barth.[50] The question that must be posed, if we are to take Barth at his word, is what was that philosophical grounding he himself found problematic? Balthasar found it in dialectic. It was a straightjacket on Barth's real concern: Jesus Christ as the single acting subject uniting divinity and humanity in his hypostasis. Dialectic cannot express the unity of the single acting subject Jesus is.

McCormack's "new paradigm" draws on a "genetic" historical approach that overcomes Balthasar's interpretation and offers the proper material, dogmatic content to interpret Barth. The problem with Balthasar, Torrance, and others is that they put their own dogmatic questions to Barth and do not stand within Barth's historical development to see how his dogmatics grew out of it. McCormack writes,

49. Ibid., 123.

50. McCormack does acknowledge in a footnote that Balthasar is only quoting Barth here, but he accuses Balthasar of doing this out of context (*Critically Realistic*, 1n1). This admission restates rather than refutes Balthasar's interpretation. He consistently affirmed that Barth's later work was a deepening of a basic christological insight that then also required, as Barth acknowledged, bidding "farewell" to the "remnants" of a previous "philosophical grounding." McCormack's interpretation, unlike Balthasar's, cannot make sense of this "farewell." What philosophical remnants did Barth jettison in this new paradigm?

> In other words, they have made their own primary concern to be Barth's as well and read it back into the development. Viewed genetically however, from a standpoint *within* the development itself, everything looks different. It was as Barth concentrated his attention on the material problems of Trinity and Christology in 1924 that solutions to methodological questions also began to emerge—something which Barth himself was only gradually aware.[51]

In this passage, McCormack finds that Barth was only "gradually aware" of his dogmatic insight. In a later passage McCormack claims he never "achieved complete clarity":

> Taking a step back, it has been shown that the trend of German language scholarship has been, for some time, in the direction of insisting that a critical correction was introduced into Barth's conception of the divine being as a consequence of his revision of election. That Barth himself did not achieve complete clarity with regard to just how revolutionary his doctrine of election could be is not to be denied. He simply wrote better than he knew.[52]

Two important dogmatic claims emerge from this "new paradigm." The first is Barth's "critical correction" in the "conception of the divine being." A full discussion of this must wait until the following chapter, but it is related to the second claim. Barth's "critical correction" is to "methodological questions." Those methodological questions are the ones raised by Kant, as Spieckermann's interpretation argued. The dogmatic material of Christology and Trinity work

---

51. McCormack, *Critically Realistic,* 20. Emphasis original. McCormack's "genetic" methodology for reading Barth raises some questions. First, what does it mean to stand "within the development itself" and do so "genetically"? What kind of historical access does this claim? We do not live in the 1920s. If we want an interpreter who did in fact stand closer "within the development itself" would it not be Balthasar? What gives historical access to these developments to a contemporary Barth researcher in a way that an interpreter like Balthasar did not have? Balthasar in fact asked Barth about these things, as we have seen from the first chapter, and he always recognized that Barth's concerns were the material dogmas of Trinity and incarnation, but he never found him answering Kantian methodological questions. Second, what gives McCormack a genetic access to these historical developments, which were not only unavailable to an interpreter like Balthasar, but even to Barth himself, since according to McCormack's interpretation he was "only gradually aware" or never completely clear on what he was doing? A strong Hegelianism is at work here, where Barth's work is best understood by placing it within Spirit's unfolding in history, producing observable results of which the author himself was only vaguely aware, but the interpreter sees clearly.

52. McCormack, "Karl Barth's Version of an 'Analogy of Being,'" 135.

in a very different realm than they did for Balthasar. They are primarily used as solutions to methodological questions put forward by the dominance of epistemology in modernity.

Although McCormack fastens upon the doctrine of election for interpreting Barth with a singlemindedness that is alien to Balthasar's more symphonic interpretation, both McCormack and Balthasar agree that Barth intensifies his Christology. McCormack rightly sees this in Balthasar.

> Decisive for Balthasar in locating the final emergence of analogical thinking in 1938 is its Christological grounding. As he put in in another passage, "In the *Church Dogmatics*, there occurs imperceptibly but irresistibly the replacement of the central concept 'Word of God' by the central concept 'Jesus Christ: God and man.'" It was the emergence of this Christological concentration in *Church Dogmatics* II/1 which allowed analogy to come to its full expression.[53]

Here McCormack interprets Balthasar accurately. He rightly identifies what matters most—Christology, but he misses the theological significance Balthasar finds in *Church Dogmatics* 2/1. Barth overcomes unpalatable theological positions that minimize and relativize the role of Christology in the theodrama: nominalism, Calvinist predestination, and neoscholasticism, by affirming God's perfections (the *de deo uno*) within the doctrine of the Trinity, and not as a metaphysical precondition for that doctrine grounded in the doctrine of pure nature. McCormack fails to mention the latter in Balthasar's presentation of Barth.

What mattered most for Balthasar is that Barth overcomes not so much dialectic but constructing theology upon a philosophical foundation that has not yet been permeated by theology. Benjamin Dahlke understands better than most why Balthasar's "Catholic Reception of Karl Barth" was so important. Balthasar opposed the *Zweistockwerkdenken* (two-story thinking) that he found afflicting Catholic theology through neoscholasticism.[54] Balthasar did not reject Scholasticism—that much should be clear from the previous two chapters. He rejected the narrowing of theology to this two-storied space where "nature" could be known separately from the dramatic economy found in the incarnation, crucifixion, and resurrection of Jesus. Then God's economy plays little to no role in the things that matter most: human action and contemplation. Barth's work pointed in a direction beyond the impasse between modernists

---

53. *Critically Realistic*, 3.

54. Benjamin Dahlke, *Die katholische Rezeption Karl Barths* (Tübingen: Mohr Siebeck, 2010), 185.

and neoscholastics. His theology was neither. It was beautiful because it expressed the form and tone of revelation. This interpretation undoubtedly served Balthasar's own theological politics, but as Dahlke also persuasively argues, the same is true of McCormack's interpretation.[55] McCormack, like Spieckermann, returns Barth to modernity.

Balthasar thought the "philosophical remnant" Barth pruned was a dialectical method of contradiction that lapsed into idealism's "identity." For McCormack dialectic is not a method; it is the *analogia fidei*, which is not, as it was for the Fathers, a biblical hermeneutic where one Scripture illumined another. The analogy of faith is an "event." He writes, "Thus the 'analogy of faith,' once realized, does not pass over into human control. It must continue to be effected moment by moment by the sovereign action of the divine freedom if it is to be effected at all."[56] This appears to be a nominalist claim, even though McCormack is no nominalist. What God has just done provides no continuity with what God may do in the very next moment unless God in his sovereign freedom yet wills it again. If this is correct, then McCormack and Balthasar's interpretations are diametrically opposed when it comes to Barth's doctrine of God. Balthasar found Barth overcoming nominalist tendencies in Reformed theology. Dialectic expresses a nominalist theology well because what God just willed can never become secure transtemporally unless God is free to will something other. Analogy assumes a metaphysical realism where the intelligibility of the created order finds transtemporal continuity, allowing us to recognize what is good, true, and beautiful. There may be dialectical moments, but such must be subordinated to analogy if we are to avoid nominalism. McCormack never finds Barth subordinating dialectic to analogy. Unlike Beintker, he does not find a shift in the lead role between them.[57] The

55. Dahlke notes that McCormack does not provide a neutral historical reconstruction but has his own "theological political interests," just as did Balthasar. McCormack returns Barth to a thoroughly Reformed universe. Dahlke is more sanguine than I am that we can reconcile these two interpretations. See Dahlke, *Die katholische Rezeption Karl Barths*, 207–210.

56. *Critically Realistic*, 17.

57. Michael Beintker developed more fully the complex use of "dialectic" in Barth, offering a modest modification and correction to Balthasar's interpretation by a careful analysis of the various uses Barth made of "dialectic." Barth never intended a logically rigorous use of the term. In fact, there is fluidity in his various usages that intentionally defy easy categorization or periodization. However, for Beintker, just as for many others who challenge Balthasar's interpretation, the key figure to understand Barth's dialectic is Kant. He writes, "Kant's philosophy—mediated through the Kant interpretation of Marburg neo-Kantianism and its interpretation via Heinrich Barth—forms the actual philosophical structure of orientation of the Barthian dialectic." He still finds a shift in the Anselm book, as did Barth and Balthasar, but it is less a "break" than a shift in which analogy takes over the leading role from dialectic. (Beintker,

predominance of dialectic is a decisive difference with the Balthasar interpretation that McCormack emphasizes: "The great weakness of the Balthasarian formula is that it conceals from view the extent to which Karl Barth remained—even in the *Church Dogmatics!*—*a dialectical theologian.*"[58] Once again, if McCormack is correct, Balthasar must be wrong about the form of Barth's theology. Both interpretations, for all their careful reading of Barth's works, cannot be correct.

A Thoroughly Modern Barth: Barth and Kantianism

Balthasar defended Barth against his Catholic critics who saw him as another modernist.[59] McCormack's " new paradigm" interprets Barth as a modernist, primarily addressing Kantian methodological questions. One difference between Balthasar and McCormack's interpretation is the philosophical context within which Barth gets read. The new paradigm emerged from careful studies of the work Barth did in the 1920s, when neo-Kantianism obviously influenced him; that is incontestable.[60] What is contestable is the ongoing significance of this philosophical foundation on Barth's later dogmatic theology and how it situates Barth within modernity. The primary question the new paradigm puts to Barth asks what he contributes to *modern* theology. Receiving Barth's work within this context necessarily pushes it in a different direction than Balthasar, who saw it in a much broader context of the patristic, Scholastic, and modern periods. He read Barth through a long tradition of retrieval that included Anselm and Aquinas, among others.[61] Although Balthasar was no reactionary against modernity, neither was he preoccupied with it. He sought a way beyond the stultifying modernist-neoscholastic debates. The new paradigm finds Barth taking the side of the former, which helps explain why the Catholic retrieval of neoscholasticism must reject Barth. Balthasar's friendship and

---

Der Dialektik in der "dialetischen Theologie" Karl Barths, 280.) For him, analogy now plays the leading role, but dialectic was never left behind. The best way to interpret the shift is as "Eine dialektische Erklärung der Analogie" (a dialectical clarification of analogy). (Ibid., 285.)

58. *Critically Realistic,* 18. Emphasis original.

59. See *The Theology of Karl Barth,* 22.

60. See Johann Friedrich Lohmann, *Karl Barth und der neukantianismus: Die Rezeption des Neukantianismus im "Römerbrief" und ihre Bedeutung für die weiterer Ausarbeitung der Theologie Karl Barths* (Berlin: Walter de Gruyter, 1995). For one of the most thorough historical analyses of Barth and his relationship to philosophy in the 1920s and 1930, see Kenneth Oakes, *Karl Barth on Theology and Philosophy* (Oxford: Oxford University Press, 2012).

61. See *The Theology of Karl Barth,* 40.

preoccupation with Barth pointed in a direction beyond those debates. His interpretation came undone. The debates have returned.

"Modernity" preoccupies the new paradigm by way of Barth's relationship to Kant. Thus Barth's contribution to modern theology has a twofold possibility.[62] Either he solves Kant's problem with the ethical subject or Kant's epistemological problem concerning the knowledge of God. The first problem is that the autonomous subject must act on a categorical imperative for which the subject has no self-interest. However, the command structure of the maxim by which the subject acts cannot escape the circular reality that it (the command) emerges from an individual's maxim that will inevitably be self-interested. The autonomous action of the individual's maxim and the universal requirements of the command cannot be reconciled. Barth's theology provides a solution at this point and sets us out on a new Enlightenment. The act no longer arises from an autonomous subject outward, but a commanding God directed toward the agent, a God who shares a similar ethical agency to what Kant attributed to the autonomous individual. Georg Pfleiderer puts it this way: "Barth's decisive concern consists in this, to represent the fulfillment of the categorical imperative rendered possible to the believer as spontaneously his own, which is [also] an uninhibited act of God's will."[63] This emphasis on Barth as affirming Kant's ethical subject is central to the teaching of the Munich school, in which Barth is concerned with a modern "realization of freedom," although Barth primarily attributes this realization to God rather than the autonomous individual. The Munich school heralds Barth as the beginning of a new Christian Enlightenment, and perhaps the most thorough call for an abandonment of Balthasar's ecclesial and dogmatic interpretation of Barth.

---

62. Here I would agree with Reinhard Hütter before he converted to Ressourcement Thomism, when he suggests something similar. He writes, "Next to the work of Korsch and a number of other German interpreters linked to Göttingen, this tendency to read Barth's theology primarily if not exclusively in relation to the Reformers, the Enlightenment problematic and Protestant liberalism can be found in the otherwise very important work of Bruce McCormack" (Hütter, *Bound to be Free: Evangelical Catholic Engagements in Ecclesiology, Ethics, and Ecumenism* (Grand Rapids, MI: Eerdmans, 2004), 246n30). In 2004 Hütter found this a problematic reading of Barth. After citing Korsch he wrote: "A reading of Barth's theology as primarily a running dialogue and controversy with neo-Protestantism and a testing and deepening of 'the fundamental insights of the Reformation in face of the development of modernity' reflects a limited, one-dimensional understanding of Barth's project" (Ibid., 85). It is unclear if Hütter still holds to this, or has any stake in it. His *Dust Bound for Heaven: Explorations in the Theology of Thomas Aquinas* (Grand Rapids, MI: Eerdmans, 2012) throws his lot in with the Ressourcement Thomists in a fundamental way.

63. Georg Pfleiderer, *Karl Barths praktische Theologie* (Tübingen: Mohr Siebeck, 2000), 262.

Trutz Rendtorff, one of Barth's last students, initiated the revised interpretation of Barth as a thoroughly modern theologian in his important essay on the "radical autonomy of God."[64] Rendtorff denies that Barth can be adequately interpreted as ever *breaking* decisively with liberal theology. He notes that "recurring expressions' like *Aufbruch* (break up), *Neuanfang* (recommencement), *Umbruch* (radical change), *Wende*"(turn), *Wiedergewinnung* (recovery), and *Anstoß* (initiation) describe "dialectical theology" since its beginning.[65] To view Barth as somehow making any decisive turn or new beginning after *Romans* 2 neglects this. For these reasons, the interpretation that finds Barth returning to the biblical and Reformed sources as a theologian of the church "cannot be accepted."[66] Instead Karl Barth's *Römerbrief* is "the first step of a new Enlightenment, which unfurls once again the process of Enlightenment, not however as historical, but rather in a radical and systematic sense."[67] The point of this new Enlightenment is not the freedom and autonomy of humanity but of God. Barth provides "dogmatic legitimation for the entrance of modern autonomy into the center of theology and church."[68] When Barth is seen as an ecclesial theologian, God's liberation, as the ultimate autonomous subject, gets missed. It can be adequately recognized only when Barth is understood as an exponent of liberal theology. Then Barth "breaks ground for a new 'Christian Enlightenment,' which is nothing less than the "secession of Christianity from its ecclesial identity."[69] No longer can we use the "formula" that "theology is a function of the church." Now we need a new formula: "Theology is a function of the historical world of Christianity. This then is the Christian form of the world of modern autonomy. Only in this connection can it be understood and worked out that Christianity has entered into its world-historical phase."[70]

One cannot help but see the influence of this nonecclesial form of Barthian theology in more recent English-speaking interpreters who interpret Barth independent of the church. It is difficult to understand why, if this is Barth, he called his great work *Church* Dogmatics. If it is correct, the clarion call Balthasar thought he heard from Barth about liberal Protestantism was woefully mistaken.

---

64. "Radikale Autonomie Gottes: Zum Verständnis der Theologie Karl Barths und ihre Folgen," in *Theorie des Christentums* (Gütersloh: Gerd Mohn, 1972), 161–81.

65. Ibid., 161.

66. Ibid., 162.

67. Ibid., 164: "Der erste Schritt einer neuen Auflkärung, die den Prozeß der Aufklärung noch einmal aufrollt, aber nicht als historischen, sondern in einem radikalen und systematischen Sinne."

68. Ibid., 179.

69. Ibid., 178–79.

70. Ibid., 181.

Far from warning Catholics about the insidious effects of liberal Protestantism, Barth completed it. God became a liberal Protestant. McCormack notes that Rendtorff's thesis "has not found universal acceptance in all of its points." Nonetheless he sees "great value" in it insofar as it reopened the question of "Barth's relationship to 'modernity.'"[71] Now that the question was "reopened," Barth studies entered into it with abandon.

As already noted, Ingrid Spieckermann's important 1985 work, *Gotteserkenntnis*, raised the second problem, the problem of the "knowledge of God."[72] She began that work stating, "With the question of the knowledge of God the new theology of Karl Barth sets a basic question for theology generally, ripping it from the traditional metaphysics as from the modern liberal self-understanding."[73] Here Barth is modern, but not with a liberal self-understanding. He addressed modern concerns, and did so in a typically modern postmetaphysical sense, particularly through his preoccupation with epistemology. As Louis Dupré has argued, "epistemology becomes a substitute for metaphysics" in the "passage to modernity." He writes, "As [modern philosophy] attributed the origin of meaning to the knowing subject, it replaced the ancient metaphysical question—Why is there Being at all?—with the epistemological one—How do I know what is?"[74] Spieckermann places Barth within "the radically changed situation of Kant's critique of reason."[75] McCormack likewise places Barth's theology "under the conditions of modernity," and inevitably finds him preoccupied with epistemology.[76]

Although the modern epistemological preoccupation differs from the preoccupation with the ethical subject in the Munich school, it is just as Kantian. The "I" is "caught" in an inescapable epistemological circle, a view of the subject Barth already developed in the *Romans* phase and continued throughout his work.[77] Barth's massive project is thoroughly modern in that its preoccupation is not metaphysics or ontology but epistemology—how might we know God after Kant? If this is the case, Balthasar was indeed a misguided

---

71. McCormack, *Critically Realistic*, 28.

72. Spieckermann, *Gotteserkenntnis*, 73.

73. Spieckermann, *Gotteserkenntnis*, 7.

74. Louis Dupré, *Passage to Modernity: An Essay in the Hermeneutics of Nature and Culture* (New Haven: Yale University Press, 1993), 160. This argument has been so well documented by others that it should be noncontroversial.

75. Spieckermann, *Gotteserkenntnis*, 23.

76. Bruce L. McCormack, "'With Loud Cries and Tears': The Humanity of the Son in the Epistle to the Hebrews," in *Epistle to the Hebrews and Christian Theology*, ed. Richard Bauckham et al. (Grand Rapids, MI: Eerdmans, 2009), 48.

77. Spieckermann, *Gotteserkenntnis*, 74.

interpreter of Barth. He could not have found in Barth a return to the transcendental predicates of being unless he seriously misread him, even if it was an interesting misreading. But if Barth is postmetaphysical, how can we make sense of the doctrine of the an- and enhypostasis, which all interpreters agree is central in Barth's thought?[78] Thomas Joseph White's legitimate question arises once again. We can no longer speak of "eternal hypostases" through an actualistic philosophy that eschews metaphysics and accepts Kant's epistemological limits. If so, we can hardly make sense of the Trinity or the incarnation. If modern epistemology is the context within which Barth must be read, then of course metaphysical entities like "hypostases" must be jettisoned. But how then can we maintain that it was this teaching, whether from Heppe or Aquinas, that was decisive for him? Can we have "an- and enhypostasis" without an account of "hypostases"? That makes no sense, as can be seen from attempts to speak about it on Kantian grounds.

Like Spieckerman, Bruce McCormack finds Barth to be thoroughly modern in that he affirms Kant's epistemology. He writes,

> With Kant, Barth believes that human knowledge is limited to the intuitable, phenomenal realm. And this means that if God (who is unintuitable) is nevertheless to be intuited (and therefore *known* in the strict, theoretical sense), God must make himself to be phenomenal, that is, God must assume creaturely form.[79]

In this passage, McCormack conflates the God/world distinction with Kant's noumenal/phenomenal. The latter distinction does not concern the relation

---

78. When McCormack states that in May, 1924, Barth made a "momentous discovery" with the anhypostasis/enhypostasis doctrine, he sets it forth in very traditional, metaphysical terms: "The central thrust of the ancient dogmas was that the Logos (the second Person of the Holy Trinity) took to Himself human flesh (i.e. a human 'nature' complete, whole, and entire) and lived a human life in and through it," (*Critically Realistic*, 327). He does place "nature" in scare quotes, but does not explain here as he will later how he sees Barth resituating "hypostasis" within a philosophical actualism. Later, in a much less traditional and more Hegelian vein, he states, "Barth was placing the orthodox Christology of the fifth century on an entirely new foundation. The strict delimitation of revelation to 'Self-revelation' is, as Wolfhart Pannenberg has rightly observed, a modern innovation. Here a point of contact with Hegel is not to be denied" (Ibid., 359).

79. McCormack, *Orthodox and Modern: Studies in the Theology of Karl Barth* (Grand Rapids, MI: Baker Academic, 2008), 111. Emphasis original. McCormack traces the influence of Kant on Barth by referring to chapter 15 of Barth's *Göttingen Dogmatics*, "The Knowability of God," which was unavailable to Balthasar. We will return to it below when we ask if Barth is this determined by Kant's epistemology. Suffice it for now to say that Barth never explicitly divides knowledge into Kant's noumenal and phenomenal distinction in that important chapter.

between God and creatures, but is a distinction found in everything that exists between the "thing in itself" (noumenal) and the "thing as it appears to us" (phenomenon). It doesn't matter whether the object is God or a spoon, we do not have access to any thing as it is in itself because our own innate subjective apparatus generates our knowledge of objects in the world. For Kant, the knowing subject only has access to the phenomenon; the noumenal is lost to us, or at least can only be inferred from the phenomenon (depending on how one interprets Kant). Our minds are either limited in, or have no, access to the thing in itself because the mind generates the conceptual structure to the sensible manifold of intuition that then renders it intelligible. Kant's "Copernican Revolution" subordinated metaphysics to epistemology. (It would be a mistake to say Kant did away with metaphysics altogether.) He wrote,

> Hitherto it has been assumed that all our knowledge must conform to objects. But all attempts to extend our knowledge of objects by establishing something in regard to them *a priori*, by means of concepts, have on this assumption ended in failure. We must therefore make trial whether we may not have more success in the tasks of metaphysics, if we suppose that objects must conform to our knowledge. This would agree better with what is desired, namely, that it should be possible to have knowledge of objects *a priori*, determining something in regard to them prior to their being given.[80]

Exactly what Kant meant here is contested. Some interpret it as a species of subjective idealism. Knowledge of an object arises not from the object, but the projection on the thing itself by the subject. Others interpret it as "epistemic humility." The "relational properties" that affect us are not to be equated with the "thing in itself," but they are made possible because of the thing in itself. The subject does not know what "substances," things-in-themselves, are, but the subject knows that they are; otherwise there would be no knowledge generated from relational properties. The "epistemic humility" interpretation posits no end to metaphysics, but resituates it. Epistemology trumps metaphysics.

Metaphysical entities pervade Kant's critiques, but the knowing subject cannot know them with certainty. His point is not postmetaphysical, but metaphysical claims are minimized by an emphasis on epistemological humility. Rae Langton explains:

---

80. Kant, *Critique of Pure Reason*, trans. Norman Kemp Smith (New York: St. Martin's Press, 1965), 22.

Kant says that there is a distinction between things in themselves and phenomena. What he says is admittedly metaphysics, but none the worse, I think, for that. He says that things as we know them consist "wholly of relations." . . . He says that we have no insight into "the inner" of things. He has a distinction between substances, bearers of intrinsic properties on the one hand; and relational properties of substances on the other. He says that we have no knowledge of the intrinsic properties of substances. This, as it stands, is not idealism, but a kind of epistemic humility.[81]

Whether Kant teaches idealism or epistemic humility is irrelevant to the fact that his phenomenal/noumenal distinction provides a very inadequate context in which to understand Barth's theology. If McCormack is correct that "with Kant, Barth believes that human knowledge is limited to the intuitable, phenomenal realm," then it can only be a fideistic assertion to then state, "and this means that if God (who is unintuitable) is nevertheless to be intuited (and therefore *known* in the strict theoretical sense), God must make himself to be phenomenal, that is God must assume creaturely form." "Phenomenal" and "creaturely" are improperly conflated here. Creaturely form has very little to do with Kant's "phenomenal," unless we understand it either as the form human creatures give to the manifold of sense intuition so that it can be conceptualized, or as the manifold of relations impinging upon human creatures, giving knowledge that there is a substance, a thing in itself, but prohibiting knowledge as to what it is. If God makes himself "phenomenal," he does not make himself creaturely. Such a philosophy could never express the incarnation. At most this means that God makes himself part of the conceptual structure of our own thought that allows us to render sensible intuitions intelligible and be humble in what we can know. The incarnation would profit us nothing ontologically if Barth were truly committed to such an epistemology. We would not need much more than our own religious symbolic concepts. That would be theology under the conditions of modernity; it would be a version of Schleiermacher. But one cannot claim on Kantian grounds that God "makes himself to be phenomenal" and then in any sense assume we have knowledge of God through the incarnation.[82] Those two claims are irreconcilable.

81. Rae Langton, *Kantian Humility: Our Ignorance of Things in Themselves* (Oxford: Clarendon Press, 1998), 2.
82. McCormack does qualify this by saying, "God does not make himself directly identical with a phenomenal magnitude but only indirectly so." *Orthodox and Modern*, 111.

If Barth's revision is that God makes himself phenomenal, his theology is at best a form of Gnosticism. God does not give himself to us in any ontological sense. God gives himself to us in gnosis, a knowledge that provides a conceptual structure allowing us to know God, or inchoate relational properties that allow us to infer a god, who would resemble Isis more than the Triune God, as Kant himself suggested. [83] "Knowledge" of God replaces any ontological participation in God as that which saves. Of course Barth points in the direction of the latter ("ontological" might cause him to stumble, but not "participation"), so it raises a further question as to how well the new paradigm interprets Barth. Can his dogmatics be adequately presented through the strictures of Kant's epistemology? They seem to produce insurmountable difficulties for a proper Christian dogma. Does it not make better sense to see the Kantian epistemology as part of the "remnants" of philosophy Barth discarded? [84]

The use of the Kantian framework here is something of a sleight of hand. On the one hand we are told Barth affirms it. On the other hand we are told he affirms it only to reject it with respect to the knowledge of God. In other words, because Barth supposedly agrees with Kant that *all* our knowledge comes from creaturely realities and creaturely realities cannot give us knowledge of God (epistemological humility), Barth must then reject any natural, human knowledge of God mediated through creatures, for it could not be knowledge of anything other than creaturely realities. No objective encounter within creation mediates knowledge of God; such knowledge comes from an encounter elsewhere. Where is this encounter then located? The answer seems to be only in God. If anyone asks how God produces this in the creature that is trapped in a phenomenal world, a reasonable answer cannot be given, because it assumes the creature might produce something. [85] How then could it be Kantian, and especially neo-Kantian, since it was so preoccupied with the "production" (*Erzeugung*) of thought?[86] Not only does this raise the

83. Kant, "On a Newly Arisen Superior Tone in Philosophy," in *Raising the Tone of Philosophy: Late Essays by Immanuel Kant, Transformative Critique by Jacques Derrida*, ed. Peter Fenves (Baltimore, MD: John Hopkins University Press, 1993), 51.

84. The same difficulties appear for Marga's important work, *Karl Barth's Dialogue with Catholicism in Göttingen and Münster*. It is invaluable as a source for understanding Barth's encounter with Catholicism. But when she sets forth the Kantian context for Barth's theology, the argument gets strained. Once again the noumenal/phenomenal distinction is transposed into a God/creature distinction. She writes, "The epistemological assumption behind such a clear assertion is based upon the Kantian framework that humans can only know, i.e. perceive and reflect upon realities that come into their sphere of knowledge as objects." Marga, *Karl Barth's Dialogue with Catholicism in Göttingen and Münster*, 99.

85. Marga states, "When faced with the Word of God, human thought, no matter how it is shaped, does not *produce* anything." Marga, *Karl Barth's Dialogue with Catholicism in Göttingen and Münster*, 140.

question how could it be human knowledge, but even more, how could it be Kantian? For Kant, and especially neo-Kantianism, if we do not produce anything, we do not know anything. Moreover if creatures produce nothing, how can we make sense of Mary's role in the incarnation? Did she not in some sense "produce" the Word as Chalcedon affirmed (*Theotokos*)?

Because the "new paradigm" finds Barth's work concerned with Kantian epistemology and ethics, it interprets his work as having more chronological continuity from *Romans* through the *Church Dogmatics* than did Balthasar. [87] Although most interpreters recognize shifts in Barth from his early liberal Protestantism to the critical *Romans* stage (1920s) to the dogmatic phases (1930sff.), in the "new paradigm" shifts are less drastic. Barth is viewed as a consistent critical, dialectical thinker answering questions Kant and/or neo-Kantians raised about our knowledge of God and ethics.

This "new paradigm" produces a substantively different interpretation of Barth's relationship to modernity than did Balthasar. Although Balthasar was not so naive as to see Barth repristinating premodernity, or think such was possible, he saw Barth ignoring the epistemological strictures erected in modernity that "policed" God as a sublime about which nothing could be reasonably known, resulting in an "anthropological reduction." The Kantian interpretation of Barth finds Balthasar mistaken. Balthasar neglects the historical significance of Barth's Marburg training, the influence of Herrmann and Cohen on his work, and the impact of his brother Heinrich. Moreover it neglects how Barth's theology completes Kantianism, which is his contribution to modern theology.

Kant or Anselm? Barth's Realist Metaphysics

Is the new paradigm correct about the Kantian context within which Barth should be understood? Barth was most likely marked in ways that he himself could not always recognize by his Marburg days. But if he were this indebted to Kant, it is a very strange Kantianism to which he was indebted. In no sense would it be possible to get around Kant's strictures against a strict theoretical knowledge of God simply by asserting that God becomes phenomenal. Barth's *Dogmatics* blatantly violates Kant's epistemological humility. He knows quite

---

86. See Johann Friedrich Lohmann, *Karl Barth und der neukantianismus*, 69–70, in which he notes how crucial the *Ursprung* is in Cohen's thought that then generates (*erzeugen*) knowledge.

87. Benjamin Dahlke succinctly explains the difference between McCormack's interpretation of Barth compared to Balthasar's. McCormack interprets Barth in terms of continuity; Balthasar interpreted him in terms of discontinuity. Dahlke, *Die katholische Rezeption Karl Barths*, 207.

a bit about God; nearly as much as Balthasar. At most, Barth could be a Kantian in his knowledge about everything except knowledge of God and then he makes an exception to Kant's epistemological limits. If that is correct, then we still have no resolution to the methodological questions his theology supposedly answered. He simply was a Kantian except when he did not want to be. This would be fideism, for we have no way to give a reason for God's existence within our knowledge. Perhaps it is precisely the irrationality of this philosophical foundation and its concomitant dialectical approach that had to be abandoned if Barth were to express the material content of the incarnation? For one of the difficulties in the newer Barth interpretation is to explain what he meant when he said he sought to rid himself of the "remnants" of a philosophical or anthropological foundation for his theology. Balthasar's interpretation can make sense of Barth's own words.

Spieckerman identifies what I find to be an insurmountable difficulty for the early (cacophonous) Barth. Like Kant, the early Barth knows the limits of human knowledge. We are trapped within a phenomenal world of our own making out of which we cannot move. The first difficulty with this epistemology is, if it were true, how could we know it? If we are trapped within such a phenomenal world, we would never be able to rise above it and know that we are trapped. Only someone who tacitly claims to have broken out of the circle would know that the rest of us remain trapped in it. The second difficulty is that how we know no longer makes sense of what we know. Knowledge arises despite what our epistemology says is possible. In other words, how we know what we know must temporarily be suspended so that what we know can be taken into account—true knowledge of God. But how that "what we know" can be known we do not know. The moment we claim to know what we know the circle closes back in upon us. Knowledge of God could only be a miracle each time. Like the Suarezian doctrine of grace and nature, grace miraculously comes to a nature completely devoid of any relation to God and miraculously elevates it. If this were Barth, then far from overcoming what Balthasar identified as the genuine problem Barth misidentified—a doctrine of pure nature—Barth restates it. But if this is Barth, he could never have attained the theological *objectivity* Balthasar discovered in Barth's dogmatic turn. Kant's epistemology simply does not allow for what Balthasar's interpretation of Barth says is possible. A third difficulty with this early Barth is that its preoccupation with epistemology cannot sustain his theological objectivity when it comes to soteriology. Epistemology does not save. Participation in the life of God does. As will be shown below, Barth says this explicitly in the later volumes of the *Church Dogmatics*.

But is this Barth? Is he such a devoted Kantian? Is he, as Thomas Joseph White suggested, a fideist? If this is Barth, then White's conclusion seems unavoidable. Barth would be a fideist who simply asserts that God speaks and we hear it even though he offers no reasons for it. White would also be correct that Barth cannot sustain Chalcedon.

Much of the evidence for the new interpretation of Barth draws on the *Göttingen Dogmatics*. McCormack finds in it the direction of the new foundation upon which Barth will construct a Kantian postmetaphysical Christology. He correlates Barth's use of the doctrine of the anyhypostasis and enhypostasis to a dialectic of veiling and unveiling in Kant's epistemology.

> The proximity to Barth's dialectic of veiling and unveiling was obvious. In that God takes to God's Self a human nature, God veils God's Self in a creaturely medium. He enters "the divine incognito"—a situation of unrecognizability. Outwardly (and inwardly!), He is a human being like any other. But the Subject of this human life—we may liken this to Kant's conception of an unintuitable, noumenal self—was at every point the Second Person of the Trinity; a Subject who, because of the veil of human flesh, remains unintuitable. Because of His unintuitability, God can only be known in Jesus where He condescends to grant faith to the would-be human knower; where He unveils Himself in and through the veil of human flesh.[88]

This correlation raises several questions. If God can only be known in Jesus when he reveals it in faith, how were Jews able to identify the same God prior to the incarnation? What are we to do with the gift of God's Name given to Moses (Exod. 3:14), about which Christian tradition saw similarities (not identities) with what many great philosophers said about God? Moreover how does this tell the biblical story well? When the *Jewish* disciples, women, and *Gentile* believers confessed Jesus to be God through worship and prayer, did they not logically have to understand in some measure what was meant by "God" in order to make such a confession? Is there not a reason the Old Testament came before the New? Jesus did reveal God more fully than had hitherto been recognized, but if no knowledge of God outside Jesus' revelation were acceptable, how would it be possible to make this confession at all? How does one recognize an "unintuitable Subject" sufficiently to fall down before "it" and offer praise? If all rational knowledge of God is denied because we have no

---

88. *Critically Realistic*, 327.

intellectual intuition of God, then we could not identify Jesus as God. Before Kant's unintuitable Subject (Isis) one can neither "fall to his knees in awe nor can he play music and dance."

Notice how Kant functions in this Barthian interpretation. His work only functions negatively. Kant is affirmed only for the purpose of acknowledging we have no knowledge of God based on metaphysical principles. Then revelation is turned into an epistemological category that resolves what Kant thought could not be resolved, but only hypothetically asserted based on the "moral proof" for God's existence.[89] Does Barth use Kant to address modern questions of epistemology? The crucial text where this use of Kant takes place is found in chapter 15 of the *Göttingen Dogmatics*. Barth referred to Kant in this chapter along with Aristotle and Aquinas. Barth neither differentiated among them nor developed any of their work with much detail. Instead he stated the obvious: theologians and preachers do not need Kant to be told that knowledge of God is a problem. The problem exists whether Kantian philosophers are right or not. Barth wrote, "The question that dogmatics has to put to preaching would be there even if philosophy could without contradiction accept or proclaim God as a possible intellectual or intuitive experience."[90] In other words, even if Kant were wrong, the problem still exists, because it is not primarily a Kantian problem. It is not a philosophical problem; knowledge of God is for Barth a *dogmatic* problem. Kant only helps identify what the theologian and preacher already know. Barth says the "Aristotelianism" of Roman Catholicism does the same.[91] Garrigou-Lagrange would agree. His use of Aristotle's philosophy to demonstrate "that God is" also denied that we have any direct intuition of God's existence. Our knowledge of God in natural theology only comes from sensible creatures from which we must "abstract" and make analogies. Kant would object to such a claim, whereas Aristotle and Aquinas would agree with it. However, all three would admit we have no direct intuition that proves God's existence. Barth recognizes that Aristotle, Aquinas, and Kant agree, which is the key point he made in this chapter. He made common cause with all three of them. We have no univocal concept of being that grants us direct access to God, but might we still have indirect knowledge, as both Aristotle and Aquinas, and through his moral proof Kant in his own metaphysics, affirmed? It was this indirect knowledge by way of analogy that the modernist oath (at its best) affirmed.

89. For some reason this interpretation ignores Kant's moral proof for the existence of God.

90. Barth, *Göttingen Dogmatics*, vol. 1, trans. Geoffrey W. Bromiley (Grand Rapids, MI: Eerdmans, 1991), 326.

91. Ibid., 345.

Kant would have opposed Catholicism's antimodernist oath. It violated epistemological humility; it violated reason's purity. It was, as Garrigou-Lagrange acknowledged, directed in part against Kantianism. If Barth were a Kantian, then he too would have to oppose the antimodernist oath. Any decent theologian would have known it challenged Kant's strictures on the knowledge of God. Yet in chapter 15 of the *Göttingen Dogmatics*, Barth did not find the antimodernist oath problematic. He notes how central it has been to Catholics since the (first) Vatican Council, and did not find it at odds with Protestant orthodoxy.[92] He explained it quite well and then stated,

> Our older Protestant predecessors took no offense at such statements. Quite the contrary. Nor need we do so, even if I say so with tongue in cheek. The decisive point is that on the Roman Catholic view the claiming of reason for the knowledge of God is an article of faith, an assertion of the church that thinks in terms of revelation. The older Orthodox were thinking along the same lines. . . . Revelation does not exclude but includes natural religion, as a major includes a minor.[93]

Natural theology works within revelation. Nature is then a *theological* concept. This interpretation of Vatican I would not be Garrigou-Lagrange's interpretation, but it was Balthasar's. Barth interpreted the oath as many Catholics do and did. It did not say we have a proof for God's existence in a natural theology based on a pure nature or a pure reason, but it says that given we know God has spoken to us, it is quite possible for a natural knowledge of God to be included under the articles of faith. In other words, because we know "That God IS" from the *Deus dixit* and the incarnation, we should not be surprised when someone comes up with a proof for God's existence as did Anselm. What differentiates Barth and Balthasar from Garrigou-Lagrange and Kant is the "realm" within which such knowledge works. Because God has spoken, there is no realm of pure nature. Barth was much less sanguine about the possibility of a convincing proof for God's existence than Garrigou-Lagrange or Thomas Joseph White, but he did not rule it out. In fact, he found something like it in Anselm. Barth certainly would not have argued that such a proof conditioned the possibility of revelation as current neoscholastics do; for Barth revelation conditioned the possibility of a natural proof.

92. Ibid., 343–44.
93. Ibid., 344.

Barth admitted that under certain circumstances he could take the modernist oath. He could do so only if he emphasizes the Vatican's sense of human creatures "*being able* to know or demonstrate." Barth said he would have to repeat this "*being able*" three times before he took the oath.[94] He realizes the Vatican teaches a possibility and not an actuality. A good Kantian could not take this vow, even with Barth's qualifications. So Barth's relationship to Kant must be more complex than the new paradigm suggests.

The problem of the knowledge "that God is" in Barth is not all that similar to what we find in Kant. Barth stated this explicitly in the *Göttingen Dogmatics* when he wrote, "For theology the real problem in all this does not lie on the side of the human capacity for knowledge." But this is exactly where it lies for Kant; he thought he knew the limits of that capacity. For Barth the problem is preachers proclaim God's Word, which he admits they do, but God's Word never becomes a mere object somehow distinct from God. God always remains subject even when God's Word is proclaimed.[95] The problem is dogmatic. God and God's Word are identical. Far from leading to postmetaphysical assertions, this requires them, which is why Anselm matters so much. Anselm's work sets Barth on a trajectory that allows for both a reasonable proof for God's existence within the Triune affirmation that God and God's Word are identical. Barth acknowledged that the proofs for God's existence have a validity after Kant's critique if we maintain their proper order: "Naturally, the sequence is as follows: Revelation comes first, and provability, the proofs, and the insight and certainty that the proofs give, come second. 'I believe in order to understand.'"[96] Barth also argued Schleiermacher's theology abandoned too quickly the Scholastic proofs for the existence of God and replaced them with anthropology.[97] Here we see Barth in the *Göttingen Dogmatics* already rethinking these matters from the *Romans* phase with the help of Anselm. Barth would certainly object to Garrigou-Lagrange's defense of the proofs. Natural theology outside revelation does too much for him. But Barth might be a better interpreter of Thomas here than the Dominican when Barth says, "The medieval and older Protestant dogmaticians never disguised in principle the fact that we cannot bring people to faith by proving the existence of God but that the proofs at best can lead only to the place where faith comes on a very different presupposition, namely, that

94. Ibid., 346.

95. Ibid., 326.

96. Ibid., 348.

97. Barth, *The Theology of Schleiermacher*, trans. Geoffrey Bromiley, (Grand Rapids, MI: Eerdmans, 1982), 268–70.

of grace."[98] Here is where Barth might be much closer to Thomas Joseph White than the latter suggested.

Barth did not significantly alter the position laid out here in the *Göttingen Dogmatics* on the relationship between natural proofs for God's existence and revelation. He developed a similar relationship in the 1931 Anselm book and made an explicit reference to its significance in the introductory claims he made in *Church Dogmatics* 2.1.[99] He explicitly claimed Anselm's proof for the existence of God was not touched by Kant's critique. What Barth opposed was Descartes and Leibniz's new foundation for this proof that assumed something like a pure reason from which God's existence could be demonstrated. As Beintker notes, for Barth Descartes began the "foundational disposition [*Grundhaltung*] of modernity, which to him also forms the foundational evil [*Grundübel*] of all modern theology: namely the certainty of the existence of God is derived from the subjective self-certainty of the perceiving creature."[100] This was what he always opposed. If Barth's later work changed its attitude toward Vatican I from what is found in the *Göttingen Dogmatics*, it is because he found Vatican I's twofold order of knowledge partook more of the "modern" understanding than he had earlier acknowledged. Such comments make it impossible to read Barth as a modern. How could he make such claims and rely on his brother Heinrich when Descartes was so important for his work?[101]

Barth never turned away from the centrality of the Anselm book as a key to interpret himself, which is what he found correct about Balthasar's interpretation. For Balthasar, Barth's work on Anselm required a realist metaphysics where theology lives from its object, but metaphysics never conditions theology. Beintker does not use the precise terminology of realist metaphysics, but he explains it when he notes, "If one considers Barth's methodological procedure in *Fides quaerens intellectum* on the background of its decided anticartesianism, then one must establish that his thinking in the Anselm book arrives to an already long-prepared resolution."[102] This resolution is a realism that takes the "leading role" away from dialectic and gives it to analogy because the impossibility of truth from the dialectical phase gives way to truth's possibility from its object. Now "objectivity implies the ability to

98. *Göttingen Dogmatics*, 348.

99. *Church Dogmatics* 2.1, trans. W. B. Johnston, T. H. L. Parker, Harold Knight, and J. L. M. Haire, ed. G. W. Bromiley and T. F. Torrance (Edinburgh: T & T Clark, 1957), 4.

100. Beintker, *Der Dialektik in der "dialetischen Theologie" Karl Barths*, 190.

101. Heinrich Barth habilitated with Cohen in Marburg in 1880 on Descartes's epistemology. See Johann Friedrich Lohmann, *Karl Barth und der neukantianismus*, 133.

102. Beintker, *Der Dialektik in der "dialetischen Theologie" Karl Barths*, 192.

speak, think, and communicate."[103] If so, suggests Beintker, then the Anselm book "seals the fate" of dialectic as "the leading form of thought" *(leitenden Denkform).*[104]

Perhaps we should not be too hasty in conceding the new paradigm for the interpretation of Barth, or look to it as the path forward for Protestant theology. Although we must not be reactionary and argue everything went wrong in modernity, and all we need to do is wait for a Benedict or Thomas to give us light, nor should we think theology must proceed under the conditions of modernity. There is no Hegelian necessity to history. Balthasar's interpretation, and his fascinating conversation and preoccupation with Barth, still provides a better way forward beyond the impasse of an entrenched *modern* Protestant or Roman Catholic neoscholastic theology. Balthasar's "theological turn to theology" should attract attention and prompt Protestant theologians to reconsider what Balthasar saw in Barth. In turn, this could have a salutary effect on the deep current divisions within Catholic theology as well. For as Balthasar rightly noted, the real divisions are no longer Catholic versus Protestant but run through each tradition making for unlikely allies.

Balthasar's interpretation places Barth's work in an ecumenical context and suggests that his dogmatic theology, his ethics, and his concern for ecclesiology, albeit not his ecclesiology per se, have something to teach both Catholics and Protestants discerning how to be Christian in and through modernity. We will take up each of these concerns in the next three chapters, examining Barth's doctrine of God, his ethics, and the ecumenical significance of Barth and Balthasar's friendship. The conversation between Barth and Balthasar will continue to be the guide through these examinations, as will the "burning dispute" between them that Balthasar identified.

103. Ibid.: "Gegenständlichkeit impliziert Sagbarkeit, Denkbarkeit und Kommunizierbarkeit."
104. Ibid., 194.

4

The Realm of God

In his 1945 essay on Barth, Balthasar identified what mattered most. The "burning matter of dispute," he wrote, "decides the realm [*Gebiet*] of the natural knowledge of God and ethics."[1] Balthasar was both for and against Barth on this all-important question of the "realm" within which knowledge of God and ethics should be pursued. He was for him in that the knowledge of God and ethics should be pursued within the actual economy God created and redeemed, and not one defined by a hypothetical pure nature.[2] He was against him in that this pursuit must take place in terms of the *analogia entis*. For Balthasar the dispute included whether the *analogia fidei* alone sufficed, or whether it must be understood within the *analogia entis*. Balthasar thought Barth had a version of the *analogia entis*, but never sufficiently acknowledged it as such.

This chapter addresses the first part of the "dispute," the knowledge of God; the next addresses ethics. Because Balthasar was for and against Barth, he affirmed much of Barth's doctrine of God, but thought it lacked something. He affirmed Barth's situating the doctrine of God's perfections within the doctrine of the Trinity in *Church Dogmatics* 2.1. For Balthasar, Barth's doctrine of God's perfections expressed God's glory better than much of the theology found in the patristic, Scholastic, and modern epochs. Although Balthasar affirmed Barth's doctrine of God, he also argued it needed the *analogia entis* in order to achieve its fullness. The chapter unfolds in two stages. The first sets forth Balthasar and

---

1. Balthasar, "Analogie und Natur: Zur Klärung der theologischen Prinzipienlehre Karl Barths," *Divus Thomas* 23 (1945): 3.

2. Ben Quash explains well the implications of Balthasar's desire to do theology within the actually existing economy in his *Theology and the Drama of History* (Cambridge: Cambridge University Press, 2005). Quash explains the advantages of "theodramatics" and states, "An appreciation of drama makes available a more adequate source of categories for giving voice to the truth of creaturely life before God than other genres (archetypically, 'epic' or 'lyric') could ever be—let alone the categories of analytic philosophy and the scholastic textbooks," (7).

Barth's theology proper, that is to say, their doctrine of God. It does so by comparing it to the postmetaphysical Barthian, and the neoscholastic, doctrines of God in order to show the ongoing significance of Balthasar's interpretation for contemporary theological debates. In this stage, Balthasar is for Barth. The second stage explains what Balthasar meant when he said that Barth's theology needed the *analogia entis*. It does so by showing how Balthasar sides with the Scholastics on the need for metaphysics, but with Barth on refusing to divide treatises on God's oneness from God's triunity.

Reordering or Retrieving Dogmatics

Balthasar was excited about *Church Dogmatics* 2.1 and 2.2 because Barth reordered doctrinal loci and did not make God's perfections or attributes the condition for the Trinity. Instead, he read them in and with the doctrine of the Trinity. For Balthasar, when Barth reordered (or retrieved) dogmatics, he dismantled neoscholasticism's two-storied theological ontology.[3] This dismantling was one of his great contributions to theology. Perhaps Balthasar was in a better position to recognize this consequence of Barth's theology because, unlike Barth, he had been trained in that neoscholasticism.

Balthasar also saw the significance of Barth's reordering of doctrinal loci for Protestant theology. The order, or form, given to dogmatic loci in both Reformed orthodoxy and neoscholasticism did not adequately express the form and tone of the divine economy. Both tacitly assumed a nominalism where an abstract, unitary God of power existed behind the Triune God manifested in the economy of salvation. This God could be known outside the divine economy, and thus too easily expressed without the heart of Christian teaching: Trinity and incarnation. For the Reformed, it was the God of the absolute decree who acted prior to the Trinitarian economy, which is true at least in the ordering found in Heppe's Reformed dogmatics that influenced Barth and which he explicitly corrected.[4] For the neoscholastics, it was a reading of Aquinas's *Summa* where the *de deo uno* was understood by some as given by

---

3. I say "retrieval" because Richard Muller has shown how Peter Lombard made a similar move. Muller states, "Lombard departs from the method of Anselm by beginning his doctrine of God with the doctrine of the Trinity and the discussion of concepts of essence and attributes folding into the discourse as a whole." Richard A. Muller, *Post-Reformation Reformed Dogmatics*, vol. 3, *The Divine Essence and Attributes* (Grand Rapids, MI: Baker Academic, 2003), 38. The relationship between Aquinas's de deo uno and de deo trino is complex and contested, but it did change the order found in Lombard.

4. For a deeper analysis of the decree in Reformed theology than one finds in Heppe, see Richard Muller, *Christ and the Decree: Christology and Predestination in Reformed Theology from Calvin to Perkins* (Grand Rapids, MI: Baker Academic, 2008.)

reason alone, distinguishing it from the *de deo trino*, and then conditioning the possibility of the latter. Balthasar argued Barth's work destroyed both the Reformed dogmatics of the absolute decree and the neoscholastic two-storied theological ontology. In their place arose a dogmatics in sync with the form of God's glory present in Scripture. Balthasar's interpretation is insightful. It fits well Barth's theological development.

Barth first attempted this reordering, or retrieval, of dogmatic loci in 1924 when he lectured on dogmatics at Göttingen, and did so by listening to Aquinas and Calvin. He made a similar move six years later in *Die christliche Dogmatik*. At both places, Thomas Aquinas's *Summa* provided inspiration. In the *Göttingen Dogmatics* he wrote,

> Of the 611 *questiones* of his *Summa theologica* Thomas Aquinas devoted only one to a discussion of sacred doctrine as such. With qu. 2 he plunged into the middle of things under the heading "The Existence of God." Melanchthon, Zwingli, and Calvin acted similarly. They were so sure of their cause that they hardly thought it worth the effort to devote more than a few pages to the concept and method of their science. To the extent that theologians increasingly lost sight of their theme and became unsure of their cause, beginning with the tragic retreat which in the theology of Schleiermacher ended with total capitulation, there flourished introductions, prolegomena, debates about scripture, inspiration, revelation, miracles, religion, and reason, and apologetic efforts to establish and justify the discipline and its theme. Not for nothing it was Schleiermacher who wrote the most famous and indeed the classical introduction to doctrine. This is an enterprise that necessarily arises out of the situation in which theology, and especially Protestant theology, finds itself. The less people have to say, the more zealously they must *pro-legein*.[5]

Here Barth attends to the *form* of dogmatics. It once began, with Aquinas and Calvin, in the "middle of things." Now, because Christianity lost confidence in its message, prolegomena condition dogmatics.

In 1924 Barth affirms, and laments, that theologians can no longer pursue dogmatics otherwise than by following the modern form with its *pro-legein*.

5. Barth, *Göttingen Dogmatics* vol 1., trans. Geoffrey W. Bromiley (Grand Rapids, MI: Eerdmans, 1991), 19

Theologians cannot return to Calvin or Aquinas. Barth is pessimistic about any alternative. In 1927, in his *Die christliche Dogmatik,* he incorporated the same quote about Aquinas, but now he is less pessimistic about an alternative approach.[6] Just as the older theology "let the truth speak for itself," so dogmatics must still assume God is the subject who speaks: *Deus dixit.*[7] This claim is nothing new in Christian tradition or among Barth's teachers. Ritschl and Herrmann could be understood as teaching something similar. God is only known when God speaks. Barth, however, distances himself from any assumption of a fideism that could suggest he is just repeating Ritschl. "If God were not the speaking subject who creates faith by his Word, then what could he be but the object of a scholarly metaphysics? We must be on guard lest with the Rischlians we deny out of hand that he might perhaps be this as well, but that is another question."[8] For Ritschl, the choice was an either-or, either revelation or Scholastic metaphysics. This was a common feature of liberal Protestantism, but in 1927 Barth expresses doubts about this either-or; his position is more tempered.[9] Barth's position here could also be read as the residual influence of his teacher Herrmann, for whom religious experience of revelation is self-authenticating.[10] Such a residual existentialism can be found in this 1927 work, which was revised in his turn to *Church Dogmatics.* Barth distances himself from Herrmann in his *Ethics* lectures in 1928–1929, as he distances himself from Ritschl here in 1927. They both claimed an end to metaphysics. Barth too would be wary of it, but the key question is—of what is he wary? Is he just repeating the liberal Protestant opposition to it? At his most profound, his concern should be understood not with metaphysics in general, nor the *analogia entis,* but the metaphysics of nominalism, as Balthasar pointed out.

The basic beginning point in *Die christliche Dogmatik* and Barth's later theology bear a strong resemblance. God speaks God's Word in the Spirit

---

6. *Die christliche Dogmatik in Entwurf,* ed. Gerhard Sauter (Zurich: Theologische Zurich, 1982), 25.

7. *Christliche Dogmatik,* 28.

8. This quote would seem at least to raise a momentary pause before Bruce McCormack's claim: "If there is a constant in all phases of Barth's development, from his student days through to the end of his life, it lay in his protest against the introduction of metaphysics into the domain of Christian theology." McCormack, "Election and the Trinity: Theses in Response to George Hunsinger," *Scottish Journal of Theology,* 63, no. 2 (2010): 210.

9. Kenneth Oakes persuasively shows how liberal Protestantism eschewed metaphysical speculation for revelation. See his *Karl Barth on Theology and Philosophy* (Oxford: Oxford University Press, 2012).

10. See Simon Fisher's *Revelatory Positivism? Barth's Earliest Theology and the Marburg School* (Oxford: Oxford University Press, 1988).

by means of human agents. Theology begins with this speech and radiates outward. It is the nature of this radiance, and what it accomplishes, that shifted. The shift occurred as Barth recognized the dangers of the metaphysics of nominalism in order to account for this Word and its effects. Barth came to see such nominalism not only in liberal Protestantism, but also in Thomism when, or if, the *de deo uno* established the metaphysical conditions for the *de deo trino*. His own ordering in *Church Dogmatics* 2.1 explicitly addressed this concern when he offered an alternative ordering of God's perfections.

Barth began *Church Dogmatics* 2.1 with a basic assumption that referred back to his Anselm book: "But if the life of the Church is not just a semblance, the knowledge of God is realized in it. This is the presupposition which we have first of all to explain in the doctrine of God." God is known in the church through its speech and acts. Theology does not begin by groping for God with a limited rationality that knows only in part; it begins with God giving God's self to us, not in part but in whole; for as the perfection of simplicity teaches, God does not have "parts." To know God is to know God. Barth learned this from Anselm. He encouraged readers to take up his book on Anselm in order to understand 2.1.[11] His presupposition is "God is actually known." He does not begin with the *pro-legein*, but the thing itself: God is and God speaks. All of *Church Dogmatics* 2.1 seeks to make sense of this actual knowledge. It does so by reversing the order of Aquinas, but nonetheless affirming all that Aquinas affirmed. That is to say, Barth did not begin with God's perfections and then move to the Triune hypostases; Barth began with the latter and interpreted the former within them. But God's perfections were still affirmed without question. Barth not only reordered Thomas's distinction between the *de deo uno* and *de deo trino*, he also moved the Reformed doctrine of election into the doctrine of God in *Church Dogmatics* 2.2. Balthasar recognized the dramatic import of this key theological reordering.

BALTHASAR READING ELECTION TRINITARIANLY: OVERCOMING NOMINALISM

This section presents Balthasar's antinominalist interpretation of Barth. Balthasar read Barth as setting forth a dogmatic theology that sensed the "form and tone of revelation." He offered a realist theology of glory that witnessed the world as "charged with the grandeur of God" because it was created in and through Christ. After his first meeting with Barth in 1940, Balthasar explicitly

---

11. *Church Dogmatics* 2.1, trans. W. B. Johnston, T. H. L. Parker, Harold Knight, and J. L. M. Haire, ed. G. W. Bromiley and T. F. Torrance (Edinburgh: T & T Clark, 1957), 4.

stated that his own attempt to write such a theology would now be superfluous. After reading *Church Dogmatics* 2.1 he realized Barth had already done it.[12] This of course did not prevent Balthasar from setting forth his own dogmatics in the form and tone of revelation, one that drew its inspiration in part from Barth.

BALTHASAR FOR AND AGAINST BARTH'S DOCTRINE OF GOD

After Balthasar's first meeting with Barth in 1940, Balthasar sent him a ten-page letter explaining his sympathy and opposition to Barth's theology. He admits his "rising interest" and "great excitement" in reading *Church Dogmatics* 2.1 through to the end. What he found of such great interest was Barth's doctrine of God, which he describes as "the first consistent 'Systematic' (pardon me) of the Scotist view of God, which for the first time radically establishes itself on the knowledge of the Personhood of God."[13] Barth more than any other theologian recognized God as a free, acting Person. He immediately states that this doctrine of God makes it impossible to enter into discussion with a "Thomism" that arose in the later Middle Ages. It is important to note that he wrote "Thomism" (*Thomismus*) and not Thomas, and qualified it by the "latter Middle Ages," for he must have had in mind the rigid manualist distinction between the *de deo uno* and *de deo trino* as a distinction between nature and grace, or philosophy and theology. Light is shed on how Balthasar reads Barth's theology established on God's Personhood when he makes a similar claim some forty-five years later in his *Theologic*.

In *Theologic* 2 (1985), Balthasar discusses the relationship between the "divine attributes" and the "hypostases" of the Trinity, which is another way of discussing the relationship between *de deo uno* and *de deo trino*. This relationship is also the discussion Barth took up in *Church Dogmatics* 2.1, treating God's perfections after the Trinity and thereby reversing the accepted method since Aquinas in both Protestant and Catholic dogmatics. In order to explain the proper relation between God's perfections and Triunity, Balthasar appeals to Barth. Barth, he writes, has "emphasized two insights with the uttermost resoluteness." The first is that the economic Trinity, and it alone, reveals to us the immanent Trinity. He then cites a passage from *Church Dogmatics* 2.1, where Barth writes, "In the inner core of the truth in which he stands

---

12. Lochbrunner, *Hans Urs von Balthasar und seine Theologenkollegen: Sechs Beziehungsgeschichten* (Würzburg: Echter, 2009), 269.

13. Balthasar wrote, "Die Gotteslehre, die Sie hier entwickeln, scheint mir, wie ich Ihnen schon sagte, die erst konsequente 'Systematik' (verzeihen Sie) der skotistischen Gottesanschauung, die zum erstenmal sich radikal auf der Erkenntnis der Personälitat Gottes begründen will." See Ibid.

before us, God stands *before himself*, . . . and, prior to that in the inner core of the truth in which we know God, God knows himself. . . . It is not self-evident that our knowledge of God attains truth as the outside of that interior truth."[14] God knows himself "prior to" standing before us. Barth clearly distinguishes the immanent from the economic Trinity here. Only as we participate in God's self-knowledge, which is prior to us, do we know God. Balthasar affirms this statement and adds, "One can accept this statement, which is correct, without having to accept Barth's refusal to acknowledge any natural knowledge of God."[15] In other words, in accepting Barth's starting point, Balthasar never accepted that it entailed rejecting metaphysics and natural theology. The *analogia entis* will still be necessary.

Balthasar then finds a second and related insight in Barth's theology: "A description of the essential properties of a *nuda essentia* of God that leaves the hypostases out of account is, in the extreme case, 'strict nominalism' and in the case of many Christian thinkers, 'semi-nominalism.'"[16] In other words, what Balthasar sees in Barth both in 1940 and 1985 is a rejection of a *deus absconditus* existing behind God revealed as Triune. Barth explicitly affirmed this in *Church Dogmatics* 2.1 in the section Balthasar cites. Barth wrote, "[God] is known in his entirety or He is not known at all. There is no existence of God behind or beyond this entirety of His being."[17] In revealing who he is, God holds nothing back. There is no "God in reserve" who might be other than the God revealed.

Balthasar draws on Barth's doctrine of God to contest a lingering seminominalism in three theological traditions: the manualist tradition of Thomism where God's oneness appears to be known prior to, and independent of, the Triune persons; in Reformed predestination with its "eternal decree"; and in Luther's Christology. He interprets Luther's Christology as dialectical, opposing the God who is revealed in Christ to the God who is always also hidden.[18] The hidden God is not the revealed God, and so God's absolute power

14. *Church Dogmatics* 2.1, 49. The full quote is, "First of all, and in the heart of the truth in which He stands before us, God stands before Himself: the Father before the Son, the Son before the Father. And first of all and in the heart of the truth in which we know God, God knows Himself; the Father knows the Son and the Son the Father in the unity of the Holy Spirit. This occurrence in God Himself is the essence and strength of our knowledge of God. It is not an occurrence unknown to us; rather it is made known to us through His Word; but it is certainly a hidden occurrence."

15. Balthasar, *Theologic*, vol. 2: *The Truth of God*, trans. Adrian Walker (San Francisco: Ignatius, 2004), 138n15.

16. Balthasar, *Theologic* 2, 138.

17. *Church Dogmatics* 2.1, 51.

18. Balthasar, *Theologic* 2, 41–45. David Luy pointed out to me that this is a caricature of Luther indebted to Balthasar's friend Theobald Beer, who was a less than accurate interpreter of Luther. See Luy,

may differ considerably from God's power ordered in the economy. Balthasar suggests that this "tears open an abyss" in theology whereby "negativity" and thereby the devil play too important a role. Balthasar is correct about some postmetaphysical Lutheranism that retrospectively reads a consistent tradition from Luther through Hegel and/or Harnack to Heidegger, a tradition that eschews metaphysics, denies divine simplicity and impassibility, and requires God to negate being in order "to be" (or "not to be") God. Oftentimes this tradition trumpets Christianity "without religion." At some point, theologians will recognize that such a theology comes closest to atheism, which some philosophers and (a)theologians are beginning to recognize.[/footnote]

THEOLOGY'S RATIO—THE DRAMATIC GLORY OF GOD

If Balthasar worried late in his life that Protestantism could not present the proper form of Christian glory, he never brought this accusation against Barth. Barth retrieved the proper form and made a contribution to Catholic theology. Balthasar never intended his engagement with Barth to be an introduction or exposition of Barth's theology alone. He sought to engage Protestants and Catholics with the *ratio* found in Barth's theology. In *Humani generis* (August 12, 1950) Pius XII instructed Catholic theologians what they were to avoid in ecumenical engagement. First, they were to avoid "false irenicism," and second "contempt for the rational and philosophical moment in theology," its "*ratio.*"[19] These two injunctions frame Balthasar's introduction in the 1951 book. They were added after the encyclical's publication, but Balthasar thought he obeyed both of them. Barth is an ideal ecumenical conversation partner because he clearly cannot be guilty of the first (irenicism), and poses, perhaps, the crucial challenge to the second. Does Barth hold the *ratio* necessary for theology in contempt? If Balthasar demonstrates that Barth has done so, then he also demonstrates that he and de Lubac maintained the proper Catholic philosophical *ratio* in their christological *ressourcement*. In other words, a christological rendering of the *analogia entis* allows for the proper role of nature within grace, without on the one hand evacuating theology of its necessary philosophical and metaphysical content, or on the other hand making metaphysics condition the christological center, diminishing theology's dramatic import. Barth's *ratio* does not reject the Catholic tradition, but resources it from Scripture and the Fathers with the proper christological

Dominus Mortis: Martin Luther on the Incorruptibility of God in Christ (Minneapolis: Fortress Press, forthcoming).

19. *The Theology of Karl Barth*, trans. Edward T. Oakes, SJ (San Francisco: Ignatius, 1992), xix.

ordering it always already assumed in practice. Balthasar wrote, "Of course we must test and probe how well Barth has made room for such an appreciation of the *ratio* in theology, but it is found at the very basis of his thought."[20] Balthasar finds Barth appreciating this *ratio*, noting the irony that while Catholics are turning away from the Scholastics, Barth turned toward them.

What is this *ratio*? Barth returns "glory" to theology after its exile from late medieval Catholic and early modern Protestant theology. Late medieval theology exiled it through its metaphysics; Reformed theology did so through its doctrine of predestination.[21] Balthasar gave three reasons why he engages Barth. First, Barth offers "the most thorough and penetrating display of the Protestant view and the closest rapprochement with the Catholic."[22] The more Barth attends to the Protestant emphasis on the Word spoken by the Father in the Spirit as the foundation for theology, the closer he comes to Catholicism. Second, "his theology is beautiful." It is this for a similar reason that it comes close to Catholicism— "*because* he strictly adheres to theological objectivism ('Faith lives from its object.')."[23] Third, "Barth focuses on the Word, fully and exclusively, [so] that its full splendor might radiate out to the reader."[24] He sees in Barth the glory and splendor of God that illumines all things, which then requires a properly Catholic philosophical *ratio* that has a place for beauty, goodness, and truth. This *ratio* is necessary to understand what Barth is doing and why it is so compelling. Clearly Balthasar sees in Barth the presence of a properly Catholic philosophical *ratio*, whether Barth affirms it or not.

Balthasar continues this line of argument in his 1965 work, *Glory of the Lord*, vol. 5: *The Realm of Metaphysics in the Modern Age*. He claims, "At the very same moment that the distinctively *Christian* glory of God would have been ready to emerge (freed from the religious aesthetics of antiquity), it is deprived of the medium by means of which it could have been manifested."[25] He then traces that deprivation. He begins with Scotus's formal conception of being. It

---

20. Ibid.

21. I am interpreting Balthasar's reading of Barth and the Reformed, which, as I noted earlier, seems consistent with Heppe's *Reformed Dogmatics*. For a fuller understanding of Reformed orthodoxy that persuasively shows it was not a system of predestination, but maintained much of the Christian Aristotelianism of scholasticism, see Richard A. Muller, *Post-Reformation Reformed Dogmatics*, vol. 1, 2nd ed. (Grand Rapids, MI: Baker Academic, 2003).

22. *The Theology of Karl Barth*, 23.

23. Ibid., 25. Emphasis original.

24. Ibid., 26.

25. *The Glory of the Lord*, vol. 5: *The Realm of Metaphysics in the Modern Age*, trans. Oliver Davies et al. (San Francisco: Ignatius, 1991), 18. Emphasis original.

makes being pure ideality and accomplishes too much and too little. The "too much" is found in the fact that "in its concept of Being it raises itself above God and the world, dominating the Absolute from the standpoint of a greater absolute." It does "too little" in that "reality . . . is silently eliminated in this realm of graded formalities and essences."[26] If being is mere concept, then it cannot adequately account for the reality of God's Triune hypostases radiating the "splendor" of God's own being into creation. Interestingly, Balthasar sees in Barth the alternative to these deprivations: "It is precisely in Barth's dogmatics that (despite all the protestations to the contrary) a feeling for 'glory' emerges in a new and elemental way."[27] This "feeling for glory" is what allows for a proper metaphysics, and thus the proper *ratio*.

Balthasar saw Barth's doctrine of God recovering an ancient theme in Christianity lost in the Middle Ages and Reformation: the radiance of God in Christ illumines all things so that no possibility exists for a "hidden God," behind the *deus revelatus* that we can somehow know outside of Christ. The proper philosophical *ratio* (metaphysics) for theology must be attentive to this illuminating glory or, it cannot truly be the proper *ratio*. Much of modern theology and philosophy lost this *ratio*. To understand the significance of Balthasar's argument, it is important to see how Barth reordered Catholic and Protestant dogmatics.

DE DEO UNO AS DE DEO TRINO

Reformed Dogmatics followed a traditional order, in which "The Existence and Notion of God" is first discussed, followed by God's attributes, and then the Holy Trinity.[28] This ordering followed Roman Catholic Scholastic thought. Aquinas moved from question 2 in the Prima Pars on the existence of God, to the attributes or perfections of God in questions 3 through 11, followed by the discussion of the Trinity in questions 27 to 43. Aquinas then went immediately into a discussion of creation. Heppe, however, did not. He separated the doctrine of the Trinity and the Triune work in creation by two intervening sections: "The Decrees of God" and "Predestination." Prior to the Triune God's work in creation and redemption, God established a hidden, inscrutable eternal decree. The doctrine of election came prior to the divine economy in

---

26. Ibid., 17.

27. Ibid., 15.

28. This is the order Heppe adopts in his *Reformed Dogmatics*, which Barth used when he had to teach dogmatics at Göttingen.

Christ. Barth did not follow Heppe because he saw in this ordering a residual nominalism Calvin's theology otherwise rejected.

In his section on God's attributes, Heppe acknowledged that Calvin rejected the nominalist distinction between God's absolute and ordered power. "This absolute power Calvin has rejected, not absolutely but relatively, abusing the method of the *Scholastics*, who constructed from it many portentous dogmas: as that God can lie, sin, etc."[29] Nonetheless Heppe still adopted an order to his dogmatics that made a distinction similar to the nominalists because of his defense of the eternal decree. It is not enough, Heppe noted, for God simply to have a "permissive will" that allowed for sin as the "Scholastics assert." God directly willed all things. Therefore, "Otiose permission of sin separated from God's will is repugnant both to the nature of the First Cause and to the divine and almighty foresight, to His nature and to Scripture."[30] Heppe's rejection that God permits sin causes some difficulty for him, in that he cannot argue God directly wills sin. He resolved the difficulty by distinguishing between "God's revealed" and "God's secret will." He wrote, "The former is that which God reveals as His will partly by the word of Law and Gospel, partly by experiences which He sends to man. The latter is God's decree, in so far as it is still hidden and is only to be revealed in the future at a definite date."[31] Heppe may have critiqued Scholastic nominalism, but he now brings it back in with his distinction between a revealed and a hidden will. By setting the doctrine of decrees and predestination between the doctrines of Trinity and creation, Heppe reveals how Reformed dogmatics subordinated Christ's mission to the eternal decree. The eternal decree rendered Christ's mission intelligible rather than vice versa. Citing the Reformed dogmatician Riissen, he stated, "We admit that Christ is the meritorious cause and foundation of the salvation decreed, from the standpoint of guilty man, but not of the decree of salvation from the standpoint of God."[32] Because the eternal decree is solely accomplished by the will of God from all eternity, it comes prior to God's economic act in Christ. God elects the elect and damns the damned independent of their response or relation to Christ. Before God is gracious to us in Jesus Christ, God makes an eternal decision. Barth explicitly rejected this teaching on election when he placed the doctrine of election within the doctrine of God.

29. Heinrich Heppe, *Reformed Dogmatics*, trans. G. T. Thomson (London: Wakeman Great Reprints, 1950), 103. Emphasis original.

30. Ibid., 90.

31. Ibid.

32. Ibid., 168.

In the *Göttingen Dogmatics* Barth already reversed Heppe's (and Aquinas's) ordering in part. The doctrine of the Trinity preceded the discussion of God's attributes, but election and predestination still come after the doctrine of God and before that of creation. Even here, however, Barth disagreed with the Reformed doctrine. He cites the Protestant Scholastic Heidegger's "definition of reprobation" in Heppe, and states that its emphasis on elect and reprobate "individuals" is the "worm in the timbers of Reformed orthodoxy" as well as a "secular error."[33] Why is it a "secular error?" The doctrine of predestination allows for a realm of human activity not defined by God's gracious act in Jesus Christ. Barth attributes a similar "secular misery" to the Catholic *analogia entis* in his infamous introduction to *Church Dogmatics* 1.1. Similar to the move Barth will execute in *Church Dogmatics* 2.2, he rejects this doctrine of election in the *Göttingen Dogmatics*, insofar as it identifies "certain people" for either election or reprobation. He insists we must "press back behind it to a better version which corresponds to the true intentions of these classical proponents [Augustine and Calvin], to objective exegesis of Rom. 9–11, and to the context of a Christian doctrine of God, and from which that 'certain people' has been expunged."[34] Barth has already begun to locate the doctrine of election in the doctrine of God in the 1920s, and Barth acknowledges that this represents a "serious departure" from the Reformed "tradition and its implications."[35] The question is, what kind of departure is it?

Barth's doctrine of election refused to divide God's act toward creatures from God's nature. Barth affirms that God's freedom is the "freedom to love." This freedom is an obviously antinominalist claim, which Barth explicitly established in *Church Dogmatics* 2.1, where he offers two important critiques of nominalism. He first critiques Ockham's "concept of being" for failing to make sense of God's perfections. Barth expresses concern that Aquinas might point in the direction of a similar metaphysics. He then critiques the relation between God's *potentia absoluta* and God's *potentia ordinata* that Ockham, and perhaps Aquinas, set forth. In his first critique of nominalism, Barth takes up God's perfections and asks how they can be consistent with God's simplicity. Since the *Göttingen Dogmatics*, Barth consistently affirmed God's simplicity and he does so here as well.[36] What concerns him about Ockham's concept of being is that it assumes the diverse perfections of God are primarily logical

---

33. Barth, *Göttingen Dogmatics*, 455.

34. Ibid.

35. Ibid., 456.

36. Ibid., 429. This also prompts him to reject the language of "divine interventionism" in *Romans* 2 in that same discussion.

concepts we attribute to God and not the essence of who God is. They are mere "names" we give our relation to God (much as they are in Schleiermacher). In contrast, Barth intends to "develop the truth of the multiplicity, individuality and diversity of God's perfections—in view of the nominalistic contesting and the semi-nominalist weakening of them."[37] In other words, he intends to strengthen rather than diminish the traditional divine perfections. He does so via "three explanatory propositions:" First, "The multiplicity, individuality and diversity of the divine perfections are those of the one divine being and therefore not those of another divine nature allied to it."[38] Here is where Balthasar read Barth well. The perfections set forth in the *de deo uno* do not describe a God other than the Triune God. They are not prolegomena known by reason alone; they are intrinsic to the Triune God. If we posit them as something known by reason that condition God's triune revelation, then we describe a God behind the God revealed in Christ, a God who gives himself only in part. Barth does not deny the perfections, or that they can be known. Instead, their importance is accentuated. They are intrinsic to God's "simple being." Second, "The multiplicity, individuality and diversity of the perfections of God are those of His simple being, which is not therefore divided and then put together again."[39] Although Barth speaks of the real, and not nominal, multiplicity of these perfections, he does not discard simplicity; he explicitly affirms "God's simple being."[40] This affirmation makes little sense without remembering he refuses to set forth the perfections outside the Triune hypostases. What the perfections describe is not God's unity prior to Trinity, because there is no such God. Any suggestions of such a God would miss the form and tone of Christian theology. If we understand that the Father is the essence of God, as is the Son and the Spirit, and the Father, Son, and Spirit are the essence of God, and yet there is only one essence, then we can understand Barth's point. These relations, like the perfections, cannot be merely "nominal" or we will fail to see who God is. The real "multiplicity" in God does not oppose God's simple essence. Third, "the multiplicity, individuality and diversity of God's perfections are rooted in His own being and not in His participation in the character of other beings."[41] God *is* these perfections even if creation did

---

37. *Church Dogmatics* 2.1, 330.

38. Ibid., 331.

39. Ibid., 332.

40. Barth is not innovative here. In the Christian tradition divine simplicity never meant God did not have "real distinctions." In fact, for Aquinas, simplicity was necessary to understand how God could have real distinctions and yet be one. See STI.28.1-3.

41. *Church Dogmatics* 2.1,,333.

not exist. They are not modes of our knowledge of God, which would not be if we were not. They do not describe God's relation to us. Here Barth has a version of the important doctrine that there is no real relation between God and creation; otherwise this third explanatory proposition makes no sense. In these three propositions Barth is not allowing his theology to be policed by modern epistemology; he is making substantive metaphysical claims. For Barth, not even Aquinas has recognized the full reality of these perfections as fitting to God's essence. Barth accused him of being a seminominalist, as the second nominalist distinction he made demonstrates.

The second nominalist distinction Barth explicitly rejected in *Church Dogmatics* 2.1 is between God's *potentia absoluta* and God's *potentia ordinata*. Barth does not reject this distinction altogether. He agrees with Aquinas that we cannot completely reject it; that would be disastrous for theology. If we collapse the *absoluta* into the *ordinata* we would tie God necessarily to creation. (The same would happen if we collapse the immanent Trinity into the economic Trinity in our speaking of God; it would amount to the same move.) Barth wrote,

> He would not be their real Lord if as their Lord He has lost or never had the power to be Lord without them, apart from the lordship exercised over them in Himself, in an infinity of very different inward or even outward possibilities. We therefore endorse the distinction between *potentia absoluta* and *potentia ordinata* in so far as it reminds us that God's omnipotence is His own power and therefore free power.[42]

Barth never revised this important passage distinguishing the *potentia absoluta* and *ordinata*. Barth then states that the distinction became problematic in the tradition when it posited the *potentia absoluta* as a *potentia extraordinaria* and assumed some "arbitrary power beside or behind a power of order which corresponds only accidentally to God's real work."[43] Barth explicitly critiques both nominalism and Luther for exploiting his distinction. He finds the nominalists transferring Thomas's hypothetical distinction to the "essence" of

42. Ibid., 539. When we see how committed Barth was prior to *Romans* 1 to a "Melancthonian epistemology," where we only know God because of God's benefits for us, that he now affirms this traditional Thomistic distinction is a key shift away from that epistemology. See Simon Fisher, *Revelatory Positivism?*.

43. *Church Dogmatics* 2.1, 41. I think this helps us make sense of Barth's critique of his earlier "divine interventionism" in *Romans* 2. See *Göttingen Dogmatics*, 429.

God. God could then "create and maintain a world ruled either by His wisdom and righteousness or equally by their opposites." You would have a multiplicity not contained within simplicity. Barth says this makes God "'wholly Other,'" and he finds it "intolerable." Likewise, with Balthasar, he thinks Luther's hidden God borders on this nominalist distinction.[44] Barth writes,

> It cannot be denied that Luther sometimes spoke of his *Deus absconditus* as if he understood by this concept a *potentia absoluta* or even more a *potentia inordinata*. The power to work miracles

44. Barth's interpretation of Luther shifted considerably from the 1927 *Die christliche Dogmatik* to the claim made here in *Church Dogmatics* 2.1. In 1927, he gave a more positive interpretation of Luther's veiling and unveiling. In that work, Barth offered an early critique of natural theology that nonetheless began by affirming Thomas Aquinas: "Nothing hinders us from saying with Thomas Aquinas, 'Every truth, which is spoken by anyone, is from the Holy Spirit.'" That would be a kind of natural theology, and Barth affirms it as such. Every truth is to be affirmed even if it does not explicitly express its connection to Christian revelation. But Barth then interprets this theologically and says that "every truth" must be precisely understood. Because truth is from the Holy Spirit, it cannot be partial. It is this claim that requires Barth to critique both natural theology and nominalism. Barth thinks natural theology too often assumes access to some God standing behind the God who is disclosed in Christ. In contrast, he does not begin theology with "God is," but with "God spoke." In so doing, he claims to be following Aquinas. He made the same move earlier in *Göttingen Dogmatics* when he wrote that the presupposition of the Bible is not that God is but that God spoke (*Göttingen Dogmatics*, 58), and relates it to Exod. 3:14, and then stated "all attributes or predicates" can "be only references back, not to the statement 'God is' but to the statement 'God spoke' (Ibid., 88). Even then he recognized that Aquinas taught something similar: "And even in Thomas Aquinas the insights one can gain into God's nature apart from revelation have the significance only of a possible and necessarily ancillary construction that pays secondary honor to the truth of revelation" (Ibid., 92). He uses this affirmation of Aquinas to reject any firm distinction between natural and supernatural theology: "We do well at this point to express the free and broad outlook of Aquinas when he said that all truth no matter who speaks it, is of the Holy Spirit," but because it will then be the "whole truth," it cannot be divided between a natural or supernatural theology. He then goes on to deny with Luther any *deus absconditus* (Ibid., 93). What is interesting in these early works is that Barth appeals to Luther as overcoming the *deus absconditus*, and this forms the basis for his critique of natural theology. When we think we have some partial knowledge of God, then we have a God in reserve, a God who does not give himself to us completely, as if each of the Triune Persons were not the fullness of God. Barth sides with Luther against "the view of a God, in that sense of standing behind his revelation, and withholding a portion." Barth cites Luther's hymn, "A Mighty Fortress is our God," quoting the line: "Fragst du, wer der ist, der Herr Jesus Christ, der Herr Zebaoth, *und is kein andrer Gott.*" Far from seeing Luther as a nominalist here, Barth interprets him as overcoming nominalism. He writes, "The hidden God (*deus absconditus*) is also the revealed God (*deus revelatus*)." (See *Die christliche Dogmatik*, 177–80.) Barth shifts from these earlier works to become more suspicious of the language of veiling and unveiling in *Church Dogmatics* 2.1 and 2, suggesting it could lead to nominalism. In *Göttingen Dogmatics*, Barth critiques his early *Romans* for its occasionalism and interventionism, which would also relate to this faulty doctrine of God. See *Göttingen Dogmatics*, 429.

alongside and behind the power active in the sphere of order and regularity has now become an arbitrary power beside or behind a power of order which corresponds only accidentally to God's real work. Understood in his sense, the whole distinction has become completely intolerable. Now that God has in fact chosen and acted as He has, now that He has revealed His capacity, it is both true and important to maintain with Thomas that this capacity is most certainly to be understood as free, but it is completely invalid to ascribe to Him a capacity different from that which He has in fact revealed in His work, and one which contradicts it.[45]

Barth goes on to argue that if this were the case we could not trust God's Word, which is of course the "presupposition" that began *Church Dogmatics* 2.1, and which he explicitly stated derives from Anselm.

If we divide *Church Dogmatics* 2.2, where Barth places the doctrine of election within the doctrine of God, from these explicit antinominalist claims in *Church Dogmatics* 2.1, we will miss seeing well what Barth is doing. When he makes the odd claim that God determines himself in the beginning of 2.2, he is not tying God to creation by making the incarnate Son the one who elects God. Such a claim would reject the distinction he affirmed between *potentia absoluta* and *potentia ordinata*. Nor is he denying a proper distinction between the immanent and economic Trinity. A better way to understand this statement is to see in it the affirmation that what God speaks in the Son reveals what God's *potentia absoluta* is, so that we can trust God. As Barth had already argued at length, God's freedom is the freedom to love. It is not an arbitrary freedom by some "wholly other," about whom we have little to no knowledge. God has no will behind his will to redeem us in the Son by which he eternally decrees that these people will be reprobate and these people will be saved. He wills all to be saved in the Son because this alone shows us who God is. In fact, early on in *Church Dogmatics* 2.2, in his explanation of what it means to say God determines himself, Barth once again rejects the distinction he found in Heppe between a revealed and a secret will of God. Since the Gottschalk controversy of the ninth century, undue speculation about the doctrine of election had unfortunately arisen.[46] Calvin, Barth argued, was no Gottschalk. He did not divide God's will from God's wisdom and righteousness. Instead, for Calvin, "we must say too, and just as definitely, that in God we are not dealing with a tyrant or a God

45. *Church Dogmatics* 2.1, 541.

46. Gottschalk was a monk who first radicalized Augustine's thought into a doctrine of double predestination, which was condemned.

of caprice." In fact, he states, "to distinguish between a *voluntas Dei ordinata* and *absoluta* is a blasphemy for which we can only recoil in horror."[47] He rejects this dogmatic decree in Heppe's Reformed Dogmatics. He reforms the Reformed, through Calvin, bringing them back into the Catholic fold, and at the same time challenges a sharp division between the *de deo uno* and *de deo trino* taught not by Thomas, but by his epigones. As Balthasar taught, the more he is Reformed, the more he is Catholic.

POSTMETAPHYSICAL BARTHIANISM: ELECTING TRINITY

Overcoming nominalism provides a better context for understanding Barth's, and liberal Protestantism's, rejection of metaphysics. If this statement is true, it has important theological, ethical, and political implications. Rather than Barth addressing questions of Kantian epistemology, making his theology essentially modern, Barth points beyond modernity for which the nominalist God was, and is, in many ways central. In order to see the significance of this point, it is important to contrast Balthasar's interpretation with a very similar postmetaphysical interpretation. It finds metaphysics putting God in a straightjacket, especially through the *analogia entis*. Rather than metaphysics conditioning the incarnation, the doctrine of election conditions it. This interpretation contains all the elements Balthasar's interpretation does, but it orders them differently, and that makes all the difference. Form matters.

THEOLOGICAL ONTOLOGY OF ELECTION

Bruce McCormack offers the most thorough postmetaphysical reading of Barth's theology. Interpreting Bruce McCormack's Barth interpretation is no easy matter. He is a subtle author who blends his own constructive theological position with his historical interpretation. The doctrine of election in *Church Dogmatics* 2.2 becomes the key for interpreting Barth, and the result is an innovative doctrine of God much less Catholic than Balthasar saw in Barth.

McCormack suggests Barth is a modern theologian who adopts its postmetaphysical philosophical perspective and then draws on the doctrine of election to explain God's own being. Like Balthasar, McCormack finds Barth reordering doctrine, but he evaluates Barth's placement of election within the doctrine of God in a markedly different way than Balthasar's interpretation. Election has taken the place of God's "existence" in Aquinas's *de do uno*. The result is a very different ontology. For McCormack, history constitutes being.

47. *Church Dogmatics* 2.2, trans. J. C. Campbell, et al., ed. G. W. Bromiley and T. F. Torrance (Edinburgh: T & T Clark, 1958), 23

He states, "What is distinctive about Barth's Christology lies in the sustained effort to think through what it means to be orthodox *under the conditions of modernity.* . . . What Barth does is to historicize and actualize the 'natures' of Christ."[48] The "conditions of modernity" include acknowledging Kant's critiques that putatively put an end to any premodern metaphysics. Far from needing any metaphysics as the condition for revelation, election alone conditions it. For McCormack, Barth's crucial turn begins where Barth states, "[Election] is part of the doctrine of God because originally God's election of man is a predestination not merely of man but of Himself."[49] What does it mean to say God "predestines" himself?[50] McCormack explains it in an important essay, "Election and the Trinity."

> Read in the light of the doctrine of the Trinity which is implied by Barth's treatment of the incarnation, the statement "Jesus Christ is the subject of election" means that Jesus Christ, the eternal Son, elects his own election *by means of the same will by which the Father elects him* and that this takes place *in one and the same eternal event.* By the same will: that means that the unity of the divine subject is not set aside by the "command" and "obedience" structure proper to the covenant of grace. What we have before us here is an eternal

48. "'With Loud Cries and Tears': The Humanity of the Son in the Epistle to the Hebrews," in *The Epistle to the Hebrews and Christian Theology*, ed. Richard Bauckham, Daniel R. Driver, Trevor A. Hart, and Nathan MacDonald (Grand Rapids: Eerdmans, 2009), 48. Emphasis original. Could Barth have ever claimed Christology is to be conditioned by modern knowledge? If I read McCormack correctly here, he would seem to neglect an important claim Barth made in *Church Dogmatics* 4.2, where Barth states, "In the inner life of God, as the eternal essence of the Father, Son and Holy Ghost, the divine essence does not, of course, need any actualization" (*Church Dogmatics* 4.2, trans. Geoffrey W. Bromiley, ed. G. W. Bromiley and T. F. Torrance [Edinburgh: T & T Clark, 1958], 113). If Barth can distinguish the "divine essence" from "actualization," McCormack's ontology does not seem accurately to describe Barth's position.

49. *Church Dogmatics* 2.2, 3

50. To say God "predestines" himself is an odd expression, and the English translation that puts it this way is not the best. Barth wrote, "Sie [Die Erwählungslehre] gehört darum zur Lehre Gott, weil Gott, indem er den Menschen wählt, nicht nur über diesen, sondern in ursprünglicher Weise über sich selbst bestimmt." Notice that two different German words, *wählt* and *bestimmt*, are used here. After stating, "the doctrine of election belongs therefore to the doctrine of God," Barth gives the reason, beginning with "because" (*weil*): "Because God by electing [*wählt*] man, not only elects them, but also in a primordial way [*in ursprünglicher Weise*], determines [*bestimmt*] himself." Barth does not use the same verbs to speak of the "election" of creatures and God's self-determination. To put them together under the common verb "predestines," as the English translation does, and suggest that they identify the same event, loses this important distinction.

act of *self*-differentiation on the part of a single, unified subject. In one and the same event: that means that there is no temporal gap between "command" and "obedience." As the act of the one divine subject in differentiating himself into modes of being, "command" and "obedience" take place simultaneously. But then, that also means that the one generated by the Father is already "joined" (on the level of his identity) to the human nature he would assume even *as* he responds in obedience. It is as joined to the human nature that he is the subject who obeys the command of the Father, i.e. as Jesus Christ.[51]

This passage is difficult to interpret, for it makes unusual claims. The first few claims are unusual in their language, but quite traditional in content. Christian theology does not customarily use the verb "elects" to speak of God's activity toward God, but McCormack is a good guide to Barth here. For Barth, election now falls under the doctrine of God and not God's relationship to creation. The Son elects his own election identical with the Father's election of the Son. This expression is also odd, but traditional in content. If I understand his claim, it is that no "temporal gap" exists between the eternal generation of the Son and the Father as the unoriginate source of that generation. The command of the Father and the obedience of the Son are the same act, or procession. That claim could be uncontroversial, depending on how we interpret the Son's "obedience." It is the next claim that is odd in expression and content and raises questions as to which "temporal gap" McCormack refers. The claim is this: the eternal generation of the Son "is already 'joined' to the human nature he would assume even *as* he responds in obedience. It is as joined to the human nature that he is the subject who obeys the command of the Father, i.e. as Jesus Christ." What could it mean to say that in the eternal generation of the Son from the Father he is already joined to his human nature? This seems to be saying the following. First, at the same eternal instance of God's self-differentiation as Trinity, he elects the Son as incarnate ("already 'joined' to the human nature he would assume") so that no temporal gap exists between the eternal processions in God's immanent Triune life and temporal missions in the economic. The Son's obedience is not only the obedience of the Son to the Father in the Triune procession; it is also *at the same time* the obedience of Jesus Christ joined to his creatureliness.

51. McCormack, "Election and the Trinity," 216. Emphasis original.

QUESTIONABLE ENTAILMENTS TO MCCORMACK'S THEOLOGICAL ONTOLOGY

If McCormack's interpretation identifies the Son's obedience in his mission with his generation in his procession, then it raises some significant theological objections; entailments would follow, whether McCormack explicitly affirms them or not, that radically revise the Christian doctrine of God. Because I don't think McCormack would affirm many of these entailments, let me put them forward in terms of questions. First, how is creation not eternal, making it a fourth hypostasis? Second, how could the *logos asarkos* (unfleshed logos) of John 1 be affirmed? Must the Son always be enfleshed, or at least on the way to enfleshment for the Son to be Son, and what is the difference between a *logos ensarkos* and a *logos sarkos* if the *logos asarkos* is denied? If the Son must be enfleshed to be the Son, how is the Son free as the Son? Has not flesh conditioned God's triunity? Third, how are the divine missions and processions not collapsed into the same temporal moment such that God cannot be God without creation? Fourth, how is creation not necessary for God's own election as Trinity? If that is the case, then fifth, how will God not be affected by creation? In other words, unlike Aquinas, where there is no "real relationship" between creatures and God, but only a logical relationship between God and creatures (which is why there is no reciprocal *analogia entis* between God and creatures, but only from creatures to God), in McCormack's Barthian interpretation, a real relationship exists from creatures to God and God to creatures. Sixth, how then will central perfections such as simplicity and impassibility not be jettisoned? If these perfections are jettisoned, God could no longer be *actus purus*.

McCormack may not affirm all the above entailments. His controversial theses were put in public for the sake of "discussion." A careful review of these theses, however, confirms the entailments, intended or not. He explicitly acknowledges his Barth interpretation would require "modifications . . . of the being and perfections of God (in CD II/1)" (sixth entailment).[52] He distances his Barth interpretation from George Hunsinger's, acknowledging Hunsinger finds more commonalty between Barth and Aquinas. Hunsinger and Aquinas distinguish God's "eternal processions" (the Triune Persons) from the "eternal missions" and affirm simplicity—God has no unrealized potentialities.[53] The question McCormack asks is how this can be if the processions and missions are distinguished? In other words, if we distinguish God's processions from the missions, then we would have to assume a potentiality in God that was

52. Ibid., 203.
53. Ibid., 205.

actualized in the missions. This interpretation misunderstands Aquinas. For Aquinas the missions are not "eternal," so that would entail no logical contradiction or ascription of potentiality to God. He thought it was possible for God to do something temporally without God actualizing a potential. Creation does not add something to, or take away from, God. McCormack does not find this logical. If God has a mission separate from the procession, then it must be the actualization of a potential, which McCormack denies. But wouldn't this raise a question about every divine temporal act? How could God create anything other than God, which is what creation itself is, on this logic (first entailment)? In other words, if the processions and missions must be held together as an eternal act, then not only the Son's humanity but all of creation would need to be eternal. Otherwise on McCormack's terms God could not act in any way, creating, redeeming, sustaining, without actualizing a potential.

McCormack has an answer. It is to abandon all "talk of ontological priority" of God. God's being is in act such that who God is is what God does. This is why his position eschews metaphysics. Citing Jüngel, McCormack affirms, "God's being is constituted through historicality." There is no ontological priority to God's "historicality" in the immanent Trinity, only a logical one. Otherwise a "metaphysical gap" opens "between God's essence and will."[54] To do that is to return to a "classical concept of substance." In order to make this argument, McCormack acknowledges he must reject a distinction between the *logos asarkos* and *ensarkos* (second entailment). Does it not also reject any distinction between the immanent and economic Trinity (third entailment)? McCormack finds the traditional distinction between the immanent and economic Trinity deeply problematic, but it does not mean he would find any such distinction problematic. Nonetheless, he interprets Barth's antimetaphysical posture as denying any distinction between God's essence and "God's decision to be God in a redemptive relationship with sinful humanity."[55] He cites as evidence Barth's statement,

> Everything *that* God is, He is insofar as He is. He essences (*west*) as Person. He is Father, Son, Spirit from eternity to eternity. As soon as we abstract from the speaking Person who *addresses* us, who addresses *us*—even if only for a moment—transposing God into a general truth or idea which is *not* a Person, we could no longer be thinking *God*.[56]

54. Ibid., 207.
55. Ibid., 210.
56. Ibid. Emphasis original.

Nothing in his quote suggests the Person God "essences" must be the incarnate Son. In fact, everything said here is quite conventional. Which Christian theologian ever said we should transpose God "into a general truth or idea"? Yet McCormack moves from this quote to the very unconventional statement, "[Barth] wants to understand the divine 'essence' in terms of willed activity directed towards the human creature." [57] The statement does not follow from the quote. Barth's quote only makes the theological judgment that God's essence cannot be thought in distinction from the Person. That restates the doctrine of the Trinity.

McCormack's commentary adds something to Barth's quote that Barth did not mention. McCormack defines God's essence as "willed activity." This willed activity is directed to human creatures such that God's relationship to them now seems necessary for God's essence. This goes further than denying a distinction between the economic and immanent Trinity; it affirms a real relationship between God and creation (fifth entailment). McCormack has evidence from Barth that says precisely this. Barth once stated, "The relation of God to the human is not accidental; it is necessarily contained in and grounded in God's *essence*. . . . God would not be God if the relation to the human were not intrinsic to Him from the start." This statement is truly astonishing, and fits well the worst characterization of Hegelianism in Barth. Fortunately, it is not found in the *Church Dogmatics*, but in the 1924 lectures at Göttingen.[58] McCormack only challenges it in that it is not yet situated within the "doctrine of election" from *Romans*. He admits Barth never uses the verb form of "essence" (*west*) after this time, and replaces it with "self-determination."[59] It is with Jesus Christ as the object and subject of election that Barth finally hits the right note. As subject of election, McCormack thinks Barth "says more" than the traditional claim that the Son wills the Father's will. Instead, McCormack surmises,

> I think he wanted to overcome the metaphysical gap introduced into theology in the West by the Thomistic distinction between the eternal processions (by which the being of God is constituted) and the eternal missions (by which God sets himself in relation to human

57. Ibid.

58. Karl Barth, *Unterricht in der christlichen Religion*, vol. 2, *Die Lehre Gott/Die Lehre vom Menschen,1924/1925*, ed. Hinrich Stoevesandt (Zurich: Theologischer Zurich, 1990), 70. Barth's more mature position in volume 4 of the *Church Dogmatics* states, "In the inner life of God, as the eternal essence of the Father, Son and Holy Ghost, the divine essence does not, of course, need any actualization" (*Church Dogmatics* 4.2, 113). Emphasis original.

59. McCormack, "Election and the Trinity," 211.

beings) by collapsing the processions and the missions into a single eternal event.[60]

To his credit, McCormack acknowledges this is his own constructive position. It is not explicit in Barth. In fact, the argument above showed that Barth explicitly stated the opposite in *Church Dogmatics* 2.1.

Much of McCormack's interpretation arises from Barth's claim that the Son is obedient to the Father, which makes obedience essential to deity. From it McCormack makes an odd statement that bears a strong affinity with that of the Ressourcement Thomists, who will be examined below. McCormack also speaks of the "conditions" that render possible God's revelation, but in a very different direction. McCormack's conditions would seem to make creation necessary for God (fourth entailment). He states,

> Barth is seeking, with his doctrine of the Trinity, to describe the ontological conditions in God for his self-revelation in time. That his self-revelation in time takes place in obedience must mean that obedience is not alien to the innermost being of God. But now notice: Barth has identified the differentiation of Father and Son with the "commanding" and "obeying" which takes place in election. In so doing, he has described the ontological conditions for the possibility of a correspondence of the history of the incarnate God to that which God is in eternity. . . . There is no longer any room left here for an abstract doctrine of the Trinity. There is a triune being of God—only in the covenant of grace.[61]

Barth offers us the "ontological conditions" for God's triunity and incarnation. Those conditions are not to be found in an *analogia entis*, but in the doctrine of election, which requires a real relationship between God's essence and creatureliness. Of course, all this discussion of God's "essence," of what God "is," of "ontological conditions," is the traditional subject matter of metaphysics. How can we speak of "ontological conditions" in God and claim not to be doing metaphysics? It may be an odd metaphysics, but it would seem to be metaphysics nonetheless.

---

60. Ibid., 214. As previously mentioned, in the *Göttingen Dogmatics* Barth affirmed how Thomas laid things out in the *Summa*, so to now read him as pointing in the direction of something this radical at that time seems unwarranted.

61. McCormack, "Election and the Trinity," 215.

This analysis of McCormack's theses for discussion certainly lends support to the entailments noted above. If they are not intended, the theses presented for discussion at least point strongly in their direction. What is striking is how thoroughly God's essence is understood as "willed activity" toward creatures. If McCormack is right, it would have required Barth to make major revisions of the earlier volumes of the *Church Dogmatics*, especially the antinominalist interpretation of God in *Church Dogmatics* 2.1. McCormack acknowledges that Barth's work was on a trajectory and he did not always go back and revise earlier portions in light of later commitments. He should have revised that earlier material, but he did not. However, we have no evidence Barth ever thought he needed to do so. Why did Barth not recognize that he should have made more radical revisions than he did? This remains inexplicable.

By correlating the doctrines of election, Christology, and the Trinity, McCormack presents a much less traditional, Catholic, and much more modern, revisionist doctrine of God than did Balthasar.[62] God's being is constituted by a primordial decision to incarnate the Son. God predestines God's own being. Election constitutes God's Triune hypostases, and Jesus Christ, the incarnate, is subject of that election. This revisionist doctrine of God is also found in Paul Jones, who, like McCormack, finds Barth radically reconstructing theology by the way he brings together "election, Christology and the doctrine of God."[63] Jones develops the trajectory McCormack saw in Barth to its logical conclusion. The divine obedience of the Son is not simply the functional obedience the Second Person of the Trinity gives to the First. It is more. Jesus' obedience in the incarnation constitutes and even changes who God is. Not only are the perfections of impassibility and simplicity rejected, but also immutability.[64] Jones writes, "It could even be said that the transformation of God's being coincides with the revelation of God's being *in* transformation."

62. George Hunsinger refers to McCormack's Barthian theology as "revisionist" and his own as "traditional." McCormack rejects this, but what he rejects seems to miss the point of Hunsinger's claim. Hunsinger is speaking about *theological* revisionism. McCormack interprets this as *Barthian* revisionism and argues his interpretation is the more "traditional" Barthian one since the "new paradigm" in contemporary German theology. That may be, but no one can deny McCormack's reading of Barth's doctrine of God demands major revisions in the Christian tradition's doctrine of God. When I use the term "revisionist," I mean it in that sense. See Bruce McCormack, "Election and the Trinity," 2, and George Hunsinger, "Election and Trinity: Twenty-Five Theses on the Theology of Karl Barth," *Modern Theology* 24, no. 2, (April 2008): 179–98.

63. Paul Dafydd Jones, *The Humanity of Christ: Christology in Karl Barth's Church Dogmatics* (New York: T & T Clark, 2008), 206.

64. McCormack does not go this far. He states that after Barth's revolution we must "ground immutability in an eternal decision" God makes ("'With Loud Cries and Tears,'" 48).

So far, he claims only to be explicating Barth's radical theological innovation, but then he takes this further. "Might it also be that the 'immanent' distinctions between God's first, second and third ways of being are *radicalized* by the Son's incarnational act? Perhaps, though one ventures here beyond the text of the *Dogmatics*."[65] To his credit, Jones acknowledges that "radicalizing" the immanent Triune hypostases via the incarnation is not explicit in Barth. However, he nonetheless finds in Barth warrant for the "transformation of God's being" by God's historical act in the incarnation. Like McCormack, act or history constitutes being, even God's.

For McCormack and Jones, Barth accentuates the doctrine of election, making it the basis by which God now chooses himself as Triune in a primordial election that collapses the traditional distinction between the economic and immanent Trinity. That God chooses such an actualized existence to constitute God's own being would seem to accentuate not only election, but also produce a new version of nominalism. God's essence is willed activity toward creatures that brings with it no known metaphysics, such as what is true, good, or beautiful, by which we know the form of God's will. Not only are creatures who they are because of an eternal decree, so is God. We have a God who actualizes an eternal decree upon himself, thereby constituting his own being. We have a God who gets "transformed," who does not appear to be simple, who at least suffers, and possibly changes, although from what to what is not entirely clear.

Balthasar's interpretation bears resemblances to McCormack's. Both correlate election, Christology, and Trinity in order to avoid a "god" behind the God revealed in Jesus. Yet a key difference remains. To put the matter succinctly, for Balthasar the Triune hypostases constitute election. For McCormack, election constitutes the Triune hypostases. For Balthasar, the divine missions are not an eternal event identical to the Triune processions. They are, of course, identical in that the immanent Trinity is the economic Trinity. But they are not identical in the sense that the immanent Trinity cannot be God without the economic missions. That the Persons create and redeem is not necessary for God's being. Otherwise God is not free to love. The missions represent an analogous movement, and of course the Triune God is subject of both. But the *eternal* processions, complete in themselves, are the source for the temporal missions. God can enter into that which is not God, temporal existence, without the temporal missions conditioning the eternal processions. The temporal missions do not actualize any potential in

65. Jones, *The Humanity of Christ*, 208. Emphasis original.

God. Election, then, does not constitute who God is, but the Triune hypostases constitute election. Rather than a radically, innovative theologian, for Balthasar, Barth retrieved a more biblical, patristic, and Catholic theology that never quite came into its own in the patristic, Scholastic, or modern eras, although it was present in them.

Either Barth is a more traditional theologian who reforms the Reformed and challenges manualist Thomism, making possible a new "rapprochement" between Catholics and Protestants, as Balthasar and many other Catholic theologians imagined, or he is a modern Reformed theologian who places the doctrine of God *within* the doctrine of election, producing such innovations within the Christian doctrine of God that much of it will now have to be revised, which is of course what characterizes modernity—the incessant need for revision because nothing can be relied upon to prepare us for the just now (the *modo*) which is about to arrive but never does.[66] For Balthasar, Barth's reordering of the doctrine of election challenged Reformed doctrines of God that divided the eternal decree from Christ's mission, and a sharp distinction between *de deo uno* and *de deo trino* in late medieval Catholic theology, both of which contributed to the emergence of modern theology. Both provide shelter for a *deus absconditus*, who as Kevin Hart notes, "haunted modernity."[67] This god is one of absolute power who may or may not be consistent with the God revealed in the Triune economy. It is a god of "transrational will," who cannot be known at all by natural reason, but only through actions that always come as miraculous events without any metaphysical continuity from one event to another.[68] By providing an alternative to the *deus absconditus*, Barth posed a challenge to a core thesis of modern theology. Barth is not a modern theologian, but one who provides a doctrine of God to heal a modern theology that too often confused the Christian God with Isis.

Debating the Form and Content of the *Analogia Entis*

Although Barth and Balthasar agreed on the relationship between the *de deo uno* and *de deo trino*, they disagreed on the role left for metaphysics once the

---

66. Part 4 of Balthasar's *The Theology of Karl Barth* was entitled "Prospects for Rapprochement." This rapprochement did not work in one direction. As early as the *Göttingen Dogmatics*, Barth wrote, "We cannot believe in the unity of the Spirit, that is, of God, and be indifferent to the universal or partial unity of the church." *Göttingen Dogmatics*, 240. He also stated, "we cannot possibly think that church history began in 1517," ibid., 241.

67. Kevin Hart, *Postmodernism* (Oneworld, 2004), 11.

68. See Michael Gillespie, *Nihilism before Nietzsche* (Chicago: University of Chicago Press, 1996).

loci had been reordered. This disagreement forms the basis for their ongoing debate about the *analogia entis*. The above discussion on nominalism, however, helps frame their debate. If the *analogia entis* entails a natural knowledge of God that conditions and therefore possibly contradicts the Triune God disclosed in the economy, then theology should be sufficiently bold to reject such a philosophical rendering of being. Barth seems to have thought that this is what the *analogia entis* entailed. Balthasar, however, construed it not as conditioning the Triune economy in this strong sense, something he feared his neoscholastic training did, but construed it as contributing to the Triune economy such that truth, goodness, and beauty were not reduced to historical relativity, or to their use-value. Balthasar affirmed the transcendental predicates of being (truth, goodness, beauty) without rejecting the important developments history brought to theology in the modern era. He thought Barth should recognize and affirm this construal of the *analogia entis*.

ANALOGIA ENTIS AND VATICAN I'S DUPLEX ORDO

Thomas Aquinas never explicitly used the term, *analogia entis*, yet due to Barth's rejection of it, the term came to designate a perceived division between Catholic and Protestant theology in the twentieth century that seldom was named as church-dividing before.[69] For some on either side of this debate, the *analogia entis* has become one more expression of the gaping chasm between Protestants and Catholics that cannot be bridged until one side either gives up its metaphysics of being, or the other side adopts it. Balthasar himself stated, as noted above, that the *analogia entis* was an essential Catholic teaching. Unlike the doctrine of a philosophical pure nature, it is dogma.

The *analogia entis* emerges from Vatican I's teaching on the *duplex ordo cognitionis* (twofold order of knowledge). It is why Barth asserted the *analogia entis* was "legitimate only on the basis of Roman Catholicism, between the greatness and misery of a so-called natural knowledge of God in the sense of the *Vaticanum*."[70] Would that Barth had said something more about its "greatness," but he did speak to its "misery." It leads, like Schleiermacher, to secularism. Barth never defended, nor explained, this assertion in any detail. His point seems to be that Schleiermacher and neoscholasticism produced a realm of

---

69. Related teachings such as the *duplex ordo cognitionis* were understood as church dividing prior to this time. Barth, to his credit, recognized the similarity between it and the *analogia entis*, but the specific expression of the *analogia entis* had not been previously understood as church-dividing.

70. *Church Dogmatics*, 1.1, trans. Geoffrey W. Bromiley, ed. G. W. Bromily and T. F. Torrance, 2nd ed. (Edinburgh: T & T Clark, 1975), iii.

nature separate from the divine economy and then argued from that realm to the economy. Balthasar thought there was something to this charge, but that it misidentified the error. He argued that Barth had a version of the *analogia entis*. In his argument, he made an intervention on both sides of the Protestant/ Catholic divide. Balthasar's intervention challenges a Catholic interpretation that understands the *analogia entis* as a purely metaphysical and philosophical condition within which the incarnation makes sense. It also challenges a Protestant interpretation that seeks to be postmetaphysical because the *analogia entis* is a purely metaphysical framework within which the incarnation must fit. Faith and pneumatology suffice without metaphysics. Once again, both sides feed off the interpretation of the other. Is the *analogia entis* a necessary line in the sand dividing Catholics from Protestants and vice versa? Any adequate answer depends on its interpretation.

The decree from Vatican I, *Dei Filius*, to which Barth referred, stated:

> The perpetual agreement of the Catholic church has maintained and *maintains* this too: that there is a twofold order of knowledge, distinct not only as regards its source, but also as regards its object. With regard to the source, we know at the one level by natural reason, at the other level by divine faith. With regard to the object, besides those things to which natural reason can attain, there are proposed for our belief mysteries hidden in God which, unless they are divinely revealed, are incapable of being known.

Like all such decrees, precisely what it teaches remains contested. For some interpreters, Barth and Balthasar included, it does not mean we have any specific natural, rational proof available to all right-thinking persons demonstrating God's existence with certainty, but in the context of faith such a proof is possible. For others like Garrigou-Lagrange, it teaches a specific rational proof known naturally outside faith. The Council did make the bold claim "that God the beginning and end of all things, may be known for certain by the natural light of human reason, by means of created things." This statement became the first proposition to be affirmed in the antimodernist oath, which under certain circumstances Barth said he could confess. The statement suggests a specific kind of knowledge of God. First, it is knowledge "by means of created things." Human creatures do not have an immediate intuition of God; knowledge "that God is" comes by way of analogy from sensible, creaturely things. We know God by abstracting from being what is unfitting to God.[71] The decree does not say if this knowledge arises from a realm of "pure nature," a point made by Balthasar. Moreover, this knowledge by the "natural light of reason" does not let us know the mysteries of the faith such as that God is Triune or incarnate in Jesus, nor is there anything in the decree that says this natural knowledge is necessary as a condition for those mysteries. Natural knowledge lets us know God as "beginning" and "end" of creatures, and from that we can deduce God's attributes or perfections.[72] The Vatican decree claims this is "certain" knowledge. Anyone who taught otherwise was to be anathematized.[73]

Garrigou-Lagrange argued such knowledge was necessary to avoid a number of modern errors: "atheism, positivism, traditionalism, fideism and Kantian criticism." The atheists and positivists refuse knowledge of God because knowledge is limited to sensible, finite, historical realities. They reject natural theology. The traditionalists and fideists argue "we can know God only through revelation or by some positive teaching received by tradition."[74] Kant was the major target that the Council had in mind because he participated in both errors, arguing that we could not move from sensible, creaturely realities to a true knowledge of God. Thus he critiqued reason to make room for faith, but the room made was for an a-rational faith.

For Garrigou-Lagrange, the Catholic Church teaches God can be known based on the specific proof of causality. Creatures are effects of God's causal agency. For that reason they bear an ontological resemblance to God that forms the basis for an analogical movement from creatures to God, the *analogia entis*. It is not just a predicamental analogy (a logical analogy in our use of terms), but also a transcendental analogy (an analogy present in the mode of being). This interpretation of the decree is contested. Gerald McCool gives a

71. Such a procedure must assume we already know something about God; otherwise how would we know what to abstract?

72. This natural knowledge of God includes a "natural love" for God, which falls under the natural virtue of justice. For this reason, Ressourcement Thomists argue prayer and certain forms of worship should be enshrined in law, and protected and promulgated by the nation-state, especially as it listens to the Catholic magisterium. For a defense of the natural love of God and its political implications see Steven A. Long, *Natura Pura: On the Recovery of Nature in the Doctrine of Grace* (New York: Fordham University Press, 2010), 146–50. Reinhard Hütter makes a similar argument in his *Dust Bound for Heaven: Explorations in the Theology of Thomas Aquinas* (Grand Rapids, MI: Eerdmans, 2012.) See his chapter, "'Democracy after Christendom'—Sovereign Secularism, Genuine Liberalism, and the Natural Love of God," 102–26. Balthasar's statement that nature alone cannot give us the means for such a Catholic civil religion obviously stands in contradiction to Ressourcement Thomism.

73. See Garrigou-Lagrange, *God: His Existence and His Nature: A Thomistic Solution of Certain Agnostic Antinomies* (St. Louis: B. Herder, 1946), 8.

74. Garrigou-Lagrange, *God: His Existence and His Nature*, 8–9.

different reading: "Although the constitution declared that natural reason had the ability to know God's existence and attributes, it did not determine whether, in point of fact, natural reason ever did so. . . . Nor did *Dei Filius* specify any definite argument through which the existence and nature of God could be established."[75] By contrast, Garrigou-Lagrange saw in the decree the defense of a specific, posteriori proof, grounded in causality, that did not need any authority to support it, neither the "testimony" of God nor the consensus of "tradition" nor even that of the whole human race, because it is present in the way things are, and such things are *naturally* intelligible.[76] That the proof is grounded in causality is contested among Thomists, as we shall see, but Garrigou-Lagrange thought this was required by the decree.

For Garrigou-Lagrange "that God is" is known primarily from rational arguments outlined in Aristotle's *Posterior Analytics*, and this *necessarily* conditions any knowledge of God that comes from revelation; the latter is based upon the former. This knowledge "that God is" is not salvific, but for revelation to be something more than fideism or historicism, it must be based on an analogy of being founded upon causality. Reason and faith are divided into two discrete, even pure realms, and here, despite all his protest against Kant, he shares an understanding of the relation between faith and reason with him. Unlike Balthasar, Garrigou-Lagrange and Kant pursue theology and philosophy within two realms, decisively distinguished from each other. Reason works from a source within pure nature; faith works within a supernatural realm. The two should not be confused. Garrigou-Lagrange writes, "Reason is placed in contrast with supernatural faith." This reason is not historically mediated but found in the nature of things themselves, for "whatever we know with certainty to be true, is due to the intrinsic evidence of things."[77] For Garrigou it was essential that the "natural knowledge of God . . . precedes supernatural faith."[78] The latter builds on the former like a foundation.

75. Gerald McCool, *Nineteenth-Century Scholasticism: The Search for a Unitary Method* (New York: Fordham University Press, 1977), 219.

76. Garrigou-Lagrange wrote, "This is why the first proposition of the Antimodernist Oath merely insists upon the natural sense of the words of the Council, as is shown by the insertion of the phrase: '*tamquam causam per effectus*' (as a cause [is known] by its effects).' This fact obliges us to assign to the principle of causality an ontological and transcendental value, for without it, reason could never rise from created things to the existence of God, as from effect to cause." Garrigou-Lagrange, *God: His Existence and His Nature*, 20. For the development of his argument based on causality see ibid., 62–81.

77. Ibid., 17.

78. Ibid., 54.

Garrigou's interpretation of the *duplex ordo* is the *Zweistockwerkdenken* (two story thinking) Balthasar challenged.

BALTHASAR'S CHALCEDONIAN ANALOGY OF BEING

Balthasar never rejected the *duplex ordo* of Vatican I, nor did he argue that metaphysics *conditions* revelation in Garrigou-Lagrange's strong sense. He defended metaphysics and natural theology on Barthian grounds. For Balthasar, Vatican I's twofold order of knowledge takes Christ's two natures as its starting point.[79] Metaphysics does not condition theology, as if human nature could condition God. In fact, if human nature conditions God, the neoscholastic position does not significantly differ from a radical Barthianism where Jesus Christ elects God. Both positions differ from the logic found at Chalcedon, in which the two natures come together into a unity without God ceasing to be God or creature ceasing to be creature, but in such a way that God conditions creatures without creatures conditioning God. The doctrine of the an- and enhypostaton affirms the nonreciprocity between God and creatures. The man Jesus has a human nature without a human hypostasis; his hypostasis is in the Second Person of the Trinity, which is why for Aquinas and Barth any analogy between God and creatures cannot be reversed. The *analogia entis* tells us how creaturely being depends upon God without in any sense affirming God's being depends on creatures.

Chalcedon presupposes intelligibility to both human and divine natures. They remain unconfused even when in Christ a single subject acts in both natures, but this single acting subject, who acts in two natures, requires that "nature" is understood as a *theological* concept, as Balthasar taught. Philosophy offered nothing like a single acting subject in two natures with one hypostasis; revelation required it. It is a *theological* concept, however, that then marks out a space for metaphysics. It also shows a "limit" to nature, which Balthasar also taught. We know nature by abstracting from what we do know about God and reminding ourselves that God is not a creature. Balthasar stated, "The theological concept of nature, which can be obtained only by the way of abstraction, is primarily a negative, limiting conception."[80] This does not make it a "vacuole." There is a *limit* that distinguishes nature from grace; neither is collapsed into each other.[81] The decisive question is how firmly this limit can be

---

79. *The Theology of Karl Barth*, 272.

80. *Karl Barth: Darstellung und Deutung Seiner Theologie* (Cologne: Jakob Hegner), 294.

81. John Milbank interprets this defense of nature as Balthasar's capitulation to external papal authority. Reinhard Hütter dismisses this as Milbank's non-Catholic unwillingness to become obedient to the

drawn, as if we can say everything on this side is nature and everything on the other is grace. Balthasar simply refuses to draw such a line.

For Balthasar, "everyday reason" thinks it can draw the limit precisely, but the more it tries, the "more difficult" the task. What constitutes something "natural" over and against the "supernatural" often eludes us because God's creation is "always already graced." But a *limit* is acknowledged. Grace is not nature, nor is nature grace.[82] Liberal Protestantism collapsed grace into nature where affirming nature (or culture) was affirming grace. Barth saw the consequences of this collapse in all its horror in Germany in the 1930s. Balthasar feared another version of it occurred after Vatican II among Catholics (without the horrifying consequences of the German Christians but also without the capacity to be critical of culture or nature rather than always blessing it).[83] At its worst, Barth's early reaction to liberal Protestantism reversed the polarities, evacuating nature and turning it into grace. The only agent was God's electing

magisterium, which makes Milbank unorthodox. It is difficult to see from Hütter's recent dramatic theological shift how orthodoxy would be possible outside obedience to the Catholic magisterium. Hütter never addresses Milbank's actual point in his argument, which is whether the kind of obedience demanded by a church divided into a juridical-legal male hierarchy, and a receptive female laity, fits with the best insights of Balthasar and de Lubac's theology? Is it an early modern innovation? Milbank's point is not that one should disobey the magisterium; he simply asks if this particular gendered rendering of it makes sense. Hütter and the Ressourcement Thomists do not appear to have time for such questions. See Milbank, *The Suspended Middle* (Grand Rapids, MI: Eerdmans, 2005) 104–5 and Hütter, *Dust Bound for Heaven*, 136–43 and 180–82. My own reading of Balthasar in the previous chapter and this one stands in sharp contrast to Milbank's dismissal of Balthasar in *The Suspended Middle*, 66–78. He says Balthasar "celebrates that, for Barth, nature is 'totally locked up' and yet in this negativity 'totally open to grace'" (66). This interpretation is similar to Steven A. Long's claim that nature is only understood as a vacuole in Balthasar. The terms Milbank places in quotations do not appear in the reference he cites for this evaluation, *Theology of Karl Barth*, 240–44, so it is difficult to know what he has in mind, or why they are in quotation marks. What is present in this section is Balthasar affirming a quote from Barth that says the opposite of what Milbank attributes to both of them. Balthasar writes, citing Barth, "faith awakens 'man to an action that is *proper* to him. This action not only lies within the scope of created nature, it actually corresponds to the highest natural determination of his creatureliness' (understood once more in the concrete Augustinian sense.) The model for how the act of faith relates to human nature is the Incarnation." (*The Theology of Karl Barth*, 140). That statement does not seem to be a claim that nature is locked in upon itself with only a bare negativity or mere repugnance that makes it open to grace. For a careful and nuanced criticism of Milbank's reading of Balthasar, see Edward T. Oakes, SJ, "On Milbank's *The Suspended Middle*," *Nova et Vetera* 4 (2006): 684–95.

82. Both de Lubac and Balthasar always affirmed nature as a "hypothetical," which Milbank rejects and sees as a capitulation to *Humani generis*. Milbank's position would be strengthened if he did not conflate pure nature and a hypothetical pure nature.

83. Balthasar explicitly feared Vatican II led only to the "blessing of culture," a point that will be discussed in the last chapter.

grace. Take for instance Keith Johnson's interpretation of Barth's opposition to the *analogia entis*. He writes, "For Barth, there simply is no natural capacity for faith, nor is there any inherent capability to hear and understand God's revelation." The only agent is God. Here is a strong rejection of any language in which metaphysics conditions revelation. Instead, for this postmetaphysical interpretation, any such natural capacity "is given to the human anew and afresh in each moment in the event of God's self-revelation."[84] Balthasar thought otherwise. *Citing* Barth, he wrote, "faith awakens 'man to an action that is *proper* to him. This action not only lies within the scope of created nature, it actually corresponds to the highest natural determination of his creatureliness' (understood once more in the concrete Augustinian sense.) The model for how the act of faith relates to human nature is the Incarnation."[85] That faith is not an "inherent capacity" in nature is true of both Protestant and Catholic theology.[86] That is the point of delimiting even a hypothetical nature from grace. By contrast, that there is no "natural capacity" for faith is not true of these traditions. If there is no natural capacity, then the only acting subject is God, and the unity of divinity and humanity in Christ cannot be communicated. Human creatures are redeemed by evacuation of their creatureliness and not by a creaturely participation in divinity.

Rather than an inherent, natural capacity, faith is a gift. For Balthasar, and Catholicism, it is an "infused" virtue *inhering* in the soul that comes to it as something more than an extrinsic event like a miracle.[87] That extrinsic understanding was the Suarezian position he rejected. But this does not make faith an inherent capacity. The *potentia oboedentialis* is not faith; it is a natural created potentiality that God can actualize so that faith inheres in the creature even as the creature participates in God. Faith is a gift that becomes inherent because God made creatures for God's self. That we have a potential for it is not known prior to its actualization. Balthasar never said this natural potency conditions faith, but after God's gracious economy has been revealed then this potency can be known; for in it we see God seeks to be *one* with human nature, which is known from the hypostatic union of Christ's two natures. We are not incarnate. Jesus Christ alone is the Incarnate One, but he is incarnate for us, to make our humanity at one with God. Barth emphasizes this oneness as well in his doctrine of reconciliation. If grace is to unite God and creatures, and

84. Keith Johnson, *Karl Barth and the Analogia Entis* (London: T & T Clark, 2011), 168.

85. *The Theology of Karl Barth*, 140.

86. At times, Milbank's "Radical Orthodoxy" would seem to deny this.

87. This was debated during Barth's 1941 seminar on the Council of Trent. It will be discussed in the final chapter below.

not be an extrinsic layer added on to an otherwise intelligible human nature, thereby repeating the two-story theological ontology of neoscholasticism, then this requires the *potentia oboedentialis* as something more than mere repugnance. Grace is proper to human nature because the latter's true end exceeds its nature, friendship with God. Aristotle's understanding of nature must be revised; for as Aristotle taught, each creature has an end, and the means to that end are inherent in the creature. An end that surpasses the natural means to it makes no sense on Aristotelian grounds. Aristotle provides a doctrine of pure nature because he did not know one hypostasis could, in fact, have two *physeis*. Karl Barth should affirm the *analogia entis*, Balthasar argued, because his theology lived from the beauty of its object.

If Balthasar reads Barth well, then the question is not whether the *analogia entis* is affirmed, for any Christian theologian who affirms the incarnation will affirm some version of it; the question is which version of the *analogia entis* is affirmed. This acknowledgment might help move Catholic and Protestant theologians beyond the stale debate Barth himself created about the *analogia entis*. If the *analogia entis* requires Aristotle's *Posterior Analytics* to make sense of the incarnation, then it will be difficult, if not impossible, to argue Christian theologians understood the incarnation well prior to the thirteenth century. If the *analogia entis* is dismissed, and we develop a postmetaphysical theology, then it will be difficult, if not impossible, to sustain the teaching of the faith emerging from Chalcedon. On this account true Christian theology begins with Barth, something against which he would have recoiled in horror.

WHAT IS AT STAKE IN THE *ANALOGIA ENTIS*?

Although Balthasar thought the disagreement over the *analogia entis* was not the most important argument to have with Barth, it did have significance. Balthasar denied a maximalist interpretation, where it is a piece of pure philosophical reasoning that came prior to, and then conditioned, theology. He also rejected a minimalist interpretation that thought it could be replaced with the *analogia fidei* without loss. In so far as Barth assumed the latter, Balthasar defended the *analogia entis*. What was he defending and why? To answer that question, a discussion of various defenses of the *analogia entis* is necessary.

WHOSE ANALOGIA ENTIS?

Although most Thomists, and many Catholic theologians, agree against Barth that the *analogia entis* is necessary for Christian theology, they do not agree among themselves as to what it is, or even if Thomas taught it. Some of the disagreements that any discussion of the *analogia entis* entails are these: Was Przywara's interpretation novel, or did if fit with the tradition of interpretation found in the Thomist manualist tradition, and upon which conciliar decrees were based? Was the Thomist manualist tradition, especially arising from Cajetan's threefold analysis of the names of analogy (inequality, attribution, proportionality) novel, or did it fit with Thomas's own teaching? Did Thomas teach the *analogia entis*? If so, was it as a predicamental logic or a transcendental reality? If it is a transcendental reality, is it a *pros hen* analogy, and therefore based upon an analogy of causality with a metaphysics of participation that emphasizes relationality, or is it an analogy of proportionality based on act and potency that must come prior to any relationality? [88] There is no agreement

88. For the question about Cajetan, see Ralph McInerny, *Aquinas and Analogy* (Washington, DC: Catholic University of America Press, 1996). He attributes to Cajetan a faulty understanding of Thomas. Cajetan misled Thomism altogether. "In short, there is no distinction between analogy of attribution and analogy of proportionality in St. Thomas Aquinas" (12). Bruce Marshall follows McInerny's argument and denies that the *analogia entis* provides genuine knowledge of God. "The metaphysics of creation deals with beings and their perfections, while the analogy of names deals with *rationes* and their logical relationships" (Marshall, "Christ the End of Analogy," in *The Analogy of Being: Invention of the Antichrist or the Wisdom of God?*, ed. Thomas Joseph White, OP [Grand Rapids, MI: Eerdmans, 2011], 299). Laurance Dewan stands against this position, affirming Cajetan's interpretation and arguing for a metaphysical rather than logical use of *analogia entis*. (Dewan, "St. Thomas and Analogy: The Logician and the Metaphysician," in *Form and Being: Studies in Thomistic Metaphysics* (Washington, DC: Catholic University of America Press, 2006) 81–95. Thomas Joseph White, Reinhard Hütter, and Steven A. Long agree with the Cajetanian interpretation against McInerny and Marshall. (See Hütter, "Attending to the Wisdom of God," in *The Analogy of Being*, 224–28) and Steven A. Long, *Analogia Entis: On the Analogy of Being, Metaphysics, and the Act of Faith* (Notre Dame: University of Notre Dame Press, 2012), 138n26.), but disagree among themselves as to what kind of analogy the *analogia entis* is. A previous generation of Thomists likewise sided with the Cajetanian interpretation. See John F. Wippel, *Metaphysical Themes in Thomas Aquinas* (Washington DC: Catholic University of America Press, 1984), 215, and Jacques Maritain *Existence and the Existent*, trans. Lewis Galantière and Gerald B. Phelan (Garden City, NY: Image Books, 1957), 32–44, and, of course, Garrigou-Lagrange. Those who argue for the metaphysical use differ among themselves over what kind of analogy this transcendental analogy is. For Long, it can only be an analogy of proper proportionality based on diverse *rationes* of act/potency, which must come prior to any relation. The *analogia entis* is not an analogy of attribution, relationality, or simple analogy of proportion or causal relation and participation. It is "analogy of proportionality" (Long, *Analogia Entis*, 2–3). Hütter, however, finds it in Thomas as a *pros hen* analogy that presumes causal relation and participation. *Pros hen* analogy assumes a primary instance by which the analogy works. Health in bodies, urine, and humans is the usual Aristotelian example, but Aquinas then supplemented it with respect to God via a doctrine of participation. Hütter writes, "Here we can see immediately why participation and transcendental analogy converge: To participate is to have partially what another is without restriction," (see Hütter, "Attending to the Wisdom of God," 230). Hütter follows closely the argument in Bernard Montagnes (see Montagnes, *The Doctrine of the Analogy of Being according to Thomas Aquinas*, trans. E. M.

among devout Thomists on these questions, so a Protestant seeking to understand why the *analogia entis* is the condition that makes revelation intelligible, and even possible, should be excused for failing to understand.

The Thomists who follow Cajetan do agree that the *analogia entis* is a necessary *condition* for revelation. For Steven A. Long, the *analogia entis* as "diverse *rationes* of act limited by potency" conditions both any relation of God and creation and any possibility of revelation.[89] "The analogy of being is the evidentiary foundation for the *preambula fidei*, as well as the precondition for the terms of revelation signifying the inner life of God."[90] The *analogia entis*, as well as a doctrine of pure nature, are necessary for faith. Long argues that no other possibility exists, "as though the revelation of God in Christ does not invite and presuppose a natural doctrine of God as a condition for the intelligibility that Christ is God."[91] Notice what he is claiming here. Long's thesis is not the

Macierowski, reviewed and corrected by P. Vandevelde, with revisions by A. Tallon [Milwaukee: Marquette University Press, 2004]). The above comments are only a few of the disagreements among the Thomists. Not mentioned are theologians who found the sharp distinction between philosophy and theology, nature and grace, a misreading of Aquinas, such as Etienne Gilson (against whom Wippel's book is directed) or Henri de Lubac. Balthasar fit much better among the latter.

89. Long finds close similarity, if not identity, between Aquinas and Aristotle on the use of analogy, unlike Montagnes, who finds Aquinas supplementing Aristotle with Platonism, as does Rudi te Velde. See his *Participation and Substantiality in God* (Brill Academic, 1995). For Long, the "diverse *rationes* of act by potency" is best exhibited in Aristotle's *Metaphysics* 10 1 and 6, 1048a30–1048b9, where he explains the analogy as "that which is building is to that which is capable of building, and the waking to the sleeping, and that which is seeing to that which has its eyes shut but has sight, and that which has been shaped out of the matter to the matter." (Long, *Analogia Entis*, 17). In other words, everything that is, is as an *act* of being that presupposes a specific potency for that act by which it is. This allows for the diverse *rationes* of act and potency. These then are related to God, not as cause, but as pure act, who has no potency. These diverse *rationes* are identical for him to Aquinas's existence/essence distinction. Thus the analogy of proper proportionality sets up this proportion between God and creatures, demonstrating God's existence: "One can say that *esse:creature* as *esse*: God insofar as in each case *esse* is act, and in each case *esse* is proportionate to the subject—proportionate to the finite subject contracted by potency, and proportionate to the infinite subject uncontracted by potency." (Long, *Analogia Entis,* 99). But how we move from the proportion everything-that-has-*esse*-is-limited-by-potency to God-who-has-*esse*-without-potency seems odd. How is this, in any sense, "proper proportionality"? For Long's claim that the analogy of proper proportionality conditions any analogy of relation or causality, and thus any God-creature relation, note the following quote: "The relation of having being from another follows upon having being. . . . It follows that the analogical formality of being is necessarily by nature prior to and indeed the condition of the relation of createdness, of the relation of efficient and final dependency, and so prior to the analogy of effect to cause which is predicated upon it. God is prior to the creature, but the relation of createdness is posterior to the being of the creature" (Long, *Analogia Entis*, 71).

90. Long, *Analogia Entis*, 102.

91. Long, *Natura Pura,* 49.

more temperate claim that God's revelation invites a natural theology. Balthasar affirmed that, and argued Barth always had it even if he refused to acknowledge it. Balthasar's interpretation would suggest that for reasons of faith we should be open to the possibility of nature giving us insight into God's existence. Long's thesis is something much more than this. God's revelation demands a natural doctrine of God as the "*condition* for the intelligibility that Christ is God." In other words, we cannot know who Christ is if we do not first have this natural knowledge. This argument is common among the Ressourcement Thomists.

Long affirms the *analogia entis* as a proper proportionality against other Thomists who argue for a *pros hen* analogy, but all agree the *analogia entis*, despite the debate over what kind of analogy it is, conditions revelation. The key word is "conditions." White too, who holds a more modest interpretation of *Dei Filius* than Garrigou-Lagrange or Long, still writes,

> My claim is that the natural human capacity to think analogically about God in his unity and existence as the cause of the world—with the help of concepts drawn from creation—is a necessary epistemological presupposition for any scriptural or dogmatic account of the incarnate Word. The *analogia Verbi* presupposes the possibility of an analogical ascription of *esse* to God as the necessary (but not sufficient!) condition, just as grace presupposes nature.[92]

Likewise, Reinhard Hütter states, "And thus the analogy of being is indeed the always already operative metaphysical condition for the surpassingly gratuitous salvific relation of God *quoad nos* to become analogically intelligible while remaining essentially *mysterium*."[93]

POSTMETAPHYSICAL THEOLOGY?

Comparing these Ressourcement Thomist theologians with one of the best examples of a postmetaphysical Barthianism will assist us in seeing the significance of Balthasar's reading of Barth for moving beyond the *analogia entis* debate. First, one more quote from Thomas Joseph White, OP sets forth in all clarity the Ressourcement Thomist position:

---

92. White, "'Through Him All Things Were Made' (John 1:3): The Analogy of the Word Incarnate according to Thomas Aquinas and Its Ontological Presuppositions," in *The Analogy of Being*, 267.

93. Hütter, "Attending to the Wisdom of God." 245.

Here I will argue that the theological analogy of the incarnate Word (the *Logos ensarkos*) is not fully intelligible, even as a specifically Christian and dogmatic notion, without the capacity to ascribe to God analogical notions of being and unity, in comparison with creatures. Furthermore, we are capable of ascribing such analogical notions only if there is a real ontological resemblance between creatures and God that is naturally intelligible to the human intellect without formal recourse to divine revelation. Consequently, the knowledge of Christ's divinity that we are given by grace implies that we have a natural capacity for knowledge of God.[94]

Contrast this claim with Kevin Hector's *Theology without Metaphysics*, which offers a "therapy" against metaphysics. He writes,

Metaphysics does violence to objects by forcing them into predetermined categories. . . . The present proposal is therapeutic in precisely this sense: it aims to make the metaphysical framework visible—and so render it optional—by setting another account alongside it and to do so in such a way that one can shake free from the sense of loss which leaves one feeling alienated from, or nostalgic for, that which metaphysics has habituated one into taking for granted. . . . The proposal, briefly stated, is to understand the Spirit's work in the following terms: after Jesus Christ had taught his disciples how to follow him, he recognized them as competent to recognize other persons and performances as doing so; the disciples, in turn, recognized still others as competent recognizers, and so on."[95]

Both these proposals share a common concern—how best to render intelligible the mystery of the incarnation. The means employed are directly opposed. White finds a specific metaphysics, the *analogia entis*, to be a necessary condition for the intelligibility of the incarnation. Hector finds metaphysics preventing the proper role of the incarnation in theology. For White, a denial of metaphysics, of an "ontological resemblance" between God and creatures, loses a proper recognition of the incarnation. For Hector, affirmation of metaphysics, of an ontological resemblance between God and creatures, does violence to

94. White, "'Through Him All Things Were Made,'" 249.

95. Kevin Hector, *Theology without Metaphysics: God, Language and the Spirit of Recognition* (Cambridge: Cambridge University Press, 2011), 10, 31–32, 38.

the incarnation.[96] White calls theologians to retrieve a proper metaphysics; Hector provides a therapy to overcome any such nostalgic longings. In its place he offers a much more modern, pragmatic politics of recognition grounded in pneumatology. Their disagreement continues, in a new and accentuated form, the disagreement Barth had with Balthasar on the *analogia entis*. It does so, however, by refusing to acknowledge the christological rendering of the *analogia entis* that Balthasar affirmed in Barth to his Catholic audience, and his critique of Barth that metaphysics must still be done within that Christology, which Balthasar affirmed to his Protestant audience. The rejection of Balthasar's presentation of Barth widens the ecclesial divide and forces upon Protestants and Catholics an either-or.

If metaphysics (the analogy of being) *conditions* revelation, then Hector's concern seems warranted. It straightjackets theology and overlooks the historical reality of Christian faith. Is the *analogia entis* what allowed first-century Jews to recognize God in Christ? What happened to the revelation given to Moses? Does metaphysics not do violence to its object if it *conditions* what revelation can say in this strong sense? Any answer depends on what we mean by "conditions." It could mean nothing more than this: if God is incarnate in Jesus Christ, uniting humanity and divinity in one, then after that fact we know one of the conditions for it is that "humanity" and "divinity" exist, and are at least in part, intelligible. We may not know that two natures are found in one Person, but we do at least know something about what natures and persons are. If this were all that the Ressourcement Thomists claimed, it should neither cause controversy, nor be church dividing. But they appear to say more. At the least, they suggest that the *analogia entis* is the *epistemological* condition rendering our knowledge of the incarnation intelligible. At most they assert the *analogia entis* is the *metaphysical* condition rendering the incarnation possible. It gives us, as Long puts it, "the precondition for the terms of revelation signifying the inner life of God." If it is the latter, how does it not lack a proper Christian humility in the face of God's mystery? Are creatures able to tell God the conditions by which God can become incarnate? Could Aquinas affirm this?[97]

---

96. Hector, *Theology without Metaphysics*, 10.

97. How could we affirm Long's position and still acknowledge that the handmaid who knows Jesus knows more than Aristotle (to paraphrase Aquinas)? Here is what Aquinas actually wrote, "Et hoc patet, quia nullus philosophorum ante adventum Christi cum toto conatu suo potuit tantum scire de Deo et de necessariis ad vitam aeternam, quantum post adventum Christi scit una vetula per fidem: et ideo dicitur Isai. XI, 9: *repleta est terra scientia domini*." "And this is clear, because none of the philosophers before the advent of Christ was able, with all of his effort, to know as much about God and the things necessary for eternal life, as a little old lady, after the advent of Christ, knows through faith; hence it is said in Isaiah 11,

If the *analogia entis* is nothing more than the obvious fact that because God was incarnate in Christ, divinity and humanity exist in some kind of natural intelligibility, then it should be noncontroversial. Balthasar affirmed it, as did Barth implicitly, when he develops his doctrine of creation as the external basis for covenant and covenant as the internal basis for the creation. For Balthasar the *analogia entis* also warrants metaphysical claims. Human "nature" must be intelligible, but it does not condition theology metaphysically. Theology does not begin with prolegomena demonstrating God's existence from either an analogy of proper proportionality or *pros hen*. If Barth misunderstood this and freighted the *analogia entis* with more baggage than it required, White and Long (at least) freight Barth's theory of human action with a theological unilateralism that is more than it ever claimed to bear. White differentiates Barth's position on analogy from the *analogia entis* by claiming Barth's position entails that "the similitude [analogy between God and creatures] is established uniquely by the unilateral activity or initiative of God in Christ, without parallel or analogy to be found in human agency *outside of Christ*."[98] Such a statement is puzzling. For Barth, drawing upon Holy Scripture, God creates in, for, and through Christ. So where is a created agency "outside" this realm? Barth never denied *human* agency. He denied it could be made sense of in some realm where it was not rendered possible by creation as the external condition of covenant, both of which occur in and through Christ. As we will see in a discussion of *Church Dogmatics* 4.3.2 in chapter 5 below, Barth went so far as to say human agents can give something to God without denying God's simplicity.

Long also caricatures Barth's position. First he sets up an either-or: either being is intelligible or there is pure apophaticism. Then he suggests a "third possibility" obviously alluding to Barth.

> Someone might ask whether there is not a third possibility. Could there not be speech about God that God Himself authorizes and that so escapes any taint of created categories? To which the response is that even human speech inspired by God remains both human and speech; and that if such speech were to be wholly denuded of any created intelligibility, it would by that fact be wholly unintelligible to the human creature and thereby cease to be speech since speech

the earth has been made full with the knowledge of God." Aquinas, *prooemium* in *Expositio in Symbolum Apostololrum*, *Textum Taurini*, 1954, http://www.corpusthomisticum.org/csv.html. I am indebted to Mark Johnson for the reference and translation.

98. White, "Introduction: The *Analogia Entis* Controversy and Its Contemporary Significance," in *The Analogy of Being*, 9.

is more than sound whose signification is either unknowable or nonexistent.[99]

But Barth affirmed precisely this—when God speaks it is always in and through human agencies. He critiqued Catholicism for evacuating created elements as the condition for God's communication, in that the bread and wine no longer remained bread and wine. In contrast, for Protestantism, God's speech worked in and through human agents without evacuating them of their agency. He never suggested God spoke somehow without the "taint of created categories." In fact, created categories are not tainted because God communicates through them, which is the basis for his high doctrine of human exaltation (more on this in chapter 5 below). Nevertheless, for Barth, "revelation is the condition that conditions all things without being conditioned." Creatures do not tell God the conditions by which God reveals himself, but when God reveals himself, and we know it, we can discern those conditions. For Ressourcement Thomism, metaphysics *conditions* revelation. Without affirming this conditioning, Christianity lapses into unintelligibility. If this conditioning of revelation is correct, then to put it whimsically, we will need to correct Scripture. Jesus would have to counter Thomas's confession in John 20:28, "My Lord and my God," with something like, "Well I know you think you know what this means, but you cannot make this confession properly until you become aware it is conditioned by the *analogia entis* found in Aristotle's *Posterior Analytics* taken up by the Thomist manual tradition after the thirteenth century." If that is the case, has not something gone woefully wrong in our understanding of the relation between grace and nature, faith and reason?

If forced to choose between this version of Thomism and Hector's therapy, I would tend toward Hector's postmetaphysical therapy. Hector begins with the claim "that although we moderns may want to avoid metaphysics, we have a hard time doing so."[100] He rightly notes how difficult metaphysics is to overcome. Caputo critiques Marion who critiques Heidegger who critiques Nietzsche who critiques Kant for seeking but failing to overcome metaphysics. Nonetheless, the effort should be made, because for Hector the history of Western metaphysics culminates in deleterious consequences: it does violence to being by forcing it into a predetermined conceptual framework.[101]

99. Long, *Analogia Entis*, 5.

100. Hector, *Theology without Metaphysics*, 2.

101. He posits (at least) three such deleterious consequences. First, metaphysics poses a threat to the self-expressive freedom of the modern, autonomous subject, and the attendant egalitarianism it produces. He affirms throughout his work the beneficial nature of the modern subject, identifying it with

Hector is specific about the metaphysics we should overcome. It is not overcoming transcendence or reality claims ("what things are like") or abandoning truth. In fact, Hector adamantly opposes any exclusive immanence, and in that sense he is willing to let others call his work, despite his provocative title *Theology without Metaphysics*, a "revisionist metaphysics."[102] But he finds metaphysics harmful at worst and unhelpful at best. He outlines Heidegger's specific historical diagnosis, according to which "metaphysics identifies the being of beings as that in and upon which they are *grounded*, and identifies this ground, in turn, with human *ideas* about them."[103] Although he begins with this historical diagnosis, he works against Heideggger's conclusion that language cannot attain its true reference when it speaks about God in terms of "being." Hector seeks an alternative to Heidegger and the apophaticism present in many postmetaphysical theologians, and does so through pneumatology mediated in a pragmatic politics of recognition. It replaces metaphysics and overcomes theologians' nostalgia for it. Nonetheless, he concedes too much to Heidegger's historical diagnosis in setting up the reason why theology must do without metaphysics.

Why should theology concede Heidegger's accusation of the "ontotheological conception of metaphysics?"[104] Because human agents identify being with human ideas and speech, this does not entail that their ideas and speech cannot attain their referent unless we somehow know a priori that such ideas and speech are always either equivocal or univocal to their referent— but this is precisely what the *analogia entis* was intended to challenge. What alternative to human ideas and speech is available to creatures? If they are inadequate, then apophaticism would seem to be unavoidable. Then Long's question is compelling as to how some human speech could be construed as God's own speech, and other human speech construed as merely human ideas about God.

To his credit, Hector knows Barth never taught what Long suggests. Hector cites Barth's statement that we speak of God only with our "creaturely-focused words," which might alleviate Long's legitimate concern. But Hector

Protestant Christianity. Second, metaphysics does violence to being, especially the being of people on the margins of society, by forcing them into a predetermined conceptual framework that refuses to grant alterity. Third, metaphysics constrains theology, especially Christology, within a predetermined conceptual structure. Metaphysical concepts function like containers that fit everything, even Christ, into their structural limitations without acknowledging they do so (*Theology without Metaphysics*, 10–12).

102. Ibid., 3.

103. Ibid.

104. Ibid., 3n4.

then finds himself in difficulty in explaining how God communicates through creatures. He interprets Barth's "creaturely-focused words" in terms of the Reformed doctrine of justification by faith alone. It is not the creatureliness of these words that matters, but solely God's grace that renders them appropriate.[105] Hector then states, "On this account, then, the analogy of attribution is itself analogous to justification by grace received in faith. This is an important departure from most accounts of analogy; another, crucial to the present project, is that analogy is here understood not as bridging a gap between two meanings—one theological, the other ordinary—as if these were separate entities, but as naming the way a normative trajectory changes as a concept is applied in ever new circumstances."[106] How is the analogy of attribution analogous to justification by faith? Does this mean our ordinary language must be supernaturally changed for it to reach its reference? How would we know when such transformation occurs? Why can a term not function with both a natural and supernatural meaning at the same time? If I understand this crucial move in his therapy, the key term is "normative trajectory changes." We do not need any metaphysical participation of our language in God such that a particular form of speech, like Christian orthodoxy, gets valorized for all time.[107] Because the proper conceptual use of our language only results from God's grace, we can never be certain that what we have at any moment speaks properly of God. What we have is a process of mutual, historical recognition where its truth is always out in front of us because its proper term is not in creaturely reality, but in God's grace. We must always be looking for the novel, and in fact the novel will be a sign of the Spirit's work. The difficulties this therapy raises are twofold. First, how does the Spirit's use of our ordinary terms differ from a pragmatic politics of recognition? Why do I need the Holy Spirit when I have the spirit found in Hegel, or Pippin, or Žižek? Second, how does the Spirit's use of ordinary terms not evacuate them and perform a miracle that provides no continuity from one moment to the next? Is a "politics of recognition" sufficient to provide that continuity?

CONCLUSION

Balthasar's presentation and interpretation of Barth avoids the either-or forced upon theologians between Ressourcement Thomism and postmetaphysical

---

105. Ibid., 141.

106. Ibid., 142–43.

107. See Hector's affirmation of Schleiermacher's argument that what was once heterodox then becomes orthodox because of "an earlier orthodoxy becoming obsolete" (85n54).

Barthianism. In its day, it led to a rapprochement between Catholic and Protestant teaching on the doctrine of God. Ressourcement Thomism and postmetaphysical Barthianism challenge that rapprochement. According to Steven A. Long, Balthasar's doctrine of God failed, because he did not develop the *de deo uno*, especially God's perfections, according to natural reason first. They emerge from a metaphysics independent of revelation that then conditions revelation. Balthasar's postmetaphysical critics make the diametrically opposed argument. He missed Barth's revolutionary revision of God's perfections. Barth's doctrine of election calls for a revision of the divine perfections much more radically than Balthasar recognized. Barth challenged the "substance" metaphysics of the patristic and Scholastic eras that provided knowledge of God's unity prior to Trinity, a challenge that now requires substantial revisions in the doctrine of God, challenging simplicity, impassibility, and the rejection of any real relation between God and creatures.[108] If Long sees Balthasar failing adequately to distinguish God's unity from God's Trinity, McCormack sees him failing to unite them. For McCormack, theology should not begin with "abstract" metaphysical speculation on God's unity and then discuss Trinity; the election of God by Jesus Christ requires theologians to reject or revise the received divine perfections, especially simplicity and impassibility. For Long, however, theology must begin with abstraction; otherwise, we lose the "purification of names predicated of God, such that only *transcendental* or *pure* perfections are predicated."[109] The *analogia entis* purifies predications. It teaches how to name God from creatures without predicating potency of God. Once "nature becomes a mere dialectical geometric point," which, for Long, it is in Balthasar because he followed Barth, then these perfections no longer do their metaphysical work. The result is theologically catastrophic. "Thus, perfections that do indeed denote limit may begin to be predicated of God in Himself (wonder; surprise; anticipation; and so on). The beginning of all this must be seen in the denial of the abstractive intelligibility of proportionate nature in relation to the analogy of being."[110] Balthasar's theodramatics posit surprise, receptivity, and risk in God, and he has been properly, and rightly, critiqued for them from a variety of theological perspectives. However, for Balthasar receptivity is a *perfection*; it is not a potentiality that allows something to be

108. The postmetaphysical interpretation of Barth often misinterprets the Scholastics and Fathers. Thomas Joseph White shows this unmistakably by showing how Aquinas rejected the term "substance" as applicable to God. See White, "Through Him All Things Were Made," 273n61.

109. Long, *Natura Pura*, 92–93.

110. Ibid., 93.

added to God. It is not a limit. The Son and Spirit *receive* their common essence from the Father, returning it without diminishment.[111] Balthasar's use of wonder, surprise, and anticipation are only predicated analogically based on the Triune relations. They do not reject Aquinas's perfections in the *de deo uno.* Like Barth, Balthasar reads those perfections within, and not prior to, the Triune economy. For Long, because Balthasar does not begin with metaphysical abstraction prior to the Triune economy, he loses God's perfections. While Long laments this Barthian influence on Balthasar, McCormack affirms it. Balthasar's theodramatics did not conceive theological ontology in terms of the doctrine of election, but his theology of Holy Saturday points in the right direction. For Long, Balthasar goes too far. For McCormack, he did not go far enough. For Long, Barth's influence on Balthasar distorts Christianity's traditional doctrine of God. For McCormack, it does not distort it enough.

Notice how these two critiques are mutually reinforcing. They do not disagree over Barth's influence on Balthasar; they disagree over its evaluation. As the preceding discussion demonstrates, their common judgment is correct in part. Balthasar was deeply influenced by Barth's theology of the divine perfections from *Church Dogmatics* 2.1. When Barth first met Balthasar, he joked that Balthasar "tows especially 2/1 in his briefcase around like a cat her youth."[112] He did so because of the sections on the divine perfections. Balthasar reiterated the importance of Barth's teaching on the divine perfections more than forty years later in his 1968 obituary for Barth. The "high point" of his *Dogmatics* was the "doctrine of the attributes of God, an archetype or role model (*Vorbild*) for every Catholic dogmatics as to how science can be combined with love, reverence, and joy."[113] Long is correct; Barth influenced Balthasar's reading of the *de deo uno.* McCormack is also correct; neither Barth nor Balthasar revised those perfections as radically as McCormack thinks they should have. Long and McCormack agree; yet their agreement misses something significant: the *reason* Barth and Balthasar refused dividing the *de deo uno* and *de deo trino* into separate realms of nature and grace as does Long, or collapsing them into a single realm as does McCormack.

---

111. Aquinas, although denying *esse receptum in aliquo* in his discussion of God's infinity (ST I.7.1 affirms a divine *esse receptum per se subsistens* in his discussion of the procession of the Divine Persons (ST I 27.2)

112. Lochbrunner, *Hans Urs von Balthasar und seine Theologenkollegen,* 279.

113. Ibid., 369.

The above argument adds something to their disagreement that neither Long nor McCormack acknowledge. Barth reordered the loci of the divine perfections and the doctrine of the Trinity in *Church Dogmatics* 2.1 to contest the seminominalism of modern theology. He did not revise the perfections per se. Neither Barth nor Balthasar was strongly committed to overthrowing Aquinas's *de deo uno*, but they held the common conviction that the *de deo uno* must serve revelation and not condition it. That is to say, what we know of God's unity must not function to undermine God's economy in Christ. Any theology that can say what needs to be said about God primarily from causality, participation, or the distinction between act and potency missed something significant: the "form" of God's economy. It posited knowledge of a god known outside that economy who may or may not cohere with the Triune God revealed in it.

If Barth is a revisionist theologian who operates under the conditions of modernity, his work will have little ability to garner ecumenical attention outside a narrow tradition of Reformed theology committed to doing apologetic theology under the conditions of modernity. Heidegger's crossing out of being will form the conditions within which we must now be theological. If Barth is the classic, Reformed, and therefore Catholic theologian Balthasar saw, overcoming the nominalist tendencies of modern theology that prevented a proper flourishing of "glory," his work will be of interest to those who do not simply think the doctrine of God has to be revised because Kant's critique of metaphysics has now attained dogmatic status, but who also continue to recognize the metaphysical realism present in Thomas. The strong version of the *analogia entis* found among Ressourcement Thomists will still be deeply problematic, as is their effort to construct a Catholic civil religion based on the natural love of God.

Barth and Balthasar's overarching concern was never epistemology, relevance, or apologetics. Nor did they pursue dogma for dogma's sake alone. God's action for us in Christ made the world different, and Christians as well as their neighbors could acknowledge and live out that difference. If that difference was not lived, something went wrong. But it was *God's actions in Christ* that made the world different, not our own superior moral abilities. Much as they refused to divide knowledge of God into two pure realms—one natural and the other supernatural—so they refused that division when it came to ethics. Ethics is not an independent discipline that follows once we get our doctrine straight, but neither is it a discipline that antecedes doctrine. They are brought together into a unity. As Barth put it, "dogma is ethics." Thinking, writing, and practicing ethics within the divine economy, rather than a preoccupation with epistemology, shaped his work. Balthasar not only recognized this, he developed it by immediately following contemplation (theological aesthetics) with action (theological drama).

5

The Realm of Ethics

The previous chapter addressed the "burning matter of dispute" between Balthasar and Barth on the "realm" within which theologians pursue knowledge of God. On this matter, Balthasar was both for and against Barth. He was for him in that the *de deo uno* cannot condition the *de deo trino* without losing the divine economy. He was against him in that the crucial identity between them did not entail abandoning a version of the *analogia entis*. This chapter addresses the other "burning matter of dispute," the realm within which theologians and Christians should reflect upon, and practice, "ethics."[1] Much like Balthasar's recognition that our natural knowledge of God should not work against God's Triune economy, he also found in Barth a way to think about ethics that overcame stale divisions between nature and grace. Ethics and theology are no more a two-tiered relation than are nature and grace. Ethics should be interspersed within dogmatic loci, and not a separate treatise grounded in nature qua nature.

Barth and Balthasar interspersed ethics throughout dogmatic loci, and generated a very different approach to ethics than that found among either the neoscholastic or the liberal Protestants. Their approach is worthy of emulation, which is to suggest neither that they produced an ethical theory or practice free of problems, nor that their work was in complete agreement. Their differences take place, however, within substantive agreements. The first is that "ethics" poses a temptation and crisis for modern theology. The second is that the remedy for this temptation is to intersperse ethics throughout dogmatic loci. The third is that dogma entails human agents capable of performing God's

---

1. This chapter does not intend to be an exhaustive analysis of Barth's theological ethics. Much work already exists that does that well. In fact, Gerald McKenny, *The Analogy of Grace: Karl Barth's Moral Theology* (Oxford: Oxford University Press, 2010) does it superbly. For a fuller analysis of Barth's theological ethics see McKenny's work. My intention in this chapter is to provide a basis to compare and contrast Barth and Balthasar on theological ethics.

goodness in the world, both within and without the church. The latter comes as a surprise to many, but it is one of the most important discussions Barth and Balthasar held over the years. They came to agreement that human agents do perform God's goodness, but the how of it remains a source of disagreement. If Barth's ethics potentially collapsed nature into grace, creating difficulties for *human* action in the realm of grace, and thus abandoning human action only to a realm of nature, Balthasar's ethics so emphasized mission and the evangelical counsels (poverty, celibacy, obedience) that it could lead to a valorization of sacrifice.

Another key difference between them is one they never resolved—what role does the church play in the human agency Christ makes possible? They differ on the following points. First, for Barth, election is of Christ and all are elected only in his election. Each Christian is equidistant from the Elect One. Balthasar's doctrine of election also finds election primarily in Christ, but some are elected to specific missions to live out obedience to him and nonidentically represent his life in ways others are not. Mary primarily fulfills this representation. She is the only person, except Jesus, whose idea and existence are united on earth, but others can approximate this unity, and the church's mission depends upon them. Second, for Balthasar, Christ and his church are differentiated, but they are one body; for Barth they are one body as well, but the Church is a form of Christ's earthly body such that it can never assume his unique singular agency into itself. Third, albeit related to the second point, Barth denounced the doctrine of the church as the prolongation of the incarnation as blasphemy. Balthasar's sense of mission depends upon that teaching. Fourth, Balthasar affirmed that some Christians were called to "go outside the camp," and be with Christ so that they become a sacrifice for others. Barth had little place for this repetition of sacrifice, even though he was open to monastic obedience, but for him, Christ alone was the prodigal Son who went into the far country. No one goes with him. Fifth, Barth always sharply distinguished justification and sanctification. The latter made no contribution to the former. Balthasar did not adhere to such a strong demarcation. Human merit in a state of grace contributed to salvation.

This chapter unfolds the above agreements and disagreements. It begins noting how Barth and Balthasar shared a sense of crisis and related it to ethics. They both addressed this crisis theologically. Theological doctrines are not somehow more particular and specific than putative universal ethical principles. Theology neither gains meaning nor justification because doctrines can be intelligible through ethics. Such a move is the modern crisis, its "anthropological reduction." For Barth and Balthasar theology, especially dogmatics, renders ethics intelligible, but they differed on which dogmas provide the context for ethics. Barth continues to suffer Catholicism by seeking to provide a Protestant dogmatics that can accomplish as much as a Catholic dogmatics, including an account of agency that is christological rather than mariological, an affirmation of evangelical counsels without their institutionalization, and an affirmation of Christ's victory that has ethical significance even if there were no church. Balthasar disagreed, and developed his own ethics accordingly.

The Crisis of Ethics: What Shall We Do?

Since his earliest work, Barth's theology was preoccupied with ethical matters. In fact, any account of Barth's theology that fails to acknowledge how tightly he wove dogma and ethics together, and the reason he did so, could only be viewed as woefully inadequate.[2] Early on, Barth recognized "ethics" could not address the crisis of modern theology. In fact ethics precipitated the crisis. Balthasar made a similar argument.

Prior to Barth's publication on Anselm (1931), he spent several summers putting together lectures on ethics (1928–1929). Those lectures, along with the 1927 *Die christliche Dogmatik*, are something of a template for what would then become the *Church Dogmatics*. Barth included whole portions of his lectures on ethics in the *Dogmatics*, sometimes with little revision. Barth never developed an independent ethics, but interspersed ethics throughout dogmatics, which is an important shift (or retrieval) that Barth produced within Christian theology. This shift is best characterized by his own words: "dogmatics is ethics."[3] Ethics is the affirmation of Christ's odd victory, declaring and witnessing to it. On December 12, 1930, Barth wrote a letter to Karl Stoevesand, in which he first noted his plan to develop a "five part work that includes an ethics dispersed over

2. I think this is one of the weaknesses in McCormack's interpretation of Barth, for all its strengths otherwise. It does not address sufficiently the ethical dimensions of Barth's theology, turning Barth's work primarily into a matter of addressing modern, epistemological concerns. Paul Nimmo and David Clough have corrected this by developing Barth's ethic within McCormack's "actualistic ontology." See Nimmo, *Being in Action: The Theological Shape of Barth's Ethical Vision* (London: T & T Clark, 2007) and Clough, *Ethics in Crisis* (Burlington, VT: Ashgate, 2005).

3. For two excellent accounts of this, see Gerald McKenny, *The Analogy of Grace: Karl Barth's Moral Theology*, especially chapter 3, "Dogmatics and Ethics," 122–66; and John Webster, *Barth's Moral Theology: Human Action in Barth's Thought* (Grand Rapids, MI: Eerdmans, 1998). Webster, more so than McKenny, finds a consistent emphasis on human action in Barth's moral theology. He also has a brief, but nuanced and persuasive, reading of Balthasar on Barth's ethics that recognizes the important place Balthasar finds for human agency in Barth. (*Barth's Moral Theology*, 14–15).

the doctrinal loci."[4] Since 1930, he envisioned a dogmatics that incorporated ethics across the loci. He began that project in all earnestness in 1931, but the foundations were laid in the 1920s, both in what Barth would reject and affirm. What shifted were the dogmatic loci within which ethics made sense.

DOGMATICS PLACING ETHICS IN CRISIS: "THE RIGHTEOUSNESS OF FAITH"

The central doctrine of Barth's theological ethics from his early to his later work can be found in the expression, "The Righteousness of Faith," or its correlate, "The Righteousness of God," which is also the title of one of his earliest essays (1916). In this work, God's righteousness primarily produces a "crisis" that calls into question any security we think we might find in ethics. The 1916 essay develops a theme that bears great similarity to Barth's work in his *Romans* commentaries. "Ethics" is how we protect ourselves from God's righteousness. We do so by building "towers," an obvious reference to the tower of Babel. Barth writes, "We are fundamentally fearful of the stream of God's righteousness which seeks entrance into our life and our world."[5] The first tower we build to ward off God's righteousness is the "righteousness of our morality." The second is "the righteousness of the state and of the law," followed by a third and fourth: "religious righteousness" and "civilization."[6] Through these towers, "we have made ourselves a god in our own image."[7] God's righteousness does not work in cooperation with these towers. It doesn't perfect or even correct them. "His Will is not a corrected continuation of our own. It approaches ours as a Wholly Other."[8] As we have seen, by the time Barth writes *Church Dogmatics* 2.1, he criticizes this language of the "wholly other," but here in this early essay, written only five years into his ten-year pastorate at Safenwil, Barth refers to God as "wholly other" in order to generate some important themes for his theological ethics, which are grounded in his dialectical approach. The most important of which is this: God's righteousness approaches us as a "wholly other," tearing down the towers we would build, especially by way of ethics, in order to secure ourselves from that righteousness.

---

4. Cited in Gerhard Sauter, "Vorwort zur Neuausgabe," in Barth, *Die christliche Dogmatik*, ed. Gerhard Sauter (Zurich: Theologischer Zurich, 1982), xvi.

5. Barth, "The Righteousness of God," in *The Word of God and the Word of Man*, trans. Douglas Horton (Gloucester, MA: Peter Smith, 1978), 16.

6. Barth, "The Righteousness of God," 17–19, 22. These "towers" bear a resemblance to the "high places" Barth will tear down by virtue of "God's righteousness" in the 1922 *Romans* commentary.

7. Barth, "The Righteousness of God," 22.

8. Ibid.

This central theme has the following correlates, which return again and again in different variations in Barth's work:

> 1. Dogma and ethics approach each other under a "crisis," where the former undoes, and establishes, the latter.
> 2. Ethics is placed under the doctrinal loci of the Reformation's doctrine of predestination, "justification by faith alone," and God's sovereign freedom. At first this sovereignty is God's freedom to be "wholly other." Later it will be God's freedom to love, defined by God's Triunity.
> 3. Once Barth situates ethics within the doctrine of the Trinity, then rather than evacuating theological ethics of all content, of all goodness, truth, and beauty, the crisis of ethics has a salutary purpose: the inculcation in human creatures of faith, hope, and charity.

Perhaps the most controversial of the above three statements is the third. For the "crisis" in Barth's early ethics raises the question whether he is able to offer a positive theological ethic at all.[9] Does his theological ethics do anything other than tear down previous towers?[10] God confronts us as a sovereign, apocalyptic

---

9. Webster demonstrates how this was an early and consistent criticism of Barth, which he finds inadequate. See *Barth's Moral Theology*, 11–39.

10. Paul Nimmo would suggest as much. He interprets Barth's statement "dogma is ethics" within McCormack's actualistic ontology. "In the actualistic context of the command of God, all previous answers to the ethical question are seen to be relativized and cannot provide a knowledge of the current will and command of God." Nimmo concedes Barth never used the term "actualistic ontology." Nimmo, *Being in Action*, 5, 65. David Clough argues something quite similar to Nimmo. Instead of moving away from crisis and dialectic as Balthasar suggested Barth did, Clough also follows McCormack in finding continuity in Barth from *Romans* on. In so doing Clough, calls for an ethics that admits of a "permanent crisis" where "God's self-revelation in Jesus Christ puts all that we think we know in question." In fact, "grace destroys all human answers to the ethical question, yet ethical reflection of any kind may witness to the divine command." Clough argues that even Jesus' humanity and divinity must be understood dialectically. This dialectical rendering of the incarnation has ethical consequences. We never arrive at a unity of ethical action between God and creatures. He writes, "If we want to affirm both that Jesus Christ was divine and that he was human, and if we accept that there is a contradiction in affirming both at the same time, then the divine/human nature of Christ is dialectical as I am using the term." But that account of dialectics is precisely the problem Balthasar argued Barth had to overcome if he were to think consistently about what mattered, the incarnation. The mystery of Christian faith declares that Christ is divine and human "without contradiction." To turn it into a contradiction rejects what mattered most to Balthasar and Barth—the hypostatic union. Clough acknowledges that Barth's ethics was an "ethics in crisis" which had two poles: the "crisis of the possibility of theology in the face of a God who cannot be comprehended by us," and the crisis of German theology at the beginning of the twentieth century in the face of Nazism. He also recognizes Barth largely left the "crisis" found in his *Romans* commentary behind him once he discovered "the absence of crisis in the work of Anselm." Clough, however, argues

power, whose actions yesterday bear little to no continuity with today or tomorrow such that ethical norms could be trusted. There is no stable, unified relationship between divinity and humanity capable of generating faith, hope, and love as a human activity.[11] As we have seen, Balthasar raised this very question about the early, cacophonous Barth. He found Barth moving beyond it, and one path through that movement was the inadequacy of Barth's early theology as it bore on ethics.

Barth's initial approach appears to make ethical action almost impossible. Barth repeatedly asks the question, "What shall we do?," but in his early work he is much better at asking it and having it elicit a crisis than he is at answering it. The radicality of his work should not be underplayed. From the 1920s into the 1940s, the crisis of ethics calls nearly every distinction between good and evil into question. As Balthasar noted, his position nearly capitulates to Nietzsche. We cannot distinguish Moses from Pharoah, Judas from St. Peter, St. Francis from Caesar Borgia.[12] In its early stages, the crisis seems to bear the mark of Ockham's razor; what is good is what God wills and we are never assured of that until God wills it. A better theological ethics emerges as Barth reorders election within the doctrine of God; then this seminominalist approach changes. Hope and love become genuine human actions, something Barth explicitly acknowledged he was unable to do justice to in his early work, but which he develops in his *Doctrine of Reconciliation*. Barth came a long way in answering the crisis ethics produced for Christianity, but his initial analysis of that crisis was profound. It was an analysis that stemmed from a question posed to him.

In September 1922, for a ministers' conference at Wiesbaden, Barth was given the topic, "The Problem of Ethics Today." Barth sees the "problem" as a

we should not leave this crisis behind, and in fact Barth did not, despite his words to the contrary. Barth moves away from "crisis" or "crisis theology" but not "from the reality of crisis or from its consequences." Thus there is no move from dialectic to analogy, and as McCormack notes, "here as elsewhere Barth is not the best interpreter of his own development." Clough obviously seeks to take us back to the Barth of the 1920s. For this reason, he dismisses what he calls Balthasar's "tidy narrative." See Clough, *Ethics in Crisis*, xi–xiii, 45, 58, 64.

11. I agree with Gerald McKenny, who makes the following judgment about the second edition of *Romans*: "Barth fails to solve the problem of ethics at this stage because the unremitting eschatological tension he maintains between the vertical and the horizontal renders it impossible to make intelligible the sanctification of human conduct on the horizontal line." *The Analogy of Grace*, 53.

12. On the distinction between Moses and Pharaoh, see *The Epistle to the Romans*, trans. Edwyn C. Hoskyns (London: Oxford University Press, 1968), 401; for Judas, see *Romans*, 391, and *Church Dogmatics* 2.2, trans. J. C. Campbell et al., ed. G. W. Bromiley and T. F. Torrance (Edinburgh: T & T Clark, 1958), 459–82; for St. Francis and Borgia, see *Romans*, 288.

crisis. This crisis is, in fact, the crisis of Western culture, and in particular that of liberal Protestantism. Barth finds it no longer credible. It substituted ethics for dogmatics, thinking that the former was the heart of Christianity. Ethics meant the continuation of progress and civilization, of "our" Western culture. The crucial question was if philosophy or theology would best advance it. Barth writes, "Fundamentally, it was a matter not of asking *what* to do, as if that were not known, but rather of finding out whether philosophy or theology, Kant or Schleiermacher, provided the more illuminating formula for the obvious—for it was obvious that what to do was to further this infinitely imperfect but infinitely perfectible culture."[13] Here is the context for Barth's ethical question: "What shall we do?," and the crisis it generated. It emerged when that "infinitely perfectible culture" collapses. Crisis originates the question.[14] We no longer know what to do. Neither Kant nor Schleiermacher provides an adequate answer to help us know how to go on. The fact that we must now ask, "What shall we do?" means something significant has changed. "Our" ethics no longer works. Barth states this explicitly,

> But since Christianity is now proved impossible as an *ethic*, or rather, since the ways of European man are now proved impossible in relation to the *ethic* of Christianity, we are faced with a need and placed before questions which make us think that the difficult asseverations of the Christian dogma of the old style correspond far more closely to the actual situation than does our predecessors' confident assertion that "following Jesus" is a simple task.[15]

What does it mean for Barth to claim in 1922 that "the difficult asseverations of the Christian dogma of the old style" fit the "actual situation" better than a Christian ethics of simply following Jesus? Is this a call to return to dogmatic theology grounded in the life of the church, so that the emphasis is on the "Christian dogma of the old style"? Or does Barth recognize modernity has stalled and needs revisions, but it is still sound?

Broadly speaking, answers can be divided between two interpretations. On the one hand is the modernist interpretation of Barth by Trutz Rendtorff and the Munich school. Although he and Balthasar greatly differ in many ways, they both see Barth as engaging modernity, albeit with vastly different

---

13. "The Problem of Ethics Today" in *The Word of God and the Word of Man*, trans. Douglas Horton (Gloucester, MA: Peter Smith, 1978), 145.

14. Ibid., 139.

15. "Ibid.," 148. Emphasis original.

consequences. Rendtorff and Balthasar would agree Barth opposes an unsavory aspect of modernity: *Der Titanismus des Menschen.*[16] They would agree that Barth avoids an "anthropological reduction." However, Rendtorff finds Barth completing modernity more so than working an alternative within it. Where they would disagree is the relation between modernity and antiquity in Barth. For Rendtorff, Barth is the first one in "theological history" to pursue theology "completely under the conditions of autonomy." On the other hand, we have the position of Balthasar. For him, Barth retrieves a version of metaphysical realism against modern elements that would deny it, precisely by offering a theological aesthetics.[17] This aesthetics should have had its moment in a "distinctively *Christian* glory of God," but was thwarted by the metaphysics of the late Middle Ages. For Balthasar, Barth's theology represents an alternative Christian modernity that had deep resonances with Christian antiquity. It was an advance over Christian antiquity because its religious aesthetics is decidedly christological.

Why such disparity in interpretations of Barth? Much of the problem can be laid at Barth's feet, especially the early dialectical Barth, when he called into question—without truly affirming—the goodness of creation. The problem arises because of the different dogmatic loci through which Barth intersperses ethics. First the dogmatic locus for ethics was a quasi-Reformed doctrine of predestination, but eventually it became his profound reordering of the doctrinal loci noted in the previous chapter. Once that reordering occurs, we find Barth explicitly revising how faith, hope, and love operate as human actions, something he admits his early work could not do.

---

16. For an important discussion of this modern Prometheanism, and Barth's relationship to it, see Anthony Baker, *Diagonal Advance* (Eugene, OR: Cascade, 2011), 20, 31–34, 204.

17. Balthasar's position finds support in Barth's *The Theology of the Reformed Confessions*, where he affirms the Reformers against Schleiermacher and the modern emphasis on the *ordo salutis* in a satiric statement: "The dark night of objectivism in which the Reformers, under the weight of medieval tradition, had still remarkably enough remained, now begins to fade, and gradually, from very far away, the pleasant morning of that day dawns on which Schleiermacher, that self-styled 'Moravian of a higher order,' will discover, as the actual finisher of that work began by Luther, that the essence of theology is the analysis of pious self-consciousness. This will be the day on which the Erlangen theologian will compose the statement that defines at least two centuries of theology: 'I, the Christian, am the most appropriate content of my science as a theologian.'" *The Theology of the Reformed Confessions,* trans. Darrell L. Guder and Judith J. Guder (Louisville: Westminster John Knox Press, 2002), 140. I am indebted to Christopher Ganski for this quote. See his unpublished dissertation, "Spirit and Flesh: On the Significance of the Reformed Doctrine of the Lord's Supper for Pneumatology" (PhD diss., Marquette University, 2011).

Barth never abandons the crisis the question, "What shall we do?" raises. We not only find it in 1922, but also two decades later, when he publishes *Church Dogmatics* 2.2.[18] The "good" is still a "problem." We do not know what to do, and so all the good does is raise the question, "What shall we do?" Once this question gets raised, it calls everything else into question. The question witnesses God's wrath against us, but God's wrath is always also God's righteousness, and that for Barth is the early solution to the problem of ethics. Dogmatics subordinates ethics, but the dogma that does so in this early phase is almost exclusively justification by faith, understood in terms of predestination. As long as that dogma addresses the crisis, human action in the realm of grace is impossible. Faith, love, and hope are only God's works, never ours. Although Barth changes in the 1950s and argues faith, love, and hope are human actions, the reason why he refused this early on should be noted. It was autobiographical.

In his 1922 essay, "The Problem of Ethics Today," Barth argued theologians thought ethics was "easy" while dogmatics was "difficult." The Sermon on the Mount represents ethics, and *Romans* dogmatics.[19] This argument is telling, in that a decade earlier it was Barth himself who played the ethics of the Sermon on the Mount against Christian dogmatics, and argued the former rather than the latter defined authentic Christianity. On December 17, 1911, his first year in the pastorate at Safenwil, he gave a controversial lecture entitled "Jesus Christ and the Movement for Social Justice" for the *Arbeitverein Safenwil* (Safenwil Labor Association). That lecture appealed to the Sermon on the Mount as a central answer to the relationship between Jesus and social justice. Christians must be socialists, Barth asserts, because socialism alone fits the Gospel. He wrote,

> One can only be continually amazed if one realizes how easily Christianity of all confessions and types has glossed over these words, while it has often been so zealously strict and precise in dogmatic questions which had no meaning in the life of Jesus. Jesus rejected the concept of private property; of that, it seems to me, there can

18. "The problem of the good calls in question all actual and possible *forms* of human conduct, all temporal *happenings* in the history both of the individual and of society. *What* ought we to do? is our question; and this *what*, infiltrating and entrenching itself everywhere, directs its attack against all that we did yesterday and shall do tomorrow." Barth, "The Problem of Ethics Today," 139. "If the What? is seriously meant, every answer that we and others may have given is continually questioned again" (*Church Dogmatics*, 2.2, 645).

19. Barth, "The Problem of Ethics Today," 147.

be no doubt. He rejected precisely the principle that what's mine is mine.[20]

A decade later, Barth questions the assumption that we can adopt the Sermon on the Mount apart from the "dogmatic questions" that in 1911 he claimed were irrelevant to Jesus' life. His 1922 claim that "the difficult asservations of the Christian dogma of the old style" fit the "actual situation" better than ethics gains clarity of meaning when read against the 1911 essay. Barth made the reverse argument in 1911: the ethics of following Jesus in the Sermon on the Mount is more important than dogmatics. The 1922 essay is a self-correction that did not stop in 1922 but culminated in his statement, "dogmatics is ethics." In order to get there, he had to first call ethics into question.

DOGMATICS IS ETHICS: PREDESTINATION, GOD'S "WHOLLY OTHER" FREEDOM AND JUSTIFICATION BY FAITH

Barth's later claim "dogmatics is ethics" never dispensed with the ethical and thus political task; it is no rupture with Barth's political and ethical concerns at Safenwil, but the relation between theology and ethics shifts.[21] First, he rejects that ethics is what allows theology to matter in everyday life. Then he begins situating ethics within diverse dogmas. In the 1922 lecture, Barth explicitly locates ethics within the doctrine of predestination. We see this in a statement that is programmatic for his work in this decade when he wrote,

> The ethical problem undeniably brings us to the reality of God—that is to say the *judgment* of God. . . . We count upon God's *grace*. But it is not our own! *Everything* depends upon that grace. But we do not bring it into being by any magic turn of our dialectic. He *is* and he *remains free:* else he were not God. "Therefore hath he mercy on whom he *will* have mercy and whom he will he *hardeneth*." From the summit of the Pauline *dialectic* this is all we can really see—the landscape of an eternal *predestination* which stretches out not only toward redemption but in the opposite direction as well.[22]

20. Karl Barth, "Jesus Christ and the Movement for Social Justice," in George Hunsinger, *Karl Barth and Radical Politics* (Philadelphia: Westminster Press, 1976), 31.

21. It may very well, however, have been a rupture with his liberal training at Marburg. Helmut Gollwitzer saw the rupture with Marburg in the unity of Barth's dogma and ethics. Helmut Gollwitzer, "Kingdom of God and Socialism in the Theology of Karl Barth," in *Karl Barth and Radical Politics*, 85.

22. Barth, "The Problem of Ethics Today," 178. Emphasis original.

Here we see the first of Barth's various dogmatic turns. The dogmas that subordinate ethics in 1922 are predestination, God's wholly other freedom, and justification by faith through grace. Because ethics collapses, dogma returns, but at this point in his work, the dogmas that return contain seminominalist hues, which is why we cannot distinguish Moses from Pharoah, Judas from St. Peter, St. Francis from Caesar Borgia. Each is who they are because of God's activity: either God grants mercy or God hardens hearts. The realm within which ethics matters is the "landscape of an eternal *predestination*."

This seminominalistic inability to distinguish good from evil haunts Barth's theological ethics throughout the early *Dogmatics* as well. However, after he revises the doctrine of predestination, then a Trinitarian theology that recognizes God's freedom is the freedom to love replaces this early seminominalistic theology. Once freedom, like election, finds its fulfillment in Jesus Christ, then love, hope, and faith provide continuity to the Christian moral life. They give it its form. Ethics is no longer only a crisis.

DOGMATICS IS ETHICS: CHRISTOLOGY

Between 1922 and 1942, the dogma by which Barth subordinates ethics gradually changed to a much more substantive Christology. The 1928 lectures on ethics reveal this change. Both the 1928 and the 1942 sections on ethics, like the 1922 essay, assume the central role of "Command as the Decision of God." But how the command works shifts; it becomes less seminominalist and voluntarist. In the 1928 lectures, Barth begins his discussion of the "Revelation of the Command of God" with the proposition: "Die Wahrheit des Guten ist keine allgemeine und theoretische und darum keine bedingte Wahrheit. Sie offenbart sich in dem konkreten Ereignis unseres eigenen Handelns als unsere Entscheidung für oder gegen das uns gegebene Gebot des Guten. [The truth of God is no general and theoretical and therefore no conditioned truth. It is revealed in the concrete event of our own action as our decision for or against the command of the good given to us]."[23] The proposition that begins a similar discussion in the 1942 *Church Dogmatics* 2.2 is also entitled, "The Command as the Decision of God," but its opening proposition has now changed: "Indem uns Gott in Jesus Christus gnädig ist, ist sein Gebot die souveräne, bestimmte und gute Entscheidung über den Charakter unsres Tuns: die Entscheidung, der wir immer herkommen, unter der wir immer stehen und der wir immer entgegen gehen.[As God is gracious to us in Jesus Christ, his commandment is

23. *Ethik* 1: *Vorlesung Münster, Sommersemester 1928, wiederholt in Bonn, Sommersemester 1930*, ed. Dietrich Braun (Zurich: Theologischer Zurich, 1973) 103.

the sovereign, exact, and good decision concerning the character of our action: the decision from which we always come forth, under which we always stand and to which we are always going.]"[24] Note that both propositions emphasize "decision" (*Entscheidung*), but whereas the 1928 emphasis is on "our decision" and "our action," the emphasis in 1942 is on "the good decision concerning the character of our actions, the decision from which we always come forth." In 1928 we are "for or against" (*für oder gegen*) the command, but this voluntarism gives way in 1942 to a more positive approach. We come forth from the decision, stand under it and come to meet it. It still stands against us, but not with the voluntarist sense of a choice for or against it. The command, now located even more firmly in the election of Christ, constitutes our actions more thoroughly than it did in 1928. However, far from making human actions less significant, the more Barth emphasized Christ's action on our behalf, the more he also emphasized human action. It is not an either-or.

Barth's God is always the commanding God, but in 1928, much like in 1922, God commands outside the divine economy.[25] We find no reference to Jesus, only to the individual believer who stands before a decision, not knowing what it is God commands. Such an ethical structure cannot distinguish between Moses and Pharaoh. Each can be considered doing what was commanded. Nor does it need Jesus; it only needs will. But in 1942 God's command no longer bears this generic, seminominalist stamp. God's graciousness in Jesus gives the command its shape. We see this in the different understandings of "claim" (*Anspruch, Inanspruchnahme*) Barth set forth in 1928 and 1942. These terms are central for Barth's ethics and reveal another important continuity. From 1928 to 1942, God "claims" the human creature, but how it occurs becomes much more christologically determined.[26] In 1928, theological ethics is conceived under

24. *Church Dogmatics* 2.2, 701.

25. The emphasis on God's command is no abstract "divine command ethics"; it is a christological ethics that incorporates human action within it by participation. The concrete specificity of Jesus eventually defines ethics, not the naked will of a commanding deity.

26. Notice the different propositions that begin the common section, "The Way of Theological Ethics," present in the 1928 *Ethik* lectures and the 1942 *Church Dogmatics* 2.2. 1928 *Ethik*: "Die Aufgabe der theologischen Ethik besteht in der Darstellung der Inanspruchnahme des Menschen durch das Wort Gottes." (German 74; English, *Ethics*, ed. Dietrich Braun, trans. Geoffrey W. Bromiley [New York: Seabury Press, 1981], 45). 1942 *Church Dogmatics* 2.2: "Die Ethik als Lehre Gottes Gebot erklärt das Gesetz als die Gestalt des Evangeliums, d. h. als die Norm des dem Menschen durch den ihn erwählenden Gott widerfahrende Heiligung. Sie ist darum in der Erkenntnis Jesu Christi begründet, weil dieser der heilige Gott und der geheiligte Mensch in Einem ist. Sie gehört darum zur Lehre Gott, weil der den Menschen für sich in Anspruch nehmende Gott eben damit in ursprünglicher Weise sich selbst für diesen verantwortlich macht. Ihre Funktion besteht in der grundlegenden Bezeugung der Gnade Gottes, sofern

dogma as "the claiming [*Inanspruchnahme*] of man through the Word of God." As Balthasar rightly noted, the later Barth replaced the "Word of God" with the concrete specificity of Jesus, noting his two natures in a single acting Subject. In 1942, Barth's theology has become much more christologically specific in its "claim" on human agency. The "claiming" remains *(in Anspruch nehmende)*, but the hypostatic union has become the source for it ("weil dieser der heilige Gott und der geheiligte Mensch in Einem ist [Because Jesus Christ is the holy God and sanctified man in one]"). God and humanity are not dialectically related in Jesus; they are one. This unity has profound ethical implications, for it is the source for ethics. Ethics is subsumed under the doctrine of God, which is why Barth placed it in the doctrine of God in *Church Dogmatics* 2.2. In so doing, Barth does not diminish human or philosophical ethics, but locates ethics within creation and redemption understood through the Triune processions and missions. He poses a question, a question Balthasar heard and addressed:, In what other realm would it be possible to pursue ethics for a Christian theologian?

ETHICS AND THE "ANTHROPOLOGICAL REDUCTION"

In the previous chapter, I argued Barth reordered dogmatics so that it expressed more fully the divine economy. Balthasar recognized the profound significance of this reordering. Both Reformed orthodoxy and neoscholasticism had not adequately expressed the divine economy in their account of ethics, because they assumed an abstract god of power who existed behind the Triune God manifested in the economy of salvation. For Reformed orthodoxy this god was the god of will who commanded the eternal decrees prior to the divine economy. The ethical counterpart of such a god would be something like the divine command theory. But of course Christology is not necessary for such an ethics; all that is necessary is a commanding will. Likewise the ethical counterpart of a god known through pure nature would be natural law, and of course Christology is unnecessary for that ethics as well.[27] Both Reformed orthodoxy and neoscholastic natural law would meet the requirements of universalizability in the context of the Enlightenment's "anthropological

---

diese des Menschen heilsame Bindung und Verpflichtung ist." (German, *Die kirchliche Dogmatik* 2.2 (Zürich: Theologischer Verlag Zürich, 1948), 564; English, 509).

27. McKenny recognizes that Barth, like Troeltsch, found the difficulty of the modern as "self-assertion" in the lingering effects of a Stoic natural law that neglected the christological reordering of nature (*Analogy of Grace*, 79). As we shall see below, Balthasar made the same argument, explicitly affirming Troeltsch.

reduction." They pose no challenge to it. Barth and Balthasar's ethics challenged that reduction. They saw the crisis.

Balthasar, like Barth, recognized that Kant's dominance on modern theology tempted it to an "anthropological reduction," a reduction that often substituted ethics for theology. Balthasar presented his account of the crisis in his important work, *Love Alone Is Credible*. Here Balthasar argued that Barth both stands within modernity and beyond it. He stands within it because like Kant he critiques reason and metaphysics in order to make room for faith. Balthasar recognizes, however, that it is a specific historical portrayal of reason that concerns Barth. After Kant, reason gets cordoned off from theology, and in turn philosophy reduces it to anthropological control. For this reason, Barth was correct to recognize reason's dangers. Barth was also correct to recognize that God and creatures cannot "share a common language" that would allow them direct access to God. Only God's "personal self-disclosure" makes that possible. Barth, however, takes this too far when he rejects the *analogia entis*. Balthasar states, "But it would have sufficed for his purpose (as it has in this study so far) simply to reject the *reduction* of revelation to a prior understanding of God's existence on the basis of reason, i.e. to an understanding of 'the divine.'"[28] Like Barth, Balthasar rejects Kant's reduction of theology to ethics, but he thinks it can be countered without abandoning the *analogia entis*. He agrees with Barth that modernity precipitates a crisis in the relationship between theology and ethics. There is a dialectical moment, but Balthasar denies the crisis must remain permanent.

Barth and Balthasar shared a desire not to make the modern move of reducing theology to ethics, while at the same time recognizing dogmatics entails the theory and practice of good human action. Both accomplished this by avoiding "the anthropological reduction" Kant brought about.[29] Frederick Bauerschmidt identifies this reduction as the "relocation of religion in the realm of practical reason." For Kant, doctrines are meaningless unless they have practical relevance; only his moral proof for God remained after his first critique, presumably calling into question all other proofs—especially the ontological proof. As we have seen, in his Anselm book Barth explicitly rejected any claim that Kant destroyed all metaphysical proofs for the existence of God. For Barth, Kant critiques Descartes, but does not touch Anselm. Rather than rendering doctrines intelligible by showing their practical import, Barth rendered ethics intelligible via their dogmatic import. He reverses Kant. To a

---

28. Balthasar, *Love Alone is Credible*, trans. D. C. Schindler (San Francisco: Ignatius, 2004), 34–36, 48–49. Emphasis original.

29. Ibid., 31–37. The original, *Glaubhaft ist nur Liebe*, was published in 1963.

large extent, Balthasar followed. His entire trilogy works against Kant's three critiques by reversing the transcendentals. In Kant's three critiques truth comes first, especially as epistemology. He first determines our epistemic limits, and only then can ethics, religion, and aesthetics be pursued. They are pursued within those limits. Balthasar reverses this process and shatters those limits. He begins with aesthetics (God's "glory"), which issues in action through the "theodrama" and only then do we explain the "logic" of it all. For Balthasar, theology does not begin in ethics or practical reason; nor must theology become postmetaphysical because "pure reason" has rendered contemplation and speculation meaningless. This Kantian reversal makes both Barth and Balthasar unusual modern theologians. They both recognized that *ethics* was the modern temptation.

Frederick Bauerschmidt explains well how the anthropological reduction can be avoided and ethics nonetheless accomplished. He agrees with Barth and Balthasar on the temptation of ethics, and then asks, "But should we draw from these criticisms the lesson that the doctrine of the Trinity has nothing to do with how we lead our lives—that it has no pragmatic value?"[30] He asks, in other words, does every practical rendering of dogma repeat the anthropological reduction? It is the right question. [31] Both Barth and Balthasar provide compelling answers to that question.

A Theological Nature: Faith, Hope, and Love

After 1942, Barth no longer subordinates ethics to a doctrine of predestination that came prior to Trinity. The doctrine of election is placed within the doctrine of God and given christological form. Now God's command provides more continuity by which necessary ethical distinctions between Moses and Pharaoh can be made. Barth is already headed in the direction of a "formed reference" so important in *Church Dogmatics* 3.4. In 1942, in *Church Dogmatics* 2.2, he writes, "And this present decision stands in unbroken continuity with all my earlier decisions."[32] How can we make sense of this continuity in the

---

30. Bauerschmidt, unpublished essay, 6, an earlier version of "Theo-Drama and Political Theology," *Communio: International Catholic Review* 25 (1998): 532–52.

31. Bauerschmidt answers "no" by turning, in part, to Balthasar's theodrama. It points in the proper direction, although Bauerschmidt argues Balthasar failed to pursue this answer as he should have. Bauerschmidt, "Theo-Drama and Political Theology," 537. Like Bauerschmidt, Kevin Mongrain recognizes Balthasar avoids the anthropological reduction a focus on praxis often brings. However, contra Bauerschmidt, Mongrain does not find Balthasar's political theology inadequate. Kevin Mongrain, *The Systematic Theology of Hans Urs von Balthasar: An Irenaean Retrieval* (New York: Crossroads, 2002), 218–20.

midst of crisis? Proposition §38 in *Church Dogmatics* 2.2 shows how: "we always originate . . . from God's decision in Jesus Christ." Jesus provides the continuity, but it is a continuity he communicates to creation. Barth now emphasizes this communication in answering the question, "What ought we to *do*?" "God's decision as it is really embodied in Him is a sovereign decision. It characterizes not only our conduct but our asking what we ought to do as a responsible decision. . . . It is not in vain that Jesus Christ is King and Victor."[33] The latter statement is important for Barth's future development of his theme, "dogmatics is ethics." Christ's kingship is one of his three offices Barth correlates to the three theological virtues, faith, hope, and love in his *Doctrine of Reconciliation*. As Barth accomplishes this correlation, he intensifies the importance of creaturely ethical action. Christ gives creatures ethical continuity because he gives creatures ethical agency. Here is where Barth and Balthasar agree. Where they will disagree is on the importance of Mary and the church for that agency, and Barth devotes an entire volume of the *Church Dogmatics* to displaying that difference (as will be discussed below).

The continuity of creaturely action is found in the "formed reference" in Barth's 1951 *Church Dogmatics* 3.4, to which he explicitly appeals when he explains the "fruitfulness" of considering dogmatics as ethics:

> The relationship or unity of ethics with dogmatics must now be made fruitful in this respect—fruitful in the question of what persists in the events of the divine command and human action, and therefore of what permits but also commands us to make the reference to these events as a formed reference, and in so doing to venture a true special ethics.[34]

The fruitfulness of setting ethics within dogmatics is found in "human action." When Barth explains this fruitfulness, we find language similar to that used in the *Ethics* lectures and *Church Dogmatics* 2.2. He states, "Two factors constitute these events in all cases." The "primary and dominant" is "God with His claim [*Anspruch*] upon man, with His decision and judgment concerning him." The "second" is "man, who is distinguished as such from God even as an active subject, who is confronted by Him, with whom God is much concerned in this event, who in his action as a free subject is plainly treated with utter seriousness

---

32. *Church Dogmatics* 2.2, 659.

33. Ibid., 2.2, 660.

34. *Church Dogmatics* 3.4, trans. A. T. Mackay, et al., ed. G. W. Bromiley and T. F. Torrance (Edinburgh: T & T Clark, 1957), 23.

by God."[35] The claim of God on the human creature is, as Barth already told us in *Church Dogmatics* 2.2, first and foremost a christological claim. Christ's obedience is characterized by faith, hope, and love. He then produces an agent "formed" by faith, hope, and love. The continuity of creaturely ethics resides in God's election of humanity in Christ, which will form the pattern for Barth's doctrine of reconciliation in *Church Dogmatics* 4. That election has ontological significance. A "new being" is made possible, in and outside the church, which can act through a nature theologically formed by faith, hope, and love.

Barth did not just happen upon faith, hope, and love in his *Church Dogmatics*. Since 1922, they were central to the question, "What should we do?"[36] Notice however, how radically Barth's account of faith changes from 1922 to his 1958 *Church Dogmatics* 4.2. In the 1922 essay, "The Problem of Ethics," he wrote,

> Faith and revelation expressly deny that there is any way from man to God and to God's grace, love and life. Both words indicate that the only way between God and man is that which leads *from* God *to* man. Between these words—and this is the inner kernel of the theology of Paul and the Reformation—there are two other words: *Jesus Christ*. These two are also dialectical. They were for Paul himself.[37]

If this were all Barth had to say about faith, he would have been incapable of affirming any analogy between Christ's faith and creaturely agency. In the 1958 *Church Dogmatics* 4.2, Barth revises this and admits a change has occurred. Now there is a way from creatures to God, which makes faith, hope, and love give more form to human agency. He states, "There is not only a way of God to man. Because there is a way of God downward to man, there is also a way of man upward to God."[38] For the early Barth faith, hope, and love form a Christian ethics because they maintain the only direction possible: from God to

---

35. Ibid.

36. The "virtues" of faith, hope, and love were always central in Barth's ethics; sometimes he referred to them as virtues and sometimes as "equivalents" to a virtue ethic. In his 1928 lectures, he wrote, "Thus faith, love, and hope are the good in human conduct and are therewith the answer of theological ethics to the ethical question—the goal that we have to reach in this last development of our thinking. Understood with a pinch of salt, this is our equivalent of teaching about 'virtues'" (*Ethics*, 61).

37. "The Problem of Ethics Today," 180.

38. *Church Dogmatics*, 4.2, trans. Geoffrey W. Bromiley, ed. G. W. Bromiley and T. F. Torrance (Edinburgh: T & T Clark, 1958), 118.

the human creature. Once he emphasizes the hypostatic union and recognizes that God's freedom is not the arbitrary freedom of the "eternal decrees," but the "freedom to love," faith, hope, and love take on a more human form.[39] He sees that the unity of divinity and humanity in Christ requires a unity of "good action" that allows these virtues to have a human form and a new direction from creatures to God, which is best seen in volume four of the *Church Dogmatics*.[40]

Barth's *Doctrine of Reconciliation* (volume 4 of *Church Dogmatics*) laid out a threefold structure correlating Christology, ethics, justification, and sanctification. These themes are not new, but they take on a new form. In fact, even more than *Church Dogmatics* 2.2 and 3.4, *Church Dogmatics* 4 offers a profound theological ethics interspersed throughout dogmatic loci. These volumes brought together key themes in Reformed theology that other theologians rendered asunder: the threefold office of Christ, his states, his Person and Work, and the theological virtues. Barth weaved them together such that each theme depended upon the other. He offered a "theodrama" that resisted any Scholastic categorization of the "pieces" of Christology or any modern division of theological labor between systematics and ethics. His *Doctrine of Reconciliation* was not a Nestorian distinction between humanity and divinity, but a lively presentation of what God has done in its unity, which is "reconciliation." Barth expressed this through a repeating triadic form, which his translator Bromily indicated:

4.1: Christ's priestly work: "very God humbling himself to reconcile," Christ's descent confronts our pride (justification), and produces faith.
4.2: Christ's kingly work: "very man exalted and reconciled," Christ's ascent confronts our sloth (sanctification), and produces love.

---

39. This can be seen developing throughout the *Church Dogmatics*. In *Church Dogmatics* 2.2, Barth discusses God's freedom as the freedom to love in the context of an explicit argument against the nominalist *potentia absoluta*: "Even if the concept freedom is filled out by that of love, it makes no essential difference, unless by both concepts we understand the one decisive thing: that the true God is the One whose freedom and love have nothing to do with abstract absoluteness or naked sovereignty, but who in His love and freedom has determined and limited Himself to be God in particular and not in general, and only as such to be omnipotent and sovereign and the possessor of all other perfections" (*Church Dogmatics*, 2.2, 249). Then he states, "The mere fact of ruling with infinite power in an infinite sphere does not make God the divine Ruler, for that is the very thing which He does not do" (*Church Dogmatics*, 2.2, 250). In *Church Dogmatics*, 4.1, he emphasizes that God is not "wholly Other." Such a description is "untenable and corrupt and pagan." God is "the one who is free in His love, and therefore not His own prisoner." (*Church Dogmatics* 4.1, trans. Geoffrey W. Bromiley, ed. G. W. Bromiley and T. F. Torrance [Edinburgh: T & T Clark, 1956], 195).

40. *Church Dogmatics* 3.4, 3.

4.3: Christ's prophetic work: "God-man, guaranteeing and attesting reconciliation," Christ is our sanctification producing hope.[41]

Early on in Barth's development of Christ's priestly work in *Church Dogmatics* 4.1, he pointed to the theological virtues as decisive in the incarnation. "God with us" always includes "in all seriousness a 'We with God.'" We are not "mere spectators," gazing upon the divine drama, for it necessarily opens up to us "the one true possibility of our own being."[42] What is this "one true possibility"? The answer to this question is as important for what it is not as for what it is. It is not epistemology. Barth explicitly rejects epistemology as the central issue in Christology; instead it is a question of ontology—the new *being*. God with us is grounded in the truth of what the particular person Jesus Christ accomplished.[43] It is the history of this concrete person who goes by this name. "Jesus" is not a principle by which creatures can answer epistemological questions. Barth wrote, "If it were a principle and not a name indicating a person, we should have to describe it as the epistemological principle of the message."[44] Once the name of Jesus is reduced to epistemology, it becomes nothing more than the "recitation of a myth."[45] Instead, Jesus offers an ontology—"The one true possibility of our own being." When he answers the question what constitutes the "one true possibility" of our being, Barth defines it in terms of the theological virtues. "This 'We with God' enclosed in the 'God with us' is Christian faith, Christian love and Christian hope."[46] This ontology is the healing of human nature God works in the incarnation through Christ's obedience, via faith, hope, and love.[47] Only in the single acting subject of Jesus does the fullness of God and humanity dwell in such a unity that we see what human nature truly is. A decisive note has already been struck early in his doctrine of reconciliation, one that will be played over and again throughout the volumes: the form "God with us" takes in human ethical agency is faith, hope, and love.

41. G. W. Bromiley, "Editor's Preface" to *Church Dogmatics*, 4.1, vii.

42. *Church Dogmatics*, 4.1, 14.

43. Ibid., 17. Barth explains "God with us" thus: "It is truth as it derives from this name [Jesus Christ] and as it points to it, and only so."

44. Ibid.

45. Ibid., 21.

46. Ibid., 15.

47. Although Barth uses the language of virtue early on when he describes the "new being" Christ effects (Ibid., 9), he warns against pursuing ethics with the theological *virtues* qua *virtues*. The reason for this is simple. Virtues, he thinks, can be known outside of Christ; faith, hope, and love cannot. This is what makes them the "one true possibility" for human being. Ibid., 3–4.

In setting this forth Barth takes up an old charge Brunner once leveled against him. For Barth, Brunner suggested, "God is everything" and "man is nothing." Barth's reply: that is utter nonsense. Instead, "God is everything" that man "may be His man."[48] The theological "virtues" constitute how humans become God's creature. Grace determines a Christian's existence in "three aspects."[49] First is faith, which is "man's recognition of God's verdict." Second is hope, which is the "placing of man under divine direction." And third is love—"Jesus Christ coming together with all men and their coming together with Him," and "the coming together of all men with one another."[50] These three aspects are correlated to the three forms of reconciliation that constitute Barth's doctrine of reconciliation, and the sins they overcome. We find this repeating threefold structure:[51]

Christology	Theological Virtue	Negation of Sin
Truly God: divine self-humiliation	Faith	Pride: The "negation of what God does for us in Jesus Christ condescending to us."
Truly Human: human exaltation	Love	Sloth: The "negation of what God did in Jesus Christ to exalt man."
Unity of God and Humanity	Hope	Falsehood: The "negation of Jesus Christ as guarantor."

This repeating structure begins with the fullness of God in Jesus Christ. An indispensable correlate of this fullness is the unity of humanity within the fullness of divinity. Barth is thoroughly Chalcedonian in affirming Christ's two natures. It is, Barth says, "factually right and necessary" as long as we don't

48. Ibid., 89.
49. Ibid., 92.
50. Ibid., 93, 99, 103.
51. Barth also had a threefold structure related to the theological virtues in his 1928 *Ethics*. It was based on the Word of God as the command of the creator, reconciler and redeemer. It too culminated in the theological virtues. See *Ethik*, 101.

begin with some pure or abstract understanding of "nature" and fit the *vere homo* within it.[52]

Barth then develops a Chalcedonian logic in some interesting and surprising ways. He reconfigures the Reformed teaching on the two states: humiliation and exaltation are no longer correlated to God's human and divine natures respectively. Instead God's humiliation is as much a marker of divinity, and exaltation of humanity. Humiliation express God's omnipotence; it is not a power to do whatever could be done but for God to enter into that which is not God without ceasing to be God. God's omnipotence is found in humility. God's freedom to love is found in condescension. Exaltation characterizes human nature. God enters into divine humiliation in order to exalt humanity. But following carefully the Chalcedonian logic, this humiliation and exaltation occur only within the single acting subject of the incarnate Christ. Barth writes, "As God who humbles Himself . . . and man exalted . . . Jesus Christ Himself is one. . . . He is the 'God-man,' that is, the Son of God who as such is this man, this man who as such is the Son of God."[53] For that reason we cannot think of ethics in terms of a human nature qua nature that has not already been incorporated into this unity. Otherwise we would not find in Christ "the one true possibility of our own being." The natures are unconfused, but in Jesus they are united in a single agency in history. They are also, for that reason alone, without contradiction. For Barth this unity reveals to us the true possibility of human ethical agency. "The concrete views of God and man which it has before it in Jesus Christ cannot be mixed but can only be seen together as the forms of a history: the reconciling God and the man reconciled by Him."[54] Barth again specifies that the "forms" of this history are faith, hope, and love.[55] As he emphasizes this form, and notes its implication for human agency, Barth explicitly acknowledges he must write more and more for his Catholic hearers. He still suffers Catholicism.

---

52. *Church Dogmatics* 4.1, 133. In *Church Dogmatics* 4.2, Barth does express reservations about misinterpretations of Chalcedon that assume we can know what "nature" means without reference to Jesus Christ. Although he affirms that the Councils always emphasized the *vere homo* as much as the *vere Deus* (25), he claims the "two natures" language can be "exposed to serious misunderstanding": "It is finally easy to read out of the word 'nature' a reference to the generally known or at any rate conceivable disposition of a being" (26). Balthasar could certainly affirm that this is exactly what happened with the accommodation to "nature" through an unqualified incorporation of Aristotle's definition of it in late medieval theology.

53. *Church Dogmatics* 4.1, 135.

54. Ibid., 136.

55. Ibid., 145.

STILL SUFFERING CATHOLICISM: MARIOLOGY, EVANGELICAL COUNSELS, ECCLESIOLOGY, SAINTS, AND SINNERS

Throughout his "Doctrine of Reconciliation" in its threefold form, Barth continues his conversation with Catholicism, making some remarkable concessions. First comes chapter 14, "Jesus Christ, the Lord as Servant," which presents the divine self-humiliation and culminates in "faith" (§63).[56] The *res* of faith is not a function of the subject, but the subject is a function of the *res*. Faith is nonetheless a human work. It is "the believer's own work," which as such is based upon its object: the work of Jesus Christ. It constitutes a "new and particular being," who is the "Christian subject."[57] This subject finds its definitive form in "love."

Chapter 15, "Jesus Christ, The Servant as Lord," focuses on exaltation and sanctification and concludes with a section on love (§68). In this chapter Barth, overthrows a great deal that often passes for Barthianism. He denies there is only a way from God to humanity without a reciprocal movement from humanity to God.[58] He offers as clear an expression of the *analogia entis* as can be found in his work: "The royal man of the New Testament tradition is created 'after God' (κατα θεον). This means that as a man He exists analogously to the mode of existence of God."[59] He explains this in the final section on love. The Christian agent now has the possibility of acting on the basis of God's own being, which is Triune. The "royal man" who *analogically exists* is first and foremost Jesus; all other human possibilities are mediated through him, but *human possibilities* are mediated. Barth emphasizes this mediation against Catholicism, assuming it cannot sustain well the priority of Christ in the *analogia entis*. Something other than Christ mediates what it means to be human. He knows that Balthasar represents a christological renaissance within Catholicism, but he suspects that Balthasar's interpretation is not the heart of Catholicism. Barth continues to read the *analogia entis* through the neoscholastic doctrine of pure nature.

---

56. For Barth, faith is "the subjectivisation of an objective *res* which in its existence and essence and dignity and significance and scope takes precedence of this subjectivisation and therefore of the human subject in it, being independent of and superior to this subject and what he does or does not do." Ibid., 742.

57. Ibid., 744–49.

58. *Church Dogmatics* 4.2, 118: "There is not only a way of God to man. Because there is a way of God downward to man, there is also a way of man upward to God."

59. Ibid., 166.

IN DEFENSE OF PROTESTANTISM: CHRIST'S AGENCY VERSUS MARY'S

Barth remains haunted by Catholicism, still making a case for the Protestant tradition against it. Protestantism preserves the centrality of God's reconciling action in Jesus and for that reason, the genuine possibility of human ethical agency, which is love. Chapter 15 is a critical response to (at least) two Roman Catholic teachings that Barth thinks fail to maintain this centrality: the representation of Christ in the Mass and saints, and the agency of Mary. Barth confesses he now writes more and more for his "Catholic readers." He does so in order to explain to them how the "Evangelical" position can accomplish what they rightly desire without losing the christological center. The argument against Barth, by Balthasar and other Catholic interlocutors, was that he lacked an adequate understanding of human agency; in particular, that Barth denied Christ's redeeming work could be represented through the Mass and among his saints without diminishing the centrality of Christ's work. Catholicism also has a key role for human action in its Marian dogmas, which form the heart of Balthasar's theological ethics. Mary, after all, gives birth to God. What higher form of human agency could possibly exist? She is also one of the key forms for the evangelical counsels. Barth affirms with Catholics an exaltation of human agency, but finds its Marian shape unnecessary and denies it can be represented in the saints or the Mass.[60] "The fact that the man Jesus is the whole basis and power and guarantee of our exaltation means that there can be no place for any other in this function, not even for the mother of Jesus."[61] In the "exaltation"

---

60. See *Church Dogmatics* 4.1, 768. Balthasar cites this passage in his 1961 "Foreword" to the 1951 Barth book, and uses it to "show how deeply Protestant Barth's thinking really is." (*The Theology of Karl Barth*, trans. Edward T. Oakes, SJ [San Francisco: Ignatius, 1992]), 398n14.) First, he quotes Barth's words about Balthasar's "christological renaissance": "In modern Roman Catholic theology, there is a promising, but, of course, unofficial movement that is apparently aiming in the direction of what we might call a christological renaissance. I am not thinking only of the well-known book that Hans Urs von Balthasar addressed to me, in which I find an understanding of the concentration on Jesus Christ attempted in the *Church Dogmatics* that is incomparably more powerful than that of most of the books that have clustered around me. For H. U. v. Balthasar has with him and under him quite a chorus of German and especially French friends who in different ways and with varying emphases all seem to wish to look again to the center, to the 'author and perfecter of our faith' (Heb. 12:2)." Barth then argues Balthasar absorbs justification in sanctification because he thinks Christ's work can be reproduced in the saints and especially in the Mass.

61. Barth writes, "The content of this book might well be regarded as an attempted Evangelical answer to the Marian dogma of Romanism—both old and new. I have nowhere mentioned this, let alone attacked it directly. But I have in fact shown that it is made superfluous by the 'Exaltation of the Son of Man' and its anthropological implications. I can hardly expect that my Roman Catholic readers—to whom I turn more and more in the *Church Dogmatics*—will accept this, but I am confident that they will at least see that there is a positive reason for my Evangelical rejection." *Church Dogmatics* 4.2, ix.

of humanity through Christ's reconciling power, Barth develops as strong a notion of what humans accomplish as found in Catholic theology, but without Marian dogmas.

Barth acknowledges "dangers" as he now emphasizes human exaltation. He admits his emphasis on exaltation could overcome the work he achieved in the past thirty years that sought to make theology about God rather than humanity.[62] He fears he could be misread, and wrongly understood as affirming mysticism, pietism, the Enlightenment, and Schleiermacher, but these are potential dangers that must be endured because Christ exalts humanity. The one danger he discusses at length, however, is not the "theological humanism" of liberal Protestantism but monasticism. It is a more worthy opponent because of its length, breadth, and reoccurrence in Christian tradition. Given how central Balthasar's retrieval of the evangelical counsels within the secular institutes was for his own theological ethics, these comments by Barth are instrumental in seeing how they agree and disagree, and how their conversation shaped each other's work.

MONASTICISM AND EVANGELICAL COUNSELS: A TEST CASE

When Balthasar left the Jesuits, he renewed his vows at the Maria Laach Benedictine abbey and wrote Karl Barth on the same day, February 22, 1950. He told Barth he had probably already heard the news of his departure, and that Arthur Frey would find it "thoroughly suitable" for an editorial. He also told him "his steps" have now been "charged with burdens and responsibilities."[63] Barth replied that he did not know: "Nobody tells me anything." He chided him (I take it in jest) for speaking evil of Frey and let him know that his letter arrived as he was working on the doctrine of marriage for his "Ethics lectures" and the "unedifying claims" about the perseverance of the saints at Trent. On a more serious note, he "commiserates" with this turn in his "path of life" and "looks forward with eagerness" to his return to Basel.[64] We should not forget that this is also the time when Balthasar is still seeking publication for his book

---

62. "The exaltation of man to God? The fellowship not only of God with man but man with God? What kind of accents are these? What associations do they conjure up? What historical images, and with them what well-known and often mentioned dangers are raised by them, and seem emphatically to warn us not to enter the way proposed? Is not this the way of theological humanism, moralism, psychologism, synergism, and ultimately an anthropocentric monism—a way which in the last thirty years Evangelical theology has scarcely begun to learn again to see and avoid in all its aridity?" Ibid., 8.

63. Manfred Lochbrunner, Hans Urs von Balthasar und seine Theologenkollegen: Sechs Beziehungsgeschichten (Würzburg: Echter, 2009), 319.

64. Ibid., 320.

on Barth, which could only add to his "burdens and responsibilities." But that expression primarily refers to his mission to foster the secular institutes and call lay Catholics to hear God's vocation to the evangelical counsels.

In the middle of his exile (1953), Balthasar sent Barth his book on Reinhold Schneider, which is the program for the secular institutes. Barth read it and replied, "Thank you for the presentation of your book on Reinhold Schneider, in which we see into [his work] so thoroughly with a concentrated power. You are astonishing!"[65] Barth then told him he plans to hold a conference on his work in heaven after he first sits at Mozart's feet for a few thousand years.[66] In the Schneider book, Balthasar affirms a new institutional form for the evangelical counsels in secular institutes. As we saw in the first chapter, he was so convinced of this mission that when required to make a choice between it and the Jesuits he chose the mission. The secular institutes were the burden and responsibility he now bore. In sending the Schneider book to Barth, he was informing him of his mission. Balthasar affirms Schneider's work for his unrelenting passion to bring Christ's influence to bear on everyday matters of politics and ethics. He traces Schneider's various works, providing theological commentary. Schneider began with the encroaching "nihilism" that concludes the evening (*Abend*) of the West (*Abendland*).[67] The sun sets on the West. Balthasar and Schneider trace this conclusion back to the colonialism that was incapable of "making plausible . . . the Christian idea."[68] Colonialism rendered Christianity unintelligible.

Balthasar also found the Reformation a source of Christianity's unintelligibility. He again critiqued the Protestant dialectic for its inability to express the proper form of Christianity: "A dialectic that remains most profoundly unchristian (and this also means: unhumanist): the Protestant protest against the Catholic 'ordering of being', the possibility of uniting heaven and earth (and idea and existence) that is portrayed and established in the Incarnation of God."[69] Uniting heaven and earth, idea and existence is the heart of Balthasar's theological ethics, both in theory, and in practice through the secular institute. He notes that this unity comes from Schneider's apocalyptic shattering of the "world of St. Thomas" that sets a "radically christological

---

65. Ibid., 326.

66. *Church Dogmatics* 4.2, 11.

67. Balthasar, *Tragedy under Grace: Reinhold Schneider on the Experience of the West*, trans. Brian McNeil, CRV (San Francisco: Ignatius, 1997), 34. I am indebted to Andy Alexis-Baker for pointing this work out to me.

68. Ibid., 41.

69. Ibid., 45.

thinking" against "thinking on the basis of the creation."[70] Schneider avoids any "purely abstract thinking in terms of natural law" and instead presents history in terms of Christ's victory, which includes an incarnation that is not tragic and a cross that is, the former limiting the tragedy of the latter. "It is not Being that is tragic; the tragic has a boundary."[71] Because being is not tragic, "the secular power must be administered under the law of the voluntary powerlessness of the Redeemer."[72] Uniting the incarnation and the cross, idea and existence, is the heart of Schneider's work, and it is Balthasar's burden and responsibility in the secular institutes. His mission is to unite what cannot be united: the evangelical counsels and the secular commandments. It is to work within the tragedy of the cross and the unity of the incarnation. Balthasar writes, "The burning concrete question posed by Schneider is this: Concrete history applies force, but the gospel forbids the use of force—does not every Christian who intervenes actively in concrete history, therefore, become guilty in relation to the gospel?"[73] But this cannot be the final word because Christ's mission is the "Christian seed" still "sprouting." It eventually ripened to the "insight that slavery is incompatible with human rights." The same may very well be occurring today with humanity's "bloody war," which Balthasar knows Schneider rejects with his pacifism.[74] Balthasar affirms much of Schneider's analysis, and especially his nonresistance, even though he cannot side with his pacifism. He does, however, affirm a version of nonresistance. Nonresistance must not be reactive; it must be theological. It is directed not against evil but offered in Christ to the Father. It is another form of the Son's obedience, another type of Ignatian indifference.

In his commentary on Schneider's work, Balthasar offers an intriguing defense of Vatican I. Its distinctions between faith and knowledge, revelation and reason should "delight Schneider." For they did away with the medieval synthesis that tempted the Church to take up the "secular sword." They made possible a new kind of engagement with the world. It is worth quoting at length Balthasar's statement on Vatican I, for it resonates with Barth's own work on the relationship between Church and world.

> Precisely this ought to delight Reinhold Schneider, because it means
> that only fragments are left after the disappearance of the temptation

70. Ibid., 51.
71. Ibid., 124, 5.
72. Ibid., 62.
73. Ibid., 128.
74. Ibid.

for the Church to take hold of the secular sword. And yet, precisely for this reason, now is the time when the walls of monasteries are opening up and the form of religious life is changing from its foundations upward: because it is more deeply than ever conscious of its social and thereby of its historical function and begins at last to understand its representative position also in the sense of a genuine responsibility for the world, without drawing arbitrary and timid boundaries between monastery and world, Church and world, and without asserting any incompatibility between obedience, which remains its essential form, and genuine responsibility and the power to make decisions. How could a Christian ever bear responsibility other than in obedience to God, to Christ and the Church, indeed, precisely out of the force of this obedience? And so, unnoticed, the image of the *nonresistant* man, that is, of the obedient man, takes center stage once more, as the image of the one who has his position in the life of the counsels but must solidify his effective power so that he becomes a model for the rulers of this world and those who bear responsibility.[75]

Here we see the program for Balthasar's secular institute, how he envisions the unity of idea and existence, and how he identifies the political and ethical significance of the evangelical counsels. Jesus' hard sayings become a "model for the rulers of this world."

Five years after receiving Balthasar's book on Schneider, within the context of an affirmation of human exaltation, Barth published a sympathetic critique of monasticism in chapter 15 of his doctrine of reconciliation. He affirms the motive behind the counsels, but not their institutionalization. He begins by noting the Reformation's rejection of monasticism: "The Reformers knew what they were about when they refused to accept it and overthrew the institutions." He then ameliorates this rejection; monasticism is not an unmitigated evil. Protestant theologians should not be quick to reject its recurring forms.

And where attempts are now made within the Evangelical Church of the present to revive monasticism in various forms, good care must be taken that in the antithesis then disclosed, and not yet legitimately overcome, there is not an imperceptible movement over to the wrong side and therefore into the shadow. This does not mean, however, that it is incumbent and legitimate to ignore *a limine*

75. Ibid., 150.

and as a whole the idea and enterprise involved, discrediting it as "monkery" and evading the question of its problem and significance even for our Evangelical life and thinking.[76]

Barth allows the heart of Balthasar's work, a retrieval of evangelical counsels for laity, to interrogate Protestant theology. He then returns the favor.

Barth distinguishes the motive and intention of monasticism from its institutions. The former should be affirmed; the latter rejected. He also distinguishes its great exponents and inferior imitators. Its greatest practitioners, Macarius, Basil, Benedict, St. Francis, Dominic, Thomas á Kempis, Ignatius Loyola, and Theresa of Avila have something to teach us, which often gets missed in Protestant criticisms. For this reason Barth critiques A. Bertholet's interpretation. Bertholet found monasticism ethically inadequate because it supposedly advocates withdrawal and abandonment of the world. To the contrary, Barth argues, for Origen and others, monasticism was marked more by "sacrificial activity and concern for the destitute and sick" than political withdrawal. Barth's argument mirrors Balthasar's. Far from "escapism," the monastic movement was largely communal and "a highly responsible and effective protest and opposition to the world, and not least to a worldly Church, a new and specific way of combatting it." The very term "secularism," he suggests, arose from "enlightened governments in the 18th and 19th centuries" who were seeking protection from the politically powerful monastic institutions. The fact that they sought such protection was a sign of the "power and vitality of the Church."[77]

Like Balthasar, Barth recognized the political and ethical nature of monasticism. To accuse it of withdrawal, sectarianism, or escapism missed its profound engagement with the world. The sectarian accusation assumed the sharp distinctions between grace and nature, theology and ethics, that they both challenged. For Balthasar, the secular institutes were the *realm* within which Christian ethics was most intelligible. Monasticism is politically charged for Barth, however, in both a positive and negative sense. He writes, "A Trappist or a Carmelite may seem very far from the world, but the monk in the form of the Jesuit can seem uncomfortably close."[78] In 1958, he still registers concerns about the Jesuits. He knew they were political, even if he did not always find their politics compelling. Nonetheless, Barth acknowledges with Balthasar that withdrawal and abstention is not a refusal to engage the world, but a necessary

76. *Church Dogmatics* 4.2, 12.

77. Ibid.

78. Ibid., 14.

form of engagement. Barth goes so far as to argue that Christians cannot be political or ethical without first undergoing some form of abstention from the world.[79]

INSTITUTIONALIZING COUNSELS

Monasticism, with its abstentions (ascesis) is necessary for every Christian, but it has its dangers, which he presents by discussing the "evangelical counsels." They raise some "crying questions," especially about the particular nature of the abstentions—sex and money—through which perfection is to be achieved.

> Are sex and property (and speech) really the occasion of particular temptation, a particular danger to Christian freedom and fitness to serve God and our neighbours? And even if they are this—as the Gospels seem to indicate, less in relation to sex, more clearly in relation to property, the unrighteous mammon—is the danger which is to be expected really met by the mechanical sealing off of these whole spheres? Is not the ordering of these inordinate desires, and its goal of Christian freedom for Christian service, really a matter of the heart, which may still be lacking in spite of this sealing off, or may be there without it?[80]

Barth, like Balthasar, acknowledges the purpose of the counsels is "Christian freedom for Christian service." Only freedom for mission renders the counsels intelligible; they became unintelligible when they are reduced to a psychological quest for spiritual development or only related to ecclesial office, which Balthasar associated with Constantinianism.[81] But contra Barth, Balthasar finds their institution essential to this freedom, even if in "secular *institutes*." Balthasar stated,

> Just as office is established in her [the church] as an abiding and often uncomfortable sign of the fact that she does not belong to herself but

79. Every Christian, Barth asserts, must have something of the monastic spirit if he or she is likewise to engage the world: "Can there be either for the Church or for individuals any genuine approach to the world or men unless there is an equally genuine retreat?" Ibid.

80. Ibid., 15.

81. Balthasar argues that the problem with the counsels in Scholasticism and Baroque theology was that they viewed holiness as individual. Like marriage today, the counsels became "bourgeois"; they were focused on self-development. But the counsels are not about spiritual self-development, they are about "being free for Christian mission." *The Laity and the Life of the Counsels: The Church's Mission in the World*, trans. by Brian McNeil, CRV with D. C. Schindler (San Francisco: Ignatius, 1993), 65–66.

to her Lord, so *spontaneous, free vocations that cannot be manipulated* are "instituted" within her by the Lord, which help her anew to achieve her own authentic "self-understanding", that is, to realize her dependence on the Lord and her task of leading her brothers in and outside the Church to him.[82]

The *institution* of the counsels among the laity makes possible a secular vocation that allows a person to participate in the "form of Christ."[83] Barth questions if the counsels produce the kind of freedom Balthasar sought. For him, they cannot if they are *instituted* as necessary for Christian perfection. Then they create a two-tiered Christianity that is unsustainable. He makes an important point. As much as Balthasar tries to deny marriage is a lesser form of Christian discipleship, he affirms its fittingness to Christian mission with great difficulty. Despite all the beauty of the counsels, at times his cajoling of persons toward the counsels borders on the obscene, such as when he argues that those who were called to the counsels but reject them for the state of marriage will always be unsatisfied and discover that their children die young; or that the difficulty those in isolated areas find in performing their mission is the lack of a good housekeeper.[84] Moreover, he now has no place for a "lay apostolate."[85] If this is what the institution of the counsels requires, Barth has a point. A two-tiered doctrine of counsels and commands cannot unite idea and existence.

For Barth, when the counsels are institutionalized, they become a law and create an unpalatable distinction between "perfect" and "imperfect" Christianity. Balthasar addressed this question in his own defense of lay monasticism.[86] He recognized the danger, which is why he argued the distinction in "states of life" only make sense in terms of mission. It was not "individual perfection" the counsels serve, but Christ. Christians who did not take the vows were likewise called to perfection, but Christians in the modern era needed a new way, a non-Constantinian way, of institutionalizing the counsels, which is what the secular institutes provide. Barth thought the counsels could not be institutionalized; they were a "matter of the heart."

82. Ibid., 17.

83. Ibid., 23.

84. Balthasar, *The Christian States of Life*, trans. Mary Frances McCarthy (San Francisco: Ignatius , 1983), 469; originally, *Christlicher Stand* (Einsiedeln: Johannes, 1977). He states that those called to the counsels but refuse the call will discover "his life will be forever unfulfilled. He will be pursued by misfortune. . . . Either he has no children or those he has die at an early age," 500.

85. Balthasar, *The Christian States of Life,* 470.

86. *The Laity and the Life of the Counsels*, 168–71.

That response is unsatisfying; it smacks of the very psychologizing of the Christian life Balthasar, as well as Barth in his better moments, eschewed. It shows one of the limitations of Barth's theological ethics. It did not need to be institutionalized for fear institutionalization would detract from the receptivity of faith. Even when he changed his teaching on faith and acknowledged it produced human action, he did not correlate it to social institutions. For this reason, his Christian ethics often lacks social or institutional flesh, even if his own living it out did not.

Barth also critiques the vow of "obedience," comparing Jesuits unfavorably to Benedictines. Obedience was the heart of all the counsels for Balthasar; everything flowed from it. It is obedience Barth finds most problematic: "For is there any relationship of man with man whose structure may try to imitate that between God and man institutionally?" This will necessarily "obscure" the "majesty of God."[87] Barth's take on obedience strikingly contrasts with Balthasar, who finds the beauty of obedience not only in the counsels, but also in marriage and between the layperson and his Christian conscience.[88] Here again we see a repeated refrain in Barth—institutionalizing the encounter between God and creatures detracts from the freedom and majesty of God, and also of creatures—echoing an old prejudice against Jesuits in Protestant Swiss culture. But now an interesting shift takes place, one that could very well be the influence of Barth's ongoing conversations with his Catholic interlocutors and especially Balthasar. He cautions that monasticism, even in its most troubling third vow of obedience, should not be dismissed too easily by Protestants *because* of God's freedom.

> If what is impossible with men is possible with God, and the Spirit bloweth where He listeth, it cannot finally be disputed that a genuine fellowship of the saints could and can take place in the form of genuine commanding and genuine obeying even in the sphere of this kind of institution.[89]

---

87. *Church Dogmatics* 4.2, 17.

88. "Thus, what the monk lives out in obedience to an 'abba' or superior as an 'exemplary sign' has its real counterpart in the situational obedience of the mature layman who listens to his Christian conscience, to the summons of Christ that comes from within the secular moment: but in such a way that sign and reality in practice exclude one another. It is indeed very impressive when one man obeys another for the sake of the gospel; it is an ascetic practice that continuously reminds the Christian in the world how demanding it can be to choose the path indicated by conscience in the 'situation.'" *The Laity and the Life of the Counsels,* 169.

89. *Church Dogmatics* 4.2, 17.

That statement is quite a concession for Barth; it differs markedly from the arguments he made previously. He affirms obedience to another as a form of freedom in response to the command of God within an institution.

Barth points to the humility and wisdom of the Benedictine rule as a faithful practice of obedience, but he still expresses a grave reservation. Barth's ultimate worry with monasticism is found in the final sentence of Benedict's Rule.

> It is a pity that the final sentence in Benedict is as follows: *Facientibus haec regna patebunt superna* [by doing this, the celestial realms will open]. This cannot be admitted for a moment. The statement must be resolutely reformulated. It is not because and as they do this that the *regna superna* will open up to them. It is because and as the *regna superna* are opened up to them in the death of Jesus Christ that they will do this in the power of His resurrection.[90]

The celestial realm is not opened because we observe the counsels, laws, or rules; the counsels, laws, or rules can be observed because the celestial realm is first opened to us. And for Barth, that opening only occurs in and through Jesus. Our hope is found in the new creature with a new direction he brings into existence. This new creature is Barth's christological ontology.

Barth affirms some of what Balthasar and Catholicism affirm with the counsels. He recognizes how essential it is for the new ethical agent to be vigilant in matters of sex, money, and language.[91] But the direction of this agency alarms him. It cannot first be from humanity to God or that would render the divine humiliation irrelevant. Agency does take a human form, even that of a human exaltation. However, a direction from humanity to God occurs only within and simultaneous to the divine humiliation. There is then a direction from humanity to God, but it must be properly ordered, which it is by the hypostatic union.

When it is properly ordered, asceticism holds forth a new way of life: "The passing of this world and its lusts (I Cor 7.31, I Jn. 2: 17) and the existence of a new man and the direction which he gives."[92] This "new direction" gets

90. Ibid., 18. Nicholas M. Healey points out that what Barth cites here is not original to Benedict's rule. 2013 Annual Barth Conference, June 17, 2013, Princeton Theological Seminary.

91. Barth writes, "Monasticism was no doubt in error when it expected relief and a solution by the simple sealing off of these spheres. As the general principle of a particular state, this could hardly be reconciled with openness to the question of God's commandment. But was it really at fault in demanding a particular vigilance and strictness in these spheres?" *Church Dogmatics* 4.2, 15.

elaborated in the final section of chapter 15, "The Holy Spirit and Christian Love." What characterizes Barth's discussion of monasticism—sacrifice, obedience, community, and freedom—also characterizes Barth's presentation of Christian love in that concluding section, for all these terms find their place within the "new direction" from humanity to God that Christ makes possible through the Holy Spirit. The new direction begins when the Holy Spirit "quickens" the sinful person by setting her in a "community" and giving her the freedom to "correspond" to God's love through its self-giving nature.

LOVE, DESIRE, AND DEATH

In this final section in chapter 15 of the *Doctrine of Reconciliation*, Barth notes a problem. Faith is always "reception," but love is "self-giving." They appear to stand in "contrast" to each other.[93] How then can the freedom found in faith lead to the self-giving found in love? Barth answers only as it takes its "basis" in the Holy Trinity.[94] This "basis of love" is found in the second part of this final section. Unfortunately, Barth explicates what love is prior to discussing its basis in the Trinity, and does so by following closely Anders Nygren.[95] Love is self-sacrificing "agape," in which one gives without expecting return. He contrasts this to a Platonic eros that seeks return. Augustine and the Middle Ages lost the tension between these two kinds of love and tried to synthesize them, but they cannot be synthesized.[96] They are a stark either-or, so stark that Christian love leads to "the wholly alien character of Christianity in relation to the world around."[97] Christian love is something purely unique—a self-giving that seeks only the good of the other.

> Christian love turns to the other purely for the sake of the other. It
> does not desire it for itself. It loves it simply because it is there as
> this other, with all its value or lack of value. It loves it freely. But it

92. Ibid.

93. Ibid., 730.

94. Ibid., 757.

95. For a good discussion of Barth's confusing statements on eros and agape throughout his *Dogmatics*, see David Clough, "Eros and Agape in Karl Barth's Church Dogmatics," *International Journal of Systematic Theology* 2 (2000): 189–203. Clough notes, "Barth states that the two are enemies of one another, but also rejects a simple opposition and attributes to *eros* qualities he identifies with *agape*" (189).

96. "The *caritas* which the Middle Ages had learned decisively from Augustine was a synthesis of biblical *agape* and antique or hellenistic *eros* in which the antithesis between the two can still be perceived but not in any sense unequivocally, the tension having been largely destroyed with all its beneficial results." *Church Dogmatics* 4.2, 737.

97. Ibid., 735.

is more than this turning. In Christian love the loving subject gives to the other, the object of love, that which it has, which is its own, which belongs to it. It does so irrespective of the right or claim that it may have to it, or the further use that it might make of it. It does so in confirmation of the freedom in respect of itself which it has in its crucial beginning. It does so with a radically unlimited liberality.[98]

Although Balthasar also interprets love as a total self-giving and affirms Nygren in part, he does not find Christian love to be so thoroughly unique.[99] Balthasar has more of a place for eros within it. Because love is commanded for every Christian, it is "therefore capable of being fulfilled substantially by everyone." He is also able to see a dim reflection of it outside of Christianity, but consistent with his emphasis on the counsels he primarily sees it in the asceticism practiced by other religions and philosophies.[100]

Barth swings between extremes. A faith marked by complete receptivity leads to love marked by complete self-giving. The force between these two motions in Barth's work is too much. It cannot hold together. Interestingly, once Barth sets forth the basis of love in the Trinity, he then critiques Nygren and presents a more defensible ethic. The basis for Christian love is the love that is God's essence, which God communicates to creatures through holy desire.

> In Himself, He is both the One and the Other. And He is this, not in any reciprocal self-seeking, indifference, neutrality or even enmity, but in the self-giving of the Father to the Son and the Son to the Father, which is accomplished by the fact that He is not merely the Father and the Son but also the Holy Spirit, and therefore as the Father is wholly for the Son, and as the Son is wholly for the Father.[101]

The self-giving love of the Trinity is neither indifference nor disinterestedness. As Kantian as Barth can sound when he lays out the "problem of love," the basis, act, and manner of love (sections 2, 3, and 4) are much more profound than either Kant or Nygren. God's Trinitarian love is generative. The Father does not lose himself in the Son, but 'gains' not only Himself but also the Spirit.

---

98. Ibid., 733.

99. Balthasar claims there is "some truth " in Nygren's eros/agape distinction. See *Theo-Drama*, vol. 5: *Theological Dramatic Theory: The Last Act*, trans. Graham Harrison (San Francisco: Ignatius, 1998), 504.

100. Balthasar, *The Laity and the Life of the Counsels*, 158, 210–14.

101. *Church Dogmatics* 4.2, 757.

Barth will take this as the pattern for Christian love and suggest that we also *give* something to God that God receives, a position Balthasar was likewise well known for; receptivity is a divine perfection. God delights in our obedience.

Once Barth sets forth the "basis" of Christian love in the giving and receiving of the Triune Persons, he then qualifies any misunderstanding love as self-giving might have created.

> This does not mean, as the matter is often represented, that there is an extinction or annihilation of the one who loves in favour of the one whom he loves. How can this be love? On this unhealthy view how can there be anything but a withdrawal from the loved one—by a departure of death?[102]

Here is where he would critique the counsels as forms of martyrdom that require death to everything that is good. Does this define Balthasar's martyrological ethic? Is it heroic and tragic in a bad sense, where the central actors must die to find new life such that death becomes the great mediator of salvation? If such an interpretation of the counsels were true, it would be a terrible irony, for it is exactly what Balthasar rejected in critiquing the German *Apokalypse*.

A heroic and tragic ethic valorizing death is also the problem with an absolute ethics of permanent crisis. It could never put forth a positive judgment about truth or goodness but only negate. Valorizing death never defined Barth's ethical practice; it could not define his theory. Love is not death; it is not the gift that makes love possible. Instead, for Barth, love will bring for the agent exercising it "exaltation, gain and joy," even happiness. He writes, "the man who loves is a happy man."[103] There is then a reciprocity to love that contradicts what Barth asserted following Nygren's sharp distinction between agape and eros. Barth distances himself from his own earlier comments, similar to Nygren's, in which he had worried Christian love would be turned into a pagan mysticism or pietism through the synthesis of agape and eros. The threat, Barth claimed, was not real. Barth had earlier taken the threat so far that, like Nygren, he refused to speak of our love for God and Jesus, and only of God's for us. This led, he now admits, to a "no less dubious antithesis (that of A. Ritschl and his disciples and his successors) according to which the work of the Holy Spirit must be reduced to the management of an eternal working-day, and with

---

102. Ibid., 787.

103. Ibid., 788. He remains Kantian in insisting that happiness cannot be the motivation or intention of love, but is an inevitable result.

the abolition of a true and direct love for God and Jesus there is basically no place for prayer."[104] Barth returns to the theme of obedience and states that without our love for God and Jesus there can be no true obedience.[105] He refers to the woman who anoints Jesus with oil as an "act of sheer extravagance" that cannot be understood by the ethico-religious puritans, and then appeals to erotic hymnody directed to Jesus and states,

> To be sure, a good deal of this smacks of religious eroticism, and it would be easy to adduce passages in which this aspect is even more pronounced. But how arid would be our hymn-books if we were to purge out all elements of this kind? And how deficient would be our preaching and teaching and pastoral work if there were no conscious utterance along these lines![106]

Barth still worries about "eros," but now he argues that admitting no place for the human actor's love of God only creates a vacuum that will be filled by a pagan eros. Barth will take this so far as to raise the question: "Is it really the case that He has caused His Word to become flesh not merely in order that He may be an act for us in His own person, but in order that we may also be an act for Him?"[107] These questions point to the human exaltation the divine humiliation generates. God does not seek passive agents who only receive. Nor does God seek only to precipitate crisis, whereby we would not know how to love what is good. God seeks the highest form of human agency. "As truly as God loves us we may love Him in return."[108] This love is our act, our freedom, our sacrifice, and our obedience. It brings life not death, and it can only be done within the community formed by the Holy Spirit.

THE CHURCH AND ITS MISSION TO THE WORLD

Barth developed the "prophetic mission of the community" in chapter 16, "Jesus Christ the True Witness." Witness and declaration occur under Christ's prophetic office. Here he offers some of his most important political and ethical analyses, and does so by returning to the theme of secularization mentioned

104. Ibid., 795.
105. Ibid., 796.
106. Ibid., 797–98. Barth continues, saying it is better "to slip up with Nicolai and even with Zinzendorf and Novalis than to be rigidly correct with Kant and Ritschl and my 1921 *Römerbrief* and Bultmann."
107. *Church Dogmatics* 4.2, 791.
108. Ibid.

previously in his discussion of monasticism. Since the sixteenth century he states, "The diastasis between the church and world" meant that the world grew increasingly secular, "turning its back on the Church with which it had contracted that doubtful union in the Middle Ages." For Barth this shows that the world "was not committed to the Church in any deep sense. . . . What human hands had built they could pull down."[109] Like Balthasar, however, for Barth this diastasis is no cause for alarm; it is the church's freedom even as it also poses a temptation. For Balthasar the diastasis, present in Vatican I, allowed for a recovery of the counsels from its Constantinian captivity to the priestly office.[110] For both of them, modernity confronts and marginalizes the Christian church through a new conception of sovereignty. Barth put it this way:

> More and more the Church has come up against the self-consciousness of modern national and regional powers with a totally new claim to sovereignty, against a modern society recognizing and proclaiming its own laws and following its own aspirations, against a modern philosophy, science, literature, art and economics which not only maintain their own particular freedom and rights against it but silently exercise them without asking any questions.[111]

This new sovereignty poses three temptations for the Church. First, it is tempted to join with "reactionary forces" and seek to reestablish its position of power; second, to "retreat to the reservations of a self-satisfying religiosity, whether in the form of the varied practices of individual piety, renewed or newly discovered liturgics or dogmatic castles in the air;" third, to make compromises and truces accepting

> the increasing secularism on an optimistic interpretation, taking it up into its own self-understanding, working away so critically at the Bible, tradition and the creeds as to appear to be in harmony with the progressive spirit of the age, to justify modern man and to offer to the adult world a suitably adult form of Christianity, thus exposing all the more obviously and palpably the alienation of the life of modern man from that of the Church and *vice versa*.[112]

---

109. *Church Dogmatics* 4.3.1, trans. Geoffrey W. Bromiley, ed. G. W. Bromiley and T. F. Torrance (Edinburgh: T & T Clark, 1961), 21.

110. Balthasar, *The Laity and the Life of the Counsels*, 162–77, especially 176.

111. *Church Dogmatics* 4.3.1, 19.

112. Ibid., 19–20.

Barth called on the church to avoid all three temptations.[113]

He then noted a fourth option that is less temptation and more promise, an option he accepts and develops throughout the third part of the doctrine of reconciliation. It is similar to the option Balthasar presented in his Schneider book. Modernity frees the church to be itself, and in so doing to serve the world without donning secular power. This fourth option admits some confusion about such a strange turn of events, but this "human confusion" (*hominum confusione*) at the undoing of the church's power is part of "God's providence" (*Dei providentia*) liberating the church for its true purpose. It sets the church "free for the service to its own cause within the secular world for which it had for the most part neglected in pursuit of its own fantasies."[114] Barth seeks to disentangle human confusion and God's providence when he explains the virtue of hope in light of the Christian community's mission.

Barth disentangles *hominum confusione* and *Dei providentia* by affirming that Christ's "future manifestation is already here and now [history's] great, effective and living hope."[115] This hope is another form of the "new being" Christ generates, but it is a new being that cannot be thought without the church.[116] That it cannot be thought without the church does not mean it has no significance for those who are not explicit members. Barth refers to the relationship between the church and the history within which it exists as "world-occurrence."[117] The interplay between God's providence and human confusion constitutes the background for world-occurrence.

God does not will human confusion, but God's providence brings out of it something it could not produce from itself. Human confusion leads to

---

113. After Vatican II, Barth thought Roman Catholics faced the temptation of accommodating the "spirit of the age," and so he posed the question to them: to what are you updating (*aggiornamento*) the church? He thought they in part resisted this ever-present temptation; Balthasar was less confident. Both Barth and Balthasar recognized their co-Christians, sometimes explicitly, sometimes implicitly, made common cause with secularizing forces against other Christians. A fuller discussion of this must wait for the final chapter. For both, however, modernity was not only a source of temptation but also of promise.

114. *Church Dogmatics* 4.3.1, 21. Barth even claimed earlier that the "Anabaptists, Spiritualists and so-called Enthusiasts . . . saw much more clearly than the Reformers themselves, being unwilling merely to accept the validity of existing relationships but trying to test them in the light of the Gospel" (28).

115. *Church Dogmatics* 4.3.2, trans. Geoffrey W. Bromiley, ed. G. W. Bromiley and T. F. Torrance (Edinburgh: T & T Clark, 1961), 681.

116. "As we have tried to explain and affirm in the preceding section, the vocation of man is his vocation to be a Christian. But we must now continue that vocation to be a Christian means vocation or calling into Christendom or the Church, i.e., into the living community of the living Lord Jesus Christ." Ibid.

117. Ibid., 685.

nothingness; God's providence to hope. For Barth, we are tempted, via Hegel, to think we can stand outside of the diastasis between nothingness and providence and resolve them through a synthesis. But this gives "nothingness" a place it does not deserve. Instead, hope is found in the third Word God speaks: Jesus Christ who not only came and was raised but will also come again.[118] This Word makes hope possible. It is a "new thing."

For Barth, it is only as the "nature of the Church" that Jesus is the new reality of world history, but the church also has a universal significance through "world-occurrence." The church, Barth acknowledges, like Jesus, "exists in the flesh, *ad extra*, within world-occurrence." Any ecclesiological Docetism must be avoided. The church exists with the same history and materiality as every other aspect of world-occurrence, but it is unique in that it exists in world-occurrence as Jesus' body.[119] Here is where things get confusing. The church is Jesus' body, and it is so in all the "flesh" of an "earthly-historical form of existence," but then Barth asserts, "it [the church] is not as He is the Word of God in the flesh, the incarnate Son of God."[120] This statement could be an innocent reminder never to reduce the singular first form of Christ's historical body, the resurrected Jesus of Nazareth, with the other forms of his body in Word, sacrament, and church, as for instance Bultmann did when he understood Jesus' body to be raised in the proclamation of the church. Yet if the church is truly flesh and body, but is not as the "Word of God in the flesh," then what kind of body is this? Barth's laudable concern is to avoid identifying Jesus' unique hypostatic union with the church and produce an ecclesial triumphalism. Jesus is always the head, the subject, of the church. He makes it possible; it does not make him possible. This concern leads Barth to reject in the strongest possible terms that the church is in any sense a prolongation of the incarnation. To call the church an extension or prolongation of the incarnation is "blasphemy."[121] As Kimlyn Bender notes, Barth fears that a strong sense of institutional mediation of Christ through the church tacitly assumes he is somehow absent and must be made present.[122]

---

118. "Jesus Christ is not a concept which man can think out for himself, which he can define with more or less precision, and with the help of which he can then display his mastery over all kinds of greater or lesser problems and therefore over the problem of this antithesis too." Ibid., 706.

119. Ibid., 723. It is no "meteorite which has fallen from a distant sphere or a pearl in its shell, but as itself a genuinely and thoroughly worldly element participating in world-occurrence."

120. Ibid., 729. Barth unmistakably affirms this: "The supreme and final thing to be said of it [the church]. . . . is quite simply that it is His body, His earthly-historical form of existence."

121. Ibid.

122. Bender writes, "Barth's understanding of Christ's presence has a direct effect upon ecclesiology. First, because Christ is present in the power of the Holy Spirit, the church does not stand as a surrogate for Christ upon earth. Barth consistently rejects any conception of the church as vicar for Christ in lieu of

Barth not only denounces an ecclesiology that affirms the church as an extension of the incarnation, he is also wary of any "sacramental mediation" of Christ's presence by the church.[123] The only one true sacrament is the crucified Christ. The church witnesses to this one true sacrament; it neither repeats nor represents it.

The extent to which Barth is willing to go with these themes is found in three judgments he makes that seem to undo what he accomplished in this section, by arguing world-occurrence can be rendered intelligible without the earthly community Christ forms, the church. Barth states,

> 1. the world would be lost without Jesus Christ and His Word and work;
> 2. the world would not necessarily be lost if there were no Church; and
> 3. the Church would be lost if it had no counterpart in the world.[124]

The first judgment is noncontroversial. The second one is confusing. Has Barth himself not argued that the church is central to the "work" Jesus Christ accomplished? Bender's excellent work on Barth's ecclesiology suggests it is. He explains the central role ecclesiology had in Barth's mature theology:

> Barth's unique reconceptualization of election has a direct affect upon ecclesiology, for if the existence of the church is grounded in election and thus in an eternal decision (even though its historical reality is actualized in the history of reconciliation), then the church is not only discussed under the rubric of the doctrine of God, as election itself falls within this doctrine, but the church itself is viewed as part of God's eternal covenantal intention.[125]

Christ's own presence." Nor is the church then defined as "sacramental mediation," as if Christ were absent. The church is characterized not by sacrament, but by "witness." "Barth can in fact assert that there is only one true sacrament, that of Christ upon the cross." Kimlyn J. Bender, *Karl Barth's Christological Ecclesiology* (Aldershot: Ashgate, 2005), 148.

123. Some Catholic theologians find a shift from Pius XII's language of the church as the extenstion of the incarnation in *Mystici Corporis* to a less triumphalist tone in *Lumen gentium*, where the church is understood as sacrament. Although appreciative of much of Vatican II, Barth's comments here would not find that particular shift significant. Nor should it be forgotten than *Lumen gentium*, as will be noted below, still referred to the church as the extension of the incarnation.

124. *Church Dogmatics* 4.3.2, 826.

125. Bender, *Karl Barth's Christological Ecclesiology*, 101.

The Realm of Ethics | 217

If this is accurate, which I think it is, then how can Barth divide Jesus' "Word and work" from the church in the way these three judgments require? Barth leaves us with an unresolvable diastasis in Jesus' own body. His church is his body, and it is his body in the world as his flesh serving the world, but the world would not "necessarily be lost" if there were no church. The church is the earthly form of Christ's body, but it is not his flesh because that flesh cannot be extended. His flesh is, as Calvin argued, located only in a specific place in heaven.

Barth's judgments produce a speculative move bordering on the seminominalism he usually rejects. He explains his three judgments in an abstract and nominalistic fashion: "Who is to prevent Him from going His own direct way to man without it [church] in His self-declaration?"[126] If this question is permissible, so are others. Who is to prevent him from saving the world by fiat (contra Anselm's aesthetics)? Who is to prevent him from electing a people other than Israel? Who is to prevent him from saving the world by becoming incarnate in a donkey? If we were to insist that God's absolute power is known outside, and in contradistinction to, God's ordained power, then such questions make sense. The ordered economy cannot be trusted because it could always be called into question by some new miraculous event of God's power unrelated to that economy. God can do whatever God can do whether it is fitting to God's character and to what God has done in Christ. But if, as Barth has argued elsewhere, we should be careful not to divide God's will and wisdom, then this makes little sense. Could it be that Barth's concerns against making the forms by which God redeems—faith, love, and hope—into an institution mislead him and place strains on his argument? We have a church that is the earthly form of Christ's body, but is not necessary for salvation, and a Spirit who calls, but need not call, the church to be Jesus' "own earthly-historical form of existence," all within a context of a "*Church* Dogmatics" that began by emphasizing the church as the location for the divine-human drama.[127] His attempt to defend Reformed Christianity *against* Catholicism and Orthodoxy reproduces a "counter" and reactive theology he rejects when he is

126. *Church Dogmatics* 4.3.2, 826.

127. §72 begins with the proposition, "The Holy Spirit is the enlightening power of the living Lord Jesus Christ in which He confesses the community called by Him as His body, i.e. as His own earthly-historical form of existence, by entrusting to it the ministry of His prophetic Word and therefore the provisional representation of the calling of all humanity and indeed of all creatures as it has taken place in Him." Ibid., 681. Barth is doing more here than the common Calvinist/Wesleyan claim that God has tied us to the church, but God has not tied himself. With his second judgment, he is speculating that there may be no church at all.

at his best. The church's opposition to the world (his third judgment above) becomes more determinative of its being than the fullness it receives from Christ's odd triumph.[128] The result is Barth does not generate an adequate institutional sense of agency for the "new being" he identified.[129]

The Ethical Fruit of Balthasar's Preoccupation with Barth: Theodramatic Ethics

Barth situates ethics within dogmatic loci, but the church as the prolongation of the incarnation is not one such locus. For Balthasar, however, the extension of Christ's mediatorial agency from heaven to earth and from earth to heaven is the basis for his thodramatic ethics. As we will see below, he affirms its necessity in the "Last Act" of his *Theo-Drama*. This teaching could lead to the very triumphalism and usurpation of Christ's mediatorial role by his earthly representatives that Barth feared, but Balthasar has also learned from Barth not to be led into this temptation. He does not reject Luther's objection that the church is also the "whore of Babylon"; he addresses that very accusation in his essay, "Casta Meretrix" (The Chaste Prostitute).[130] Balthasar's Christology

---

128. "In the sphere of Romanism and Eastern Orthodoxy we have examples of the transgression of this upper limit of the ministry of the community to the extent that in them the Church ascribes to itself, to its life and institutions and organs, particularly to its administration of the sacraments and the means of grace entrusted to it, and in Romanism to its government by the teaching office, certain functions in the exercise of which it is not only not subordinate to Jesus Christ but is ranked alongside and in practice even set above Him as His vicar in earthly history, its ministry of witness being left far behind as it shares with Him an existence and activity which are both human and divine, and human in divine reality and omnipotence." Ibid., 36.

129. Bender points out that Barth rejects the church as an extension of the incarnation at the same time that he affirms a version of the *totus Christus*. See *Church Dogmatis* 4.2, 59–60; Bender, *Karl Barth's Christological Ecclesiology*, 149. Bender also notes that Barth does analogize from ecclesiology to Christ's an- and enhypostatic relation (151). He concludes, "There thus exists an ongoing tension in Barth's thought between perceiving the church as an event and as an institution, and this unresolved tension is in fact a dialectical relation in which the church exists as the unity of an invisible event and a visible historical manifestation, with the second dependent upon the first in an anhypostatic–enhypostatic relationship, in that the second exists only in dependence upon the first, though it does have a real and true, and therefore visible and historical existence through the first" (154). Bender's book is the best work we have on Barth's ecclesiology. I think he has identified a significant tension that creates difficulties for Barth. Bender does not find the difficulties as problematic as I do.

130. Balthasar explores the theme of the church as "chaste prostitute" not only from Luther's criticism but from within Catholicism itself. He writes, "Without endangering the immaculateness, holiness, and infallibility of the Church, one must look the other reality in the eye and not exclude it from consideration. Much would be gained if Christians learned more and more to realize at what price the holiness of the Church has been purchased." See "Casta Meretrix," in *Explorations in Christian Theology,*

demands such an ecclesiology. As William Cavanaugh notes, with Balthasar's Christology, "What we see when we see Christ is the entire drama of sin and salvation acted out on the stage of his one person." Cavanaugh draws out the implications of Balthasar's Christology for an ecclesiology that affirms the church as a prolongation of the incarnation without four unsavory consquences that teaching can have. It does not ignore the church's sins. It does not equate Christ's unique hypostatic union with the church. It does not identify the church's infallibility with its institution and fallibility with its people (something Balthasar may not have always avoided well) and it does not conclude to a triumphalist ecclesiology.[131] Neither does it take solace in an invisible church that cannot be identified, for this too, Cavanaugh recognizes, would lose the dramatic import of Balthasar's work, which is what makes Balthasar's moral theology possible.

BALTHASAR AS MORAL THEOLOGIAN?

Balthasar is not often thought of as a "moral theologian," but such a judgment misses the importance of his conversation with Barth and the "burning dispute" between them. Balthasar's refusal of a sharp distinction between nature and grace meant ethics could not take place in a realm independent of God's glory in Jesus. Like Barth, Balthasar conceived and practiced ethics within a realm always marked christologically. He followed Barth's lead; dogma is ethics. Few theologians, including Barthians, accomplished this as well as Balthasar. Too often we find essays on Barth's dogmatics or his ethics, but seldom the simultaneous interplay he performed. This is understandable; his approach does not fit disciplinary divisions in academic life well. Nor is it easy to cultivate the sources of knowledge necessary for such a monumental task. Balthasar, however, recognized what Barth was doing and took up the task.

In his 1951 Barth book, Balthasar noted that one of the ways to Barth's *Umbruch* was "ethics." The early Barth only stressed God's ethical agency in the sphere of grace. This precipitated a crisis in our understanding of ethics, but in his initial attempts at ethics, Barth did not produce an adequate understanding of human action in the sphere of grace. Balthasar recognized Barth was no "Molinist," where God elects solely based on God's foreknowledge of the creature's good deeds. Barth rejected that Jesuit approach and instead followed

vol. 2: *Spouse of the Word*, trans. A. V. Littledale with Alexander Dru (San Francisco: Ignatius, 1991), 198. I am grateful to Frederick Bauerschmidt and William Cavanaugh for reminding me of this important point.

131. William Cavanaugh, *Migrations of the Holy: God, State and the Political Meaning of the Church* (Grand Rapids, MI: Eerdmans., 2011) 141–69.

more closely the Thomist/Dominican route.[132] Balthasar acknowledges Barth affirms "an authentic creaturely freedom" yet "it remains subordinate to the all-determining sovereign freedom of God."[133] He had the *soli Deo* but never the *ad omnia*. Balthasar draws a surprising conclusion from this critique of Barth. For Barth, because God alone acts in the realm of grace, ethical human action is consigned only to a natural realm because it has no role in the realm of grace.[134] Insofar as this characterized Barth's ethics, he repeated exactly what Balthasar thought he failed to identify as the real problem within Catholic theology—a doctrine of pure nature. Barth failed to have an adequate place for an authentic secondary causality in the sphere of grace.[135] As we will see in the final chapter, this disagreement stems from Balthasar's participation in Barth's 1941 Council of Trent seminar.

Balthasar repeated this theme when he published his *Theology of History* the year after his exile from Basel ended (1957). He stated even more clearly what he had been saying for two decades:

> Karl Barth, in defining the man Christ as "man *for* men" and describing the rest of humanity as "man *with* men", is undoubtedly making an extremely profound statement (that the human *nature* of Christ is totally monopolized by the redeeming *action* of God and must be understood in terms of it). But this does involve the danger of looking upon the oneness of Christ and mankind as merely analogical. It would lead on to the conclusion that the "brothers" cannot, as is envisaged in Catholic teaching, participate in God's action in Christ—Incarnation, Cross, Resurrection. If the *analogy* between Christ's uniqueness and mankind in its multiplicity is not to annul the *identity* of their nature, then the ascent of human nature into God must be more deeply grounded in the descent of God into human nature. Only then does the inclusion of the redemption of the many within the uniqueness of Christ become intelligible.

---

132. Balthasar, *The Theology of Karl Barth*, 130.

133. Ibid., 131.

134. Ibid., 132.

135. Ibid., 133. Balthasar then concludes: "If it is true that the creature in its creatureliness and autonomy is a secondary cause and, on the other hand, if it is also true that freedom must be interpreted in terms of the economy of grace, then only one conclusion is possible. Contrary to Protestant doctrine, we are forced to conclude that the causality of the creature achieves its true character and its fullest maturity in the order of grace." Ibid., 135.

> The humanity of Christ, as Saint Thomas says, is the *instrumentum conjunctum* for the salvation of human nature as a whole.[136]

What Barth rejected as blasphemy, Balthasar affirms as necessary for the theodrama—Christ has brothers and sisters who can indeed "as is envisaged in Catholic teaching, participate in God's action in Christ—Incarnation, Cross, Resurrection."

Apart from the strange three judgments Barth made about the relationship between Jesus' Word and work and the church, it would be difficult to say this rightly characterizes Barth's theology after *Church Dogmatics* 4.3. To some extent, Barth concedes the point Balthasar presses. If the relationship between divinity and humanity is to have its unity in Christ properly understood, then there must be a human ascent within the context of the divine descent. The previous sketch of Barth's exaltation of human action that (supposedly) outdoes the Marian account in Catholicism is a response to Balthasar's critique. It was intentionally written in response to his Catholic interlocutors, but the inability to explain how the "new being" is ecclesially and institutionally constituted, for Balthasar, would still leave little to no room for human agency in the realm of grace. Barth needed correction.

The correction does not flow only from Balthasar to Barth. Balthasar's careful preoccupation with Barth also allowed him to see a weakness in Catholic theology and ethics. Barth influenced him to affirm and cling to the christological center in metaphysics, ethics, and all other secular engagements. In that same 1957 work Balthasar wrote,

> There are three things we cannot do: [1] we cannot carry on with natural metaphysics, natural ethics, natural jurisprudence, natural study of history, acting as though Christ were not, in the concrete, the norm of everything. [2] Nor can we lay down an unrelated "double truth", with the secular scholar and scientist on the one hand and the theologian on the other studying the same object without any encounter or intersection between their two methods. [3] Nor, finally, can we allow the secular disciplines to be absorbed by theology as though it alone were competent in all cases because Christ alone is the norm.[137]

---

136. Balthasar, *A Theology of History* (San Francisco: Ignatius, 1994), 16–17. Emphasis original.

137. Balthasar *A Theology of History,* 18–19.

He made a similar argument two decades later, when discussing the Christian states of life and how they relate to secular disciplines. Each is pervaded with a theological wisdom and particular charism to which it should remain open.[138] Much as Barth worried that the *analogia entis* would lead to a "secular misery," so Balthasar recognized that a "double truth" that cordoned theology off from secular disciplines, and grace from nature, would do the same. He cautioned against thinking theology could absorb every secular discipline, which it obviously cannot. Barth would certainly agree, but both insisted Christ was the "concrete norm," and that entailed relating everything to him. [139]

Balthasar acknowledges everything—ethics, metaphysics, secular disciplines—cannot be reduced to the particularity of Christology, but neither can Christ be left out of any of them. Sciences by their nature seek universal laws and in so doing abstract from concrete particulars. Abstraction is necessary, but it is also a source of error if it occurs at the expense of the particular. For Christian theology, the concrete particular is Jesus of Nazareth, who affects every aspect of creation. Everything then, must be related to him, but this does not happen identically in each case. Not everything is "equidistant" from this christological center. Disciplines will be variously related: "There are some in which the uniqueness of Christ totally eclipses the abstract general laws, practically replacing them, and others, whose relative autonomy persists practically untouched, only having to submit, as it were, to occasional indirect supervision."[140] Balthasar's *Theo-Drama* displays the relationship between Christ and most of the practical and theoretical concerns that are concerned with ethics: sex, economics, power, race, war, and so on. All are discussed within Christ's dramatic action. It is, however, not "ethics" per se. For Balthasar, no such thing exists within Christianity; his theodramatic approach is "transethical" because "Jesus' main achievement cannot be called simply ethical: it consists in his *allowing* something to happen, in *letting* himself be plundered and shared out in Passion and Eucharist."[141] It is, as we saw in his book on Schneider, Jesus'

---

138. "Proper to revelation, then, is a supernatural, theological penetration of all earthly sciences without exception: cosmology and astronomy, physics, biology, pharmacology, botany and zoology, history, psychology and other intellectual disciplines. As natural sciences, these sciences are not sufficient unto themselves; they are permeated by divine wisdom. . . . It is not surprising, therefore, but rather to be expected, that every earthly discipline and skill that is closed upon itself and refuses to open to supernatural wisdom . . . leads ultimately to folly; for there is, for every natural gift bestowed on man by God, a grace-filled charism that marks its perfection." Balthasar *The Christian States of Life*, 423.

139. Balthasar, *A Theology of History*, 20. Balthasar writes, "There is nothing in him which does not serve God's self-revelation. As the center of the world, he is the key to the interpretation not only of creation but of God himself."

140. Ibid.

nonresistant, surrendering obedience that forms the heart of a theodramatic "ethics."

Despite his critique of "ethics," Balthasar directly addressed it. He did so, however, consistent with the Barthian theme "dogmatics is ethics." In 1975 Balthasar wrote an essay on Christian ethics entitled, "Nine Theses in Christian Ethics" for Joseph Ratzinger's 1975 *Prinzipien christlicher Moral*. It began, "The Christian who lives by faith has the right to base his moral activity on his faith."[142] His first thesis stated,

> Christian ethics must be elaborated in such a way that its starting point is Jesus Christ, since he, as the Son of the Father, fulfilled the complete will of the Father (= everything that must be done) in this world. He did this "for us" so that we might gain our freedom from him, the concrete and plenary norm for all moral action, to accomplish God's will and to live up to our vocation to be free children of the Father.[143]

This first thesis could easily be read as the central theme of Balthasar's *Theo-Drama*. It sets forth a rich moral theology within central christological loci that includes analyses of vocation, mission, action, and freedom. These are the key components to Balthasar's moral theology, and Barth's as well. Barth likewise correlated freedom and obedience, but Balthasar's correlation comes with this important difference: The freedom Christ brings forms the basis for human action that can nonidentically repeat his obedience as a graced, natural action. Grace comes to human nature and completes it so that it can fulfill its purpose, its "vocation." The (natural) freedom necessary for morality and the (graced) obedience to Christ's mission through human institutions mutually support each other. Balthasar repeatedly emphasized, especially in the *Theo-Drama*, this "acting arena" for human freedom that Christ won through the cross, resurrection, and ascension. For Balthasar, Christ gives himself over to human mediation in a way that Barth found troubling.

---

141. Balthasar, *Theo-Drama*, vol. 3: *Dramatis Personae: Persons in Christ*, trans. Graham Harrison (San Francisco: Ignatius),, 29.

142. His essay, "Neun Sätze zur christlichen Ethik," first appeared in *Prinzipien christlicher Moral*, ed. Joseph Ratzinger (Einsiedeln: Johannes, 1975), 67–93. It was translated and published as "Nine Theses in Christian Ethics," in *Readings in Moral Theology*, no. 2: *The Distinctiveness of Christian Ethics*, ed. Charles E. Curran and Richard A. McCormack, SJ (New York: Paulist Press, 1980), 190–207.

143. Balthasar, "Nine Theses in Christian Ethics," 191.

The "acting arena," or "realm," within which a graced natural action occurs requires attention to Balthasar's theology of mission and its relationship to the secular institutes. They are necessary to understand not only his life and the decisions he made, but also the ethics and political theology in the *Theo-Drama*. If Barth set ethics within the doctrine of election, Balthasar placed it within mission. He left the Jesuits, despite his deep and abiding commitment to Ignatius, to purse the mission of the secular institutes because he thought they were of such tremendous importance to engage the modern world politically and ethically. He recognized how difficult such an engagement would be because of what modern European Christianity had rendered asunder: the mission of "administering the earthly realm" and that of "the saint." Reinhold Schneider's work helped him see their unity.

POLITICAL THEOLOGY?

Balthasar also had the example of Karl Barth before him as someone who engaged the world against the distorted political sovereignty of their generation, uniting dogma and ethics. Balthasar praised his courage. Barth's public stand against Nazism was primarily done through lectures and writing, which got him in trouble with the Swiss government. He joined the Swiss military to fight against Germany if they invaded Switzerland. He joined the *National Widerstand*, which swore an oath not to lay down arms even if the Swiss government did. He sent Balthasar an invitation to join this group. We have no evidence that he responded; it appears he did not join.[144] Although he admired Barth, Balthasar never explicitly followed his form of political and ethical engagement.

Perhaps Balthasar engaged politics differently than Barth, and yet consistently with Barth's insight that dogmatics is ethics? Undoubtedly Barth's political engagement was significant, less because he thought the Swiss should take on the German military, and more because of his public witness. He helped form the Confessing Church and wrote much of the Barmen declaration. He tried to mobilize the church to resist. He sent a copy of "Theological Existence Today!" to Hitler.[145] He drafted but never sent a letter to call German Christians to refuse participation in the German military and its war making apparatus.[146] He lectured to thousands, wrote public editorials, and regularly

144. Conversation with Hans Anton Drewes, April, 2011.

145. Frank Jehle, *Ever Against the Stream: The Politics of Karl Barth 1906–1968*, trans. Richard and Martha Burnett (Grand Rapids, MI: Eerdmans, 2002), 47.

146. Eberhard Busch, *Karl Barth: His Life from Letters and Autobiographical Texts*, trans. John Bowden (Philadelphia: Fortress Press, 1976), 289.

provoked the Swiss government for their putative neutrality in World War II with little concern for the consequences. He accused them of capitulation. The Swiss authorities tapped his phone during the war years, and no member of the Swiss Federal Council attended his funeral.[147] He was a courageous and public witness. Balthasar's public witness was much more local. It occurred through the form of life Christ made possible through vocation and election to perfect love. "It is through this love" he wrote, "—not through speeches, axioms, organizations, and *aggiornamento*—that the world is redeemed. And since Christ has given us everything that is his, he also gives to those who belong to him the form of his own life."[148] The ethical task is to conform our existence to this form, which is done through the "Christian states of life."

The importance of this mission can be seen in Balthasar's critique of "political theology." He did not reject it out of hand. It is one of eight "trends of modern theology" that he affirms in part. Each of these trends recognizes theology is "stuck fast on the sandbank of rationalist abstraction and want to get it moving again." He thinks they "converge" on "theo-drama;" it is necessary to complete them. [149] Without the theodrama, "nature" will be defined without Christ, and any politics or ethics that acts based upon such an understanding of nature can only be inadequate. Balthasar made a similar argument in his 1969 publication *Convergences*, where he did not dismiss "political theology," but emphasized a christological center if it is to be truly political. He wrote, "Jesus' life as a whole is political theology." Only a focus on his "total obedience" can give rise to a proper political theology.[150] Theodrama completes political theology by "opening up an horizon beyond the immediate horizon of the state." This "opening up" is what the apostles did, and it allowed them to subject the state to "eschatological critique." The state is not an actor in the theodrama. To look to it for a "political" stance will entail a truncated political theology.

Balthasar critiques any "Constantinian imperial theology," whether it would be of the left or right. It arises when theology's mission is reduced to the "political."

---

147. Jehle, *Ever Against the Stream: The Politics of Karl Barth 1906–1968,* 1.

148. Balthasar, *The Laity and the Life of the Counsels,* 239.

149. Balthasar, *Theo-Drama,* vol. 1: *Prolegomena,* trans. Graham Harrison (San Francisco: Ignatius, 1988), 25. The other trends are "theology of 'event' (Barth and Bultmann), of history, of praxis, of dialogue, futurism, functionalism and role." Balthasar seeks to take what is good in these and complete them with what is lacking, which is a theology of mission.

150. *Convergences: To the Source of Christian Mystery,* trans. E. A. Nelson (San Francisco: Ignatius, 1983), 42.

The dramatic situation in which the Christian is consciously, and the world and its history are unconsciously, involved goes far beyond the category of politics. It complements the latter with a dimension which, depending on how one looks at it, can be described as ineluctably tragic or utopian (whether in a meaningless or a meaningful sense) or as ultimately bringing reconciliation.[151]

That Balthasar invokes "tragedy" here points to his important work, already mentioned, on Reinhold Schneider. Balthasar originally wrote this work in 1953, three years into his exile from his secular institute in Basel. He then revised it toward the end of his life in 1988. It is a crucial work for understanding his theological ethics as well as his vision for the secular institutes. Dedicated to the "secular institutes," it sought to present the "tragedy" of synthesizing "two missions that are equally original and yet stand in a deadly mutual conflict: the mission of the one who is entrusted with the task of administering the earthly realm and the mission of the saint as the real symbol of the kingdom of God that descends into the world." Christ and Mary unite these two missions in their being and bequeath its unity to the church. This unified mission was, Balthasar notes, the "guiding image for the secular institutes."[152] The purpose of the work is "to combine the radicalism of the gospel with a total, active involvement in secular work, enduring in their own selves the conflict described here."[153] Balthasar both followed and supplemented Barth's significant revision and/or retrieval of an ethics that primarily makes sense within the particular contours of Christian doctrine, but he did so by cultivating instituted communities where laity would live out that ethics, uniting in themselves these two missions. It is a heroic and chivalric ethic that differs significantly from Barth's, especially since it is primarily for those elected to the perfection found in the evangelical counsels of celibacy, poverty, and obedience.

Balthasar situated ethics not only within dogma, as did Barth, but also within a specific sociality—lay institutes within the church and the mission entrusted to them. Here he developed something beyond Barth's theological ethics. It is within this practical context that his theodramatic "ethics" best makes sense, and this new context meant an abstract nature could not be the realm to think or practice ethics. No such realm exists. Whatever could be practiced in such a realm would be unintelligible from the perspective of the divine economy. Some other economy would inevitably characterize it.

151. Balthasar, *Theo-Drama* 1, 40. He makes a similar point in *Convergences*, 43
152. *Tragedy under Grace*, 11.
153. Ibid.

THEODRAMATIC ETHICS

Chapters 2 and 3 made reference to a controversial statement Balthasar made in his 1951 Barth book, acknowledging "pure nature" cannot "answer" essential human questions concerning "ignorance, hardship, concupiscence, disease, death, marriage, community, State, the eschatological fate of the soul, resurrection of the body, Last Judgment and eternal bliss."[154] Gutwenger in 1953 and Steven A. Long in 2010 pointed this out as an error Balthasar made because Barth led him astray. Despite criticism, Balthasar never relinquished the judgment that pure nature could not provide a faithful context for ethics. In his 1977 publication *The Christian States of Life*, he argued a transition happened in the understanding of "nature" once Aristotle was introduced into Christian theology. Aristotle's introduction misled Catholic philosophy into thinking his doctrine of nature could describe nature qua nature without theology. The result was "fallen nature" took the place of a theological concept of nature, producing a significant shift in the theory and practice of Catholic moral theology with respect to private ownership, sexuality, and moral freedom.[155] These moral issues were no longer addressed from within the divine economy, but from a pure nature that often was conflated with fallen nature.

That pure nature could not address important ethical and political questions did not mean Balthasar found the questions themselves unanswerable; his trilogy addressed all of them in varying degrees. Nor did it mean ethics would be pursued solely in a realm of grace. That was never an option; ethical questions are unanswerable via a philosophical rendering of nature alone, but they are answerable through a theological one that maintains a central role for philosophy. Nature could neither be "pure" nor evacuated by grace. Because it cannot be evacuated, Balthasar set ethics within the transcendental predicates of being (beauty, good, true), which is how the *analogia entis* contributed to his theodrama, an element for which Barth had no interest. Balthasar placed the

---

154. Balthasar, *The Theology of Karl Barth,* 283. *Karl Barth: Darstellung und Deutung Seiner Theologie* (Cologne: Jakob Hegner, 1951), 294.

155. Balthasar, *The Christian States of Life,* 91n21. He writes, "It is surprising that the utterances of classical theologians on this subject are so little known to more recent scholars of natural law within the Catholic Church. This fact—which often leads them, for allegedly apologetic reasons, to misconstrue and distort the whole range of patristic and scholastic literature at least to the time of Thomas Aquinas, while such impartial researches as Carlyle and, for the most part, also Troeltsch are able to assess it correctly—has its basis in a concept of natural law that became possible only with the post-Reformation hypothesis of a *status naturae purae* that was to be distinguished as a state in its own right from all the concrete states defined above: original state, state of grace and state of redemption. As we shall see, the application of this concept of nature to earlier times led to deep-seated misunderstandings." *The Christian States of Life,* 105. See 105–19 for his important excursus on these misunderstandings.

theodrama and the human pursuit of the good between the aesthetics and logic in order to situate ethics within contemplation of God's glory and truth, but also to differentiate it from the receptivity of aesthetics and the demonstrations found in logic.[156] He brought beauty, goodness, and truth into a complex unity. The logic of truth is unsustainable without the performance of the good.[157] Contemplation immediately issues in action, an action embedded in divine action, but one that is always also human action. Bringing together theological dramatics and the good makes for a profound moral theology.

To call the *Theo-Drama* a moral theology is, in part, imprecise. It is obviously not an ethics per se, but that merely restates Balthasar's claim that Christianity is transethical. The *Theo-Drama* is, in Balthasar's own terms, a five-part drama between heaven and earth that consists of a prolegomena (volume 1), anthropology (volume 2), Christology (volume 3), soteriology (volume 4), and doctrine of the Trinity (volume 5).[158] The first volume establishes central themes in moral theology: the good, freedom for it, and a theory of action.[159] The last volume addresses Karl Rahner's accusation that Balthasar's theology is "gnostic," and offers insight into what he intended and why he thinks this charge is inaccurate.[160] Like Barth, its purpose is an ethics of witness. Balthasar wrote, "Following Aquinas, we have tried to erect theology on the articles of faith (and not vice versa): on the Trinity, the Incarnation of the Son, his Cross and Resurrection on our behalf, and his sending of the Spirit to us in the apostolic Church and in the *communio sanctorum*." Only on the "basis of such a theology," he continues, is it possible for human creatures to "give witness in their lives and in their deaths" to "the highest gift of God."[161] Witness and death are closely related for him, perhaps too closely. By the time he comes to the end of the *Theo-Drama*, he will argue that death is "transformatory." A critical question that must be posed to Balthasar's performance of Barth's "dogmatics is ethics" is if it valorizes self-sacrifice. Does death finally have too much of a positive role to play? Has Balthasar peered into the *Apokalypse* too long? Perhaps, but an adequate answer requires an examination of what he meant by

---

156. *Theo-Drama* 1, 19. "This good is something done: it cannot be contemplated in pure 'aesthetics' nor proved and demonstrated in pure 'logic.'"

157. *Theo-Drama* 1, 20. "The *good* which God does to us can only be experienced as the *truth* if we share in *performing* it." emphasis original.

158. *Theo-Drama* 5, 13.

159. *Theo-Drama* 1, 19.

160. John Milbank repeats this accusation in his *The Suspended Middle* (Grand Rapids, MI: Eerdmans, 2005).

161. *Theo-Drama* 5, 14.

a "transformatory death." It is finally eucharistic, related not only to the church but to the church's offering of all creation to the Father in the Son through the Spirit. This offering is the final act of the *Theo-Drama*.

Theo-Drama traces the good, beginning with articles of faith in volume 1 and culminating in the eschatology of volume 5, in which we discover heaven and earth were always united because Christ united them. The theodrama is the realization of that unity, the bringing together of "idea" and "existence." Much like Barth's ethics, Balthasar's theodrama is an ethics of declaration and witness. The church plays a central role, but a decisive difference is found in how the church is the body of Christ.

The role of the church in Barth's dogmatics bears similarities and dissimilarities to its place in Balthasar's theodrama. For both, it is the acting arena in which God addresses humanity. For Barth this is primarily done through the threefold Word—the Word preached, written (Scripture), and revealed. These three forms are not "three different Words of God." They are one Word in three forms that cannot be fundamentally divided .[162] No analogy exists for the unity of these three forms except for the mystery of the Holy Trinity. He wrote, "Dogmatics is the scientific self-examination of the Christian Church with respect to the content of its distinctive talk about God."[163] Barth offers a different account of dogma than Balthasar, for whom it is a deposit entrusted to the church and readily identifiable. For Balthasar, dogma is not an event. For Barth, dogma is an event that occurs when the threefold forms of God's Word coincide; then "dogmatics is ethics." The event of the Word, when it occurs, entails the self-involvement of its hearers that generates good action founded upon, and inculcating, faith, hope, and love. But for Barth, this event cannot be insured through any institutional church or objective office, especially a hierarchical one. Jesus always stands over and against the church, even if it is the earthly form of his body. Unlike the Roman Catholic tradition, to which Balthasar always adhered, the church is not,

---

162. *Church Dogmatics* 1.1, trans. Geoffrey W. Bromiley, ed. G. W. Bromiley and T. F. Torrance, 2nd ed. (Edinburgh: T & T Clark, 1975), 121. "The revealed Word of God we know only from the Scripture adopted by Church proclamation or the proclamation of the Church based on Scripture. The written Word of God we know only through the revelation which fulfills proclamation or through the proclamation fulfilled by revelation. The preached Word of God we know only through the revelation attested in Scripture or the Scripture which attests revelation."

163. Ibid., 3.

even analogically, comparable to the mystery of the incarnation.[164] For Barth, however, the key to the church is not office or institution but prayer.

As thoroughly as Barth rejected the church as the prolongation of the incarnation in the concluding section of his doctrine of reconciliation, Balthasar affirms it in the "Last Act" of the *Theo-Drama*.

> The Church is the prolongation of Christ's mediatorial nature and work and possesses a knowledge that comes by faith; she lives objectively (in her institution and her sacraments) and subjectively (in her saints and, fundamentally, in all her members) in the interchange between heaven and earth. Her life comes from heaven and extends to earth, and extends from earth to heaven.[165]

For Balthasar, if the church is not the prolongation of the incarnation, there is no theodrama. For it begins in Christ, where God and humanity are reconciled, and extends to all of creation, which participates in the eucharistic surrender to God both in the secular and sacred realms. Balthasar's theory of action and analogy of finite and infinite freedom in *Theo-Drama* 1 only make sense within this acting arena. It is the crux of his criticism of Barth for failing to have an adequate account of human agency in the realm of grace, and thus colluding with a doctrine of pure nature. If the church as Christ's body is not extended in time, creation loses its purpose. It becomes devoid of theological significance. For Balthasar, in opposition to Barth, creation has different gradations of proximity to the christological center.

Balthasar emphasizes that any adequate reception, and therefore enactment, of God's gift of grace requires a commitment to the distinction found in the "Christian states of life": priest and laity, counsels and

164. As *Lumen gentium* 8 puts it, "Christ, the one Mediator, established and continually sustains here on earth His holy Church, the community of faith, hope and charity, as an entity with visible delineation through which He communicated truth and grace to all. But, the society structured with hierarchical organs and the Mystical Body of Christ, are not to be considered as two realities, nor are the visible assembly and the spiritual community, nor the earthly Church and the Church enriched with heavenly things; rather they form one complex reality which coalesces from a divine and a human element. For this reason, by no weak analogy, it is compared to the mystery of the incarnate Word. As the assumed nature inseparably united to Him, serves the divine Word as a living organ of salvation, so, in a similar way, does the visible social structure of the Church serve the Spirit of Christ, who vivifies it, in the building up of the body." See http://www.vatican.va/archive/hist_councils/ii_vatican_council/documents/vat-ii_const_19641121_lumen-gentium_en.html. I am grateful to Francesca Murphy for this quote.

165. *Theo-Drama* 5, 131.

commandments. The church lives objectively in its priestly structure and subjectively in the call to perfection found in the saints and counsels, but also among all the church's members. Balthasar sets forth a chivalric ethic that calls laity to profess the evangelical counsels in order to witness to the unity of what cannot be united until Christ returns: the secular and the religious, earth and heaven. These witnesses are the theological vanguard embodying the unity that will characterize the last act, an act that is already accomplished even if we cannot yet see it. From Barth's perspective this raises the question whether Balthasar's chivalric ethic provides an adequate space for the agency of the laity. He was suspicious of the Catholic distinction between the perfection of the counsels and its tacit assumption of a lesser form of Christian discipleship for the laity. Balthasar works diligently to avoid this assumption, not always successfully. A decisive difference between them focuses upon the doctrine of election.

Barth places the doctrine of election within the doctrine of God. Jesus is the Elect One and in him all are equally elect. For Balthasar all are equally elect as well in Christ, but then gradations of election occur as each is called to perform her or his mission.[166] The gradations begin with Mary; she is elect unlike all other humans.[167] For Barth election has no gradations; everyone is equally distant from the Elect One. Freedom does not consist in one person realizing this perfection more so than another. For Balthasar freedom exists precisely in such a realization. Some more perfectly exercise the freedom to follow in the state of Christ than others, who then depend upon that freedom for their own participation in it. The state of election is primarily the state of the counsels (poverty, celibacy, obedience), following Christ's hard sayings. The counsels differ from the secular state, but in the mission of the secular institutes the two are united. Both the religious and the secular are called to perfection, but the election to the counsels provides the condition for the secular state that is not reciprocated.[168] Balthasar's ethics is heroic and therefore tragic in a way

---

166. Balthasar, *The Christian States of Life*, 158: "Thus it has become even more evident that the state of election is preeminently the *state of Christ*."

167. *Theo-Drama* 3, 273.

168. "This does not mean that he [the married person] is a less worthy Christian than they [the religious] are, for, even when God's gifts vary, his election bestows on each individual only what is best. Both states—the lay state, which achieves its fulfillment in the married state, and the state of election—condition one another and are intimately related to one another; not, however, as two equal and complementary halves are related, but as the special state, which emanates from the general one and returns to it by way of sacrifice and mission, is related to the general state that is what it is—a genuinely Christian state—only because of the special state." Balthasar, *The Christian States of Life*, 249.

that Barth's is not; those who are elect to merge the secular with the counsels follow Christ most closely. They are called to go "outside the camp."

For Balthasar Christ's mission to go "outside the camp" (Heb. 13:12) forms the heart of the Christian understanding of the good. This theme from Hebrews pervades his work in a way similar to Barth's use of the prodigal son pervades his. Just as for Barth the Son's going "into the far country" defines his mission, so for Balthasar his going "outside the camp" does, which is true both of the procession of the Son in the immanent Trinity and the mission of the Son in the economic. Balthasar draws upon Thomas Aquinas to explain this.

> *Thomas Aquinas* describes this identity by saying that in Christ the *processio* within the godhead, which constitutes the Son as the Father's dialogue partner, is identical, in God's going-out-from-himself toward the world with the *missio*, the sending of the Son to mankind. (This *missio* is completed by the sending of the Spirit into the world, proceeding from both Father and Son).[169]

Secular persons who profess the counsels share this movement even more so than priests or laity in the secular state. In a way that can easily be construed as autobiographical, Balthasar writes,

> Marriage and priesthood tend to require a manageable roster of duties and rights with which the Christian is familiar, that are satisfying to him, and by the accomplishment of which he is able to please God. The religious knows no such finiteness. It is his function in the Church to open all closed ideals and pastoral goals to the always limitless demand of Christ. In the parish and the diocese, he is an element of Christian unrest; when all tasks have been neatly assigned, he is there as the uncomfortable "seamless robe", the disturber of the peace, the disrupter of all plans. By this state of life, he shares in a special way in Christ's expulsion and abandonment "outside" the camp, which he, too, experiences; within the Church, his position is analogous to that of the Church as a whole within the world: the position of a stranger who can never be completely at home here.[170]

---

169. See *Theo-Drama* 1, 646. Emphasis original. He cites *Summa Theologica* Ia 43 1–8.
170. *The Christian States of Life*, 379.

Perhaps laity who have not professed the counsels can perform this task, suggests Balthasar, and perhaps many of his comments about Barth's life reveal that he thought Barth himself did. But without the state of life the counsels bring, this essential participation in Christ's mission to the world cannot be accomplished. This mission forms the heart of the theodrama.[171]

Once Balthasar establishes this "mission" as the heart of the theodrama, three elements then constitute the transition from aesthetics to dramatics: "form, word and election."[172] Drama cannot occur without dialogue, so the emphasis on "seeing the form" in the aesthetics must now be supplemented with the Word "understood as expression, as a ground that makes itself known." Like Barth, the Word "declares" itself, allowing creatures the freedom to witness to it. Although the expressed Word makes itself known, it also requires freedom to hear, receive, and enact it. Any predestination that denies such freedom is for Balthasar a species of Gnosticism.[173] It is what worried him about Calvinism, a worry Barth's Reformed theology alleviated in part. Along with freedom is the "in-sight (intel-lectus)" that comes from understanding the Word, "faith" to receive it which is a human act, and "attentiveness." Attentiveness recognizes that language is universal; it discloses being as beautiful, true, and good. Every language assumes this same disclosure of being, even though it only does this in terms of a particular language.[174] The specific words of a language occur against the backdrop of a universal form. Form and word must finally come together. When they do, one is "touched" or "enraptured," which is "election."[175] From this election emerges each Christian's mission. Everyone is called to use her or his freedom to participate in Christ's mission within his or her particular state. The extent to which each individual accomplishes this is the extent to which she or he becomes a "person."[176]

By person, Balthasar means something distinct that cannot be understood without its Trinitarian analogy. Only Christ is fully identical in his Person with his mission, but it is mission that constitutes each individual's "personhood." To become a person then is a task; it is not inherent based on dignity, rationality, autonomy, linguistic capability, race, gender, class, or some such identifiable

171. *Theo-Drama* 1, 647–48/

172. *Theo-Drama*, vol. 2: *Dramatis Personae: Man in God*, trans. Graham Harrison (San Francisco: Ignatius, 1990), 21.

173. Ibid., 17.

174. Ibid., 22–25.

175. Ibid., 27–31

176. This is, of course, controversial. For criticisms and defenses of it, see Steffen Lösel, *Kreuzwege: Ein ökumenisches Gespräch mit Hans Urs von Balthasar* (Zurich: Ferdinand Schöningh, 2001) 164–66.

marker. It is to bring together idea and existence. We are each summoned to participate in the freedom God gives us in order to receive and thereby enact our mission. This summons constitutes not only our personhood, but also our humanity. For Balthasar the drama also always remains "unfinished." Human creatures have "degrees" in their "full humanity" based on their exercise of freedom to achieve perfection within a given historical context.[177] In explaining this anthropology in *Theo-Drama* 2, he writes, "man, in his inner, noumenal life-form, is critically shaped by his freedom, and it is only by responding to the personal and impersonal challenges of the world around him that man's freedom is provoked and summoned to realize itself." [178] A person's mission in the actual world in which one lives realizes freedom, but the realization of our humanity and personhood only finally makes sense against the background of Balthasar's eschatology in *Theo-Drama* 5, when he discusses "The World in God."

Once again the key theme is Christ's mission to go outside himself for others, bringing heaven and earth together in union. Christ has already accomplished this unity. When he does so, we do not discover "a 'different' world replacing the first." Instead, "'the new heaven and the new earth' found in Is. 65:17; 66:22 and Rev. 21:1 . . . are the result of a transformation effected by God and with God as its goal."[179] The transformation is found in Christ: "Christ's body has become finally and definitively eucharistic . . . its being is not for itself but for the other."[180] Creatures participate in this realization of Christ's mission when they too become eucharistic, pouring themselves out for others. Because the "Idea" of each one, as well as the "Idea" of every mission, has always and forever will be "in Christ," each has a mission to embody his life in service to the world. This call to realize a mission is what it means for us to be created in, through, and for Christ.[181]

In his eschatology, Balthasar raises two questions about the realization of mission: first, "How far can the task that on earth, is never fully completed, or only superficially so (and sometimes not at all) be regarded as being fulfilled in heaven?" All earthly performances of our mission remain unfulfilled, except for Christ and Mary's, so the time of heaven is necessary to fulfill it. Second, "How is it possible for creatures to be embedded in God in such a way that

---

177. In no way, of course, does Balthasar suggest that this gradation of "person" warrants or legitimates unequal or oppressive treatment. Such an implication of his position would be uncharitable and miss how "person" functions.

178. *Theo-Drama* 2, 37.

179. *Theo Drama* 5, 380.

180. Ibid., 382.

181. Ibid., 392.

they attain perfection without losing their creaturely nature?"[182] God's act does not overwhelm the creature and evacuate her nature in a gnostic destruction of materiality; God's act establishes creaturely freedom. It does so both on earth and in heaven. The drama does not end with earthly existence; it continues in God's final, eschatological rule. We are always becoming what we are to be. Balthasar provides three responses to these questions, which form the structure for the first part of *Theo-Drama* 5, in which we realize that the eschatological theodrama is not future but also always present.

The central point in his responses, consistent with his understanding as to how creatures are in God on earth and are still freely acting agents, is that there is never a movement from outside to inside God. Creation is always within God, even though it is genuinely creation and therefore other. There is no pure natural realm outside God. The Trinity contains creation within itself without denying creation's genuine freedom to be other than God and realize its mission(s), and thus effect a transformation where heaven and earth are united. This was always the goal of the divine economy, which Balthasar seeks to express in his theodrama. He explains this goal by first emphasizing the "fullness of life within the Godhead in a super-essential way."[183] This fullness includes the potentialities in creation that are truly potential for us, but which are not as such for God. In God there is no potentiality, but there is receptivity. God can receive not only God's own being from others—Father, Son, and Holy Spirit—but also from creation, without making creation a fourth hypostasis. A "superessential being" cannot be added to by receiving being, so receptivity does not deny God's essential perfections such as simplicity, immutability, and impassibility. Balthasar affirms Aquinas's perfections within the context of orthodox Christian theology and sets forth their importance for good human action. Second, he offers a "theology of the world" in its "pilgrim condition" that requires a "transformatory death" for it to reach its "ultimate, though unimaginable, state 'with' God."[184] The term "transformatory death" is troubling. Given that Balthasar subjected German Idealism's "apotheosis of death" to serious criticism in his *Apokalypse*, the return of a "transformatory death" is puzzling, but the language used is eucharistic. The world is united and "handed over" to God. This death and handing over is the basis for freedom. Third, potentiality and transformatory death allow for genuine human freedom. It finds its place in God because of the "infinite distinction between the Divine Persons."[185] To explain this freedom grounded in God's infinite

182. Ibid.
183. Ibid., 394. He explains this in ibid., 66–99.
184. Ibid., 394. He explains this in ibid., 99–118.

distinction, Balthasar appeals to "dialectic:" "We must speak in dialectical terms of the highest presence of something that is beyond all that we can grasp."[186] God remains "incomprehensible" even in heaven, so that the freedom we exercise on earth to realize the idea of our mission can be extended into heaven.[187] Balthasar's eschatological vision points to a unifying of heaven and earth that was always present, but can only now come into focus. It allows for a genuine human freedom without positing a two-tiered system of nature and supernature. But it unites them without losing human action by collapsing nature into grace, as he thought Calvinist doctrines of predestination tended to do. There is genuine drama, but to exercise our freedom, to achieve our unique mission is not simply a means to something; it is always already a participation in something Christ accomplished. Like Barth, for Balthasar declaration and witness become essential "ethical" categories.

Between the prolegomena of *Theo-Drama* 1 and the eschatology of *Theo-Drama* 5, Balthasar offers ethical reflection on creaturely mission on earth as it is in heaven. Because religious who take vows of poverty, celibacy, and obedience live in a "bridal state or existence," their lives form the normative pattern within which all other Christian states are rendered intelligible.[188] Mary is the central image of such human action because like Jesus her mission and person are identical. The receptivity of mission constitutes her agency as person. This receptivity is key for Balthasar's theory of human action, found in *Theo-Drama* 2:

> While he [the human agent] finds himself on the stage as soon as he comes into the world, he also has a part in shaping it. He does this through the measure of his receptivity, which enables him in an earthly way to receive heavenly things and give birth to them, and through the measure of his freedom to keep the kingdom of heaven away from the earth or, conversely, to cause it to come nearer. Ultimately, therefore, the stage is entirely assimilated into the spiritual dimensions of the actors themselves.[189]

185. Ibid., 395. He explains this in ibid., 247–321.

186. Ibid., 396.

187. Ibid. "God's infinite life is a freedom that cannot be plumbed; its rooms cannot be 'beheld': we are to hurry through them as in a 'race' that will never end."

188. *Theo-Drama* 1 offers the "conditions that render action possible," which requires moving from a dramatic "role" to "mission." This assumes the priority to the saints: "The saints are the authentic interpreters of theodrama." They set "a standard of interpretation not only for the life-dramas of individuals but ultimately for the 'history of freedom' of all the nations and of all mankind." *Theo-Drama* 2, 14.

Barth thought he could advocate a similar agency without Mary, but an important difference between their accounts of agency is the gradations within election. These gradations also entail different ecclesiologies. For Balthasar, the gradations entail a hierarchical church, but even the hierarchical Petrine office depends upon the Marian vocation to holiness. For Barth, any such gradation denies his central claim that only Christ is the Elect One, and all are equally elect in him. As head of the church, he also stands above the body; all its parts are equidistant from the center. For Balthasar, head and body are one within a hierarchical ordering. As one reality, Christ and his body constitute a single acting subject extending to all of creation. For Barth Christ and the church must always remain divided if Christ's rule is not to be usurped by secular authority.

Conclusion

Is Balthasar's emphasis on the church as the extension of the incarnation blasphemous, and would Barth really have thought it was? One of Barth's concerns, of course, is to have an ecclesiology that is capable of acknowledging the church's sins and thus capable of reform. He affirmed Vatican II for this precise accomplishment and admonished Protestantism for failing to have any such reform. Balthasar, as we shall see, was not as taken by Vatican II as was Barth, but not because he had a triumphalist ecclesiology where the church never erred. He could also speak, like Luther but with a significant difference, that the church was the "whore of Babylon": for Balthasar, she was the "chaste prostitute." If the church fails to look this "reality in the eye," then it fails to see at "what price" it has been purchased. Balthasar's theodramatic ethics never precluded ecclesial reform; it is part of the drama.

Barth and Balthasar interspersed ethics throughout dogmatic loci, and brought about a very different approach to ethics than is found either among the neoscholastic or the liberal Protestants. They both retrieved a strong eschatological sensibility to the Christian life, which resulted in the ethical importance of attentiveness, declaration, and witness. They both understood the church as the acting arena within which Christian ethics should be pursued. Dogmatics, like the theodrama, occurs within the context of the church, which makes arguing over ecclesiology all the more important. What began in turmoil and conflict, Balthasar's preoccupation with Barth, ended in common reflections about the renewal and unity of the church. Barth and Balthasar worked from 1939 until 1968 to understand and address the "puzzling cleft" that divided Protestants and Catholics. If the church is the acting arena within which

189. *Theo-Drama 2*, 188

Christian ethics makes sense, the church's divisions were all the more troubling. If modern theology reduced theology to ethics, then overcoming the church's divisions could not be had through a liberal sensibility where doctrine divides but ethics unites. Instead, theological differences must be stated precisely. They cannot be remedied by ignoring their existence. The above differences will not be adjudicated and resolved in the final chapter. They cannot be resolved because they remain church dividing. Yet tracing the "rapprochement" between Barth and Balthasar from the 1941 Trent seminar to their joint 1968 lecture on church unity will at least contribute to illumining why these differences matter, where they might be based on misunderstandings, and where frank and honest conversation must continue.

6

The Realm of the Church: Renewal and Unity

If the "burning matter of dispute" between Balthasar and Barth, Catholicism and Protestantism, was the "realm" within which we contemplate, practice, and pursue the knowledge of God and ethics, and if the church was a central component of that realm, then the division between Catholics and Protestants become all the more important. When he was in exile from Basel from 1950 to 1956, Balthasar thought nothing was as important as addressing this split. In fact, his book on Barth begins by taking up an important phrase Barth used to describe the fracture: *rätselhafte Riss*, which can be translated as a "puzzling crack" or "enigmatic cleft." Neither Barth nor Balthasar could be reconciled to this *Riss*. Neither sought to render it intelligible. The split was, is, and remains puzzling. Recognizing the enigma of the cleft creates its own crisis, albeit one that cannot be resolved by human agency alone. Nonetheless, Christians were required to declare the oddness of their divisions and witness to a unity that Christ accomplished, although it was seldom seen. To that end, Barth and Balthasar spoke unapologetically from the heart of their traditions. Barth began his approach to ecumenism with a self-described "dogmatic intolerance" of others' positions.[1] What must have surprised Barth, and took him a while to recognize, was the Catholic interest in his theology. Balthasar helped him make sense of it. From their first substantive engagement with each other in Barth's 1941 seminar on the Council of Trent, to their last public lecture on Ash Wednesday 1968 to the Ökumenischen Gesprächskomissionen der Schweiz [Swiss Ecumenical Dialogue Commission], Barth and Balthasar were thrust into an ecumenical conversation about which they both had suspicions and reservations, but that they also could not ignore.

---

1. See Eberhard Busch, *Karl Barth: His Life from Letters and Autobiographical Texts*, trans. John Bowden (Philadelphia: Fortress Press, 1976), 215 for Barth's insistence that this is how ecumenism should begin.

INITIATING THE ECUMENICAL CONVERSATION

Without knowing he had done so, Barth began the ecumenical conversation seven years before he and Balthasar met. Balthasar's preoccupation with Barth centered on ecclesial divisions and the harm they do to the church's witness. The first line of his Barth book presents it as a "confessional conversation [Gespräch] among theologians," and he begins with a quote from Barth's Church Dogmatics 1.1 (1932) about the "puzzling crack" (rätselhafte Riss) that has gone through the church for over four hundred years.[2] The title of the first chapter, "Zerrissene Kirche" (the torn or divided Church) plays off this Barth quote.[3] The Riss is the basis for the Zerrissene, but what exactly is torn? Gaining some clarity on that is the first step in understanding what can only be an enigma — a divided church.

The Barth quote comes from a section in the first volume of Church Dogmatics, where he compared the Reformed emphasis on proclamation with the Catholic emphasis on Eucharist. Barth, who is not yet writing for Catholics, encourages his assumed Protestant readers not to recoil at Catholic terms for the Eucharist such as fieri (to become) and nova forma (new form) when applied to the "earthly elements" of bread and wine that become "the body and blood of the Lord." Although he sides with the Reformation rejection of transubstantiation, he also acknowledges that what occurs in Reformation preaching is as realistic as what Catholics claim takes place in the Eucharist. He writes, "We only show our failure to understand what it means that the earthly reality acquires this new nota by the Word of God if we regard this view of the new becoming as less realistic than that expressed in the Roman Catholic doctrine of transubstantiation or the Lutheran doctrine of consubstantiation."[4] Reformed preaching claims a communication of God's presence as high as Catholic or Lutheran doctrines of the Eucharist. In order to explain this Barth cites the Council of Trent. By "priestly consecration" the bread undergoes a "conversio totius substantiae panis in substantiam corporis Christi Domini nostri et totius substantiae vini in substantiam sanguinis eius [a conversion of the whole substance of bread into the substance of the body of Christ our Lord and of the whole substance of wine into the substance of his blood]."[5]

2. "Diese Buch ist ein Beitrag zum konfessionellen Gespräch unter Theologen." Karl Barth: Darstellung und Deutung Seiner Theologie (Cologne: Jakob Hegner, 1951), 9. The English translation of the Dogmatics puts this as "puzzling cleft." Fr. Oakes translates it as "mysterious split."

3. This was the exact same title as in the 1941 manuscript.

4. Church Dogmatics 1.1, trans. Geoffrey W. Bromiley, ed. G. W. Bromiley and T. F. Torrance, 2nd ed. (Edinburgh: T & T Clark, 1975), 89.

5. Ibid.

Barth only critiques this for setting aside the earthly elements, which, he argues, does not occur in Reformed preaching. Because Christ is truly divine and truly human for eternity, and he is the acting subject in proclamation, the *human* "willing" (*Wollen*) and "accomplishing" (*Vollbringen*) cannot be set aside.[6] The "willing and accomplishing" is true not only of the divine–human Christ, who is the subject, but also of the earthly human preacher. It is "irrelevant," Barth argues, to ask about the "co-existence" or "cooperation" of the "two factors" (Christ and the preacher) because they are harmonious and thus one and not two. We don't need an account of secondary causality because the human and divine are united through the hypostatic union. Only in a "state of disobedience" could they be considered as two distinct causes rather than one. As will be shown below, the disagreement over secondary causality began in Barth's 1941 Trent seminar. It was a disagreement Barth and Balthasar never resolved. Barth allowed for a *significando causant* (the sacrament causes by signifying) but rejected secondary causality. Balthasar thought this was a distinction without a difference. Because Barth affirmed the former, he tacitly affirmed the latter, whether he acknowledged it or not. He constantly questioned why Barth's teaching on preaching did not entail the representation of Christ similar to the Catholic Mass.

Throughout this section of Barth's *Dogmatics*, which must have intrigued Balthasar since he began his own conversation with Barth at this point, Barth does not dismiss real presence, nor deny the validity of Catholic orders of ministry. He even defends the possibility of apostolic succession and the episcopal office as *vicarius Christi* against his former teacher Harnack.[7] "The difference between Roman Catholic dogmatics and ourselves, which, of course, we must always keep in view, cannot refer to the fact of this vicariate or succession, but only to its manner." The difference in manner is that the human element gets lost in Catholic dogmatics. Barth's argument should surprise his Catholic detractors. The accusation neoscholasticism brought against Barth is what he brought against Catholicism. Barth asks if the vicariate not only represents (*Vertretung*) Christ, but much more replaces (*Ersetzung*) him.[8] Does it, like the Eucharist, make the human element a mere accident of a substance which has been so completely changed that it is taken to be Christ rather than representing him? They are not two that become one, but they are two with one setting the other aside; the divine evacuates the human. Barth's criticism is

---

6. *Die kirchliche Dogmatik* 1.1 (Zurich: Evangelischer, 1932), 6.

7. *Church Dogmatics* 1.1, 97.

8. "Inwiefern liegt hier noch eine Vertretung und nicht vielmehr eine Ersetzung Christi vor?" (*Kirchliche Dogmatik* 1.1, 99).

precisely the same Catholics brought against him—the human, the creaturely, gets displaced.[9] He also acknowledges that Roman Catholicism never explicitly sets forth such a theology of replacement.

> Roman Catholic dogmatics is naturally aware of the lordship of Christ as a lordship not only in His Church but also over His Church. But where can this lordship of Christ over His Church take concrete shape in this system, where can it come into proper play, when all its power has already been fully transferred to the Church, when its power is simply present in the Church? And if it has no play of its own, is it distinguished in any way but name only from the power that is exercised in the Church by men without break, hindrance, or limit?[10]

Barth sets Jesus' role over and against the church, rather than within it, which does not fit seamlessly with his previous argument that the Word and proclaimer are one, not two. He denies to the Catholic Eucharist what he affirms for Reformed preaching. However, Barth's point is that office and institution never guarantee unity between Word and proclaimer. It is an event.

Barth concludes this section citing Augustine, from whom he derives the church as constituted by prayer more so than office. Even more important than liturgy and Eucharist, he suggests, is petitionary prayer. The church can only be what it is called to be when it prays. We must not assume we already have what we need to be church by its offices, but pray (*oret*), for the proper word of proclamation; office alone does not guarantee it. After insisting on the importance of prayer for a proper ecclesiology, Barth then asks the question with which Balthasar began his "confessional conversation" in the 1951 Barth book. It is the key question Barth put to Catholicism:

> Is Christ's action, real proclamation, the Word of God preached, tied to the ecclesiastical office and consequently to a human act, or conversely, as one might conclude from this *oret*, are the office and act tied to the action of Christ, to the actualising of proclamation by God, to the Word of God preached? From the standpoint of our theses this question is the puzzling cleft [*rätselhafte Riss*] which has cut right across the church during the last 400 years.[11]

---

9. Anne Carpenter pointed out to me that this does not adequately present Catholic teaching. Aquinas explicitly states that the bread is not "annihilated." See *Quaestiones quodlibeta* V, ques. 6, art. 1.

10. *Church Dogmatics* 1.1, 97–98.

Balthasar's "confessional conversation," as well as his presentation of Barth's work, begins here. He does not react to, or dismiss, Barth's question to Catholicism, but calls for self-examination among Catholics to determine if a "cause of offense" still remains on their part. And he acknowledges, with Barth, "this whole project must begin with the admission that unity can only be the grace of the Church's Founder; this is no human product."[12] Here is an ecumenical theme about which they agreed. Unity is Christ's gracious action and not a result of human ingenuity. They also agreed that disunity is not God's will, but an enigma, and therefore something could be done about it. Where they disagreed was whether much of what Catholicism taught was supplementary and illuminating of unity in Christ, or distracting and dispensable, potentially usurping his place.

COUNCIL OF TRENT

Karl Barth's Seminar on the Council of Trent began on April 24, 1941, nearly one year to the day after he and Balthasar first met face to face.[13] Barth began by claiming,

> In each time the necessary task to engage the phenomenon of Roman Catholicism is placed before the Protestant Church and for the Protestant theologian. As long as a Protestant Church and theology is and will be, it stands over and against the Catholic Church, which for it forms its greatest question.[14]

This seminar did not position the Reformation against Catholicism as if they constituted a simple either-or in terms of the law of noncontradiction. The sixteenth century period often gets interpreted this way, and perhaps those who lived through it experienced it as such and conceived it in these terms. We should not forget, however, that the Protestant-Catholic split was only emerging during this period. The lines were not clearly demarcated; they were blurred and confused. Luther carried around an image of the Catholic

---

11. Ibid., 99.

12. Balthasar, *The Theology of Karl Barth*, trans. Edward T. Oakes, SJ (San Francisco: Ignatius, 1992), 7.

13. Recall from chapter 1 that they first met on April 29, 1940.

14. Council of Trent *Protokolle*, 1a, 1st Session, April 24, 1941. The Council of Trent *Protokolle* consist of 108 pages, all of which were handwritten, except one typed *Protokoll*. Because they are not numbered, I will refer to them based on the PDF file Hans Anton Drewes graciously provided for me, where they appear in fifty-four pages with a side a and b. I will give both the page number of the PDF file and the date the session was held.

Reformer Savonarola with him until he died. Catholics made attempts to reform Catholicism prior to, during, and after the rise of the Protestant Reformers. Catholics invited Protestants to attend the Council of Trent in 1553.[15] Protestants never rejected the one, holy, *catholic*, and apostolic church. Nonetheless, the sixteenth century produced a strong either-or in terms of the mutual anathemas Catholics and Protestants eventually hurled at one another.

Brad Gregory finds these mutual anathemas unsurprising and reads them in terms of the logic of noncontradiction. He writes,

> The Tridentine counter-flood of Counter-Reformation anathemas raged against the torrent of Reformation denunciation of papist errors. There is nothing odd or mysterious about this. It simply reflected a clear understanding on all sides of the logical necessity that contrary truth claims cannot all be true. But it also had the cross-confessional effect of placing unprecedented emphasis on interior assent to the propositional content of doctrinal truth claims, whatever they were. It risked making Christianity seem more a matter of what one believed than of how one lived—of making the faith a crypto-Cartesian matter of one's soul and mind, *rather than* a matter of what one does with one's body.[16]

Gregory makes a fair historical judgment, but it was not how Barth conducted his seminar on Trent. It neither set forth an either-or, nor bifurcated doctrine and life. Nor did Barth and Balthasar find the Protestant-Catholic split unmysterious. It was, and must be, an "enigmatic crack." To render it "unsurprising" would be to make a significant theological mistake.

Barth's seminar focused on Trent's 1547 seventh session. It began with the *proemium* (preface) to "Canons on the Sacraments in General," and examined in detail its thirteen canons. These canons follow those on justification, and do so for theological reasons. Because the sacraments "begin, augment or restore justification," the council fathers found it necessary to follow the canons on justification with those of the sacraments.[17] Barth emphasized two things about

15. Guy Bedouelle, *The Reform of Catholicism, 1480–1620*, trans. James K. Farge (Toronto: Pontifical Institute of Medieval Studies, 2008), 50.

16. Brad Gregory, *The Unintended Reformation: How a Religious Revolution Secularized Society* (Cambridge, MA: Belknap, 2012), 155.

17. *Proemium* to Session 7, Council of Trent, "Canones de sacramentis." "Ad consummationem salutaris de justification doctrinae, quae in praecedenti proxima sessione uno omnium partum consensus promulgate fuit, consentaneum visum est, de santissimis Ecclesiae sacramentis agere, per quae omnis vera

these canons on the Catholic side. First, all seven sacraments are necessary. Second, and Barth adds this to the first protocol at the beginning of the second session, although the sacraments are the *conditio sine qua non* of justification, they are not the only way Trent claimed grace was communicated.[18] The preface stipulated sacraments "begin" or "augment" justification. Barth saw different means of communicating grace in those two terms. If they begin grace, the sacraments work without the promise of faith or the need for proclamation. If they augment it, they assume something other than sacraments alone, something such as proclamation.

The *proemium* and thirteen canons constitute less than two full pages of text, yet Barth devoted the entire summer semester to those two pages. The seminar met once per week. A student leader led the discussion and another took notes and recorded it. Throughout the seminar students were asked to address three questions:

> First, how do we agree with the canon; that is [how do] we [also] say no to the rejected conception [the anathema]. Second, in what decisive different sense can we not join in the rejection, which underlies, or primarily underlies the canon? Third, what is our positive proposition, which we have to place over and against the canon?[19]

The Reformed found common cause at places with what Trent rejected. Take for example this report on canon 5. The canon stated, "If anyone shall say that these sacraments have been instituted for the nourishing of faith alone: let him be anathema." The seminar first agreed with the canon. Sacraments do not only nourish faith. They communicate grace, which "means for men the forgiveness of sins, salvation, and for God the establishment [*Aufrichtung*] of his honor and glory. The glory of God and salvation of men is what the sacrament is about. . . and that is more than a mere nourishment of faith. So we speak

---

iustitia vel incipiet, vel coepta augetur, vel amissa reparature." Henrici Denzinger, *Enchiridion Symbolorum: Definitionum et Declarationum De Rebus Fidei Et Morum* (Friburg: Herder, 1942), 843a.

18. "Zum Beginn ergänzt Prof. Barth das Protokoll des letzten Sitzung dahin, dass nach dem Proemium die Sakramente wohl als condition sine qua non, aber nicht als die einzige Möglichkeit der Gnade." Council of Trent *Protokolle*, 4b, 2nd Session, May 8, 1941.

19. Council of Trent *Protokolle*, 36b, 10th Session, June 26, 1941. "1. Inwiefern gehen wir mit dem Canon einig, d.h. sagen wir nein zu der ihm verworfenen Auffassung? 2. In welchen bestimmten andern Sinn, der dem Canon auch zu freunde liegt oder vielmehr primär zu freunde liegt, können wir obex Verwerfung nicht mitmachen? 3. Wie lautet position unser Satz den wir dem Canon gegenüber zu stellen haben?"

with canon 5 a *no* against fideism." Balthasar agreed that the canon set forth "a point against fideism," but it was also to be understood in a second sense, which the seminar participants rejected: "According to the Roman teaching, the Sacrament bestows a *charakter christianitatis*." According to the seminar participants, Protestants reject this character.[20] Then they rephrased the canon, putting together their own proposition:

> The sacraments are actions [*Handlungen*] in which God himself places Jesus Christ before us and through that creates faith in us. We have thus avoided the appearance as if the sacraments worked by their own laws [*eigengesetzlich*]. God remains subject of the sacramental event, even if the Church is the acting subject.[21]

Perhaps this approach to the canons is evidence of Barth's dialectical method at its best. Students were not to dismiss the canons out of hand. They discovered where they agreed, where they disagreed, and how they would formulate their concerns as clearly as Trent.

If Gregory is correct that Trent tempted both Catholics and Protestants to reduce Christianity to belief rather than a way of life, Barth's seminar and work avoided this temptation as well. The previous chapter explained how Barth united doctrine and life through his efforts to show how "dogmatics is ethics" without reducing doctrine to ethics. Balthasar followed his lead. Both found Trent avoiding this as well, but only when it was interpreted within Catholic practice. The fifth seminar session discussed the relationships among the seven sacraments, setting forth how they relate to the Christian life. Correspondences were drawn among the virtues, sacraments, and what they opposed. These correspondences bear striking similarities to how Barth structured his own doctrine of reconciliation, correlating Christology, the theological virtues, and the sins they opposed. In the seminar, the correlation emerged from the first three canons, which state that Christ instituted all seven sacraments, that they differ from the sacraments of the Old Law, and that they contain different dignities. This is all the canons assert; none of the correspondences noted below are spelled out in the canons, but they are the context in which the sacraments are practiced. Any strong distinction between sacramental and moral theology was inappropriate.

Here are the correlations they made:[22]

20. Council of Trent *Protokolle*, 37a, 10th Session, June 26, 1941.

21. Council of Trent *Protokolle*, 41b, 10th Session, June 26, 1941.

22. Coucil of Trent *Protokolle*, 13a–b, 5th Session, May 21, 1941.

Sacraments	Virtues	Sins
Baptism	Faith	Original Sin
Penance	Justice	Mortal Sin
Unction	Courage	Venial Sin
Ordination	Prudence	Ignorance
Eucharist	Love	Malice
Confirmation	Hope	Impotence
Marriage	Temperance	Concupiscence

After setting forth these correlations, the seminar participants noted differences among the sacraments. For instance, baptism, confirmation, and ordination offer an "indelible character," but the others do not. Likewise, baptism and penance produce a change in state from sin to grace; they obviously have more dignity than the others, which Balthasar emphasized. Barth did not affirm this sacramental-moral theology, but his own *Dogmatics* works much like his seminar on Trent. He affirms what can be affirmed, rejects what he thinks must be rejected, and then restates much of it through his own propositions.

That the seminar spelled out a tacit moral theology shows they understood something Balthasar consistently emphasized. The decrees of Trent had to be interpreted against the backdrop of the fullness of the Catholic sacramental life. The decrees are not a sacramental theology, but presuppose one. It also shows how carefully Balthasar listened and responded to his Protestant questioners.

Balthasar's Barth book is a Catholic self-examination taking into account the questions raised in Barth's seminar. Balthasar listened attentively and responded by posing to them some of his own. The fruit of those responses appear in his Barth book, which he completed shortly after the seminar. It is a profound act of theological humility. For instance, Balthasar makes the following claim in the Barth book: "Even though, of course, the truth of the Councils of Trent and Vatican I will never be overtaken or even relativized, nonetheless there are still other views and aspects of revelation than those expressed here."[23] In other words, Trent and Vatican I did not say everything that needed to be said, even if what they said were true. Balthasar never sought to set aside those truths, but new questions required the development of answers consistent with what was said there, drawing on the full panoply of Catholic teaching. The difficulty with the "Fathers of Trent," he suggests, is that they failed to express this full panoply. They "gave a medieval answer to a modern question." Their answers were "correct," but they may not have understood the "question" put forward by the Reformers. They didn't speak the same language as their questioners and only responded in "Medieval-ese."[24] Their medieval answers to modern questions meant a loss for Catholicism, because the partial truth in the Protestant questions was not adequately addressed. Balthasar finds "truth" in Protestantism, but it lacks something because it is not yet integrated within Catholic truth.

An exchange Balthasar had with Barth during their seminar in the eighth session, June 12, 1941, brings to light what he meant by saying Trent did not say everything that needed to be said. The student seminar leader presented on canon 7 from the "Sacraments in General." That canon states:

> If anyone shall say that grace, as far as concerns God's part [*quantum est ex parte Dei*], is not given through the sacraments always and to all men, even though they receive them rightly [*etiamsi rite ea suscipiant*], but only sometimes and to some persons: let him be anathema.[25]

The student leader interpreted this as stating that the sacraments "work by themselves," and that this could possibly exclude "divine cooperation" (*göttliche Mitwirken*). He recognized that for Catholics, "God gives the sacraments their effectiveness," but once God gives this effectiveness the sacraments work "almost automatically, unconditionally and according to their own law [*eigengesetzlich*]." The term, *eigengesetzlich,* poses a problem for the seminar participants. They return to it on several occasions. The leader goes on to note that this canon acknowledges believers must "receive [the sacraments] rightly," but if this were to be taken seriously then the canon would not mark out a context within which the sacrament works by itself (*eigengesetzlich*). The leader interprets the expression *gratiam dari semper et omnibus* (it gives grace always and to all) as stating the sacrament works by itself. The *eigengesetzlich* is interpreted

23. Balthasar, *The Theology of Karl Barth*, 11.

24. Ibid., 11.

25. Latin citations of Trent come from Denzinger, *Enchiridion Symbolorum*, 299–301. English translations come from Denzinger, *The Sources of Catholic Dogma*, trans. Roy J. Deferrari (London: B. Herder, 1957), 261–63.

in terms of the canon's assertion that the sacrament works "without reservation" and "independently." Balthasar granted that this is the Catholic position, but he emphasized that it is so only as "it identifies the objective as compared to the subjective, personal act." The theme of an objective institution correlated with a personal mission, so important in his *Theo-Drama,* is already present in his thinking. Despite how the canon might be read, he insisted, "Standing in the realm of the Sacrament's own laws should not receive an impersonal coating; it is a standing of men before God."[26] The canon could be wrongly interpreted to suggest such an "impersonal" standing, but Balthasar reminds the seminar that the canons alone do not constitute the fullness of Catholic teaching. They are responses to particular issues raised by what the Reformers rejected; they arose because of the "counter."

Barth's response expressed "astonishment that a personal note should be attached to the *dari gratiam.*" He found the "rightly received" in the canon unintelligible because the sacrament works "according to its own law." How can Catholics claim the sacraments work by themselves and that they also require a personal reception? It would be better to exclude the personal dimension. Balthasar replied, "These canons only seek to delimit and therefore push the point of contention to the foreground." Here is where we see the influence of Barth's seminar on Balthasar's theology. Throughout the seminar, Balthasar emphasized the limited purpose of the canons of Trent. They are not in error, but nor are they exhaustive. They were set forth in a context of polemic and counterassertion that did not always present the positive teaching that lay beneath them. They defended something that was under threat; in this case, the objective character of the sacrament, but they did not say all that needed to be said. They did not emphasize its personal and subjective character as well, which was intrinsic to Catholic practice. When Barth concedes the point but still finds missing "the word of faith," Balthasar once again emphasizes that the canons do not present an exhaustive sacramental theology. He "underscored the fact again that no actual theology of the sacrament is to be sought here. These canons are only appendices, for the purpose of demarcation." [27]

Both in the seminar reports and his Barth book, Balthasar addressed the best of the Protestant questions. He did so by explicitly rejecting a simple antithesis of Reformation–Counter-Reformation. That antithesis had for too

---

26. Council of Trent *Protokolle*, 32a, 8th Session, June 12, 1941.

27. "Herr Dr. Balthasar unterstreicht erneut die Tatsache, das hier keine eigentliche Theologie des Sackramente zu suchen sei. Diese Canones seien nur anhangsweise, zur Abgrenzung." Council of Trent *Protokolle*, 32b–33a, 8th Session, June 12, 1941.

long inhibited the conversation, leading to Catholic identity being defined by its anti-Protestantism and Protestantism by its anti-Catholicism. Balthasar's own ecumenical breakthrough was to recognize this reactive ecclesiology lacked the full truth necessary for a positive performance of Christianity. Barth also rejected such a simple antithesis in the conduct of his seminar, requiring students to explain where they agreed with Trent, where they disagreed, and how they would positively state a similar proposition. Balthasar also discerned a movement beyond this antithesis and wrote in his Barth book:

> Perhaps today we are beginning to move beyond the era of stale antitheses—Reformation and Counter-Reformation—with Catholics trying to be more catholic and not "anti-Protestant" and the Protestants more biblical and "evangelical" and not "protesters". At any rate, as long as the split [*Riss*] in the Church continues, we are daily being admonished for a guilt we have yet to settle.[28]

Here is where he saw the fruit of ecumenical engagement with Barth. It was what he was for in his Reformed theology that motivated him, not what he was against. The more Barth could be Reformed without being "counter," the closer he came to Catholicism. The same logic applied to Catholics. Without his attentive and engaged participation in Barth's Trent seminar, Balthasar could not have seen this possibility. It did not mean he rejected Trent. What it taught was true. Balthasar always affirmed it. Toward the end of Barth's life, after Vatican II, Balthasar worried that some of its interpreters understood it as a rejection of what was taught at Trent. Balthasar argued, however, that Trent needed to be understood within the fuller context of Catholic teaching.

THEOLOGICAL DIFFERENCES

Although Balthasar and Barth refused a simple antithesis between Protestant and Catholic theology, they never downplayed their significant differences. The 1941 seminar focused on these differences, which stressed three points of disagreement:

> 1. The seven sacraments and their relation to Christ and the magisterium.
> 2. The difference between *significare* and the Catholic language of *continere*, *conferre* and *ex opere operato*.

---

28. Balthasar, *The Theology of Karl Barth*, 19; *Karl Barth: Darstellung und Deutung Seiner Theologie*, 29.

3. The nature of the *charakter indelebilis* sacraments produced, and whether grace is an "inherent quality" in the soul.

Each will be examined in turn.

1. THE SEVEN SACRAMENTS AND THEIR RELATION TO CHRIST AND THE MAGISTERIUM

The first three sessions of the seminar were devoted to setting forth the canons, exploring the rejected propositions, and responding to them from a Reformed perspective. The first reference to Balthasar occurs toward the close of the third session after all thirteen canons had been set forth.[29] A student reported that the Catholic Church found itself in difficulty by claiming Christ instituted all seven sacraments. He could not have done so because the first reference to unction is found in the letter of James. The student reported:

> It is quite clearly indicated here, that New Testament exegesis does not have the final word on this question, and also that tradition does not have it either. Rather the ecclesial magisterium and its infallibility, gives to the thesis its final steadfastness and is regarded as the real source of revelation.[30]

The student suggested, and Barth later agreed, that Catholicism has three sources of revelation: Scripture, tradition, and the magisterium. The suggestion caused Balthasar to enter into the fray for the very first time. The student reported,

> Dr. Balthasar indeed corrected the question of infallibility and the interpretation of revelation. There is here in fact not three but only two rails that cross and meet, not revelation, tradition, and interpretation through the assistance of the Holy Spirit. What was proclaimed *ex cathedra*, was always already present in the Roman Church, even if it was only latent and not expressed.[31]

In other words, Balthasar objects to the Protestant claim that the magisterium is a source of revelation. It gives expression to revelation, which is always already

---

29. The numbering of the seminar sessions in the *Protokolle* is odd. This third session is numbered as "4 Sitzung, May 15, 1941," which means it comes one week after the second session on May 8th, when one would expect it to be the third session.

30. Council of Trent *Protokolle*, 20a, 7th Session, June 5, 1941.

31. Council of Trent *Protokolle*, 11b, 4th Session, May 15, 1941.

latent in the tradition. Balthasar's intervention caused a response from Barth as well. "Professor Barth, however, is of the view that this does actually concern revelation."[32] This names a, if not the, key disagreement they had throughout their long friendship. Does the Catholic magisterium claim for itself the power of revelation, and thus stand over Christ? Or does it only identify that revelation and thus express obedience to Christ? The seminar session then came to an end without further discussion of this important point. After this session Balthasar became much more vocal.

The seminar repeatedly returned to the question whether Catholicism acknowledged Christ was the sole revelation of God. The seventh session prompted Balthasar to affirm the Catholic Church to be as christological as the Reformed, which the Reformed participants question because of canon 4. It states explicitly that all seven sacraments are necessary. They are not necessary for each individual's justification, but through them, or the desire for them, the "grace of justification" is obtainable. Barth already addressed this in his comments on the *proemium* in the second session of the seminar, noting that Trent taught all seven are necessary, but not that they were exclusive. The sacraments are necessary for us, but not for God, who can dispense the grace of justification based on desire for them rather than the actual participation in them. In order to explain how the "desire" for the sacraments justifies even when the material reality is absent, Balthasar appealed to the biblical story of the two thieves on the cross. The one thief desired Christ and therefore the sacraments even though he did not have them. The seminar lodged a "Protestant objection" against Balthasar's interpretation. The "desire" found in canon 4 did not stipulate that the desire was for Christ, but for the sacrament. Protestants would affirm the soteriological significance of such a desire, but only as it is for Christ. Catholics, they observed, made the desire "directly" for the sacrament and therefore only "indirectly" for Christ. Balthasar in turn objected that they were making a distinction that did not exist in Catholic theology, a distinction between desire for Christ and the sacrament.[33] This disagreement displays the significance of Barth and Balthasar's difference over the relationship between Christ and his church. This difference was never resolved. It also played itself out in a discussion of infant baptism, which was a thread throughout the seminar.

Barth and the seminar participants did not contest that sacraments are necessary, but they did question in what sense they are.[34] They emphasized that for Protestantism faith makes them effective, rather than the Catholic

---

32. Ibid.

33. Council of Trent *Protokolle*, 24b, 7th Session, June 5, 1941.

approach, which suggests they work as long as those who receive them present no obstacle. Barth acknowledged that this Catholic teaching went back to Augustine and was the basis for infant baptism. Because a child cannot have faith, baptism works as long as no obstacle is present. For Barth, this teaching bases the sacrament not on the presence of faith, but on the absence of any hindrance. How then, questions Barth, can the Catholic position also affirm canon 7, where the sacraments must be "rightly received" (*rite ea suscipiant*)? If the sacraments work *ex opere operato*, and do so based solely on no objective hindrance, receiving them in faith has no place. Because Protestantism makes faith necessary for the sacraments, it is better to say, claims Barth, that they "signify" (*significare*) grace rather than that they "confer" (*conferre*) it. Balthasar denied this distinction. The eighth seminar session on canons 5 through 8 highlighted the difference between *significare* and *conferre*.

2. THE DIFFERENCE BETWEEN SIGNIFICARE AND THE CATHOLIC LANGUAGE OF CONTINERE, CONFERRE, AND EX OPERE OPERATO

Canons 5 through 8 were the basis for the seminar's eighth session, one of the liveliest recorded. Canon 5 rejects the claim sacraments nourish "faith alone," with which the Reformed found agreement. Canon 6 affirms sacraments "contain" grace and do not only "signify" it, which prompted disagreement. Canon 7 emphasizes that this grace is given to all who receive the sacraments "rightly" (*etiamsi rite ea suscipiant*) and not just to those whom God wills to give it, which prompted puzzlement. Canon 8 states this grace is "conferred" *ex opere operato*. More than any other session Barth and Balthasar directly engaged each other over the language used in these canons. The heart of the seminar's discussion and disagreement centered on the extent to which the Protestant insistence on faith for the validity of the sacrament was consistent with the Catholic language that grace is "conferred" *ex opere operato* as long as the recipient offered no hindrance. In other words, how does canon 7 fit with canons 5, 6, and 8? The test case for this was infant baptism.

The student leader started the eighth session asserting that these canons teach, "The sacraments mediate grace apart from the faith of the believer."[35] Balthasar objected. "It is false to say that faith would not be necessary for

---

34. "Auch wir Protestanten bestreiten die Notwendigkeit der Sacrament keinesweges—auch wer fangen wie die Katholischen mit der Tatsasche an, dass es Gott gefallen hat, sein Wort als verbum invisibile und visible an unser gehen zu lassen. Die Sacramente gehörhen so gut zur Offenbarung wie das Wort, da das Evangelisum Ereignis und nicht Theorie ist." Council of Trent *Protokolle*, 24a, 7th Session, June 5, 1941.

35. Council of Trent *Protokolle*, 25a, 8th Session, June 12, 1941.

the reception of the sacrament. A *dispositio* is still at least required." He then went on to explain that for Catholics, "sanctifying grace would not be possible without faith in God."[36] Canon 7 insists that the sacrament be "rightly" received. Barth once again expressed surprise and stated he was unconvinced by Balthasar's explanation. He pressed the language of "*rite* [rightly]." What was to be understood by a "'worthy' reception" of the sacrament? He raised this question because Catholic teaching claims a "*conferre* apart from dignity." Balthasar answered, "Then it no longer confers grace." He explained canon 7 more fully, which stated: "If anyone shall say that grace, as far as concerns God's part [*quantum est ex parte Dei*], is not given through the sacraments always and to all men, even though they receive them rightly, but only sometimes and to some persons: let him be anathema." In order to explain why the Catholic teaching was not contradictory, Balthasar pointed to the *quantum ex parte Dei* of canon 7. "God is always ready," he stated, to give grace to all. Those who do not yet have a proper disposition, and nonetheless prevent no obstacle to reception, will receive the grace of the sacrament. They receive a "character" that is "identical with that of the church."[37] In other words, the faith of the individual who presents no obstacle is born by the church. This character requires the doctrine of implicit faith that Calvin and the Reformed tradition rejected, and the central instance of this is infant baptism, which Catholics and the Reformed accepted. For Balthasar infant baptism is not the norm, but an exception that is permitted because of this "character." His argument highlighted how inconsistent Reformed practice and theology were. It allowed infant baptism but denied implicit faith. This inconsistency was not lost on Barth. It prompted an ongoing conversation between them. We have a letter from Balthasar to Barth shortly after the seminar that discusses infant baptism along with the important expression *significando causant*. The discussion of infant baptism reoccurred in Barth's 1960–1961 course on the sacraments in the Lutheran tradition and in his unfinished *Church Dogmatics* 4.4. Before tracing the intriguing discussion about infant baptism that occurred between them for over a quarter of a century, attention must be given to their interaction in the seminar over the expression *signifcando causant*. It helps understand their ongoing discussion of infant baptism.

Canon 6 uses the term "signify" to explain how sacraments work. However, it correlates the term "signify" with "contain" and "confer." The grace that they signify is contained in, and conferred by, the sacraments.

---

36. Council of Trent *Protokolle*, 25a–b, 8th Session, June 12, 1941.
37. Council of Trent *Protokolle*, 26a, 8th Session, June 12, 1941.

Reformed theology, according to the seminar participants, has no problem with "signify," but found "contain" and "confer" troubling. "Protestant theology," they explained, "sees the sacraments as a sign where the grace is only contained in them as it exceeds the sign." The term "contain" neglected this excess. What did it add to "signify" that illumined anything? If the sacraments "signify" grace, why must they also "contain" and "confer" it? Isn't "signify" sufficient?[38] Balthasar acknowledged the point but emphasized the fuller Catholic teaching that interprets the sacraments as *significando causant* (that expression is not in the canons.) They signify grace, but they signify it by causing it. Barth "regretted" this way of putting it because the "signify" and the "cause" were distinguished from each other. He stated, "If the signifying were the cause, then we could extend the palm of peace." Balthasar once again emphasized the "counter" that made Trent possible. The formulation in canon 6, he stated, "was chosen against an opponent" who had divided the sign and the grace it contained. Barth denied that any Protestant actually put forth this distinction. They agreed the distinction between sign and cause should not occur. Trent presented Protestants as dividing them; Protestants presented Catholics as the culprit. Each misunderstood the other. Barth concluded,

> What a fearful misunderstanding occurred in the sixteenth century when the Reformers proclaimed a sacramental doctrine supposedly in opposition to the *continere* and *conferre*, and Trent supposedly in opposition to the *significare*! The Protestants did not understand that the Catholics spoke of a *significando* causare, whereas the Catholics had not paid attention that the Protestants said, significando *causare*.[39]

Because of this statement, Balthasar thought Barth should concede the sacraments as a "cause" of grace worked through human means. Human nature expresses agency in the realm of grace.

Balthasar returned to this discussion and pressed Barth further in a letter he sent him in the summer of 1941, shortly after the seminar. He asks why Barth accepts the *significando causant*, as he did in the Trent seminar, but not

---

38. Council of Trent *Protokolle*, 29a, 8th Session, June 12, 1941.

39. "Welch fürchterliches Missverständnis wäre doch hin 16 Jahrhunert passiert, wenn die Reformation eine Sakramentslehre verkünden hätten, vermeintlich im Gegensatz zum 'continere' und 'conferre' und das Tridentum vermeintlich im Gegensatz zum 'significare'! Die Protestanten hätten nicht verstanden, dass die kath. Kirche 'significando causare' redet, während die Katholiken nicht darauf achteten, dass die Protestanter sagten: 'significando causare.'" Council of Trent *Protokolle*, 30b–31a, 8th Session, June 12, 1941.

the *causa secunda*. For Balthasar, the two are inextricably linked. If Barth accepts that the sacraments cause by signifying, he should then accept that God uses them as secondary causes. If God uses them as secondary causes, human agency mediates grace. To press his point, Balthasar asked, "Is it irksome for Rembrandt to use a brush?" Moreover he finds that the *causa dispotiva* of the Middle Ages, along with the "doctrine of character (understood ecclesiologically), were best illuminating" for what occurs in the sacraments. He also suggests to Barth that his theology of proclamation is similar to Trent's doctrine of the sacraments, which "does not want to say that the sacrament somehow becomes the function of faith." In other words, if preaching does what Barth claimed it did, then he already had a teaching similar to the Catholic *ex opere operato*. Balthasar saw a similarity between their disagreement on secondary causality and their ongoing debate between the *analogia entis* and *fidei*. Both Barth and Balthasar give priority to God, but Barth wrongly conceived of the *analogia entis* as a "diacritical point, as a naked eye-to-eye between the Person of God and the human person." He would understand it better if he saw that it "acknowledges the absolute priority of God's Person (and his worldly media)." Balthasar then relates the *significando causant* to infant baptism. It is a "limit case" and not "normative." Yet it is proper, and how it is so must be explained. Barth "should learn from this limit: *agere sequitur esse*" (action follows being).[40]

Barth and Balthasar's discussion picked up on these same themes twenty years later, as Barth prepared to teach a seminar on the Eucharist, drawing from the Lutheran confessions in the winter semester 1960–1961.[41] He wrote Balthasar and asked him for references. Balthasar provided some and sent him his *Sponsa Verbi*, the second volume of *Skizze zur Theologie*. Barth read it with interest and wrote back to Balthasar excited that he named infant baptism "the most momentous decision of all church history. " Barth tells Balthasar that he "immediately incorporated" it into his discussion of baptism in *Church Dogmatics* 4.4.[42] He does so by considering once again how faith is necessary for the sacrament, and how this distances the Protestant position from any Catholic doctrine of *ex opere operato*. However, he concedes, Protestant practice is inconsistent with its theory because of infant baptism. It lacks a carefully articulated theological rationale. Although Barth had rejected Calvin's teaching

40. Lochbrunner, *Hans Urs von Balthasar und seine Theologenkollegen: Sechs Beziehungsgeschichten* (Würzburg: Echter, 2009), 280–81.

41. Ibid., 347.

42. See Barth, *Church Dogmatics* 4.4, trans. Geoffrey W. Bromiley, ed. G. W. Bromiley and T. F. Torrance (Edinburgh: T & T Clark, 1969), 167.

on infant baptism since 1938, the particular argument he makes in *Church Dogmatics* 4.4 repeats much of what Balthasar argued.[43]

In *Sponsa Verbi*, Balthasar argued that the early church had not given adequate reflection on ecclesiology, and this is what accounted for both infant baptism and Constantinianism. They lost the importance of personal mission so important for Balthasar's theological ethics, collapsing the personal, subjective mission into the objective element of sacrament and office:

> It is this unreflective consciousness that alone explains, after a fashion, what is most difficult to grasp of all the various decisions in the Church's history (though they were, in fact, not conscious decisions): that of infant baptism, more pregnant for the future even than the paradoxical *"In hoc signe vinces"* of the Constantinian era, in which the Cross, the sign of the divine helplessness, was made the standard behind which the Church marched onto the field of earthly battle. It is easy to understand how, later on—by appealing to Tradition as a source of revelation—theologians sought for a primitive justification to legitimize a Christianity that one did not enter into by personal decision but was unconsciously "born into", as one was incorporated by circumcision into the "carnal" people of the promise; it was going to be infinitely difficult not to take this practice as the model for the *opus operatum*.[44]

The difficulty with infant baptism was that it misled theologians to use it to describe how the sacrament worked *ex opere operato*. It offered only an objective doctrine without the personal element of mission. It viewed baptism as a "carnal" practice of incorporation into an inheritance.

Barth's controversial discussion of baptism in *Church Dogmatics* 4.4 cites Balthasar's statement at a critical juncture, drawing upon and expanding themes Balthasar raised. Barth leads up to this citation by setting forth a positive theological teaching on baptism. It is "the twofold answer of man to the divine justification and sanctification, cleansing and renewal, which have taken place for him and been revealed to him in Jesus Christ." This twofold answer is defined as "renunciation and pledge." The decision for baptism does not emerge from a clear alternative between two possible paths between which someone chooses. "Hercules at the crossroad" is not the pattern for baptism.

43. See Busch, *Karl Barth*, 286.

44. Hans Urs von Balthasar, *Explorations in Theology*, vol. 2: *Spouse of the Word*, trans. A. V. Littledale with Alexander Dru (San Francisco: Ignatius, 1991), 17.

The deed is already fulfilled in Christ, and the human "yes" points to the "renewal" already accomplished, which is its "pledge" and therefore the only real possibility. All other options are impossible. What is renounced in baptism is the "impossible."[45]

Although baptism is not a choice between two equally possible alternatives, it is nonetheless a human decision and Barth finds this absent in the tradition. He states,

> We may thus say that it is in wholly free, conscious and voluntary decision that there takes place in baptism that renunciation and pledge, that No on the basis of the justification of sinful man effected in Jesus Christ, that Yes on the basis of the sanctification accomplished in Him. If only it were enough merely to make what would seem to be so self-evident a statement! If only we could make this the conclusion to the second point in our description of the event of baptism! Unfortunately this is not so.[46]

Why can this not be the last word? Why must more be said? The problem, Barth states, is that a "higher authority" from "Church history breaks into the theological discussion." At this critical point Barth quotes Balthasar's *Sponsa Verbi:* infant baptism is "the most momentous of all decisions in Church history." For Barth, it denies the freedom of the human subject.[47] Although baptism is not a human decision between two equally possible options, it is a human act by a human agent. He is not denying infants are human, of course, but that they are not yet able to enter into a covenant because infants cannot renounce or pledge. Like Balthasar, Barth associates infant baptism with Constantine.

> Infant baptism might well have been practised relatively early—possibly even in the New Testament churches, as many investigators believe. Nevertheless, it became the general rule, which

---

45. *Church Dogmatics* 4.4, 162.

46. Ibid., 163–64.

47. Ibid., 164. See also165: "The result is that theology to-day is confronted by the brute fact of a baptismal practice which has become the rule in churches in all countries and in almost all confessions, and in which that which ought to be regarded as self-evident is not only no longer self-evident but has been forgotten and even intentionally ignored. In this practice the baptised person has his place as an object of the community's action but there can be no question of any renunciation and pledge as the act of his own free decision. Hence he has no function, no active part. He is not a subject, and baptism cannot be understood seriously as a common work."

the Reformation churches also accepted, only in the course of the greatest historical transformation which Christianity had thus far undergone, namely, that associated with the name of Constantine I, when the Church entered into an ontological unity with people, society, state and empire, which found its ripest form in the mediæval *Corpus Christianum* with its two distinct but not separated dominions. Whether this unity has really broken up today, or is in process of breaking up or crumbling away, is a question which need not concern us here. What is beyond dispute is that the continuity and existence of the Church within this unity stood or fell with the rule of infant baptism.[48]

The citation from Balthasar's *Sponsa Verbi* forms the basis for Barth's discussion and critique. Infant baptism became a "fact" in church history because of "Christendom."[49] It was a fact the Reformers, like the Constantinian Church, accepted without subjecting it to theological analysis.

Themes from the Trent seminar reappear here in Barth's negative evaluation of infant baptism. He emphasizes that for Luther and Calvin, faith is indispensable for baptism, but they were inconsistent with their own insights and reacted angrily against anyone who challenged the practice of infant baptism. For Barth their anger was a sign they overly reacted and failed to offer calmly considered theological reflection.[50] He then critiques Luther's *Greater Catechism*:

> It is worth noting that in the corresponding place in the *Greater Catechism* the reference to faith is abandoned and there is mention only of the Word of God in the water. And how are we to harmonise with this premise, which is still quite plain in the *Greater Catechism*, the later saying in the section dealing with infant baptism: "We thus say further that for us the greatest stress does not lie on whether the one baptised believes or not"? Baptism is valid, we are now told, even though there is no faith. It is not invalid because improperly received.[51]

48. Ibid., 168.

49. Ibid., 167. "The presupposition, however, was a recognition of the validity of the powerful fact of Church history whereby infant baptism had long since become the rule in Christendom."

50. Ibid., 172.

51. Ibid.

The "rightly received" from the Trent seminar appears here again, but now as a critique of Luther's *Greater Catechism*. He does not have even this negative Tridentine qualification. Barth then claims Luther can put this teaching forward only on the basis of the Catholic *ex opere operato*. If he found Trent confusing on the relationship between faith and the valid reception of the sacrament, he found the Reformers just as confused, if not more so.

For Barth, Calvin, who is usually a stricter thinker than Luther, is even more "inconsistent" on this question.[52] He defends infant baptism by neglecting the faith that he taught elsewhere was necessary for it. Barth does not reject infant baptism out of hand, but argues neither Catholics nor the Reformers offered a satisfying theological defense. Such a defense would require that it be shown to be "commanded, necessary and permitted."[53] Neither Calvin nor Luther met this requirement. He asks,

> What is the heart of Luther's proof? It is undoubtedly the powerful and very true thought that where God's work is done and His command is uttered, the question of the completeness of the answering faith and obedience of man, indeed, the question whether there is any such faith or obedience, is of secondary importance, and even an uncertain or indeed a negative response cannot alter the objective reality of the divine work or the objective validity of the divine command.[54]

This is Luther's major premise: God's command brings about its fulfillment. It has an objective character, which Barth affirms. But there is also a minor premise Luther sets forth—*Fides creatix divinitatis in nobis* (Faith creates divinity in us). Barth questions if the major and minor theses hold together. Infant baptism neglects the minor and only affirms the major. The result is the following: "If this intrinsically true thesis [the major thesis] is to have any force here, it has to be granted that not merely in baptism generally, but also in infant baptism, we may count on a divine work and a divine command which relativise the question of the faith of the recipient."[55] Barth's concern was not that the sacrament was treated objectively, but that it was exclusively so treated.

Calvin defends infant baptism on grounds different from Luther, grounds Barth finds even more objectionable. Baptism, like circumcision, shows a

52. Ibid., 173.
53. Ibid., 175.
54. Ibid., 177.
55. Ibid.

"hereditary right" to the covenant. His defense is similar to Balthasar's equation of infant baptism to "carnality." Barth objects, "The people of the new covenant, however, is not a nation. It is a people freely and newly called and assembled out of Israel and all nations. It is not made up of succeeding generations. It is not recruited through procreation and birth. Those who join it are 'born, not of blood, nor of the will of the flesh, nor of the will of man, but of God.'"[56] Barth then examines biblical and traditional support for the practice and finds them all wanting. He concludes with a lengthy admonition to the church that echoes Balthasar's argument but radicalizes it more than Balthasar would have done, for Barth still rejects implicit faith and any indelible character borne by the church, which for Balthasar made infant baptism possible as an exception. Barth's conclusion is worth repeating in its entirety:

> Enough of this tiresome matter! Theology can and should do no more than advise the Church. It would be as well for the Church, of course, if it would occasionally ask seriously for the advice of theologians, and if it would then listen to it no less seriously. In this matter of infant baptism, our advice has not been sought, and there is only the faintest hope that it will be heeded. This advice cannot be that in its baptismal practice the Church should continue with a supposedly good conscience on the way which was entered in hoary antiquity and which has been obstinately pursued through all the vicissitudes of history. Theology cannot say to the Church that if it continues on this way it is acting in obedience and may thus have a good conscience. It cannot share with the Church the responsibility which the Church has taken on itself by introducing this practice, and which it constantly takes on itself by maintaining it. This practice is profoundly irregular. It is true that through the centuries and up to our own time the Church has not been destroyed by it (any more than by corrupt preaching or so many other corruptions). But it would be most dangerous—of all arguments for infant baptism this is the worst—to appeal to the fact, or to rely on it, that this practice will not harm it in the future. In the history of Israel the patience of God manifests its greatness and therewith also its limits in certain great judgments and disasters which were made unavoidable by the obstinacy of Israel. There can be no guarantee that a Church which is only too faithful to its ancient errors will forever escape these. To all concerned: to

56. Ibid., 178.

theologians, for unfortunately even theology has not yet realised by a long way that infant baptism is an ancient ecclesiastical error; to Christian congregations and their pastors; to Church leaders, presbyterial, synodal or episcopal; to all individual Christians, however simple, let it be said that they should see to it whether they can and will continue to bear responsibility for what has become the dominant baptismal practice, whether they might not and must not dare to face up to the wound from which the Church suffers at this genuinely vital point with its many-sided implications, whether they could not and should not undertake measures for its healing which do not bear the character of compromise, and which ought not, therefore, to be the last to call for consideration.[57]

Barth warns the church that infant baptism may very well be its downfall. John Howard Yoder argued Barth moved more toward a free church ecclesiology in his later *Dogmatics*, but this judgment is incorrect. Barth made a similar argument decades earlier; it was not something he came to late in life. What is intriguing about this later argument was the influence Balthasar had on it, which was most likely not Balthasar's intended result. As shown earlier, he critiqued Barth for his "Anabaptist" theology of baptism in his "preoccupation" with him in the late 1930s. Nonetheless, it was Balthasar's argument that formed a critical piece of Barth's claim that Reformed theology and practice were inconsistent when it came to infant baptism. Discussions initiated in the Trent seminar led to conclusions that found their way into the last incomplete volume of the *Church Dogmatics*.

3. THE NATURE OF THE CHARACTER INDELEBILIS SACRAMENTS PRODUCE

Balthasar acknowledged infant baptism was irregular, but he nonetheless found it permissible because of the "character" it formed in any recipient who did not prevent an obstacle. In his obituary for Barth in 1968, Balthasar referred to Barth's doctrine of baptism in the fragment of 4.4 as "very radical to catholic ears."[58] For Balthasar, infant baptism was a permissible exception because of its ecclesial character. Canon 9 stated explicitly that baptism, confirmation, and orders "imprinted on the soul a sign, that is, a certain spiritual and indelible mark, on account of which they cannot be repeated." The nature of this

---

57. Ibid., 194–95.
58. Lochbrunner, *Hans Urs von Balthasar und seine Theologenkollegen*, 369.

indelible character led to some of the more interesting agreements between the Protestant participants and the Catholic canon.

The agreement is found in the "ontological character" of this indelible sign. The seminar leader for session 12, drawing on Hebrews 1, reported agreement that this character is Christ. However, the seminar leader continues, based on Eph. 3:17, this character is also for us. Christ as the head gives it to the church. Because Christ is this sign, and he shares it with his church,

> the church cannot be destroyed. It is indelible, unrepeatable, or as Augustine formulated it, *quae ecclesia perpetua mansura* [the church continues uninterrupted]. The church cannot pass away because it shares in this character. Because it cannot be destroyed, no one can build the church again. If anyone sets up a church he is foolish for the foundation of the church is unrepeatable.

The seminar participants then offered some interesting observations relating the Reformation and ecclesiology. "The Reformers did not found a church. It cannot be newly established, but only reformed. The Reformers asserted: 'We are the old Church. There is no second church next to the Catholic Church. We are the true Church.'"[59] They agreed with Trent that on these grounds, baptism is unrepeatable.

Although they agreed Christ is the indelible character by which creation itself comes into existence, they disagreed, based on Hebrews 1 and Colossians 1, whether humans bear this character. For the Reformed participants, Christ alone is the "image of God," and that means the "image" is not in us but only in him. It has no basis in humanity qua humanity.[60] This leads to two criticisms of Catholic teaching. One concerns natural theology. Barth and the participants do not reject it. They do not posit it as a genuine possibility. One cannot reject something that doesn't exist. Because the world is already disposed to Christ, natural theology is impossible.[61] Christ's character inextricably marks the world. There can be no nature left unmarked. The second concerns the "inhering" of this character in the individual soul.[62] Because Christ is the "character of the hypostasis" (Heb. 1:3) it does not inhere in us, but we in it. That Christ is the "character" distances Protestant from Catholic teaching, because the latter makes salvation dependent upon something present in the human person qua

---

59. Council of Trent *Protokolle*, 50a–b, 12th Session, July 10, 1941.

60. Ibid., 50b–52b, 12th Session, July 10, 1941.

61. Ibid., 51b, 12th Session, July 10, 1941.

62. Ibid., 52a, 12th Session, July 10, 1941.

person independent of Jesus, which for Barth is the quintessence of liberal Protestantism. The seminar leader drew attention to the lack of any mention of Christ in canon 9. Because the sacraments work *ex opere operato* and produce this character, he questions if faith in Christ matters at all. Simply participating in the church's structural mediation of grace redeems.

Balthasar was unconvinced this properly interpreted Catholic theology. He sought to correct it by explaining how the character is mediated by the sacraments via the *communicatio idiomatum*. The sacraments should not be thought of as merely external forms. When it comes to the sacraments, he states, the "inner is not only inner and outer is not only outer." Like Christ's two natures, the external and internal mutually communicate. Balthasar then explains that Catholicism does not teach grace is "guaranteed" simply because someone belongs to the church. It is the overlapping of the inner and outer from which "the reality of the character arises." The character is Christ; it is the *res* that is grace. But this *res* is genuinely mediated through creaturely means so that it can inhere in creatures. He then tries to explain the nature of this indelible character provided by the sacrament. It cannot be adequately explained only in physical or moral terms. He states, "To say it gives rise to something ontological is perhaps an unfortunate expression. There is no great value in distinguishing between the physical and moral. The character lies beyond these realms."[63] Balthasar drew the following diagram on the black board:[64]

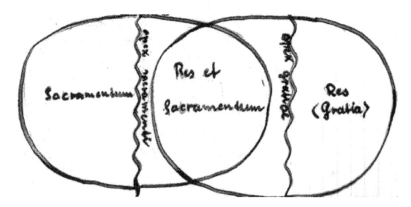

Figure 1

63. Ibid., 53a, 12th Session, July 10, 1941.
64. The diagram comes from the Council of Trent *Protokolle*, 53 a, 12th session, July 10, 1941.

The *sacramentum* is the sign and the *res* is the actual grace. The external sign and the internal grace come together to form the character. One cannot be had without the other. The *sacramentum* always refers objectively to the *res*, but it does not guarantee it. Only when it is rightly received does that occur, but rightly received it does produce a character. "The character," he stated, "functions there at this decisive point between the *res* and *sacramentum*.[65] Balthasar's drawing of the sacrament shows the identity between it and Christ. The sacrament can only be understood as a representation of Christ's personal unity of divinity and humanity mediated to creatures.

With that the seminar ended. The seminar leader thanked all the participants and concluded: "With a word of thanks to everyone who participated, especially to Herr Dr. Balthasar who offered so much that was instructive and interesting, and with a word of regret, that both our guest and the seminar leader [Barth] do not stand in a more prominent position and by that means our conversation would be yet more fruitful."[66] The student seminar leader expresses the wish that Barth and Balthasar held positions in their churches where their conversation would bear fruit.

VATICAN II

Perhaps the student leader could be considered prophetic. Neither Balthasar nor Barth sought ecclesial positions, and few observers in the 1940s or 1950s would have found them influential in healing the "enigmatic crack" in, or between, their respective churches. Barth was involved in the church struggles while this seminar was going on, and was alienated from nearly every corner of church and society. Two years earlier, he caused a "scandal" by referring to the "natural paganism" of the German Christians. In that same year his works were banned in Germany. He wanted to issue a public letter calling all German Christians to refuse military participation or to sabotage Germany's military efforts, but even his closest allies in the church struggles thought this was "too unusual, too novel, too bold." He chided Swiss neutrality and its ecclesial supporters and advocated for armed resistance.[67] Although he had immense influence theologically, he did not have the ear of Catholic and Protestant church leaders in Switzerland or Germany.

---

65. Ibid., 53a, 12th session, July 10, 1941..
66. Ibid., 54b, 12th session, July 10, 1941.
67. Busch, *Karl Barth*, 289, 305, 298.

UNLIKELY ECUMENISTS

Nor did Barth's comments in the decade following the church struggles endear him to ecumenical leaders. His critical comments at the 1948 World Council of Churches offended many. Six years later Barth was still offending Catholics. In March of 1954 Barth held a question and answer session in Stuttgart and was asked about Protestant conversions to Catholicism. Unbeknownst to him, his answers were recorded and published in the *Deutschen Volksblattes*. Barth stated that conversion to Catholicism was not something a "decent" (*anständig*) person would do. This prompted a rather blunt letter from Balthasar admonishing Barth. He wrote, "Why must you always speak so poisonously about us? Could you not hold a little reciprocity? Do you not hold Frau Kaegi [Adrienne von Speyr] to be a 'decent person'?"[68] Balthasar's admonition prompted one of Barth's longest and most apologetic letters in return. He noted that he had no idea his words were being reported and he quoted from his own handwritten notes giving an account of what he actually said at the question and answer session in Stuttgart. The question put to Barth was, "How are Roman Catholicism and the Reformed Confessions decisively separated?" Barth responded by raising four critical points he put in the form of questions:

1. The Sovereignty of Jesus Christ over and against the church?
2. The freedom of grace over and against human performance?
3. The right and duty of the entire community over and against the official representatives?
4. The peculiarity of the Spirit over and against the work of the sacramental institution?

He told Balthasar these questions formed the answer he gave, and then quoted two sentences from his notes. The first read, "The Roman system is monistic with a domination of the Church, of works, offices, and sacraments." The Catholic reporter presented all this, clearly showing Barth's anti-Catholicism. He did not publish the second sentence: "But has our Protestantism justification to reproach the Roman Church?"[69] Barth then tells Balthasar that his statement about "decent persons" not converting was pastoral, to assuage fears by some in the audience about high profile Protestant converts, "poets and those aesthetically inclined," to Catholicism. He concludes by writing: "in short: James 3: 2–12," which is James's admonition about how the tongue gets us in trouble. He asks Balthasar to send him a note acknowledging "that you will not

---

68. Lochbrunner, *Hans Urs von Balthasar und seine Theologenkollegen*, 330.

69. Ibid., 331.

be eternally angry with me."[70] Although toward the end of his life, Barth said that if he were born a Roman Catholic he would not convert to Protestantism, he consistently repeated his claim that individual conversions from one church to the other were of no consequence. They did nothing to heal the "enigmatic crack."

If Barth's theology and life did not put him in a position to address the "enigmatic crack" between Protestants and Catholics, Balthasar's fared worse. His preoccupation with Barth had not endeared him to many Catholic leaders. They feared he conceded too much to his Protestant friend. His difficulties with incardination in the 1950s worked against his influence over ecclesial matters. Did Vatican II change all that? In one sense, it could be viewed as a vindication of Balthasar's preoccupation with Barth. After Vatican II, Balthasar was to be made cardinal, which did not occur only because he died a few days before the ceremony. The ex-Jesuit who struggled to find a diocese in which he could be incardinated was to be given the red hat. How is that not vindication? If it were vindication for Balthasar, was it not also indirectly vindication for Barth? Balthasar had personally presented his copy of the Barth book to Pope Pius XII in May 1952, who supposedly called Barth "the greatest theologian since Thomas Aquinas and the most influential in the twentieth century."[71] At Vatican II, the Catholic Church followed the way Balthasar and others pioneered by engaging Protestantism as something other than heresy, drawing on biblical and patristic theology to do so, and providing alternatives to the dominant hold of neoscholasticism, which was the very theology that had delayed the publication of Balthasar's Barth book. Unlike Trent or Vatican I, Vatican II offered no anathemas. The "counter" did not define it. But Balthasar never found vindication in Vatican II. Instead, he lamented much of it, finding it a dilution of Catholic theological substance. This lament has led some to see a shift in Balthasar from his early openness to ecclesial unity to a later Catholic triumphalism, but this perceived shift is a mistaken interpretation.

Jürgen Moltmann finds Balthasar turning away from an initially positive ecumenical engagement to a "return ecumenicism" (*Rückkehrökumene*) because "he had to absorb everything within the Catholic distinctive."[72] Steffen Lösel compares statements Balthasar made in 1951 with those in 1980, and finds a

---

70. Ibid., 331..

71. Although this statement is widely reported, tracking down a direct citation from Pius XII where he said this has so far not been forthcoming. One reference can be found in James B. Torrance, "Karl Barth," in *The Encyclopedia of Religion*, ed. Mircea Eliade, vol. 2(New York: MacMillan, 1987), 68.

72. Steffen Lösel, *Kreuzwege: Ein ökumenisches Gespräch mit Hans Urs Balthasar* (Zurich: Ferdinand Schöningh, 2001), 12.

marked difference from his earlier hope for an end to division to a retrenchment into an "all or nothing" Catholic approach.[73] As an example, he cites Balthasar's early statement that a conversation with Barth "in the full sense is necessary," a conversation whose "end" may question if the "split" (*Trennung*) between Catholics and Protestants continues to be worthwhile.[74] Balthasar speaks of "common guilt" (*gemeinsamer Schuld*) and hopes God gives grace so that the division might cease. In *Theodramatik* 3, however, Lösel finds Balthasar "assessing the situation as much more pessimistic," citing these words:

> Church history is at a growing disintegration of ecclesial unity, without any corresponding movement to return to visible unity. However much one strives, today more explicitly than ever, for an ecumenical movement for such a return, it is of an almost supernatural difficulty, because the reference point for the sought after unity can no longer be sought in common.[75]

Lösel's analysis seems undeniable. Balthasar's early preoccupation with Barth and Protestant theology held forth promise that the "enigmatic crack" did not have to be, but he did not find Vatican II healing that rift. Despite what so many witnessed as a possible ecumenical convergence, Balthasar saw the opposite. Lösel wonders if the reason for Balthasar's shift was his "angst" over theological pluralism.[76] This fits a common interpretation that finds Balthasar moving toward a conservative reaction against his earlier openness. The postconciliar tension between Rahner and Balthasar, as well as that between their respective journals, *Concilium* and *Communio*, lends itself to a "progressive" versus "conservative" interpretation that fits nicely within Catholic culture wars. It must be said, however, that Balthasar denied such an interpretation in his lifetime. When questioned by a reporter on Swiss television in 1984 about the changes he made post–Vatican II, Balthasar answered by adopting Rahner's words as his own. He said, "Earlier we were on the left. All of a sudden we were on the right. We have, of course, not changed at all."[77]

So what accounts for Balthasar's seeming shift from an openness to healing the Protestant–Catholic split to asserting that "the sought after unity can no

73. Lösel, *Kreuzwege*, 17.

74. Balthasar, *Karl Barth: Darstellung und Deutung Seiner Theologie*, 30. Lösel, *Kreuzwege*, 16.

75. Lösel, *Kreuzwege*, 16. Balthasar, *Theodramatik*, vol. 3 (Einsiedeln: Johannes), 425ff.

76. "Ist est die Angst vor dem Pluarlismus, die den späten Balthasar dazu bewogen hat, Abstand seiner Forderung des konfessionellen Gesprächs zu nehmen?" (Lösel, *Kreuzwege*, 18).

77. Lochbrunner, *Hans Urs von Balthasar und seine Theologenkollegen*, 14.

longer be sought in common?" Statements made during and shortly after Vatican II show that Balthasar was less worried about pluralism (after all, truth was "symphonic" for him), and more alarmed that Vatican II underwrote the very kind of Catholicism Barth feared. His putative shift was not away from his earlier engagement with Barth but because of it.

A LIBERAL PROTESTANT CATHOLICISM?

Moltmann and Lösel are correct that Balthasar insisted upon absorbing all things into the "Catholic distinctive," but they are wrong to see it as a shift. Careful reading of Balthasar shows it was a position he always held. Because Catholicism was as christological as Barth's theology, it could answer Protestant questions and absorb Protestant distinctives without losing its own. What Balthasar did not foresee was the threat liberal Protestantism was for Catholicism. Rather than a Catholic christological renaissance that demonstrated the heart of Catholic theology was as christological as Barth claimed for Reformed theology, Vatican II represented for Balthasar the encroachment of "liberal Protestantism" within Catholic theology. Schleiermacher rather than Barth opened the Vatican windows to the world.

Balthasar had initiated a preoccupation with Protestant theology and paid a significant cost for it in the 1940s and 1950s. Protestantism preoccupied him while he was in exile from Basel in the early 1950s. He thought it so important that he turned down a teaching position so he could devote time and attention to it. His attention to it was not out of an irenic desire for unity. He thought Catholicism could do better what Barth attempted to do, affirming a christological center, without throwing out so much of the theological and philosophical tradition Barth and Protestantism jettisoned. For Balthasar, Vatican II was not vindication, but loss, which is evident in the last lecture he gave with Barth. If Trent reacted against Protestantism and did not set forth the true heart of Catholic teaching, but assumed it, Vatican II reacted by adopting too much liberal Protestantism in engaging modernity, and neglected what Catholics should have learned from Barth about their own tradition.

If Barth's work from the 1930s through the 1950s treated the ecumenical movement with suspicion, the work at the end of his life opened toward it. He was invited to attend Vatican II, but was unable because of illness. He did go to Rome afterward and had a private meeting with Pope Paul VI. He wrote an essay on Vatican II, *Ad Limina Apostolorum*, when he was eighty years of age, having studied carefully its Latin texts. He went to Rome with ten sets of questions, one of which had to do with *aggiornamento*. He asked, "What does *aggiornamento* mean? Accommodation to what?" He wondered aloud if

Catholics were "aware of the danger" of the "repetition of the errors committed in modern Protestantism." He seemed particularly troubled by *Lumen gentium* and asked, "Is it so certain that dialogue with the world is to be placed ahead of proclamation to the world?"[78] He also asked publicly what had happened to the denunciation of those who rejected natural theology at Vatican I.

> Now, on the other hand, where in the documents of Vatican II is there a natural theology or an anathema against those who reject it? All the concern over the relationship of faith to reason, of nature to the supernatural, etc., which occupied the fathers of Vatican I exclusively does not seem to exist any longer for the fathers of Vatican II.[79]

He raised these questions and held seminars on the teaching from Vatican II, to which he invited Joseph Ratzinger, whose visit Balthasar arranged. He also denounced the anti-Catholic Swiss article in its constitution and declared that the pope is not the antichrist. He concluded his life's vocation in his last lecture by calling for "renewal" as the only way toward unity. Barth insisted that church unity only comes through "renewal," which also means "repentance." Protestants, he warned, should be less concerned about Rome's renewal and more with their own: "the way to the unity of the Church can only be the way of her renewal. But renewal means repentance. And repentance means turning about: not the turning of those others, but one's *own* turning."[80] Barth made considerable steps toward the ecumenical movement, steps that would have been far from anyone's expectations at the 1948 World Council of Churches. Yet he did so by raising a caution—to what will the Roman Catholic Church measure itself when it concludes its own "reform"? Will it repeat the errors made by the Protestants, or will it measure itself christologically?

After spending nearly three decades denying Barth's claim that liberal Protestantism and Catholicism were two sides of the same coin, Balthasar for the first time feared Barth might be right. He made his concerns explicit in his published celebration of Barth's eightieth birthday in 1966 and his obituary for Barth in 1968. In the birthday celebration, Balthasar acknowledged that Barth was an "uncomfortable partner in ecumenical conversation [*Gespräch*]."[81]

78. Barth, *Ad Limina Apostolorum: An Appraisal of Vatican II*, trans. Keith R. Crim (Richmond, VA: John Knox Press, 1968), 20, 27.

79. Ibid., 53.

80. Ibid., 78–79.

81. Lochbrunner, *Hans Urs von Balthasar und seine Theologenkollegen*, 352.

His relentless critique of modern, liberal Protestant theology made him such. Unfortunately, Balthasar argues, much of Vatican II was more interested in being modern than honoring Barth's concerns. Balthasar made this intriguing statement: "In terms of the Council, he will feel confirmed in his grim analysis of Catholicism in the first volumes of his great *Dogmatics*, which in proximity, even in a secret identity, of the Catholic and Schleiermachian liberal principles again and again he unsparingly underlined."[82] Balthasar continued, explaining how some have suggested Barth has "had his time," but this is incorrect. If we "resist" this interpretation, he continues, "We will have then discovered perhaps with amazement that Barth actually did not at all have his time." For Balthasar, in 1966, Barth's theology has not yet had its day; it has not yet seen vindication, and the reason he gives is that Barthians, and now Catholics, failed to acknowledge the significance of Barth's shift from being modern to questioning modern theology.

Barth himself was "once terribly modern," Balthasar wrote, but his "breakthrough" (*Durchbruch*) called that into question. He did not express himself well at first. It took time to find the right challenge to modern theology, but he did find it.

> What he wanted to say, and what he always said more clearly and classically, is that the Word of God in Jesus Christ is the lord of man and the world, that this Word brings death to the old man, so that he can be raised with its divine power to the new from the grave, that the salvation of man finally lies beyond himself in this saving Word, that through the grace of faith man is able to apprehend; that the word of God, as it is presented to us in Scripture and proclamation, is powerfully sufficient to interpret itself for men and to make it understandable. It bears thus the measure of its truth in itself and is not dependent on that, when it wants to be understood by men and to be measured by their measure.[83]

Toward the end of Barth's life, Balthasar returns to the controversial 1932 preface to the first volume of *Church Dogmatics* and wonders if Barth saw something he had not recognized. Jesus Christ should be the measure that measures nature and culture, but a modern Catholicism and Protestantism constantly reverses the measure and the measured.

82. Ibid.
83. Ibid., 352–53.

In the 1932 preface, Barth claimed he now had a "better understanding of many things," especially the problem with "philosophical existentialism" as the foundation for theology. By that statement he meant that theology began with an account of human existence and moved from it to God. The errors of that movement preoccupied him as early as the winter semester of 1923–1924 in his lectures on Schleiermacher, who initiated the transition to philosophical existentialism, replacing the prolegomena of the Scholastic proofs for the existence of God with an elaborate anthropology as theology's beginning point. For Barth, replacing the proofs with an anthropology was a deadly move. Intended or not, Schleiermacher turned Christology into nothing more than "the triumph of humanity, or enhanced humanity."[84] At this point, prior to his public disagreement with Wobbermin, Barth affirmed Aquinas's starting point in opposition to Schleiermacher: "Not simply following the logic of the matter itself like a Thomas Aquinas, he does not seek to say what Christianity is and ought to be in its own context, let the world say what it will about it."[85] Schleiermacher tried to replace the Scholastic proofs for the existence of God with the feeling of absolute dependence, and in turn could not sustain his best efforts at maintaining the christological center, which Barth admits Schleiermacher sought to do. Schleiermacher was a Christocentric theologian.[86] By replacing the proofs with the feeling of absolute dependence, Schleiermacher attempted to make Christian theology relevant to modernity. The result was a "secularization of the Christian life."[87]

In his criticism Barth wrote:

> Nothing remained of the belief that the Word or statement is as such the bearer, bringer, and proclaimer of truth, that there might be such a thing as the Word of God. Schleiermacher knows the concept of the *kerygma*, but naturally a kerygma that only *depicts* and does not *bring*, that only *states* or *expresses* and does not *declare*. Truth does not come in the spoken Word; it comes in speaking feeling.[88]

84. Barth, *The Theology of Schleiermacher*, trans. Geoffrey W. Bromiley (Grand Rapids, MI: Eerdmans, 1982), 90, 193, 200.

85. Barth, *The Theology of Schleiermacher*, 245.

86. He recognized Schleiermacher was a brilliant theologian and a "sincere Christian." Likewise he acknowledged Schleiermacher sought a "real Christology," that made Jesus "absolute." But he failed, and this was the "wound" in his system. He failed because he denied language could adequately express God's Word. Instead "music" replaced words. Ibid., 70–71, 76, 106, 183.

87. Ibid., 193, 35.

88. Ibid., 210. Emphasis original.

In response to this, Barth called for a "theological revolution," which requires a "basic No to the whole of Schleiermacher's doctrine of religion and Christianity."[89]

When Barth produced the first volume of the *Church Dogmatics*, he confessed that such a philosophical existentialism had too much characterized his earlier efforts at dogmatics, and now he wanted to develop it without any hint of that foundation. The *Church Dogmatics* was not the first effort at that revolution, but it was its fruit. It is undeniable that thinking with Anselm helped him in that revolution. Anselm provided a theological beginning similar to, but different from, the Scholastic proofs. It was a beginning rooted in a confidence in speaking of God, a beginning founded on dogma and not an elaborate anthropology that then warranted speaking of God. This beginning point helps make sense of the title: *Church Dogmatics*. Contra Schleiermacher, and with Anselm, Barth's revolution undertook a careful analysis of the church's dogma. He had earlier stated this was a terrible lacuna in Schleiermacher. "We are appalled by the fact that Schleiermacher seems not to have seriously considered at all the meaning of the church's dogma before replacing it with his own substance."[90] In 1924, he stated forthrightly if Schleiermacher was right about Protestantism, the only option was to return to Roman Catholicism.[91] It was a judgment he never relented from. Late in life, he found Bultmann's fascination with Heidegger and existentialism nothing more than a "Schleiermachian renaissance," which troubled him.[92] What unites them, he wrote, was "the consciously and consistently executed anthropological starting point which is the focus of their thought and utterances."

If Schleiermacher represented the replacement of Scholastic proofs for God's existence by an anthropological starting point neglecting the church's dogma, then exploring "Anselm's proof for the existence of God in connection to his theological program" would be an antidote.[93] Anselm's proof was not touched by Kant's so-called postmetaphysical critique of the proofs, and therefore theologians did not need to cower before Kant's critique. He did not sweep away the so-called proofs for God's existence and destroy metaphysics. He only demolished Descartes and Leibniz's use of that proof within a strict and truncated account of reason. Properly understood within the context of

89. Ibid., 259.

90. Ibid., 240.

91. Ibid., 259.

92. Ibid., 268–70.

93. The quote is the subtitle to Barth's 1931 publication, *Fides quaerens intellectum: Anselms Beweis der Existenz Gottes im Zusammenhang seines theologischen Programms* (Munich: Chr. Kaiser, 1931).

fides quaerens intellectum, Kant's postmetaphysical critique lacked any persuasiveness.[94] Theology did not need to follow Schleiermacher; it could begin with Anselm's proof. In the early 1930s, Barth returned theology to an earlier Scholastic foundation, a proof for the existence of God, but with a decided twist. The proof was not merely natural, it was established within the realm of grace. For that reason, it was as aesthetic as it was logical. The proof was "fitting" to how God had redeemed the world.

Barth held a seminar on Anselm in 1930, which is certainly not his sole "breakthrough," but Barth referred to it as crucial, and Balthasar, for obvious reasons, agreed with Barth's assessment. That seminar issued in Barth's book on Anselm, which Balthasar obviously found significant both for Barth and for his own work. Anselm's significance through Barth on Balthasar should not be a surprise. Barth begins his Anselm book explaining that Anselm's proof necessitates theology, for it is founded not upon *utilitas*, but *pulchritudo* (beauty). Anselm's proof is concerned with the "aesthetics of theological knowledge."[95] It issues from faith, which knows that God's will is never arbitrary. Thus from faith, theology can and must reason to God's existence.[96] Anselm's proof, then, provides a different foundation for theology than Schleiermacher, one that can finally eschew existentialist prolegomena. From his 1932 preface to *Church Dogmatics* to the end of that extraordinary enterprise, he strove to rid theology of this foundation, of any "philosophical existentialism." He called for a choice—either the Word or philosophical existence as the theological starting point. In 1932 he wondered aloud—in his now infamous passage about the *analogia entis*—if Catholicism itself really offered an alternative.

If Barth offered a choice between a theology founded upon the Word or upon a philosophy of existence, Balthasar rejected the choice. Both were possible as long as the latter did not condition the former. He learned from Barth to be attentive to any philosophical reduction of Christianity that made the affirmation of being the essence of Christianity. He thought Barth was wrong about Catholicism; he misunderstood it. It was as christological as Barth's theology. It could affirm what he affirmed and offer a more profound

---

94. See the final paragraph of ibid., 199.

95. Ibid., 15–16.

96. Interpreting Anselm sympathetically, Barth writes, "Corresponding to the basis in faith there has to be a reason in knowledge; to the ontic a corresponding noetic necessity. The way to the latter he finds in the confidence based on faith and faith alone that there might be a valid use of the human capacity to form concepts and judgments and that therefore there could be a valid noetic rationality." But, he insists, Anselm neither begins with an "autonomous human reason" nor with "the data of general human experience." Barth, *Fides quarens intellectum*, 52–54.

philosophy of existence that did not lose the christological center. But after Vatican II, Balthasar began to have his own doubts. In 1966 and then again in 1968, Balthasar expressed those doubts, finding Catholic theology trending toward a neo-Schleiermachian theology that lost the central insight of Barth: theology begins with an aesthetic knowledge that seeks to express the form and tone of the glory of God revealed in Christ. Instead theology would begin with something putatively more secure, something seemingly readily available to human creatures: nature, culture, existence, being, transcendental anthropology.[97]

Published only four days after Barth's death, Balthasar's obituary sets forth themes similar to his published greeting on Barth's eightieth birthday. Once again we find a criticism of Schleiermacher:

> The name, Karl Barth, stands for an epoch. He and no other broke through the rigidity, or shall we say, the agile, amorphous front of the thousand-footed Protestant liberalism, and that could not be done otherwise than through a massive, blazing protest, presented in prophetic antitheses. Against all the diluted speeches on religion and religious culture, he placed the one and exclusive word: the Word of God.[98]

Balthasar acknowledges Barth's great interest in Vatican II and his approval of the conciliar document, *Dei Verbum*. He also states that three days before his death, "[Barth] proposed to me, cheerful as always on the telephone, that we jointly put together a brochure, which connected a lecture from him and one from me, with a twofold dedication, and send it to the Holy Father."[99] This was "one side" of Barth, the "Mozart, catholicizing Barth." But then Balthasar's obituary takes a turn that once again alludes to Barth's criticisms of Catholicism in his early *Church Dogmatics*. Once again he does not dismiss Barth's criticism. It is not only born out of misunderstanding. He wrote, "There is however, to our shame, another side; the sharp and relentless analyses of Catholicism especially in the first volumes of the *Dogmatics*, have been proven right in many

97. Although no one would accuse Steven A. Long of affirming liberal Protestantism, note the odd similarity between it and his statement: "It is on the basis of the being of creatures that the truth of the proposition that God exists is demonstrated." Long, *Analogia Entis: On the Analogy of Being, Metaphysics, and the Act of Faith* (NotreDame: University of Notre Dame Press, 2012), 3. Of course this is for him a philosophical and natural theological affirmation, whereas for liberal Protestantism it is the source for revelation as well, but the similarities are striking.

98. Lochbrunner, *Hans Urs von Balthasar und seine Theologenkollegen*, 369.

99. Ibid., 370.

postconciliar developments in the Catholic Church in an almost frightening way."[100] For someone who spent three decades defending the *analogia entis* against Barth's rejection, this admission is stunning, but even here Balthasar does not concede Barth's point entirely. What the postconciliar developments demonstrate is what happens when the *analogia entis* gets "misused." Then, Balthasar says,

> It leads in fact easily to a *Kulturseligkeit* [blessing of culture] or "turning to the world," which whether now appears in the name of the order of creation (evolution) or of the Gospel and Christology (as "transcendental anthropology"), can lead even further to the degeneration, which stands before us everywhere today.[101]

In response to this, Balthasar admonishes his hearers with two important lessons he learned from Barth. First, he writes that the older Barth "witnessed these developments [of Vatican II] with the greatest concern" and warned Catholics not to make the same mistakes Protestants did: "For Heaven's sake do not commit the same foolishness that we did in the last century and have repented bitterly: learn from the history of liberal Protestantism." This lesson led to a second, ecumenical lesson. Barth was a courageous person and theologian.

> He looked around already in 1945 and saw what in the meantime many other ecumenically minded Christians learned to see: that the fronts today to a large extent pass straight through the churches. The critical line ran there, where the faith in Jesus Christ as the only mediator between God and men (1 Tim. 2:5) and, we explicitly add, personal love to him is maintained or abandoned.[102]

Rather than decreasing the importance of ecumenical endeavors, Balthasar's admonitions make them more important. Catholics and Protestants must find a way to find each other—*in Christ*.

How did the *analogia entis* get misused? A cue to Balthasar's answer is found in his 1978 publication *Theo-Drama* 3, where he wrote,

> However *analogia entis* may be defined in philosophical detail, it means that the terms employed cannot be traced back to a generic

---

100. Ibid., 371.
101. Ibid.
102. Ibid.

concept (for example, as if both God and the creature were to fall *under* the heading of "being as such": this is the danger of Scotism and late scholastic rationalism). . . . Quite simply, this means that the person of the Logos in whom the hypostatic union takes place cannot function, in any way, as the ("higher") unity between God and man: this person, as such, is God.[103]

Balthasar's consistent defense of the *analogia entis* integrated Barth's christological center into a Catholic fullness. After Vatican II, he feared Catholicism was becoming the caricature Barth saw in the 1920s, affirming God by affirming ourselves. Balthasar's theology was always caught between these two poles: convincing Catholics they were as christological as Barth's Reformed theology, and convincing Protestants they could affirm the *analogia entis* and thereby glimpse the whole creation as God's good gift in, through, and for the glory of the mystery that is the hypostatic union.

"The Church in Renewal" and "Unification in Christ"

Barth died while preparing a lecture on ecumenism in response to a request from Professor J. Feiner, to be given during the week of world prayer. After his death, the first few handwritten pages of the lecture were found on his desk. His last public lecture was held in tandem with Balthasar on Ash Wednesday, 1968 for the Swiss Ökumenischen Gesprächskommissionen. Barth spoke on the theme, "The Church in Renewal," and Balthasar addressed "Unification in Christ." Twenty-seven years after Balthasar attended his Trent lecture, Barth and Balthasar addressed Vatican II together.

BARTH'S CALL FOR RENEWAL

Barth's lecture primarily responded to the conciliar documents *Lumen gentium* and *Gaudium et spes*. As in *Ad Limina Apostolorum*, he finds the former helpful and the latter troubling. He divided his lecture into three parts. First, he affirmed the definition of the church from *Lumen gentium,* and then he added to it. The church is, *Populus Dei peregrinans, qui est corpus mysticum Christi* (The pilgrim people of God, which is the mystical body of Christ.) It is the mystical body of Christ because "it receives, takes and has a share in the mission of the Son of

---

103. On this point I am indebted to Peter Casarella's important essay, "Hans Urs von Balthasar, Erich Przywara's *Analogia Entis*, and the Problem of a Catholic *Denkform*," in *The Analogy of Being: Invention of the Antichrist or the Wisdom of God*, ed. Thomas Joseph White, OP (Grand Rapids, MI: Eerdmans, 2011), 203.

God becoming human." The church exists not for itself, however, but in service to all people as a "particular people" that always "wanders" within creation to its destination.[104] Second, he discussed "renewal in the church." It is *semper reformanda*, which is not "innovation" (*Neuerung*) but renewal (*Erneuerung*) through a constant return to its source and origin, Jesus Christ. Third, Barth offered some comments about the "structures of the church in renewal." It comes as no surprise that the key image he draws upon for ecclesial structures is John the Baptist. The church exists, like John, to serve and witness. It points away from itself and to Christ. This prompts Barth to express some worries about the sharp hierarchical distinction between clergy and laity in *Lumen gentium,* but he admits it provides more of a place for the work of the laity than did Calvin. He adopts the key word *aggiornamento,* and states, "The church in renewal is the people of God in '*aggiornamento.*'" He then redefines it in order to challenge possible misuses of the term by Catholics. *Aggiornamento* should signify "the adaptation [*Anpassung*] of the church's life to the life of another," which is first that of the "triune God in his action in the world and in the church." He questions if this is the life to which *aggiornamento* applies, or if it is not much more "neoprotestant," especially with the insistence on the "dignity of the human person" in *Gaudium et spes.* More than opening a window to modernity, *Gaudium et spes* may be "removing the roof": "A house that is completely open has no roof." The church must be open to its Lord. It must have many open windows, but if too many windows are built, it ceases to be a house.[105] Then it will serve a different lord. The church's structure is that of a "free, living people," free for service, for God and humanity. The opposite of this freedom is Babylonian captivities: a "captivity of power, of mammon, of brutal force," and then Barth adds, "and of course much more dignified but also more effective, captivity to the Spirit of the age, to the modern."[106] Like Balthasar, Barth worried this might be the outcome of Vatican II, especially if *Gaudium et spes* sets the agenda. Barth adds that the church in renewal must be joyful, obedient, and praying. Liturgy and Eucharist are important, but prayer is above all.[107]

---

104. Karl Barth, "Kirche in Erneuerung," in *Einheit und Erneuerung der Kirche: Zwei Vorträge Karl Barth und Hans Urs von Balthasar* (Freiburg: Paulusverlag, 1968), 10.

105. Ibid., 15.

106. "die Gefangeschaften der Zeitgesiter und der Modern." Ibid., 16.

107. Ibid., 18.

BALTHASAR'S INTEGRATION

Balthasar addressed the question of "unification in Christ." He republished this lecture in a 1969 work, *Entfaltung: auf Wegen christlicher Einigung* (Integration: On the Paths to Christian Unity).[108] He acknowledged the "confused" and "contradictory" stances internal to Catholicism and between Catholics and Protestants that emerged from Vatican II's engagement with modernity. Catholics seek to go "behind tradition" and hear the Word of God, but they do not want to hear the eschatological tone in that Word, which speaks of the Christian's "alienation" in the world. Modern Catholics domesticate the eschatological and hear primarily "openness to the world."[109] This loss of eschatology is his concern, more so than any fear of pluralism. He denies Scripture alone can bring unity because of the multiplicity of its witness. He admonishes his audience not to fear that multiplicity for it is like a "kaleidoscope" that brings the apparent divisions into a unity. Christian truth is like that kaleidoscope; it is never a singular essence. Here is where Moltmann and Lösel inadequately identify Balthasar's apparent ecumenical shift. His concern is not that the ecumenical movement brings in too much pluralism, but that it abandons too much as secondary and extraneous in order to produce a unity based on the "essentials" of the Christian faith. Balthasar's concern is best found in this lengthy quote:

> A word about the Evangelical-Catholic controversy in general is appropriate here. The present ecumenical dialogue, although it is frequently understood as a cooperative search for Christian truth in focus on the mutual Lord, is understood also as a radical reduction to the allegedly "essential", along with the elimination of all dispensable additions which disturb the understanding. It is clear that the Catholic partner will draw the shorter straw under these conditions for the Reformation already lightened the ship of all its alleged 'ballast' four hundred fifty years ago, and today, in the face of the events within the Catholic Church, it speaks, not without satisfaction, of a "need to catch up" [*Nachholbedarf*].

---

108. Balthasar, *Entfaltungen: Auf Wegen christlicher Einigung* (Munich: Kösel Gmbh, 1969). The English translation is *Convergences: To the Source of Christian Mystery* (San Francisco: Ignatius , 1988.) Balthasar's lecture was given the chapter heading, "The Multitude of Biblical Theologies and the Spirit of Unity in the Church," 75–110.

109. Balthasar, *Entfaltungen*, 19.

The "need to catch up" is what concerns Balthasar. He worries about the "abandonment of Catholic goods (allegedly those of the 'Counter-Reformation' above all)." Abandoning those goods was never his intention. However, he sees promise in "Evangelical and Anglican movements" because they do not throw all this out as "ballast." Instead we find "new appropriation of Mariology, the Holy Mass as a sacrifice, the ecclesiastical teaching authority and the literally interpreted life of following Christ in the evangelical counsels—while in the Catholic camps it is contemporary to throw all these things, like cheap trifles, into the rubbish."[110] The latter statement shows the real concern Balthasar had for church unity. He hoped the truth of Protestantism would be folded back into the truths of Catholicism. His vocation was to call laity to follow Christ through the evangelical counsels, to venture "outside the camp" and embody Christ's difficult teaching of perfection through creative forms of mission. What he saw taking place was the opposite: the loss of Catholic truths in search of some Protestant "essence," but this was the source for the demise of Protestant Christianity. A Catholic repetition of reducing Christianity to its essence and losing the symphony of its truth could hardly turn out different. Barth's warning needed to be heeded.

Balthasar made two references to Barth in his lecture. The first affirmed Barth's insistence that any unity is only a unity in Christ.

> After everything that has been said we can first of all—from the highest observatory, so to speak—venture the statement that a Christian truth which divides the Church is an internal contradiction, an "impossible possibility", as Karl Barth would say: for Christian truth *per definitionem* can only be unifying for the Church. For this reason, Catholics and Protestants owe each other "mutual exhortation (*paraklesis*)."[111]

But Karl Barth's exhortation to Catholics can be a temptation for the reduction of the symphonic character of Christian truth to some singular essence. Balthasar also wrote,

> Karl Barth's invectives against the "Catholic And" can be important and even indispensable as earnest brotherly exhortation—particularly when they protest against something secondary being put in the

110. Ibid., 36. *Convergences*, 109.
111. Balthasar, *Entfaltungen*, 35. *Convergences*, 106.

place of something primary—but they can also prejudice, too quickly and unnecessarily, a necessary integration.[112]

Here is the fruit of Balthasar and Barth's conversation for ecumenical unity. The key term is "integration." How do we integrate without reducing Catholic truth to some putative essence? How do we allow the rich diversity of Christian truths from the past to inform the present, even truths from the Council of Trent, Vatican I, and the Protestant Confessions? If they are from Christ, they cannot be contradictory. Any apparent contradiction can only be an enigma. We may not yet see how they hold together, how they might converge or integrate (*entfalten*). If we throw much of this out as nothing but ballast, no convergence is necessary.

Conclusion

Much had taken place in Barth and Balthasar's lives in the years between their first meeting in 1940 and their last public lecture in 1968. Barth published *Church Dogmatics* from 2.2 on. Balthasar began his work on the trilogy, publishing much of *Herrlichkeit*. They corresponded, vacationed, traveled to Rome, exchanged presents and manuscripts, and had numerous private meetings. What began with an effort to demonstrate the superiority of each one's respective tradition, culminated in an ecumenical rapprochement that showed how much Protestants and Catholics needed each other if Christianity was to be grounded upon the Word God spoke in Christ. Barth's early approach to ecumenism began with "intolerance." In 1931 he wrote, "Genuine and profitable discussion is only possible where there is a confrontation involving real dogmatic intolerance. For it is only there that one confession has something to say to the other."[113] From this odd beginning and from their mutual exhortations, Barth and Balthasar wittingly and unwittingly produced a theological renaissance centered on Jesus Christ that influenced the doctrine of God, theological ethics, and ecclesiology. Their influence on the latter still awaits fuller elaboration, but they agreed on this point: Catholic and Protestant ecclesiology goes awry when it begins with the "counter." If Catholic identity is predicated upon opposing Protestant errors, it will need those errors for its own identity. The same, of course, is true for Protestantism. I fear this is what occurs in contemporary Protestant appropriations and Catholic rejections of

---

112. Balthasar, *Entfaltungen*, 35. *Convergences,*107.

113. Eberhard Busch, *Karl Barth: His Life from Letters and Autobiographicsl Texts*, trans. John Bowden (Philadelphia: Fortress Press, 1976), 215.

Barth's theology. The "counter" remains decisive. The result is the construction of reactive ecclesiologies. Renewal and unity result when each affirms and confesses from the heart of its tradition, but then each also listens attentively to the other's affirmations. Affirmation does not reject disagreement; it allows it to emerge without making the disagreement essential for identity. Protestants need not reduce the richness of Catholicism to some putative essence to find unity, for that only asks Catholics to abandon their tradition for Protestantism. Catholics need not treat Protestants like flat-footed fideists whose only option is conversion to a Catholic metaphysics created in the manualist tradition. Neither Catholics nor Protestants should give quarter to their coreligionists who explicitly or implicitly side with secularizing forces, either through a misplaced *aggiornamento* or a reductive essentializing of Christianity, especially to ethics, which is always ready at hand in a secular culture. Beginning with Barth's dogmatic intolerance and Balthasar's desire to save Barth, they traveled a long way together. It was a remarkable journey. We do not need to start at the same place they did. The last thing we need is Barthians or Balthasarians, Protestants or Catholics, who repeat the early decades of the twentieth century and approach each other with dogmatic intolerance, or simply the desire to save and convert the other. The question their friendship poses is how to affirm Christ as the center of our common faith and allow that center to radiate into all things, without allowing those things to somehow usurp the center. Our task is not to take up where they began but where they ended.

7

Conclusion

This work began arguing that Catholicism haunted Karl Barth. Theologians should be grateful for it. Had he not suffered Catholicism, he would not have been motivated to turn to dogmatics. Barth sought a robust Protestant theology that could dogmatically stand on "its own two feet" as much as Catholic theology did. In pursuing it, he moved beyond modern theological categories, returning to, without repristinating, the dogmatic tradition. Balthasar affirmed Barth for turning toward the Scholastics, toward Anselm and Aquinas, when Catholics were turning away from them toward "openings in modern thought."[1] Balthasar also discovered that the more Barth turned toward Protestant dogmatics, the more Catholic he became.[2] He endeavored, despite all the obstacles, to show this to Catholics and Protestants alike, and he sought to show it to Barth.

What did Balthasar try to show us? First, that the issue of the *analogia entis* was not the primary issue. The *analogia entis* was unavoidable for any christological theologian. It could get misused, but that did not take away its usefulness. Barth's preoccupation with the *analogia entis* was not where the fruit of their relationship can be found. It is too much of a secondary matter. Kenneth Oakes makes the astute observation that many of the efforts theologians have made to supplement Przywara's *analogia entis* with Barth's *analogia fidei* and vice versa are "redundant." As he puts it, "Przywara's *analogia entis* needs no supplement of revelation and Barth's theology needs no supplement of ontological claims and concerns."[3] The *analogia entis* was never a metaphysical framework of being within which both God and creation were conceived.

1. Balthasar, *The Theology of Karl Barth*, trans. Edward T. Oakes, SJ (San Francisco: Ignatius, 1992), 40.

2. Balthasar, *The Theology of Karl Barth*, 23.

3. Kenneth Oakes, "The Cross and the *Analogia Entis* in Erich Przywara," in *The Analogy of Being: Invention of the Antichrist or the Wisdom of God?*, ed. Thomas Joseph White, OP (Grand Rapids, MI: Eerdmans, 2011), 170–71.

What Christian theologian (surely not even Duns Scotus) would have intentionally been that shortsighted? If it became that, as Balthasar acknowledged it could, it was misused. Likewise, revelation always assumes creaturely conditions (conditions of being if one prefers) within which it makes sense. Whoever denied that? Would that we could move beyond these caricatures. Would that Barth listened more patiently to his younger colleague in order to identify more carefully where he disagreed with Catholic (nonessential) teaching, and how he agreed with it. Balthasar identified Barth's real concern as the assumption that knowledge of God and ethics could be pursued in some putative neutral, natural realm. There is nothing more modern than that. The fruit of their conversation is found in the retrieval of God's perfections within, and not as a condition for, God's Triunity, and in the recasting of ethics within God's ordered economy. It is also found in the inheritance of an important controversy they bequeathed us: How shall we best think, speak, and act on the relationship of Christ and his church to make sense of the divine economy? That conversation is much more important than rehearsing, one more time, debates over the *analogia entis*.[4]

Second, knowledge of God and ethics make no sense upon the foundation of a doctrine of pure nature. They will then lose what matters most—in Christ, God elects the human creature to be reconciled with God. Because Barth did not recognize where the Catholic error was located, he failed to develop an adequate account of human agency within the realm of grace. Balthasar feared that grace evacuated human nature. Toward the end of his *Dogmatics*, Barth emphasized such a human agency. In fact, he worried that Catholicism evacuated nature with its doctrine of transubstantiation. A richer conversation than that of the *analogia entis* can be taken up by pursuing the question of which realm knowledge of God and ethics should be pursued, and how dogmatics affects natural theology and ethics. Is there a pure nature that provides the foundation for revelation? How is that possible? To what extent is such a nature an excuse to rule?

Both Barth and Balthasar help us think and practice Christian ethics in a new way, one that retrieves the dogmatic task as an ethical task. If God creates, preserves, and redeems the world as the Holy Trinity, then creation, preservation, and redemption occur through, in and for the Person and mission of the Second Person of the Trinity. Ethics cannot be pursued well by positing some space outside that only "locus" for creaturely existence.

---

4. George Hunsinger's *The Eucharist and Ecumenism* (Cambridge: Cambridge University Press, 2008) is a start in that direction.

Third, Barth and Balthasar saw in liberal Protestantism, even in its Catholic appropriation, a methodological starting point in human nature and/or culture that could not be troubled by Christian eschatology and therefore missed something significant; it missed the dramatic form and content of Christian theology. Once theology was reduced to an anthropological starting point, theology's dramatic character would be lost.

Balthasar recognized Karl Barth as a theologian saved from "liberal Protestantism." Barth's work should be a warning to Catholics. Drawing on Barth's theology, Balthasar admonished Catholics: "Learn from the history of liberal Protestantism."[5] He found Barth moving much closer to Catholicism toward the end of his life, and he presented Barth's "Catholic" side to Catholics and Protestants. It is true that after Vatican II, when he went to church, Barth often attended the Bruder Klaus Catholic Church, but we don't have statistics on his frequency.[6] After Vatican II, Barth found Catholics more capable of reforming the church than the Reformed. He never abandoned an understanding of the church as *semper reformanda*, and saw it present in some of the Vatican II documents. He affirmed much of the Catholic teaching on the church in *Lumen gentium* but worried about *Gaudium et spes*. He also acknowledged a rapprochement between his understanding of Reformed Christianity and Catholicism that was not present in liberal Protestantism. It was incapable of reform. However, as was evident in the previous chapter, Barth wrote strong critiques of authority in Roman Catholicism early and late. Its authority structure was "secular," usurping the place of Christ.[7] What Balthasar

5. "Macht doch um Himmelswillen nicht heute die gleichen Dummheiten, die wir im letzten Jahrhundert gemacht und aufs bitterste gebüßt haben: lernt aus der Geschichte des liberalen Protestantismus!" Lochbrunner, *Hans Urs von Balthasar und seine Theologenkollegen: Sechs Beziehungsgeschichten* (Würzburg: Echter, 2009), 371.

6. The "Karl Barth Guide Map" available at the Karl Barth Archives has the "Bruder Klaus Church" as the third site to visit to "meet Karl Barth." It states that Barth "influenced its final architecture. He very much appreciated the fact that even before the Second Vatican Council the priest here no longer had his back turned toward the congregation. His friends and family even feared he would convert to Catholicism and become a Catholic. However, he denied their concern: 'Clearly, I would never become a Catholic.'" Eberhard Busch, *Karl Barths Lebenslauf: Nach Seinen Briefen und autobiografischen Texten* (Munich: Chr. Kaiser, 1976).

7. For Barth, Roman Catholic authority not only sets itself up as equal to the authority of Christ, but "even set above Him as His vicar in earthly history, its ministry of witness being left far behind as it shares with Him an existence and activity which are both human and divine, and human in divine reality and omnipotence." *Church Dogmatics* 4.3.2, trans. Geoffrey W. Bromiley, ed. G. W. Bromiley and T. F. Torrance (Edinburgh: T & T Clark, 1961), 836. For an invaluable discussion of this passage and Barth's ecclesiology, see Kimlyn J. Bender, *Karl Barth's Christological Ecclesiology* (Aldershot: Ashgate, 2005). Barth's understanding of authority led him increasingly to a "free" church polity. Whereas Balthasar saw

affirmed, Barth denied to the end. The church is not the prolongation of the incarnation. This theme recurs from the early to later volumes of the *Church Dogmatics*. Barth consistently set his ecclesiology of witness and mission against Roman Catholic and Orthodox hierarchies.

After Vatican II, Balthasar feared Barth might be right, not about his critique of hierarchy, but about a misuse of the *analogia entis*. Catholicism was tempted by liberal Protestantism. The *analogia entis* could get misused where affirming one's own being was to affirm God. Such a starting point provided a secure foundation for modernity against eschatology's troubling judgment. If so, Barth's time had not yet come. His criticism had not yet been heard. Catholicism took on too much of exactly what Barth critiqued, repeating the errors of liberal Protestantism, which always of course ends in secularism. Retrieving the doctrine of pure nature against modernity offers no alternative to that end for Catholics. Revisiting the relationship between Barth and Schleiermacher as an apology for a modern Barth offers no alternative to that end for Protestants. Listening and noting well the conversation between Barth and Balthasar will by no means solve all the difficulties Christianity faces in our hypermodern era, some brought on internal to the faith and others external to it. It might, however, help us discover what they discovered. The enigmatic cleft dividing us is not only unintelligible, but damaging to Christian mission. At least their conversation should remind us that Christian faith, along with its necessary insistence upon reason, is best pursued through friendship, friendships across ecclesial divides.

Finally, Barth and Balthasar's friendship and conversation is a powerful example how to pursue the church's unity. This work began suggesting the friendship between Barth and Balthasar has ongoing potential for ecumenical fruitfulness. Revisiting that friendship, it was suggested, could have tremendous benefits as we seek to move beyond a liberal unity that rejects too much and a conservative retrenchment that accepts too little from the gains theologians such as Barth and Balthasar achieved. The ecumenical fruitfulness of their conversation and friendship is discovered in the questions they put to each other, which required them to take the other's work with utmost seriousness. Barth's question to Balthasar and Catholicism in general was this: Is *Jesus* disclosed as the Lord of his church and creation in your theology? Balthasar

Barth moving in a Catholic direction, John Howard Yoder claimed he moved increasingly toward the Anabaptists. Are such seemingly divergent interpretations of Barth nothing more than theologians reading into his massive work their own convictions? Perhaps. Or perhaps something more interesting is at work here, something unexpected. Perhaps Yoder and Balthasar were both correct. The more Catholic Barth became, the more his theological witness to Christ took on an Anabaptist form.

answered yes, and in turn asked Barth: Is Jesus disclosed as the Lord of his *church* and *creation* in yours? Is everything radiated by Christ's presence? Their questions assume this basic agreement: Christian unity is only a unity in Christ. If we first seek Christ, unity will inevitably follow. If we do not yet have unity, it must be that he is not yet our first desire and end. If the *analogia entis*, metaphysics, dialectic, nature/grace distinction, *potentia oboedentialis*, *finitum non capax infiniti*, ecclesial structures, ethics, or doctrine does not serve that end, it has no necessary place in the theodrama. This approach to unity is certainly how Barth put it, and Balthasar agreed. He added, however, that Christ as our end brought with it many forms and styles presented in Christian tradition that we abandon at our peril. We never seek some "essence" of Christianity as the basis for unity. No tradition should be asked to abandon anything essential to its witness to Christ; every tradition must be tested by it. This premise provides the primary condition for their understanding of renewal and unity in the church.

Although relatively simple, this premise has vast implications for the church's task. The task cannot be, as Balthasar worried was happening after Vatican II, unity by subtraction where each tradition removes what the other might find offensive. Then the church will inevitably slide into the lowest common denominator of liberal Protestantism's perennial quest for the singular "essence" of Christianity, which will repeat the anthropological reduction. Balthasar explicitly rejected this quest for Christianity's "essence," and found it to be Protestantism's downfall. He worried Catholicism was becoming influenced by it. For Balthasar the essential witness to Christ is not a singular essence but a rich composite affecting every aspect of life; it can be nonidentically repeated by saints and those entrusted with the secular realm until everything is gathered together and handed over to the Father in the eucharistic sacrifice. This witness requires the form of a vast dogmatics or theological aesthetics, dramatics, and logic, in which everything gets implicated in everything else, all of it being radiated from the center. Once that center gets acknowledged, a fruitful exchange can occur. Then the question can be asked, how does our performance of that "everything" relate to the center?

Balthasar found Barth's performance unsatisfactory in relating *everything* to the radiating center. Barth denied Christ's performance could be repeated in the saints or represented in the Mass. Balthasar sought to save Karl Barth, not in the sense that he thought Barth needed salvation, but that his theology needed to be expanded without loss by some essential Catholic teachings and practices that radiated from that center, bringing all of creation into its light. He recognized Barth's work clung to the radiating glory of Christ at its center more than many Catholic and Protestant theologians of their generation, but his clinging to it, albeit admirable, did not always allow everything to come into view. Rather than illuminating that everything, his theology could blind it in an apocalyptic blaze—a "Christomonism" or "Christological constriction" that did not allow others their proper role in the theodrama. Likewise Barth sought to save Catholic theology, asking whether it was radiated by that center or whether some lesser light illumined it. Could it say "Jesus" as much as it said "nature"?

If Barth were preoccupied with modernity and epistemology, any concern for ecumenical convergence would be secondary if not tertiary. Yet he spent the last few years of his life, his last few public lectures and seminars, preoccupied with the theme of ecclesial renewal and unification, which was no new theme. Balthasar recognized its presence in the first volume of the *Church Dogmatics*, and took up a conversation with Barth based on it. Barth saw that the divisions between Protestants and Catholics could only be called an "enigmatic crack." Such recognition did not cause him to embrace the ecumenical movement, as his strident tone at the 1948 World Council of Churches demonstrated, but it did lead to a more hopeful ecumenical openness. Such openness was, in part, the fruitfulness of his friendship with Balthasar. This fruitfulness is potentially being lost by a retrenchment on the part of some Catholic and Reformed theology, the former recovering neoscholasticism against modernity, the latter revisiting Barth's affirmation of modernity and undergoing a Schleiermacher renaissance. Such retrenchment is no more helpful than unity through subtraction by a liberal Protestant quest for minimal essentials (whether it be a Catholic or Protestant quest.) If these trends are the future for both Catholics and Protestants, they will be nothing but a return and repetition to the debates in the mid to late forties that swirled around Balthasar's preoccupation with Barth. At their worse, God forbid, perhaps we could repeat the sixteenth century. Then secularism not only will, but also should, result. If people who follow Christ, hear the Word, and share the Eucharist use the power to rule against each other, then we should expect deleterious consequences. We will not have learned much from these two unlikely friends. What we should learn is that our divisions should never be rendered intelligible, and we should never be satisfied with them. They are, and always will be, like evil itself, puzzling, enigmatic, and absurd. Although individual conversions from one side to the other are understandable in certain contexts, Barth is correct. They do no good in healing the split and recognizing the enigmatic character of the *Riss*. Conversions that mimic the "counter" of the sixteenth century are theologically dangerous. Despite their original intent, Barth and Balthasar's friendship and conversation point in a better direction.

Bibliography

Aquinas, Thomas. "Prooemium in Expositio in Symbolum Apostolorum." In *Corpus Thomisticum: Sancti Thomae de Aquino Expositio in Symbolum Apostolorum.* Edited by Roberto Busa, SJ. Textum Taurini, 1954. http://www.corpusthomisticum.org/csv.html.

———. *Quaestiones quodlibetales* V, Ques. 6, Art. 1. Translated by Alfred J. Freddoso.
http://www3.nd.edu/~afreddos/translat/aquinas4.htm.

———. *Summa Theologica.* English translation by Fathers of the English Dominican Province. Three volumes. New York: Benziger Bros., 1947.

Baker, Anthony. *Diagonal Advance: Perfection in Christian Theology.* Eugene, OR: Cascade, 2011.

Balthasar, Hans Urs von. "Analogie und Dialektik: Zur Klärung der theologischenPrinzipienlehre Karl Barths." *Divus Thomas* 22 (1944): 171–216.

———. "Analogie und Natur: Zur Klärung der theologischen Prinzipienlehre Karl Barths." *Divus Thomas* 23 (1945): 3–56.

———. *Apokalypse der deutschen Seele: Studien zu einer Lehre letzten Haltungen.* Three volumes. Salzburg: Anton Pustet, 1937–39.

———. "Der Begriff der Natur in der Theologie." *Zeitschrift für katholische Theologie* 75 (1953): 453–61.

———. *The Christian States of Life.* Translated by Mary Frances McCarthy. San Francisco: Ignatius, 1983.

———. *Convergences: To the Source of Christian Mystery.* Translated by E. A. Nelson. San Francisco: Ignatius, 1983.

———. "Einigung in Christus." *Freiburger Zeitschrift für Philosophie und Theologie* 15 (1968): 171–89.

———. *Entfaltungen: Auf Wegen christlicher Einigung.* Munich: Kösel Gmbh, 1969.

———. *Epilog.* Einsiedeln: Johannes, 1987.

———. *Explorations in Theology,* vol. 2: *Spouse of the Word.* Translated by A. V. Littledale with Alexander Dru. San Francisco: Ignatius, 1991.

———. *The Glory of the Lord,* vol. 5: *The Realm of Metaphysics in the Modern Age.* San Francisco: Ignatius, 1991.

———. *Karl Barth: Darstellung und Deutung Seiner Theologie.* Cologne: Jakob Hegner, 1951.

———. "Karl Barth und der Katholizismus." *Theologie der Zeit* 3 (1939): 126–32.

———. "Die Krisis der protestantischen Theologie," *Stimmen der Zeit* 132 (1938): 200–1.

———. *The Laity and the Life of the Counsels: The Church's Mission in the World.* Translated by Brian McNeil, CRV with D. C. Schindler. San Francisco: Ignatius, 1993.

———. *Love Alone is Credible.* Translated by D. C. Schindler. San Francisco: Ignatius, 2004

———. "Neun Sätze zur christlichen Ethik." In *Prinzipien christlicher Moral,* edited by J. Ratzinger, 67–93. Einsiedeln: Johannes, 1975.

———. "Nine Theses in Christian Ethics." In *Readings in Moral Theology,* no. 2: *The Distinctiveness of Christian Ethics,* edited by Charles E. Curran and Richard A. McCormick, SJ, 190–207. New York: Paulist, 1980.

———. "Patristik, Scholastik und wir." *Theologie der Zeit* 3 (1939): 65–104.

———. *Theo-Drama,* vol. 1: *Prolegomena.* Translated by Graham Harrison. San Francisco: Ignatius, 1988.

———. *Theo-Drama,* vol. 2: *The Dramatis Personae: Man in God.* Translated by Graham Harrison. San Francisco: Ignatius, 1990.

———. *Theo-Drama,* vol. 3: *Dramatis Personae: Persons in Christ.* Translated by Graham Harrison. San Francisco: Ignatius, 1991.

———. *Theo-Drama,* vol. 5: *Theological Dramatic Theory: The Last Act.* Translated by Graham Harrison. San Francisco: Ignatius, 1998.

———. *Theodramatik,* vol. 3: *Die Handlung.* Einsiedeln: Johannes , 1980.

———. *Theologic,* vol. 2: *The Truth of God.* Translated by Adrian Walker. San Francisco: Ignatius, 2004.

———. *A Theology of History.* San Francisco: Ignatius, 1994.

———. *The Theology of Karl Barth.* Translated by Edward T. Oakes, SJ. San Francisco: Ignatius, 1992.

———. *Tragedy Under Grace: Reinhold Schneider on the Experience of the West.* Translated by Brian McNeil, CRV. San Francisco: Ignatius, 1997.

Barth, Karl. *Ad Limina Apostolorum.* Zurich: Evangelischer, 1967.

———. *Ad Limina Apostolorum: An Appraisal of Vatican II.* Translated by Keith R. Crim. Richmond, VA: John Knox, 1968.

———. *Die christliche Dogmatik im Entwurf.* Edited by Gerhard Sauter. Zurich: Theologische , 1982.

————. *Church Dogmatics* 1/1. Translated by Geoffrey W. Bromiley. Edited by G. W. Bromiley and T. F. Torrance. 2nd edition. Edinburgh: T & T Clark, 1975.

————. *Church Dogmatics* 2/1. Translated by W. B. Johnston, T. H. L. Parker, Harold Knight, and J. L. M. Haire. Edited by G.W. Bromiley and T. F. Torrance. Edinburgh: T & T Clark, 1957.

————. *Church Dogmatics* 2/2. Translated by J. C. Campbell, Geoffrey W. Bromiley, Ian Wilson, J. Strathearn McNab, Harold Knight, and R. A. Stewart. Edited by G. W. Bromiley and T. F. Torrance. Edinburgh: T & T Clark, 1958.

————. *Church Dogmatics* 3/4. Translated by A. T. Mackay, T. H. L. Parker, Harold Knight, H. A. Kennedy, and J. Marks. Edited by G.W. Bromiley and T. F. Torrance. Edinburgh: T & T Clark, 1957.

————. *Church Dogmatics* 4/1. Translated by Geoffrey W. Bromiley. Edited by G. W. Bromiley and T. F. Torrance. Edinburgh: T & T Clark, 1956.

————. *Church Dogmatics* 4/2. Translated by Geoffrey W. Bromiley. Edited by G. W. Bromiley and T. F. Torrance. Edinburgh: T & T Clark, 1958.

————. *Church Dogmatics* 4/3.1. Translated by Geoffrey W. Bromiley. Edited by G. W. Bromiley and T. F. Torrance. Edinburgh: T & T Clark, 1961.

————. *Church Dogmatics* 4/3.2. Translated by Geoffrey W. Bromiley. Edited by G. W. Bromiley and T. F. Torrance. Edinburgh: T & T Clark, 1961.

————. *Church Dogmatics* 4/4. Translated by Geoffrey W. Bromiley. Edited by G. W. Bromiley and T. F. Torrance. Edinburgh: T & T Clark, 1969.

————. *The Epistle to the Romans.* Translated by Edwyn C. Hoskyns. Oxford: Oxford University Press, [1933] 1968.

————. *Ethics.* Edited by Dietrich Braun. Translated by Geoffrey W. Bromiley. New York: Seabury Press, 1981.

————. *Ethik 1: Vorlesung Münster, Sommersemester 1928, wiederholt in Bonn, Sommersemester 1930.* Edited by Dietrich Braun. Zurich: Theologischer, 1973.

————. *Fides quaerens intellectum: Anselms Beweis der Existenz Gottes im Zusammenhang seines theologischen Programms.* Munich: Chr. Kaiser, 1931.

————. *Göttingen Dogmatics*, vol. 1. Translated by Geoffrey W. Bromiley. Grand Rapids, MI: Eerdmans, 1991.

————. "How My Mind Has Changed." *Christian Century*, Sept. 20, 1939, 37–38.

————. "Jesus Christ and the Movement for Social Justice." In *Karl Barth and Radical Politics*, edited and translated by George Hunsinger, 19–37. Louisville: Westminster John Knox, 1976.

————. "Kirche in Erneuerung." In *Einheit und Erneuerung der Kirche: Zwei Vorträge von Karl Barth und Hans Urs von Balthasar.* Freiburg: Paulusverlag, 1968.

————. *Die kirchliche Dogmatik* 1.1. Zurich: Theologischer Verlag Zürich, 1932.

————. *Die kirchliche Dogmatik* 2.2. Zurich: Theologischer Verlag Zürich, 1948.

————. *Offene Briefe 1909–1935.* Edited by Diether Koch. Vol. 5 of *Gesamtausgabe.* Zurich: Theologische , 2001.

————. "The Problem of Ethics Today." In *The Word of God and the Word of Man*, 136–82. Translated by Douglas Horton. Gloucester, MA: Peter Smith, 1978.

————. "The Righteousness of God." In *The Word of God and the Word of Man*, 9–27. Translated by Douglas Horton. Gloucester, MA: Peter Smith, 1978.

————. "Roman Catholicism: A Question to the Protestant Church." In *Theology and Church: Shorter Writings: 1920–28*, 307–33. Translated by Louise Pettibone Smith. New York: Harper and Row, 1962.

————. *The Theology of the Reformed Confessions.* Translated by Darrell L. Guder and Judith J. Guder. Louisville: Westminster John Knox Press, 2002.

————. *The Theology of Schleiermacher.* Translated by Geoffrey Bromiley. Grand Rapids, MI: Eerdmans, 1982.

————. *Unterricht in der christlichen Religion*, vol. 2: *Die Lehre von Gott/Die Lehre vom Menschen 1924/1925.* Edited by Hinrich Stoevesandt. Zurich: Theologische, 1990.

Bauckham, Richard, Daniel R. Driver, Trevor A. Hart and Nathan McDonald, eds. *The Epistle to the Hebrews and Christian Theology.* Grand Rapids, MI: Eerdmans, 2009.

Bauerschmidt, Frederick Christian. "Theo-Drama and Political Theology." *Communio: International Catholic Review* 25 (1998): 532–52.

Beattie, Tina. *The New Catholic Feminism: Theology and Theory.* London: Routledge, 2006.

Bedouelle, Guy. *The Reform of Catholicism, 1480–1620.* Translated by James K. Farge. Toronto: Pontifical Institute of Medieval Studies, 2008.

Beintker, Michael. *Der Dialektik in der "dialetischen Theologie" Karl Barths: Studien zur Entwicklung der Barthschen Theologie und zur Vorgeschichte der "Kirchlichen Dogmatik."* Munich: Chr. Kaiser, 1987.

Bender, Kimlyn J. *Karl Barth's Christological Ecclesiology*. Aldershot: Ashgate, 2005.

Betz, John R. "After Barth: A New Introduction to Erich Przywara's *Analogia Entis*." In White, *The Analogy of Being*, 35–87.

Bromiley, Geoffrey W. "Editor's Preface." In Karl Barth, *Church Dogmatics 4/1*, pages vii–viii. Translated by Geoffrey W. Bromiley. Edited by G. W. Bromiley and T. F. Torrance. Edinburgh: T & T Clark, 1956.

Busch, Eberhard. *Karl Barth: His Life from Letters and Autobiographical Texts*. Translated by John Bowden. Philadelphia: Fortress Press, 1976.

———. *Karl Barths Lebenslauf: Nach Seinen Briefen und Autobiografischen Texten*. Munchen: Chr. Kaiser, 1976.

Casarella, Peter. "Hans Urs von Balthasar, Erich Przywara's *Analogia Entis*, and the Problem of a Catholic *Denkform*." In White, *The Analogy of Being*, 192–206.

Cavanaugh, William. *Migrations of the Holy: God, State and the Political Meaning of the Church*. Grand Rapids, MI: Eerdmans, 2011.

Clough, David. "Eros and Agape in Karl Barth's Church Dogmatics." *International Journal of Systematic Theology* 2 (2000): 189–203.

———. *Ethics in Crisis: Interpreting Barth's Ethics*. Burlington, VT: Ashgate, 2005.

Dahlke, Benjamin. *Die katholische Rezeption Karl Barths*. Tübingen: Mohr Siebeck, 2010.

Denzinger, Henrici. *Enchiridion Symbolorum: Definitionum et Declarationum De Rebus Fidei Et Morum*. Friburg: Herder, 1942.

———. *The Sources of Catholic Dogma*. Translated by Roy J. Deferrari. London: B. Herder, 1957.

Dewan, Lawrence. *Form and Being: Studies in Thomistic Metaphysics*. Washington DC: Catholic University of America Press, 2006.

Dupré, Louis. *Passage to Modernity: An Essay in the Hermeneutics of Nature and Culture*. New Haven : Yale University Press, 1993.

Ernst, Victor. "Karl Barth und kein Ende." Editorial. *Kirchen-Zeitung Luzern*, Nov. 25, 1948.

Fink, Urban. "'Ihr stets im Herrn ergebener Hans Balthasar:' Hans Urs von Balthasar und der Basler Bischof Franziskus von Streng." In *Hans Urs von Balthasar—ein grosser Churer Diözesan*, edited by Peter Henrici, 93–130. Fribourg: Academic, 2006.

Fisher, Simon. *Revelatory Positivism? Barth's Earliest Theology and the Marburg School*. Oxford: Oxford University Press, 1988.

Frey, Arthur, and Max Fischer. *Zeitgenössische Betrachtungen zur Jesuitenfrage.* Zurich: Evangelischer, 1953.

Ganski, Christopher. "Spirit and Flesh: On the Significance of the Reformed Doctrine of the Lord's   Supper for Pneumatology." PhD diss., Marquette University, 2011.

Garrigou-Lagrange, Reginald, OP *God: His Existence and His Nature; A Thomistic Solution of Certain Agnostic Antinomies.* Vol. 1 Translated by Dom Bede Rose. St. Louis: B. Herder, 1934.

———. *God: His Existence and His Nature*, vol. 2. St. Louis: B. Herder, 1946.

Gillespie, Michael. *Nihilism before Nietzsche.* Chicago: University of Chicago Press, 1996.

Gockel, Matthias. *Barth & Schleiermacher on the Doctrine of Election: A Systematic-Theological Comparison.* Oxford: Oxford University Press, 2006.

Gollwitzer, Helmut. "Kingdom of God and Socialism in the Theology of Karl Barth." In *Karl Barth and Radical Politics*, edited and translated by George Hunsinger, 77–120. Louisville: Westminster John Knox, 1976.

Gregory, Brad. *The Unintended Reformation: How a Religious Revolution Secularized Society.* Cambridge, MA: Belknap, 2012.

Gutwenger, Engelbert. "Natur und übernature." *Zeitschrift für katholische Theologie* 75 (1953): 82–97.

Hart, Kevin. *Postmodernism.* Oxford: Oneworld, 2004.

Healey, Nicholas M. "Barth and Aquinas." Paper presented at the 2013 Annual Barth Conference, Princeton Theological Seminary, Princeton, New Jersey, June 17, 2013.

Hector, Kevin. *Theology without Metaphysics: God, Language and the Spirit of Recognition.* Cambridge: Cambridge University Press, 2011.

Hegel, G. W. F. *Phenomenology of Spirit.* Translated by A.V. Miller. Oxford: Oxford University Press, 1977.

Henrici, Peter, SJ. "Hans Urs von Balthasar: A Sketch of His Life." In *Hans Urs von Balthasar: His Life and Work*, edited by David Schindler, 7–44. San Francisco: Ignatius, 1991.

Heppe, Heinrich. *Reformed Dogmatics.* Translated by G. T. Thomson. London: Wakeman Great Reprints, 1950.

Hunsinger, George. "Election and Trinity: Twenty-Five Theses on the Theology of Karl Barth." *Modern Theology* 24 (2008): 179–98.

———. *The Eucharist and Ecumenism.* Cambridge: Cambridge University Press, 2008.

Hütter, Reinhard. "Attending to the Wisdom of God – from Effect to Cause, from Creation to God: A *relecture* of the Analogy of Being according to Thomas Aquinas." In White, *The Analogy of Being*, 209–245.

———. *Bound to Be Free: Evangelical Catholic Engagements in Ecclesiology, Ethics, and Ecumenism.* Grand Rapids, MI: Eerdmans, 2004.

———. *Dust Bound for Heaven: Explorations in the Theology of Thomas Aquinas.* Grand Rapids, MI: Eerdmans, 2012.

Jehle, Frank. *Ever Against the Stream: The Politics of Karl Barth 1906–1968.* Translated by Richard and Martha Burnett. Grand Rapids, MI: Eerdmans, 2002.

———. "Karl Barth und der Publizist Arthur Frey. Zur Geschichte einer Freundschaft." In *Karl Barth im europäischen Zeitgeschehen (1935–1950) Widerstand-Bewährung-Orientierung*, ed. Michael Beintker, Christian Link und Michael Trowitzsch, 213–28. Zurich: Theologischer, 2010.

Johnson, Keith. *Karl Barth and the Analogia Entis.* London: T & T Clark, 2010.

Jones, Paul Dafydd. *The Humanity of Christ: Christology in Karl Barth's Church Dogmatics.* New York: T & T Clark, 2008.

Jüngel, Eberhard. *Barth-Studien.* Zurich: Benzinger, 1982.

Kant, Immanuel. *Critique of Pure Reason.* Translated by Norman Kemp Smith. New York: St. Martin's Press, 1965.

———. "On a Newly Arisen Superior Tone in Philosophy." In *Raising the Tone of Philosophy: Late Essays by Immanuel Kant, Transformative Critique by Jacques Derrida*, edited by Peter Fenves, 51–82. Baltimore, MD: John Hopkins University Press, 1993.

Kilby, Karen. *Balthasar: A (Very) Critical Introduction.* Grand Rapids, MI: Eerdmans, 2012.

Langton, Rae. *Kantian Humility: Our Ignorance of Things in Themselves.* Oxford; Clarendon Press, 1998.

Lochbrunner, Manfred. *Hans Urs von Balthasar und seine Theologenkollegen: Sechs Beziehungsgeschichten.* Würzburg: Echter, 2009.

———. "Hans Urs von Balthasar und seine Verbindung mit dem Bistum Chur." In *Hans Urs von Balthasar – ein grosser Churer Diözesan*, edited by Peter Henrici, 55–92. Fribourg: Academic Press, 2006.

Lohmann, Johann Friedrich. *Karl Barth und der neukantianismus: Die Rezeption des Neukantianismus im 'Römerbrief' und ihre Bedeutung für die weiterer Ausarbetiung der Theologie Karl Barths.* Berlin: Walter de Gruyter, 1995.

Long, Steven A. *Analogia Entis: On the Analogy of Being, Metaphysics, and the Act of Faith.* Notre Dame: University of Notre Dame Press, 2012.

—. *Natura Pura: On the Recovery of Nature in the Doctrine of Grace.* New York: Fordham University Press, 2010.

Lösel, Steffen. *Kreuzwege: Ein ökumenisches Gespräch mit Hans Urs von Balthasar.* Zurich: Ferdinand Schöningh, 2001.

Lubac, Henri. *Medieval Exegesis*, vol. 1: *The Four Senses of Scripture* Translated by Mark Sebanc. Grand Rapids, MI: Eerdmans, 1998.

Lumen Gentium. Vatican: The Holy See. November 21, 1964. http://www.vatican.va/archive/hist_councils/ii_vatican_council/documents/vat-ii_const_19641121_lumen-gentium_en.html

Luy, Dominus Mortis. "Martin Luther on the Incorruptibility of God in Christ." PhD diss., Marquette University, 2012.

Marga, Amy. *Karl Barth's Dialogue with Catholicism in Göttingen and Munster: Its Significance for His Doctrine of God.* Beitrage zur Historischen Theologie. Tübingen: Mohr Siebeck, 2010.

Maritain, Jacques. *Existence and the Existent.* Translated by Lewis Galantière and Gerald B. Phelan. Garden City, NY: Image Books, 1957.

Marshall, Bruce D. "Christ the End of Analogy." In White, *The Analogy of Being*, 280–313.

McCool, Gerald. *Nineteenth-Century Scholasticism: The Search for a Unitary Method.* New York: Fordham University Press, 1977.

McCormack, Bruce L. "Election and the Trinity: Theses in Response to George Hunsinger." *Scottish Journal of Theology* 63 (2010): 203–224.

—. *Karl Barth's Critically Realistic Dialectical Theology: Its Genesis and Development 1909–1936.* Oxford: Oxford University Press, 1997.

—. "Karl Barth's Version of an 'Analogy of Being': A Dialectical No and Yes to Roman Catholicism." In White, *The Analogy of Being*, 88–144.

—. *Orthodox and Modern: Studies in Karl Barth.* Grand Rapids, MI: Baker Academic, 2008.

—. "'With Loud Cries and Tears': The Humanity of the Son in the Epistle to the Hebrews." In Bauckham et al, *The Epistle to the Hebrews and Christian Theology*, 37–68.

McInerny, Ralph. *Aquinas and Analogy.* Washington, DC: Catholic University of America Press, 1996.

McKenny, Gerald. *The Analogy of Grace: Karl Barth's Moral Theology.* Oxford: Oxford University Press, 2010.

Milbank, John. *The Suspended Middle.* Grand Rapids, MI: Eerdmans, 2005.

Mongrain, Kevin. *The Systematic Theology of Hans Urs von Balthasar: An Irenaean Retrieval.* New York: Crossroads, 2002.

Montagnes, Bernard. *The Doctrine of the Analogy of Being according to Thomas Aquinas.* Translated by E. M. Macierowski. Reviewed and corrected by Pol Vandevelde. Edited with revisions by Andrew Tallon. Milwaukee: Marquette University Press, 2004.

Muller, Richard A. *Christ and the Decree: Christology and Predestination in Reformed Theology from Calvin to* Perkins. Grand Rapids, MI: Baker Academic 2008.

———. *Post-Reformation Reformed Dogmatics.* Vol. 3, *The Divine Essence and Attributes.* Grand Rapids, MI: Baker Academic 2003.

Nichols, Aidan. *Scattering the Seed.* London: T & T Clark International, 2006.

Nichtweiß, Barbara. *Erik Peterson: Neue Sicht auf Leben und Werk.* Herder: Freiburg im Breisgau, 1992.

Nimmo, Paul T. *Being in Action: The Theological Shape of Barth's Ethical Vision.* London: T & T Clark, 2007.

Oakes, Edward T., SJ. "On Milbank's The Suspended Middle." *Nova et Vetera* 4 (2006): 667–96.

———. *Pattern of Redemption: The Theology of Hans Urs von Balthasar.* London: Continuum, 1997.

Oakes, Kenneth. "The Cross and the *Analogia Entis* in Erich Przywara." In White, *The Analogy of Being,* 147–71.

———. *Karl Barth on Theology and Philosophy.* Oxford: Oxford University Press, 2012.

O'Regan, Cyril. *The Anatomy of Misremembering,* vol. 1: *Balthasar and the Specter of Hegel.* New York: Herder & Herder, 2011.

Peterson, Erik. *Theologische Traktate.* Munich: Kosel, 1950.

Pfleiderer, Georg. *Karl Barths praktische Theologie.* Tübingen: Mohr Siebeck, 2000.

Quash, Ben. *Theology and the Drama of History.* Cambridge: Cambridge University Press, 2005.

Rentdorff, Trutz. "Radikale Autonomie Gottes: Zum Verständnis der Theologie Karl Barths und ihre Folgen." In *Theorie des Christentums,* 161–81. Gütersloh: Güttersloher Gerd Mohn, 1972.

Spieckermann, Ingrid. *Gotteserkenntnis: Ein Beitrag zur Grundfrage der neuen Theologie Karl Barths.* Munich: Chr. Kaiser, 1985.

Stanley, Timothy. *Protestant Metaphysics after Karl Barth and Martin Heidegger.* Eugene, OR: Cascade Books, 2010.

Torrance, James B. "Karl Barth." In *The Encyclopedia of Religion*. Edited by Mircea Eliade. Volume 2. New York: MacMillan, 1987.

Velde, Rudi A. te. *Participation and Substantiality in Thomas Aquinas*. Leiden: Brill Academic, 1995.

Webster, John. *Barth's Moral Theology: Human Action in Barth's Thought*. Grand Rapids, MI: Eerdmans: 1998.

White, Thomas Joseph, OP, ed. *The Analogy of Being: Invention of the Antichrist or the Wisdom of God?* Grand Rapids, MI: Eerdmans, 2011.

———. "Classical Christology after Schleiermacher and Barth: A Thomist Perspective." *Pro Ecclesia* 20 (2011): 229–63.

———. "Introduction: The *Analogia Entis* Controversy and Its Contemporary Significance" In White, *The Analogy of Being*, 1–34.

———. "'Through Him All Things Were Made (John 1:3)': The Analogy of the Word Incarnate according to St. Thomas Aquinas and Its Ontological Presuppositions." In White, *The Analogy of Being*, 246–79.

———. *Wisdom in the Face of Modernity: A Study in Thomistic Natural Theology*. Ave Maria, FL: Sapientia Press, 2009.

Wippel, John F. *Metaphysical Themes in Thomas Aquinas*. Washington DC: Catholic University of America Press, 1984.

Witte, J. L., SJ. "A Talk With A Giant." *America*, September 25, 1948.

Wobbermin, Georg. "Das Wort Gottes und der evangelische Glaube." In *Vom Worte Gottes. Bericht über den dritten Theologentag in Breslau vom 5.8.10. 1930*, edited by Ernst Lohmeyer, 46–65. Göttingen: Vandenhoeck & Ruprecht, 1931.

Index of Names and Subjects